DOWNLOAD!

HOW THE INTERNET TRANSFORMED THE RECORD BUSINESS

PHIL HARDY

OMNIBUS PRESS
London / New York / Paris / Sydney / Copenhagen / Berlin / Madrid / Tokyo

To Dave Laing
Dave and I have collaborated and argued for some 40 years over a wide range of projects. Whether I was writing about Doug Sahm or the music industry, he has always been my first port of call.
Thank you Dave.

Copyright © 2012 Omnibus Press
(A Division of Music Sales Limited)

Cover designed by Fresh Lemon

ISBN: 978.1.780.38614.0
Order No: OP 54846

The Author hereby asserts his/her right to be identified as the author of this work in accordance with Sections 77 to 78 of the Copyright, Designs and Patents Act 1988.

All rights reserved. No part of this book may be reproduced in any form or by any electronic or mechanical means, including information storage or retrieval systems, without permission in writing from the publisher, except by a reviewer who may quote brief passages.

Exclusive Distributors
Music Sales Limited,
14/15 Berners Street,
London, W1T 3LJ.

Music Sales Corporation,
180 Madison Avenue, 24th Floor,
New York NY 10010, USA.

Macmillan Distribution Services,
56 Parkwest Drive
Derrimut, Vic 3030,
Australia.

Typeset by Phoenix Photosetting, Chatham, Kent
Printed in the EU

A catalogue record for this book is available from the British Library.

Visit Omnibus Press on the web at www.omnibuspress.com

Contents

Acknowledgements		v
Beginnings		vii
Chapter 1	The CD Boom	1
Chapter 2	Seeking To Monetise Intellectual Property: The First Rise And Fall Of EMI	10
Chapter 3	The Creation Of WMG	26
Chapter 4	Would You Like To Dance? EMI And WMG	43
Chapter 5	Bertelsmann Gets Itchy Feet	64
Chapter 6	Profit Warnings From EMI	76
Chapter 7	Mostly Digital	95
Chapter 8	A Revolution In Retailing	114
Chapter 9	Digital Problems Galore	130

Chapter 10	The Conglomerates Think Again About The Music Business	146
Chapter 11	The Rise And Fall Of Sony BMG	161
Chapter 12	WMG, The Bronfman Era	183
Chapter 13	EMI Finds Independence Lonely	204
Chapter 14	Transforming EMI: The Hands Era, Part One	217
Chapter 15	Battling Citigroup: The Hands Era, Part Two	243
Chapter 16	Hopes For The Future, Legislation And New Business Plans	262
Chapter 17	Rush To Market: The Sale Of WMG And EMI	290
Chapter 18	Battling The Regulators	316
Endings		344
Appendix: The Guy Hands Memos		349
Bibliography		367
Notes And Sources		370

Acknowledgements

This book owes its existence to ASCAP's seat planner for the awards ceremony it mounted in London in 2011. I was seated beside the COO of the Music Sales Group, Chris Butler, and in the course of the ceremony, after talking of matters East Anglian, we discussed the current state of the music industry. I told him I was writing a book about such and he invited me to submit it to Omnibus, the book publishing division of Music Sales. Here it is.

In writing my book I relied extensively on *Music & Copyright*, the newsletter I and Dave Laing set up in partnership with the *Financial Times* in 1992, and the online newsletter *theviewfromtheboundary* I created in 2009. The contributors to these, notably James Bourne, Dave Laing, John Qualen and Gary von Zuylen, have helped enormously. I have also leant heavily on US and UK trade papers, *Billboard* and *Music Week*. Recent years have also seen the emergence of a number of websites and online newsletters devoted to the music industry. The chief ones of these that I have used are *Hits Daily Double*, *Digital Music News* and *Music Void*. I have also been lucky to have been advised by a variety of industry players, some of whom have spoken to me on the record and many who have spoken about industry practices and policies off the record. The bibliography further details the books, magazines and articles that helped me make sense of the issues. These represent the "usual suspects".

I have also made extensive use of information provided by the International Federation of the Phonogram Industry (IFPI), the global trade body of the record industry. In particular I have relied on its annually published *Recording Industry in Numbers* (RIN), which is the best and most detailed statistical survey of the record industry. Unless stated otherwise all recorded music statistics are from RIN with the dollar equivalents converted at the appropriate historical rate. I have also used the yearbooks and/or reports of various national record industry bodies, such as the BPI (UK) and the RIAJ (Japan). The global market shares quoted are those published by IFPI between 2000 and 2004. All other market shares, except those for the US which are from Nielsen SoundScan, were calculated by me at *Music & Copyright* and *theviewfromtheboundary*.

Once a book becomes more than an idea it needs help to make the jump to reality. Here I must thank my agents, Michael Sissons and Fiona Petherham at PDF. Michael poured cold water on ideas at appropriate moments and Fiona was encouraging at (different) appropriate moments. Thank you. Chris Charlesworth and Lucy Beevor shepharded the book into production, polishing here and there. Thank you.

And then there's my family: Thank you Emily, Joe and Steph.

Beginnings

*S*itting at his desk Eric Nicoli, the chairman and chief executive of the EMI Group, brushed a chocolate crumb from his chin. If the phone call he was about to make was successful, EMI would jump from being the fourth to the third largest music company in the world with strong prospects of becoming the second. Outside, it was a surprisingly mild spring day; inside the office the atmosphere was electric. As the clock ticked down to 14.30, Nicoli's assistants and advisors shuffled their papers, waiting for the phone's pprppp. When it came, Nicoli paused and then decisively pressed the button on the intercom, waited for the crackle to fade, breathed deeply, paused again and began his sales pitch: "Good morning Edgar..."

Whoa...

This is neither the story nor the style of *Download*.

Download chronicles the making of the new record industry, from the boom years of the CD revolution of the late 1980s to the crisis of the present day, with particular stress on the last decade. As such it follows the actions and reactions of the major international record companies, five at the beginning of the story, now three, as they trudged their way through the digital Slough of Despond, bewildered by the fleet of foot digital innovators far more responsive to the changing marketing conditions through which (recorded) music was consumed and valued.

Download has no substantial heroes or villains, no individual or group who shaped the transformation that the industry is undergoing. Books have been written in which captains and swashbucklers of industry fight the good fight, in the course of which character flaws and strengths are uncovered, the hero finds victory (or defeat) and the reader is given an insight into how a particular area of human activity is structured and its problems are exposed.

Characters lie at the heart of such books. The record and related industries have within it characters enough. Some of these, Edgar Bronfman, Jr., Ahmet Ertegun, David Geffen and Eric Nicoli, are known to the public. Others, Lyor Cohen, Zach Horowitz, Doug Morris and Mo Ostin, are less well known. But these characters, however powerful they may be, particularly within their companies, have been powerless to halt the loss of control that has characterised the recent history of the music business. Recent years have also thrown up a new set of characters: Apple's Steve Jobs, for whom music was a way to reinvigorate a faltering computer company, and Terra Firma's Guy Hands and Access Industries' Len Blavatnik, venture capitalists bent on finding new ways of monetising recorded music. Each has their significant place in my story, but the real story *Download* tells is the structural change that has, almost surreptitiously, taken place within the music business. This change, for reasons I explain in detail, has left the captains of the record industry as unable to act as they were unwilling. In effect they became mere, but very well paid, observers of the shrinking of their domains.

Digital has been the elephant in the room, the palpable but difficult to understand presence that has affected everything it has come into contact with. Once information and intellectual content morphed from analogue to digital and became a series of bits and bytes, change was the name of the game for the businesses they inhabited. Book publishing and the film, music and newspaper industries, to name but a few, are currently undergoing radical transformations because of it. Hence the shift from DVDs to film (and television) on demand, from books bought at Borders or Waterstones to e-books from Amazon, from newspapers to news and comment available on the Internet.

Beginnings

Music was the canary in the mine of this transformation. Digital music files were relatively small and, once the Internet moved from dial-up to broadband, people could copy and share such files with ease. This often involved piracy and the unauthorised use of copyrighted material. Such uses hardly helped an industry stumbling enough, but piracy was not the central problem, rather its far greater impact on the digital world was a feature of the shift from analogue to digital. An analogue copy, a tape of an LP or CD, was inferior to the original and, moreover, the copying process involved was cumbersome. To all intents and purposes a digital copy was the same as the original and the actual copying was far easier, with numerous technology and computer companies banging on consumers' doors, seeking to be the one to make the process idiot proof. At the same time peer-to-peer (P2P) networks – file-sharing services that required only an Internet connection and P2P software – were competing to make searching and transferring files trouble free. Below (and in even greater detail in the ensuing chapters) I show how the digital revolution undermined business practices and traditions long established to deal with the market for physical products and left the major record companies puzzled as how to react to, let alone take advantage of, the digital revolution. One by one their aces, especially control, and their function as financial backers were trumped and their powers and revenues severely clipped.

To give the narrative a focus and a spine, *Download* follows the efforts of the two smallest of the major international record companies, EMI and the Warner Music Group (WMG), to either merge or buy the other. First attempted in 2000, EMI and WMG's bids at merger/acquisition initially stemmed from their individual situations but soon they were swept up in an industry-wide crisis, which, more often than not, they misinterpreted in the simple hope that by becoming bigger they would become safer. Both companies had been liberated from larger corporations with varying degrees of success. Accordingly, they saw the key issue as being size and entered into a decade-long courtship which sought to make them more competitive with the two larger majors, Sony Music Entertainment (SME) and the Universal Music Group (UMG). In fact all the majors were involved in (attempted) mergers and takeovers. SME bought out Bertelsmann's 50% stake in Sony BMG while UMG, which had earlier become the leading major through its purchase of PolyGram, significantly increased the size of its music publishing arm through the purchase of Bertelsmann's music publishing company BMG MP.

The issue of size was significant. Indeed, as the digital music market grew in importance, it became clear that first-mover advantage was dependent not on making a deal with digital distributors or retailers, as EMI of all the majors was most willing to do (*see* Chapter 7), but on what could be brought to the table, the size of one's repertoire. Hence, once a commercially viable, legitimate digital music business was in place, a wide range of problems notwithstanding, it was UMG, the largest record company (with about a one-third share of the global recorded music repertoire) that was the must-have partner. In 1998, Bertelsmann's then CEO Thomas Middelhoff, in a speech given at the Bertelsmann Management Conference, famously noted that: "The position of the biggest media company is of no value in and of itself. But in clearly defined market segments, market leadership is associated with disproportionately high profits." The record industry is one such segment. UMG was able to turn this advantage for a while into greater revenues and margins in the physical market, however, it was unable to transfer its dominance of the physical market fully into the digital market. As we shall see in great detail, the digital revolution created far more problems than opportunities for record companies. *Download* follows the interaction of the majors and their individual efforts as they attempted to come to terms with a business environment in which the old verities no longer held.

The CD boom, which marked the start of the digital revolution, brought with it a clutch of new entrants to the music business. Rock'n'roll wouldn't last – it was just noise – had been the view of the investment community, but after the success of The Beatles the blinkers fell off. Rock, pop, call it what you will, might be noise but it was a direct line to the burgeoning youth and leisure markets. And so corporations and private equity companies started to look at record companies with a new interest, an interest that exploded in the wake

Beginnings

of the CD boom, bringing a mix of professionalism and opportunism to the music business and giving financial weight to the increasingly widely heard mantras of "intellectual property" and "content creation". The corporate bodies blew hot and cold about music – sometimes it was seen as central, at other times peripheral. The venture capitalists were more opportunistic, regularly investing in start-ups that used music without licences. They had a greater belief in the possibilities of monetising the fast-changing music business. Sometimes they were successful, for example the consortium that bought WMG in 2004, sometimes not, as in Terra Firma's disastrous acquisition of EMI in 2007.

In *What Is History* E.H. Carr used the example of Cleopatra's nose to question whether it was her beauty or social forces that brought down the Roman Republic. He rejected the theory that had Cleopatra's nose been longer and Mark Anthony not been attracted to her there would have been no affair and hence the Second Triumvirate would not have broken up (and the Roman Republic would have remained in place). Carr's point was that it was generally social forces not individuals that made history and only a few people were able to shape the social forces that carried them to historical greatness. Others disagreed, opting for "the Great Man" as the driving force of history. The view of this particular book is that it was structural and social forces, not heroes or villains, that determined the reshaping of the record industry in the 21st century.

The story of the creation of the new record industry is one of a complex change taking place against a background of shifting patterns in the creation, consumption and distribution of music. That much is evident, but what of the how and the why?

The digital revolution offers the essential starting point. Many commentators have stressed the various ways in which the industry responded to the opportunities and threats digital posed as being little more than burying its head in the sand. Digital is associated with piracy, solution lawsuits, digital rights management (DRM) and lobbying for new legislation, etc. Digital is associated with new entrants to the market; solution: make them pay a high price of entry, make them wait, try to maintain control of distribution, etc. Steve Knopper's *Appetite For Self-Destruction* captures this process in great detail, offering a compelling and thorough account of opportunities missed and deadend streets taken. But it doesn't quite explain – the why is assumed rather than articulated.

In retrospect the reason is simple: *the unforeseen consequence for the record industry of transforming the creation and distribution of recorded music, the core activity of record companies, from an analogue format to a digital one was a loss of control of the creation and marketing of that product.* This did not seem to be the case initially in the shift from vinyl to CD that the digital revolution ushered in. All seemed wonderful: consumers re-bought music they had on vinyl albums at far higher prices; record companies were suddenly seen as key conduits to the increasingly important leisure markets and their executives were suddenly highly valued. And so the scramble for market domination started, leading to Middelhoff's comment quoted above.

Middelhoff's belief marked Bertelsmann's brief thrust for market domination of the record industry, during the course of which it forged an alliance with Napster, the first industry outsider to see a key unforeseen consequence of the digital revolution: easy file-sharing. Considered the enemy by the collective record industry, Bertelsmann, the parent company of BMG, then the smallest of the majors, briefly saw Napster as a means of leap-frogging to front place. For a short period, before caution set in, Bertelsmann ran with the uncertainty of what Napster might represent. Subsequently a clutch of new entrants to the music business, including iTunes, Spotify, Amazon, Live Nation, Pandora and various ISPs, were allowed to challenge the record companies for control over the distribution and dissemination of their product, with some, notably Apple, taking a threatening degree of control.

In the past the cost of entry into the record industry had been high, requiring recording studios, pressing plants, distribution hubs and so forth. Once a recorded music track became a computer file rather than being coupled to a physical format (a cassette, a disc) such entry costs fell dramatically. Moreover, such was the range of possibilities of this de-coupling that the identities of the new power brokers would change, almost on a monthly basis, as new business plans were announced and trounced and companies and concepts bit the dust. Virtually all the key long-haul actors came from outside the industry. And when they came from within it, it was artists and their representatives that were empowered by the digital revolution at the expense of their past paymasters, the major record companies. And it was the new entrants and the established acts, rather than record companies, that profited. As Apple re-invented itself and made billions of dollars from music with its iPods and iTunes, record companies faced declining revenues. Even worse, it soon became apparent that the digital revolution also meant smaller profits for record companies because the margins on growing digital sales were far less than those on declining physical sales.

A recurring feature of the past 20 years of crisis within the record industry has been actual and would-be mergers and restructurings and cost-cuttings, with the metaphor of closing the stable door after the horse has gone springing to mind. The first such move, the purchase of PolyGram by the smaller UMG, was an expansionist act: UMG got bigger through the purchase of PolyGram rather than through incremental growth. All the subsequent mergers and would-be mergers were defensive. They were entirely focused on cost-cutting and restructurings of activities in the physical marketplace. The reason generally put forward for this was that record companies, used to the munificent profits of the CD revolution, simply couldn't see beyond the CD and envisage a digital future. Thus, so the story goes, they first attempted to swat away the digital upstarts and then made it difficult for such newcomers to make deals with them.

This was more than a "head in the sand" view. Despite the huge attention given to digital matters by the media and financial communities, with the record industry always being presented as the canary in the mine, record companies' digital revenues at the start were tiny compared to their revenues from physical sales (we'll come to digital profits later). By their own guidelines, record company executives did the right thing by their shareholders. Just as executive bonuses were performance based, which meant that investment in the future might require a tightening of the belt, so shareholders, outside of specific industries, such as the military where the customer base was cost unconcerned, were antagonistic to research and development expenditure concerning the future. In 2005, according to international record industry trade association IFPI, digital accounted for only 5.5% of the trade value (the monies received by record companies from retailers) of recorded music sales. Digital was the future: by 2010 that had risen to 29% globally and was scheduled to represent more than 50% in the US. However, making the transition from Plan A, an industry based on the sales of physical product in which the record companies had a high degree of control, to Plan B, an industry based on online and subscription sales over which the industry had limited control at best, was difficult.

To ask record company executives to make decisions that favoured the digital at the expense of the physical when the physical represented significantly greater revenues and profits (and the bonuses of the majority of record company executives were based on current performance) was to demand the impossible of executives inhabiting a decades-long mindset that *control* was requisite. Hence, powerless to return the digital genie to the bottle, they eventually became reluctant partners in businesses created and controlled by others, with little space left for them to act beyond complaining about the stance taken by ISPs or the business terms offered them by Apple. Failing that, Canute-like they returned to the policy of delay, as in the case of Spotify, whose US launch was postponed by a year due to the unwillingness of the majors to licence it.

Anyway, the battle was lost from the start. Record companies, especially the majors – the one group particularly enriched by the CD revolution – always had to backtrack. They had little power over the digital interlopers. In a desperate attempt to keep some control the majors wanted digital rights management (DRM), an encryption system inserted on recordings which would limit what a user could do with it, including denying him the ability to make a copy of the recording. Apple didn't. Chalk that up to a victory for Apple. Even more unfortunately, at the same time in the more profitable physical market the majors had to get used to ever smaller cheques from Wal-Mart when it sought to simply pay less for the albums it bought from the majors, threatening to reduce the shelf space given to CDs if it didn't get its way. But it did anyway: sales at Wal-Mart accounted for 20% of the majors' revenues in the US while music accounted for a mere 2% of Wal-Mart's revenues. No contest.

When it became apparent that going digital had lost them control of their product, that litigation was no solution and that P2P was here to stay, the majors could do little but cut and paste themselves. This is the basic rationale for the drawn out period of mergers and cost-cutting that dominated the era and continues to do so today. While the majors sought to buy and sell each other, on both the physical and digital fronts the Wal-Marts and Apples made hay, offering record companies continued sales, but lower revenues and smaller profits, on their terms.

After the arrival of Napster, there followed a period of disdain and hostility from the record companies and artists, during which a growing number of digital companies sought to insert themselves into the distribution chain. Most met with little success, as the majors delayed and/or sought high upfront licences for the use of their repertoire. The major exception was Apple, which in February 2010 announced that over 10bn tracks had been downloaded from the iTunes store since its launch in April 2003. This represented gross revenues for the music industry over a seven year period of around $7bn. At a September 2009 Apple presentation it was announced that total cumulative sales of iPods exceeded 220m and in August 2011, Apple's market capitalisation reached $337bn, overtaking Exxon Mobil (which had held the top spot since 2005) and Microsoft, briefly making it the most valuable company in America. At the same time, as noted above, other new industry players benefitted from the ready availability of music files online, while network operators benefitted hugely from the movement of music and other digital content files across networks, whether legitimate or otherwise. There were no such comparable increases in value for record companies. Rather, revenues in the record industry fell 32% from a trade value of $23.35bn in 2000 to $15.93bn in 2010.

Change is disruptive and difficult to handle. In 1962, in his book *The Structure of Scientific Revolutions*, Thomas Kuhn introduced the idea of the Paradigm Shift. It's an idea which has been widely used since. Kuhn's point is simple but precise: science does not progress through a linear accumulation of new knowledge, but through periodic revolutions, in which the nature of scientific inquiry within a particular field is abruptly transformed. Kuhn identifies three distinct stages of this process. The first is *prescience*, which lacks a central explaining paradigm. This is followed by *normal science* when scientists create central paradigm by "puzzle-solving". Kuhn notes this period is extremely productive: "when the paradigm is successful, the profession will have solved problems that its members could scarcely have imagined and would never have undertaken without commitment to the paradigm." Moreover, during this period the failure of a result to conform to the paradigm is seen not as refuting the paradigm, but as the mistake of the researcher or an interesting exception to the general rule. As such findings grow, the science in question reaches a *crisis*, at which point a new paradigm, which subsumes the old results along with the anomalous results into a new unified framework, is accepted. Kuhn calls this *revolutionary science*. Kuhn further argued that it was impossible to understand a new paradigm through the conceptual framework and terminology of another, older paradigm. In other words, locked into one view of the world it is impossible to foresee another until the anomalous findings that stem from the earlier view grow so problematic as to make it unworkable.

Kuhn used this theory to explain the difficulties of the Copernican revolution, which required a shift in world view from one in which the earth was the centre of our universe to one in which the sun was and the earth merely a planet travelling around it. I make use of it to explain the difficulties in the record industry – difficulties that are spreading to a wide range of content-based activities, for example the newspaper and book industries – confronted by disruptive change. Previously control of the access to owned content (through its manufacture and distribution) was paramount. In the digital world content creation, not the control of its distribution, is what matters.

In its beginnings the record industry (*prescience*) was dominated by confusion (about what a record was, a cylinder or a flat disc), disputes about patents and their ownership. The era of *normal science* was ushered

Beginnings

in by the matrix exchange agreement of 1907 between the US-based Victor Talking Company and the UK-based Gramophone Company, which brought a degree of regularity to the floundering industry (*see* Chapter 2). Each undertook not to sell "Talking Machines, records and accessories" on the other's patch, and to notify each other of changes in price and policy. In addition to the non-interference pact, the so called "beautiful agreement" between these nascent giants provided for the exchange of the master recordings of each other's releases, and the mutual use of the famous "His Master's Voice" listening dog trademark. The agreement lasted in name for almost 50 years. As time wore on and new companies entered the industry – a move the agreement was meant to prevent by depriving them of repertoire – the agreement became increasingly difficult to keep in place but, at its simplest, it enshrined control through the ownership of repertoire and the control of its manufacture and distribution. Even the terminology of the industry reflected these verities. Thus a company that manufactured and distributed its own repertoire was a "major" and a company dependent on another (usually a major) for such was termed an "independent". Sometimes, a major owned its own retail outlets, as EMI once did in the UK with its chain of HMV shops, but retailers were invariably deemed to be the companies' friends. Both made money through the sale of recorded music (even though, through their various record clubs, the majors were also in competition with record shops. A further reflection of this was that US trade publication *Billboard* rarely carried stories about record clubs. This was because the editors of the magazine did not want to offend record retailers, who were their main subscribers, and for whom stories about the growing sales of the record clubs represented a decidedly unwelcome truth).

Various benefits flowed from the majors' control of the physical manufacture and distribution of their copyrights. It made physical piracy more difficult: pressing plants were costly to set up and easy to monitor. Similarly the shared concerns and experiences of record companies and retailers allowed for co-operation across a wide range of matters. Artist, record company and retailer were a family, sometimes in conflict – over discounts for example – but always aware of a shared interest.

When it didn't challenge control, change was seen as a good thing, especially when new formats led to greater sales. The format wars of the early days were reprised in the war of the speeds when RCA introduced the 45 rpm disc and Columbia the 33⅓ rpm long player. Initially each company rejected the other's format but when the opportunities that vinyl represented (Remember those LP sleeves of teenagers' bedrooms scattered with 45s out of their sleeves? Impossible in the shellac era.) were recognised and gramophone manufacturers made multi-speed players, the industry embraced the new formats. There was resistance to the CD, which required closing long established pressing plants and building new ones; EMI did not adopt the CD immediately, refusing to pay the royalty demanded by Philips and Sony as its developers. However, such debates were hidden from public view. The CD was borne from within the record industry: CD storage was set at 75 minutes because Sony's Norio Ohga demanded that a CD be able to play Beethoven's *Ninth Symphony* in its entirety. (In a similar fashion the Sony Walkman, which extended the life of the cassette, was introduced in 1978 so Sony co-chairman Akio Morita could listen to operas during his frequent plane trips.)

The bonanza that ran for most of the 1980s after the CD's introduction seemed to prove two things: controlled change was good and format change was particularly good as consumers replaced existing record collections with the same titles in the new formats. So taken was the industry with technological change as a market stimulus that it returned to the strategy (unsuccessfully) several times, with MiniDisc, DAT, DualDisc, the pocket CD, etc.

But not all change was good. Consider MTV. MTV was built on the copyrights of record companies, their promotional videos. Just as radio broadcasters in the US did not pay record companies to play their copyrights, so MTV obtained the videos (largely) free of charge. Fittingly, as a mark of the change it represented, MTV went on air in the US on August 1, 1981 with Buggles' 'Video Killed The Radio Star'. The glee of the record companies at this new promotional platform soon turned bitter (as it would again later, following the success of iTunes and the fearsome conditions Apple demanded of them). As MTV grew and grew the record companies saw it as a new entrant to the market that was getting rich off the back of their copyrights. Within a decade MTV became the eighth largest cable channel, available in over 50m homes in the US, and the most influential music broadcaster there. In addition it had five overseas operations. Its annual revenues were some $500m, 80% of which came from advertising, and a profit margin of 34%, far higher than that of any of the major international record companies. MTV was a decided success, with record companies only receiving any payment for the exclusive use of new videos for limited periods of time.

The response of the record companies was delayed but predictable. In 1994, the five largest record companies, Sony, WMG, EMI, PolyGram and BMG, announced that they planned to open a series of music video-based television channels in Europe, Asia and Latin America in competition with MTV, which (then) claimed a worldwide reach of 251m households. The prototype for the new channels being planned by the five majors was the highly successful German channel Viva that was launched in 1993 with Sony, Time Warner (WMG's owner), EMI and PolyGram as equal partners with German broadcaster Frank Otto. The new channels would allow the majors to control both the creation and distribution of their music videos. News of them followed the case brought against the majors by MTV Europe, which accused them of operating a cartel and "abuse of a dominant position" through the UK collecting society Video Performance Ltd (VPL) by charging too much for the videos that were the mainstay of its programming (in Europe broadcasters pay both producers and writers for the use of their copyrights). Little came of the majors' proposed channels, in great part because of the concerns of the US regulatory authorities, however the idea eventually led to Vevo, which, jointly funded by UMG and SME in 2010, quickly became the world's most watched online music video service.

"Change plus control being is for the industry" was the (initial) message the CD revolution sent to record company executives. "Without control, change is threatening" was the message of MTV. The problem was that change had unforeseen consequences. The CD revolution began with a few local difficulties, the MTV revolution offered immediate hope of a new promotional tool and a way to further weave recorded music into the fabric of society, but in the end neither resulted in a significant ancillary revenue stream for the companies upon whose copyrights it depended. Like Kuhn's puzzled scientists, record company executives were faced with the dilemma of whether to look back to certainties of the past, or forward to a decidedly uncertain future. Faced with gazing into the abyss, they blinked and, caught like a rabbit in a car's headlamp, were transfixed, unable to move.

The change that MTV represented was minor. For the majors mostly it meant envy at MTV's success, garnished with a realisation that it offered a new promotional platform. The changes that the Internet represented were seismic, affecting the very foundations of the industry. The CD boom, made possible by the digitisation of analogue recordings, brought a financial bonanza to record companies and their executives, but the unforeseen consequence of the digitisation process was that the record companies lost control of the distribution of their product, forever, and their power over their artists was severely diminished as others entered the music industry, often with very different agendas to those of record companies. That would only become visible when digital met the Internet. But first the industry wallowed in the CD boom.

Chapter 1

The CD Boom

No one asked what "digital" meant, or cared.

Stan Cornyn in *Exploding*

The CD sold so well. And it created this gigantic boom in the industry. And everybody got rich. And people just got incredibly accustomed to this. To the point where in the late '90s, the only way that you could get the one song that you liked was to buy the 15 to 18 dollar CD at the Tower Records.

Steve Knopper, in *Appetite For Self-Destruction*

The first impact of the CD was on physical sales. It's best to get the figures over quickly. In 1986, for the first year ever, over 100m (137m) CDs were sold worldwide and the retail value of all recorded music sales was $14bn (at the average 2004 dollar exchange rate). Ten years later in 1996, 2,162m CDs were sold worldwide, an increase of 1,444%, and the value of global recorded music sales was $34.7bn, an increase of 148%. In effect, the CD created a new music market, one in which consumers replaced existing records they already owned on vinyl or music cassette with CDs. (When the CD bonanza faded and with it the value of global recorded music sales, which fell year on year for the first time in 2000 to $37.2bn, the industry attempted another replacement solution, introducing various new formats, the most notable being DAT [digital audible tape] and the MiniDisc; however the strategy met with little success in the commercial market.)

The story of the CD is impressive enough told in figures, but it was far more than that. The CD represented a cultural revolution in the process of music consumption and production (and storage – think of all the strangely shaped CD storage racks on sale at Ikea and elsewhere and the storage cabinets advertised in the back pages of rock magazines). It also changed the economics of the record industry, both within, in terms of the new monies that suddenly started washing around record companies, and without, when the far higher revenues of music companies made them considerably more attractive targets for investors. Music was always a sexy business but now it was a profitable business too, and in the wake of those perceived profits there began a dance of takeovers and mergers. The most revealing of those were by electronics group Philips which in 1989 floated 16% of PolyGram, its music division, valuing PolyGram at $5.6bn. Previous corporate raiders had mostly used borrowed money and accordingly the information gleaned about their targets was rarely published in any detail. However, to raise the necessary funds to finance its purchase of Island, the home of U2 and Bob Marley, and the planned (and agreed) purchase of A&M Records, the home of The Carpenters and The Police, PolyGram issued an Initial Public Offering (IPO) seeking funds from a wide pool of investors to provide itself with capital for future growth, repayment of debt or working capital. Such an offering requires the company in question to make public its business practices in far greater detail than when it tapped private finance of corporate partners for additional funds. The details revealed in the IPO were staggering. Adam White, then international editor-in-chief at US trade paper *Billboard*, recalled the impact of the IPO prospectus:

> Suddenly, the PolyGram prospectus seemed to set new horizons of information. Before that, there was relatively little publicly available data about record companies' activities: just headline figures, and often, not even those. Indeed, some years before, I remember being berated by Warner Music's

The CD Boom

Nesuhi Ertegun for my estimate in Billboard *of the group's international revenues; he was upset at what were, he said, inaccurate numbers – and yet he wouldn't tell me the accurate numbers, even on background! Anyway, the PolyGram document featured real sales and profit numbers, regional breakdowns of sales, profit margins, number of employees, legal settlements and more. This seemed like a new currency, literally and metaphorically, for the music business.'*

In its bland prose the prospectus describes a *new* highly profitable record industry ushered in by the CD:

Sales in the recorded music industry in unit volumes have resumed a steady upward trend since 1984 after a substantial decline in the period 1979 to 1983, and have recently exceeded their prior peak levels achieved in 1978. Since 1984, the value of sales industry-wide has increased at a faster rate than unit volume growth, due in part to the introduction and acceptance of CDs, which are substantially higher priced than vinyl records and tapes.

This new record industry was also well run, but still competitive:

Since 1983, PolyGram and other major record companies have emphasized, among other things, the strengthening of financial and other controls of their operations in order to reduce operating costs and improve margins, while competing intensely to obtain (through acquisition or otherwise) artists, management, production personnel and recorded music catalogues in order to gain a larger share of the recorded music market.

After noting that the US and Canada, which in 1988 accounted for over a third of recorded music sales in the world, accounted for only 16% of PolyGram's revenues (compared to Europe's 66%), the document also detailed why the IPO was necessary:

Because of the size of the recorded music industry and the international diversity of music tastes, it has been difficult in recent years for recorded music companies to increase market share meaningfully through organic growth,

> *rather than acquisition. In order to increase its presence in the popular music market in the United States (where PolyGram's popular music market share has been lower than in other major markets) and elsewhere and otherwise to enhance its popular music operations, PolyGram acquired Island as of July 1, 1989 and agreed to acquire A&M as of January 1, 1990. The aggregate purchase price for these acquisitions is approximately $732 million ... PolyGram acquired Island and agreed to acquire A&M in order to increase its presence in the popular music market in the United States ... and elsewhere and otherwise to enhance its popular music operations.*

Bingo: the CD brought rising profits – in 1988 PolyGram's rose 85% following a 37% rise in 1986 – and new opportunities. Nobody was to know that the advent of the digital era also brought unforeseen consequences for the industry, down to the recording process itself, but more of that later. And, being digital, the CD revolution also transformed piracy.

A recurring element in the development of the record industry has been the effect of change on both the producers of recorded music and the formats in which recorded music has been presented to consumers for purchase. A classic example of this was the battle of the speeds that followed RCA's development of the 45 rpm single at the same time that Columbia introduced the 33⅓ long player (LP). Each new format required consumers to replace their existing record players to accommodate the new discs that played at different speeds. Both formats had their advantages: the robust 45 rpm disc became the single for some 50 years, while the LP, with its longer playing time, became the preferred format for classical music, Broadway shows and (later) the rock (concept) album. In the case of the battle of speeds, after a period of uncertainty both formats were accepted and multi-speed players were brought to the market. Such co-operation was easier to achieve because both parties were committed to music (content) as well as hardware. The introduction of stereo followed a similar compromise, with one of the competing systems (Westrex's) being chosen by the technical bodies of the major record companies as the one to be used by all of them. This compromise was in marked contrast to the VHS versus Betamax battle of film recording and playback machines in the 1970s. Both systems came to the market at the same time to the general confusion of all.

Philips and Sony (which then had no record company interests) avoided conflict by pooling their technologies (and patents) to produce a format that was universally adopted. The cost of the development of the CD was borne not by the record companies but by the electronics divisions of Sony and Philips, which then benefitted from the sales of the new CD players, also receiving a per copy royalty from all the companies issuing CDs. However, there was an inherent degree of conflict between the interests of the technologists (the hardware people) and the content companies (the software people), which reached its peak in the debates about digital rights management, which took place between 2004 and 2008, with content owners wanting restrictions and hardware manufacturers seeing them as impediments to the ease of use of their machines. Sony, the Japanese electronics company which entered the record industry through the purchase of Columbia from US broadcaster CBS in 1988, would commonly be described as sitting on both sides of this fence; however, the debate was largely conducted *sotto voce*. This was in contrast to the situation that followed the introduction by Sony of its Betamax videocassette recorder, which allowed users to make copies of copyrighted material broadcast on television.

In 1976, a number of Hollywood studios sued Sony, which then did not own either a film studio or record company, for secondary liability for copyright infringement by Betamax users. The case, *Sony Corp of America versus Universal City Studios Inc*, was the first to set the owners and creators of intellectual property (rights holders) against hardware companies, each with radically different agendas. In the digital age such battles would become commonplace. In 1984, the Supreme Court of the United States ruled that the making of individual copies of television shows or movies for purposes of time-shift viewing did not constitute copyright infringement but was fair use. The Court also ruled that the manufacturers of home video recording devices could not be liable for infringement if the device in question was "capable of substantial non-infringing uses". The broader legal consequence of the Court's decision was to establish a general test for determining whether a device or service with copying or recording capabilities infringed copyright law. That question would become a central issues of the subsequent copyright infringement cases raised against P2P file-sharing services, such as Grokster, Kazaa and LimeWire, with content owners claiming copyright infringement and the P2P networks claiming that, while their services might be mis-used, they offered so many "substantial non-infringing uses" that the infringements were ancillary rather than central.

Philips was eventually to exit the music industry, selling PolyGram to UMG (*see* Chapter 4). In contrast, seeking the secrets of synergy – a mantra of the period – Sony bought both a film and record company to fuel its expansion. As part of the cost of the dream of synergy, Sony accepted the conflicting pressures from its hardware and software division, always looking for ways to meld company loyalty and market prospects to overcome divisional concerns. That was not the case when it was different companies rather than different divisions of the same company, as in the battle between Apple and the record companies. For Apple, for whom the iPod delivered enormous profits, iTunes was a way of marketing the iPod. The record companies, whose profits stemmed from the sales of music not music players, had different priorities. They wanted variable pricing to generate higher profits from the most popular tracks and to allow a wider range of marketing possibilities for their repertoires as a whole, whereas Apple wanted simplicity and to make iTunes *the* destination point for digital transfers, be they sales or simple transfers of tracks from CDs to iPods. Apple didn't mind that the iTunes service could be used to copy a consumer's own (or "borrowed") CDs to his or her iPod.

Format changes brought in their wake significant cultural changes and made possible dramatic increases in the revenues of record companies. The hundreds of album sleeves showing teenagers sprawled on the floors of their bedrooms surrounded by sleeved and unsleeved singles testified to a new way of consuming music and identified a new target audience. Similarly the Dansette – a small record player, the size of a large handbag or small briefcase – also often a presence on such album covers, indicated portability as a concern of that new audience, a concern that would harden into a requirement, following the introduction of the Walkman and, even more bizarrely, the shoulder-needing boombox with its deep bass sound. Stereo also extended the stretch of the music market. With it came smaller speakers and players that replaced the huge consoles of the 1950s. As hi-fi reached the mass market so it also broke out of the living room, making the secret consumption of music feasible and, in turn, creating a new genre: "the bedsitting room folkie".

Stereo also changed the economic parameters of the record market. Strong consumer resistance had made it difficult for record companies to increase their prices previously. The advent of Hi Fidelity releases in the 1950s led to the start of the acceptance of the idea that "enhanced sound" would cost more. The arrival of stereo, with its manifestly superior sound quality and promotional literature about the costly R&D that brought it about, signalled a significant increase in the price of albums, after several years of, much resisted, small incremental price rises. The CD's ease of use, sturdiness (especially compared to a vinyl album) and the perceived – if often challenged (*see* Chapter 7) – "better quality" of digital sound made it an immediate hit with consumers. At the same time, the CD's higher price and reduced royalty rate – the industry negotiated an introductory lower rate with performers to compensate for its investment in the CD – produced a bonanza for record companies. If the CD was sexy, the higher prices that could be charged for it were even sexier. The US retail price of a front line cassette or LP in the 1970s and early 1980s was $8.98. The CD hit the street with a price tag of $16.95. The prices came down after a while but, under pressure from record companies (notably the majors' MAP campaign, *see* Chapter 8), they remained high, even after the costs of their manufacture and distribution had fallen appreciably.

Questions over the price of CDs would be a recurring irritant for record companies. In 1992, for example, an investigation into CD pricing was mounted in the Netherlands and the UK following protests from consumer organisations in both countries. In the UK CD pricing was the subject of investigations by a parliamentary committee and a government agency, the Office of Fair Trading. The suggested retail price of premium CDs (new releases by established artists) in the UK, then, was the equivalent to between $20 and $22, prices that were unfavourably compared with US CD prices by the UK Consumers Association and several newspapers.

The parliamentary Committee on National Heritage held three public sessions during which record company executives, artist managers and retailers were cross-questioned. The managers of Simply Red and Dire Straits denied that royalties paid to top artists affected the price level of CDs while the heads of top specialist retail chains argued that record companies should cut their wholesale prices by £2 ($3.16). In their defence, the chairmen of PolyGram UK and EMI Records said that comparisons between the UK and US markets were not relevant. The size of the US domestic market allowed for real economies of scale, they said. Separately, the Dutch lobbying group Konsumenten Kontact claimed that the average retail price of CDs in the Netherlands was 17% higher than in Germany. Depending on discounts, full-price CDs cost between $22 and $25 in Holland. After receiving the Konsumenten Kontact report, the Ministry of the Economy sought information from Dutch record companies about their CD pricing policies and the related issues of parallel imports and discounting practices. In response, representatives of the Dutch music industry pointed out that CD prices in the Netherlands were lower than those in France and Scandinavia.

In Europe, these issues and the related one of parallel imports made the headlines, but did little more. A more significant question concerning price was that raised by the European Commission when it was called upon to examine the various merger and takeover attempts attempted by the major music industry players from 2000 onwards. The Commission's concern was not with how high (or low) the price of CDs was, but with the general uniformity of the price of a premium CD from any record company. The Commission's disquiet was less to do with value than with possible price collusion (*see* Chapter 11). In contrast, in the US, the attempt by the majors to keep CD prices high at smaller record retail outlets at a time of serious discounting by mass merchandisers through the Minimum Advertised Price scheme, met with fierce opposition from the Department of Justice and was eventually terminated.

Such problems, and a host of others, awaited record companies down the line, but the first problem raised by the CD revolution was how to unleash the full value of intellectual property that it indicated. The documents published in support of the PolyGram IPO showed just how swollen were the profits of record companies following the introduction of the CD. Buying and selling record companies might be even more profitable, as the contrasting histories of EMI and the Warner Music Group were about to make clear.

Chapter 2

Seeking To Monetise Intellectual Property: The First Rise And Fall Of EMI

EMI, or Electric and Musical Industries Ltd as it was (then) formally known, was created in June 1931 by the merger of the UK Columbia Graphophone Company and the Gramophone Company, companies that could trace their origins back to the beginnings of the record industry. As was the case with the cinema, the early days of the record industry were bedevilled by patent wars to such an extent that the record industry can legitimately claim to have many fathers, notably Thomas Edison, Alexander Graham Bell, Charles Sumner Tainter and Emile Berliner. At the same time, the various rights to the resulting machines and the recordings they could play were sold and licensed on (often conflicting) territorial bases. The Columbia Graphophone company was established in the US in 1895 and in 1897 opened an office in the UK as part of its general expansion into Europe. Separately, the Gramophone Company was established in London in 1898.

Both companies quickly expanded their reach, selling locally recorded music and imported American recordings throughout Europe and beyond. In 1898 the Gramophone Company made its first recordings and opened branches in Germany, France, Italy and central Europe. Additional offices were established in Russia in 1900, in India in 1901, in Japan in 1902, and in China in 1903. The company had its first major artist when opera singer Enrico Caruso recorded 10 songs for it in 1902. The increasing popularity of recorded music was evidenced by the ownership of a gramophone by one-third of British households by 1913. As a result of the First World War, the Gramophone Company lost its Russian and German operations.

As a branch of an American company, the UK Columbia Graphophone company had access to its parent company's recordings and in turn supplied the American company with recordings it made. But until 1907 the Gramophone Company had no such certain access to American repertoire. That was secured through a little publicised 1907 licensing agreement concluded between the Victor Talking Machine Company and the Gramophone Company.

At a meeting senior representatives of the two companies concluded the Matrix Exchange Agreement (MEA), under which the world would be divided into red and green sectors with the red assigned to Victor, the green to the Gramophone Company. Each undertook not to sell "Talking Machines, records and accessories" on the other's patch, and to notify each other of changes in price and policy. A mark of the significance of the agreement was that special world maps were printed to show the details of the arrangement. On a Mercator projection of the world, two vertical lines were drawn. One was at longitude 30W, enfolding the Americas and bending at the top to take in Greenland, all coloured red. The centre of the map, Europe, Africa and the Indian subcontinent belonged to the British company and was coloured green. A second line, at 170W, gave the Philippines the bulk of China, Japan and Indo-China to Victor. In addition to the non-interference pact, the so-called "beautiful agreement" between these nascent giants of the record industry provided for the exchange of the master recordings of each other's releases, and the mutual use of the famous "His Master's Voice" listening dog trademark. (In 1922, the UK Columbia Graphophone Company bought up its US parent and the 1907 agreement was extended to cover both companies.)

Later agreements were less easy to achieve because of the growing rivalry between the partners themselves, the zeal of US Government anti-monopoly lawyers and the activities of a new generation of companies that the MEA had meant to prevent entering the record business. Nonetheless, the agreement shaped the development of the industry until the early 1950s: 1907 marked the end of the feverish adolescence of the industry, and the beginning of its history as one of the most successful and idiosyncratic modern industries, a history based on the highest possible degree of *control* over the production, manufacture and distribution of its primary product, recorded music.

By the end of the 1920s, recorded music was a profitable business to be in. In the UK, the Columbia and Gramophone duopoly saw considerable growth which after the interruption of the world war continued until the arrival of the Great Depression. In 1928–9 and 1929–30, the two companies had combined profits of £1.7m and £1.45m respectively; in 1930–1 these fell to a mere £160,000. Just prior to the Wall Street crash, two film companies, Paramount and Warner Brothers, seeking to increase their access to music rights and reduce their music costs following the coming of sound, separately began exploratory takeover talks with the Columbia Graphophone company, only for these to come to nothing following the collapse of confidence in the US economy.

The first serious talks about amalgamation between the two British companies took place at the end of 1929 with the idea of creating a holding company within which the Gramophone Co and Columbia could retain their autonomy. One reason for this was the very different styles and methods of doing business of the two companies. The Gramophone Company, with its haughtily superior His Master's Voice trademark, handed out its dealerships in the manner of appointments to royalty; it was a starched collar company. Columbia was the informal operation, orientated more to popular than classical music. One commentator at the time summed up the contrast: "The Columbia men had a strong tendency to arrive late, and often drunk, for meetings but they were quick to make decisions ... (while) the Gramophone

Company was run by a cumbersome committee system with lengthy agendas." Such cultural differences would become a feature of the mergers and restructuring of the 2000s.

The merger discussions only gathered momentum when in the second half of 1930 the sales of the companies dipped alarmingly and profits fell by 90%. The two British companies rushed to huddle together for warmth against the cold wind of the Depression and EMI was created, becoming the world's largest record company. For all the cultural difference, the two parties were well matched: the Gramophone Company had a higher turnover and greater profits, while Columbia had the larger network of overseas branch companies, notably in South America and Asia. Immediately following the merger EMI opened its Abbey Road studios, which later, after it had achieved legendary status, it briefly considered selling in 2010 at a time when it was desperate for funds to prevent a takeover by Citigroup (*see* Chapter 13).

Another new British record company of the 1930s was Edward Lewis' Decca Records. Established in 1931, Decca quickly became EMI's major competitor through its policy of cheaper priced recordings and independent access to the all important US repertoire, buying the American label Brunswick and so securing the services of Bing Crosby: "Leading Artists – Lowers Prices" ran Decca's advertising campaign of 1933.

EMI's inefficiency reduced its competitiveness in the UK in the 1930s. The changed situation that followed the Second World War threatened to destroy it as an international record company. The basis of EMI's existence as a worldwide recording organisation was the MEA of 1907. This cartelisation of the world by the Victor Talking Machine Company and the Gramophone Company had survived the many changes of identities of its signatories, because it underwrote two essential truths of the trading interests of the various parties. It reduced the possibility of international competition from any third party by making it very difficult for such a company to gain access to any American or British recordings beyond its own. Equally importantly, the agreement reflected the basic strength of its signatories. RCA and Columbia, the American heirs to Victor's signature, were given virtual control of the world's largest market, the Americas, while EMI, heir of the Gramophone Company's signature, was given the rest of the world in which to market and distribute its own and American product. But, if the 1907 agreement enshrined the isolationist stance of the pre war United States and the Imperial heritage of Britain, 1945 was not 1907. Moreover, the growing international popularity of US repertoire since the 1930s very much strengthened RCA's hand.

Columbia made it clear that it had no intention of supplying EMI (its one-time owner) with product when the MEA ran out in 1952. RCA, which (then) held the threatening trump card of 27% of EMI's shares, was the only source EMI could turn to. However, the blinkers of isolationism were removed by the Second World War: having rescued Europe, it was now the duty of every American company to profit from the undertaking. Hence, just as the Coca Cola lorries had followed the American troops across Europe, giving birth to bottling plants along the way, in the wake of the Marshall Plan came the expansion of US companies into Europe to the extent that being a multinational company became the norm in the world of US commerce rather than the exception, particularly in the field of entertainment. Accordingly, the lengthy negotiations initiated by EMI in 1946 to extend the MEA beyond 1952 were bound to fail, even though to demonstrate its loyalty to RCA, EMI took the commercially damaging decision not to introduce the 33 rpm long playing record, which had been developed by Columbia and was opposed for several years by RCA, until 1952, two years after its rival Decca.

In 1946, learning that MGM, the record division of the movie company, was proposing both to record and make its product available outside the US, EMI quickly signed a licensing deal with it in the face of stiff competition from Decca. The deal enabled EMI to release MGM recordings in the UK. But the amount of repertoire involved was minor compared to the losses involved should the MEA end. With pressing plants in Australia, Denmark, Finland, France, Germany, Greece, India, Italy, the Netherlands, New Zealand, Norway, Pakistan, South Africa, Sweden, Switzerland and Turkey, EMI was desperate for matrices to press up. The fall in sales as a result of the loss of the Columbia matrices in 1952–3 was 1.2m and over 3m in 1953–4. Although Columbia supplied far less matrices to EMI than did RCA, in the final year of the agreement EMI calculated that Columbia accounted for some 25% of EMI's record sales throughout the world. In the same year RCA's recordings accounted for 50% of EMI's worldwide sales. With this projected double loss in mind, in 1952 EMI negotiated an extension of the 1907 agreements that heavily favoured RCA, which by the month was becoming surer of the value of the European and Asian markets that could potentially be opened to it.

The new agreement continued the British/American exchange of repertoire, but with the proviso that while EMI retained the rights to existing RCA matrices throughout the world, it got no international rights on any new matrices supplied for use in the UK. At the end of the five year agreement EMI was to delete all its RCA recordings from its catalogue within a year. Given a period of grace by the new agreement, from the end of 1952 RCA began the process of transforming itself into a worldwide record company, opening factories in Australia, Greece, Italy and Spain, the first American pressing plants to be set up outside the Americas.

How was EMI to feed its worldwide factories? A paper prepared for the EMI board in 1952, *The Importance of America to our Record Business*, once again pointed out the worldwide popularity of American music and artists and hence of EMI's need for continued access to US repertoire, for both its branch companies and the domestic UK market. In the discussions it provoked two options were outlined: either buy a US company or set up a US subsidiary (as Decca had done). Finally accepting that the days of "the beautiful agreement" were numbered and that if it set up a US subsidiary it would be hard to find anyone to take on the necessary manufacturing and distribution, EMI decided to buy an American company. Two years later with a new chairman and CEO, Sir Joseph Lockwood, EMI did just that.

The choice was not very wide. The larger US companies were now EMI's rivals and allied to Decca and Philips, while most of the independents were too small or too specialised. It needed a medium-sized company operating in the mainstream of American popular music and capable of producing a fair number of hit records. It considered Mercury, but it was ruled to be too small and too specialised. There was only one company left, Capitol Records, the fourth largest record company in the US, which was co-founded by disc-jockey Glenn Wallichs in 1940 and had a current roster that included Frank Sinatra, Nat King Cole and Dean Martin, all of whom were licensed to Decca in the UK. Capitol was making a profit of about $730,000 (£300,000) a year and its shares stood at $11.50. In 1955, a desperate EMI offered $17 per share, valuing the company at $8.5m, and the deal was soon concluded. However, EMI acquired only 96% of Capitol and accordingly concluded an MEA with its new partner, which was subsequently renewed and amended until EMI took full ownership of Capitol in 1978.

The deal quickly paid off. In January 1956, EMI began to represent Capitol in the UK and in February it had its first number one with Tennessee Ernie Ford's 'Sixteen Tons'. In that year Capitol's contribution to EMI's overall revenues was in excess of $35m (£12.5m), an increase of 37% compared to 1955. Access to American repertoire now secure, EMI started making significant profits. Whereas in 1945–6 turnover and post-tax profits were £7m and £165,000 respectively; in 1961–2, following the explosion of popular music that rock'n'roll represented, these had risen to £82.5m and £7.4m and sales of recorded music accounted for 50% of the company's revenues compared to 2% in 1945–6.

Lockwood turned to rebuilding its international presence, reviving its companies in Europe and elsewhere and creating new ones, such as the joint venture with Toshiba in Japan, TOEMI. At the same time Lockwood commenced the modernising of EMI's marketing and distribution activities. In the UK, for example, where previously EMI's prestige HMV releases were available only at carefully selected dealers, he made the company's Columbia and HMV releases available at all record stores and changed the policy at EMI's stores to one where they stocked all records released, not only EMI ones. At the same time he modernised the distribution of EMI recordings, scrapping the company's own distribution system in favour of using the trains that made the morning newspapers available everywhere in the country for delivery by breakfast time. He concluded an agreement with WH Smith, which

Seeking To Monetise Intellectual Property

had started to sell records in its newsagent stores, to collect the record packages from stations along with their newspapers and deliver them to record shops.

The buying of Capitol solved the bulk of EMI's supply-side problems, but it soon became apparent that Capitol was a very reluctant conduit to the US market for its parent company's UK hits. That difficulty began with The Beatles. Despite the group's huge success in the UK and continental Europe in 1963, in which the group had three UK number ones, they were rejected as being "too British" by Capitol executives. Other US record companies were not so cautious. Thus, in 1964 when the group had 18 Top 40 entries, six of these were on labels other than Capitol (Swan, Vee-Jay, Tollie and ATCO). Under the MEA agreed with Capitol, EMI contracted to supply masters to Capitol and Capitol to EMI in return for a licence fee equal to an agreed percentage of the retail sales price in the country of manufacture. The catch was that each company retained the rights of first refusal to the other's product. Accordingly, when to EMI's consternation Capitol chose not to release the Beatles' first recordings offered to them, it couldn't do anything but complain. (The normal practice was that if a recording achieved a specified degree of success in its home market, particularly the market in which the company was based, such as being a Top 10 hit or achieving sales in excess of a certain number, licensees [such as Capitol] and branch companies were required to release the record.)

While Capitol changed its tune by releasing Beatles records from early 1964 onwards and subsequently picked up both Peter & Gordon and The Seekers, its initial hesitation over The Beatles was not an isolated incident. It had rejected both Cliff Richard, who emerged in the UK in 1958 but who would always struggle in the US, and The Dave Clark Five, who had a series of hits between 1964 and 1967 on the Columbia subsidiary Epic. Mercury got recordings by EMI artists Freddie & The Dreamers and Atlantic released Acker Bilk's UK chart-topping 'Stranger On The Shore', in 1962 the first ever recording by a British act to top the American charts. The most active US company releasing British Invasion acts was Imperial, which issued material by The Hollies, The Swinging Blue Jeans and Billy J. Kramer, all EMI acts. Finally, MGM profited by Capitol's lack of interest in Herman's Hermits and The Animals. Other UK companies did not have the "Capitol problem". Philips, for example, was far more successful than EMI in securing US releases for its British artists. Dusty Springfield, The Walker Brothers, Manfred Mann, The Troggs and Esther & Abi Ofarim all appeared quickly and efficiently on Philips or Fontana in America. In a similar way, British Decca put out hits by The Rolling Stones and The Moody Blues on their New York based London label. Meanwhile, Warner Bros., whose artists appeared in Britain through Pye, had that company's artists for America, notably The Kinks and Sandie Shaw.

Later EMI would lose the US rights of major acts, including Pink Floyd and Queen, to other US companies. But just as important as EMI's difficulties in exploiting its non-US repertoire in the US was its general failure to sign US talent consistently. This meant, as we shall see later in more detail, that EMI's US market share was never more than 10% for any significant period of time. The result was endless restructurings and high visibility signings in various attempts to solve the ongoing problem of never signing enough talent in the world's largest talent pool and so never having enough high profile US acts to sell around the world through its well developed, but increasingly under-used distribution and marketing machine.

Notwithstanding these issues, the 1960s and early 1970s were a period of exceptional growth for EMI. In 1962 revenues and pre-tax profits were a respectable £82.5m and $4.4m respectively; by 1970 these had risen to £225m and $21m. Most of this came from EMI's record division and a significant part of that from the exploitation overseas of UK recordings, a good proportion of them by The Beatles, to whom they paid a derisory royalty. In recognition of this new focus in 1971 the company formally changed its name from Electric & Musical Industries to EMI Records Ltd. A company press release explained: "It is felt that such a change is appropriate for two reasons: first because our present name no longer reflects our wide span of activities and interests; and secondly, the initials EMI have become our primary means of identification throughout the world."

This growth was not confined to EMI. The global record industry as a whole grew dramatically in the 1960s, rising almost fourfold from $663m in 1960 to $2.33bn in 1970. The growing size and profitability of the record industry attracted the attention of corporate America. In the 1960s a number of corporations entered the world of intellectual property, including Transamerica, Gulf & Western and most notably Kinney, beginning a process that would grow at an ever increasing rate over subsequent decades (*see* Chapter 3).

EMI took a very different view to the growing pile of money it was accumulating. Following the UK fashion of the time, which undervalued intellectual property in favour of bricks and mortar, it focused its investments in mostly non-music areas. Thus, the Grade Organisation, one of the UK's largest entertainment and leisure groups, was bought in 1966, followed by the Blackpool Tower Company and the Associated British Picture Company, owner of Elstree film studios, one of the UK's largest film companies and holder of a controlling interest in Thames Television. This division, The Leisure Division, was headed by Bernard Delfont and by 1979 it was a major profit centre for EMI, which was now the largest entertainment company in the UK.

The one area in which EMI did not invest seriously was music. This was despite the increased competition from EMI's US rivals who by the end of the 1960s were establishing UK branches and signing acts directly rather than licensing them from UK companies. Thus, for example, Led Zeppelin and Rod Stewart were signed directly to US record companies. Although EMI maintained its UK market share of around 17% in the 1970s, it lost global market share as the market fragmented and niche music, such as punk and its successor new wave that were popular in the UK, found little international success. On top of this, despite ongoing investment from EMI, Capitol lost substantial market share in the US, which had reasserted its place as the world's premier talent pool.

In two minds, an increasingly troubled EMI couldn't decide whether to sell its music division or whether it wanted to bolster its US reach. It first considered a merger. However, after lengthy negotiations, Gulf & Western eventually withdrew a $75m bid for 50% of EMI Music. This spurred EMI to shore up its US presence. In the 1960s the unprecedented US success of The Beatles, who between 1964 and 1985 were responsible for over 25% of Capitol's sales, and to only a slightly lesser extent The Beach Boys, had largely hidden Capitol's indifferent performance. But by 1970 The Beatles had disbanded and The Beach Boys fragmented, resulting in a decline in sales, and Capitol found itself facing new competition and a different marketplace. Ariola (which was eventually to form the basis of BMG) shifted its distribution from Capitol to RCA in 1974, in 1977 Capitol failed in its attempt to buy ABC. A year later, with disco all the rage, PolyGram, still in expansionist mode, bought the upstart Casablanca. Accordingly when in 1979 United Artists came on the market EMI bit (the deal and its making is detailed in full in David Kronemyer's posts at www.musicindustrynewswire.com). However, the purchase was not a great success and had little impact on EMI's problems in the US.

Perhaps a better solution could be found at home. Enter Thorn, a company best known for its lighting, consumer electronics, domestic appliances and engineering businesses, which came to the rescue of EMI in 1979. A music company that had, largely on the back of profits from recorded music, diversified into ever widening areas of activities, EMI had fallen on hard times in the 1970s. Its medical body scanner, which enabled the examination of parts of the body previously only examinable via surgery, won it plaudits but lost it money – £30m in the course of 1977–8 – while its music activities were seriously threatened by new entrants to the marketplace and structural changes within the music business. These changes were particularly felt in the UK, EMI's home market, which from the mid-sixties onwards was seen as a major talent pool. At the same time, although global recorded music sales continued to grow in value in these years this was was largely because of the weak US dollar: sales declined in real value and units. Moreover, what growth there was was largely driven by disco, a genre in which EMI was notably unsuccessful. As a result EMI's music-related profits fell from £33m to £2m between 1977 and 1979 and its overall pre-tax profits fell from £75m in 1977 to £29m in 1979.

However, if the prime reason for the merger of Thorn and EMI was to prevent the bankruptcy of EMI, the prime reason for the subsequent de-merger in 1996 was to unlock the value in EMI for its shareholders. At the time of the merger, value resided in bricks and mortar; at the time of the de-merger it resided in intellectual property

Some of the causes of EMI's troubles at the end of the 1970s and earlier 1980s were common to the industry as a whole following the decline in the value of recorded music sales. There were also problems specific to European-based companies: the US was the world's largest recorded music market and, *pace* Beatles and Swinging London, the most important global repertoire source. EMI (and later PolyGram), as noted above, had continual problems with its US operations. Its weaknesses were largely hidden by the CD bonanza, but when the unforeseen consequence of the digital revolution, the fall in physical sales, came it would lead to a series of management changes, restructurings and a desperate search for a merger partner.

Following the merger, the new company, Thorn EMI, began a process of rationalisation in which music, retail and rental were identified as core activities. Within five years the company's hotel and leisure interests (including the Blackpool Tower), film interests and its once successful medical division were sold off. In their place the new CEO Jim Fifield ploughed money into the music business, buying music publisher SBK Entertainment World for $377m in 1988 (which brought with it Martin Bandier who was to lead EMI Music Publishing [EMI MP] to world domination before leaving the company in complicated circumstances in 2007), subsequently setting up a separate SBK label. While SBK's music publishing gave EMI MP an extra lustre, the SBK label, despite its initial hit with Wilson Phillips, faded fast. More successful was the purchase of 50% of the independent Chrysalis company in 1989 (and the other half in 1991), Virgin Records in 1992 and increasing its stake in its Japanese joint venture TOEMI to 55% in 1994.

However, as it expanded its music interests and the arrival of the CD brought unheralded profits, it became increasingly apparent that the value of the group's music assets could never be fully realised in such a hybrid company as Thorn EMI.

The PolyGram IPO prospectus of 1989 unveiled for many the previously hidden value of recorded music as intellectual property.

This was further reflected in the general realisation within the mature economies of the world of the far slower growth of manufacturing. According to *Copyright Industries in the US Economy*, which was commissioned by US-based lobbying group the International Intellectual Property Alliance (IPPA), the copyright industries of the US accounted for 4.3% of the Gross Domestic Product (GDP) of the US, or $348.4bn, in 1997 and that over the period between 1977 and 1997, the value of the share of GDP taken by the core copyright industries – which include film and music companies that create copyrighted works as their primary product – grew four times as fast as that of the remainder of the economy, 6.3% compared with 1.6%. *Copyright Industries in the US Economy* further noted that within the US, employment in the core copyright industries more than doubled over the 20-year period, from 1.5m to 3.8m. Compared with 1996, the value of the exports and foreign sales of the core copyright industries in 1997 grew by 11% to $66.85bn and as such was responsible for generating more foreign revenues for the US than other leading industrial sectors. These include the chemical industry ($66.4bn), motor vehicles and automotive parts ($58.34bn), agriculture ($57.3bn) and electronic components and equipment ($54.29bn).

A similar survey, the *Creative Industries Mapping Document*, was published by the UK government's Department of Culture, Media and Sport (DCMS) in 1998. This was the first ever attempt to measure the economic contribution of these industries to the UK. It led to the creation of a Creative Industries Task Force to investigate issues that impacted on the creative industries and make recommendations for change in areas such as skills and training, finance for creative venture, intellectual property rights and export promotion. The report valued the total revenues of the UK music industry in 1995 at £3.6bn. A second report, valuing the revenues of the music industry in 2000 at £4.6bn, was issued in 2001. The introduction, by Chris Smith, the minister for DCMS, captured the new sense of the significance of the creative industries and their growing economic importance:

Just over two years ago, we published the first ever Creative Industries Mapping Document. *The need then was to raise awareness of the industries, the contribution they made to the economy and the issues they faced.*

Today, the term is more widely used and understood; in a knowledge economy the importance of these industries to national wealth is more commonly recognised; and the special needs of these industries are reflected more in policy development at national, regional and sub-regional levels. The creative industries have moved from the fringes to the mainstream ...

This Mapping Document *demonstrates the continuing success of our creative industries. They are a real success story, and a key element in today's knowledge economy. All of this is, of course, founded on original creativity – the lifeblood of these industries. The most successful economies and societies in the twenty-first century will be creative ones. Creativity will make the difference – to businesses seeking a competitive edge, to societies looking for new ways to tackle issues and improve the quality of life. This offers the UK enormous opportunities. We have a well-deserved reputation for creativity; we can draw on both a strong historical base and vibrant contemporary developments...*

I want all businesses to think creatively, to realise creativity is not an add-on but an essential ingredient for success.

I want our creative industries in particular to continue to seize the opportunities of a fast-changing world, to think "out of the box", to innovate, to be flexible and swift, and to strive to realise their full potential.

In an even more pragmatic fashion regional and sub-regional bodies had begun exploring the economic possibilities offered by cultural activity. Thus, in 1984, I wrote the report *The Value of Music To London* for the Greater London Enterprise Board, highlighting the value to the London economy of music activities. Similarly in other cities, councils started to look to culture as a source of employment. As the value of culture became more widely accepted, the employment opportunities it offered, particularly to small businesses, became a growing concern of regulators and lobby groups.

In the UK, a more immediate reason for the newfound belief in the economic value of intellectual property was the success of EMI in the late 1980s and early 1990s. Throughout the 1970s, EMI reported profits in the region of between £20m and £30m; however, in the late 1980s and early 1990s these rocketed to between £246m (1993–4) and £365m (1998–9). The prime reason for this, as we saw earlier, was the CD, the success of which was common to all the major record companies.

It took the City rather longer than EMI's shareholders to see the increase in the value of music. One reason for this was that there were few publicly quoted companies that dealt exclusively (or even primarily) in intellectual property, another that the perceived value of bricks and mortar assets outside of a few specialised areas, such as armaments and computer software, was not yet widely established. In the City, the few companies that traded primarily or significantly in (recorded) music were looked after by analysts who specialised in the rather broad area of "leisure". Thus, when as the editor of *Music & Copyright* in the 1990s I wanted to speak to a city analyst about any of the increasing number of issues that the music business raised, I would end up speaking to someone who "looked after music" as part of his or her brief of overseeing the leisure industry, a sector that ranged from hotels to brewing and all in between. A decade later, such analysts were replaced, almost it seemed at the wave of a Harry Potter wand, by media specialists for whom the music industry quickly became a special, and quite sexy, fiefdom in which the financial pages of the newspapers had their own page three equivalents accompanying news about the corporate activities of EMI, UMG and the like.

The signal event that revealed the huge potential of the music industry for City folk was the IPO of PolyGram in 1989. Henceforth, takeovers and mergers became central to the music business and in response, following the money as it were, financial institutions soon learnt the ways of what had previously been seen as an arcane practice. Within a decade, market forecasts and actual market shares, briefings for analysts, new business models and digital opportunities, would become an essential part of the new language the record industry was learning to speak.

Following the de-merger from Thorn as a standalone music company EMI sought to educate the potential investors as to the value of intellectual property with intensity. It won the battle, but the cost of the victory, as we shall see, was that when global recorded music sales went up or down, when the level of piracy was reported as growing and, most of all, when EMI's global or (more often) US market share fell, so the EMI share price suffered. Would becoming a bigger company, especially one with a successful US arm, provide the necessary insulation?

Chapter 3

The Creation Of WMG

Legend has it that Warner Bros. Records was formed because of Tab Hunter. A Warner Bros. contracted actor, Hunter had a 1957 hit record with a cover of Sonny James' 'Young Love', a number one in the US for six weeks. However, the record was released on Dot Records, which was owned by rival film company Paramount. Hunter's hit led to Warner enforcing its contract with the actor, stopping Dot from releasing an already recorded album and the setting up of Warner Bros. Records, which would eventually grow into the Warner Music Group (WMG), to release the album.

Most of the newly minted record companies of the 1950s grew out of a specific music; folk, for example, was the starting point for Elektra Records, which is now part of WMG. They started small and local and grew or withered according to whether or not they were successful. This was not the case with Warner Bros., which like the other film studios, such as 20th Century Fox, United Artists and Columbia Pictures, established record labels to handle soundtracks and other movie related recordings. Warner started with high hopes for its record label. Under its first head Jim Conklin, a former head of Columbia Records, it was a nationwide company from the start with branches in the major cities of the US. It would lean on the film company – its first hit was 'Kookie,

Kookie (Lend Me Your Comb)' in 1959, as featured in the company's hit television series *77 Sunset Strip* – but it would be an all-round record company. The trouble was it had no hits.

The signing of the Everly Brothers, lured to WMG by the possibility of film work – teen idol Ricky Nelson had just made his film debut in *Rio Bravo* in 1959 – changed that, giving the company a string of hits starting with 1960's 'Cathy's Clown'. Others followed as the roster slowly expanded, but the most noteworthy development came in 1963 when Frank Sinatra, being wooed by Warner for a multi-picture film deal, merged his loss making Reprise label with Warner Bros. Records as part of that agreement, receiving a one-third stake in the new Warner-Reprise company in the process. Sinatra brought with him members of the "Rat Pack" – notably Dean Martin and Sammy Davis Jr – and, even more importantly, Mo Ostin, the head of Reprise, who was to guide the new company to huge success.

Under WMG's new CEO Mike Maitland, Ostin was appointed head of Reprise and Joe Smith, a former disc jockey, head of Warner Bros., thus establishing the two label/unit set-up that would provide its basic structure (and something to be copied by other record companies). A modest man, usually in a suit, Ostin and the more gregarious Smith transformed WMG, signing UK acts that the other USA companies had passed on, such as The Kinks and Sandie Shaw, reviving Sinatra's recording career and reaching sales of $20m in 1964. The pair then plundered San Francisco and Laurel Canyon, signing the likes of Grateful Dead and Joni Mitchell and buying Autumn Records, while Maitland began opening international branches, creating Warner Bros. Canada in 1966. By then, the 74-year-old Jack Warner was losing control of the film studio – he had failed to block the making of *Bonnie And Clyde*, a film project he hated – and investors were circling.

US investors, deal makers and private equity groups saw a value in intellectual property far earlier than their European counterparts. Their first great success was the film studios' catalogues. Seen as being of little value – what cinema owner in the 1950s would want to put on a 1934 or 1948 box office success? – as the studios ran short of cash, they were sold in the early 1950s to syndicators who reaped a bonanza from the content-greedy television networks that exploded in the 1950s and 1960s. One such was Eliot Hyman's 7 Arts, which in 1950 had bought Warner Bros. back catalogue. In 1967, financiers Serge Semenko and Charlie Allen put together a deal under which Seven Arts bought the Warner Bros. film and record companies for $32m with the idea of selling them on at a profit.

To increase that profit, Hyman, Semenko and Allen sought to expand Warner's music interest, music rather than film being by then the company's main revenue source. Enter Atlantic. From lowly beginnings in 1947, Atlantic became a giant in the 1950s with a blend of rock'n'roll based on urban black rhythms and, unusually for an independent, a number of distribution and productions deals. Unlike many of its contemporaries, who failed to see the shift in music trends, Atlantic continued to prosper in the 1960s, first with southern soul and then with a wide range of (mostly) white rock acts. In tandem with their growing success its three owners, Nesuhi and Ahmet Ertegun and Jerry Wexler, feeling a need for financial security, sold Atlantic for $17.5m to W-7 Arts. Subsequently, decidedly unhappy with what they regarded as too small a received amount, they sought and got great power and money from Warner Communications Incorporated (WCI), as the new company was called. Warner Bros.' own executives were also seen as valuable, some more than others. As W-7 Arts was being shopped around it was discovered that the negotiations concerning Ostin and Smith's renewal contracts had not been concluded. CEO Maitland, about to go on holiday, was called back from the airport to conclude the negotiations. The pay scale for executives with clout was rising and stock options became an essential part of an executive's life once he moved into the upper tiers of management. In 1969, Kinney a conglomerate whose businesses included funeral parlours, parking lots and a talent agency, bought W-7 Arts and the benefits increased further.

Stan Cornyn, the head of publicity at Warner Bros., explains: "Over the heads of his label leaders, Steve Ross [the head of WCI] spun financial incentives, like a lamé lasso. Ross's general rule was if one of his labels made a profit, WCI would take half of it, but would leave the other half for the label to divvy up among its execs. The label's chief exec got to do the divvying but he could take a maximum of half (a quarter million) for himself. The other quarter million was spread over the company's employees. Ross's generosity fell over many of us."

Thus began the creeping perception within the record industry and the financial community that it was executives who were the real stars, the men (it was almost always men) who knew the real value of the talent contracted to the company and how to maximise the output of that talent. This was in the early 1970s, and as time went on such rewards became increasingly "generous" and the numbers of those due them grew, as deals and more deals created increasingly complex organisations, structures and fiefdoms at Warner and those companies seeking to emulate its success. A further reflection of this was a new species of biographies and (usually ghosted) autobiographies, books about and by record company executives. The books took two different tacks. Some told the stories about legendary record men of the past, such as John Hammond and Jerry Wexler, people who recognised talent and had style. Thus, Bob Dylan, initially a poor-selling act for CBS' Columbia label, was dubbed "Hammond's folly", Hammond being the man who signed him (and had the power to do so). The culmination of this approach was George Tow's profile of Ahmet Ertegun, which ran across two issues of the *New Yorker* magazine in 1978. It treated Ertegun as a glorious example of a "record man" and a prince of high society with a firm grasp of low life realities. A second strand was inaugurated by Clive Davis in 1975 with *Clive: Inside The Record Business*. These books were about managing talent, about executives with "vision", who, for example, could turn a company around by repositioning it (as Davis claimed he did by transforming CBS into a rock oriented company after "seeing the future" at the Monterey Pop festival of 1967).

The Kinney Corporation was an example of a 1960s conglomerate. Through a series of mergers and acquisitions it was transformed from a funeral service company into a media entity (with parking lots on the side). Another such company, this time with beginnings in insurance, car-financing and small manufacturing interests, was the Transamerica Corporation. It too wanted to get into the entertainment business, merging with film and record company United Artists in 1967 and a year later buying Liberty Records for $38m. After Kinney assimilated Warner 7 Arts in 1969 (at a cost of $400m, allowing Hyman, Semenko and Allen to make that profit) the company was promptly re-organised. Under the guiding hand of would-be media emperor Steve Ross the funeral services were sold off, the real estate assets (including the parking lots) were put into a public company, National Kinney Corporation, while the intellectual property elements (notably its film and music interests) were restructured as WCI.

Ross focused on rebuilding Warner's film division. Accordingly, he watched rather than controlled, as Ostin, Smith and Jac Holzman (after WCI bought his Elektra Records for $10m in 1970) made WEA, as the music division was renamed, the most successful US record company, surpassing Columbia in the pre-CD era. In those years WEA set up its own distribution, made its services available to a growing number of record companies in the US and opened branches overseas.

This growth didn't come without problems. People wanted to protect their fiefdoms. Thus, however attractive the idea of one back office servicing all the WEA labels in a variety of ways might seem to the centre, the label divisions wanted and got, until the much changed world of the late 1990s, complete control of their activities. Similarly, jealous of each other, the label divisions, Warner, Electra and Atlantic, competed with each other for new signings, of acts and distribution deals. Thus, Warner and Atlantic established separate branch offices in the UK, soon to be followed by Elektra. Similarly, when Warner executive Phil Rose arrived in Australia to begin setting up an Australian subsidiary, he discovered that only one week before, Atlantic had signed a new four-year distribution deal with a local company, Festival Records. This made the smooth running of WEA International more difficult. In 1970, Nesuhi divided the world between himself and Rose, making Rose responsible for WEA International in most of Latin America and Asia and taking control of WEA International in Europe and Brazil. By the late 1980s WEA International accounted for over 50% of WEA's revenues.

One reason for Warner's success was the explosive growth of the value of record industry sales. Between 1970 and 1980, the global value of recorded music sales at retail prices rose from $2.3bn to $11.4bn. All the majors benefitted from this trend, but Warner more than most. Its executives, while squabbling among themselves, were decidedly artist friendly.

Cornyn again: "Director Ed Thrasher and I created a massive billboard to stand above the Sunset Strip, with the faces not those of record acts but of Mo and Joe, whom we labelled The Gold Dust Twins. Pure self-pride. 'Why are these men smiling?' was our headline."

It's hard to think of any other record company in which such a celebration of its executives would be so well received by artists, their managers and the general public (let alone have the money and chutzpah to raise such a billboard). Columbia could boast in press adverts of the time that "The Man can't bust our music" and present Clive Davis, its then CEO, as the man who saw the future and changed the direction of Columbia by signing rock acts rather than pop acts, but it was The Gold Dust Twins and the savvy Ahmet Ertegun with whom managers wanted to associate and Warner the family of labels they wanted their acts to be on.

Witness the famous anecdote concerning the mythic British-based supergroup Scorpio. Cornyn again, in 1978: "Bidding wars for hot acts like James [Taylor], and especially supergroups from England, had become hotter than pizza ovens on Super Sunday." When managers Dee (Peter Frampton) Anthony and Brian (Yes) Lane spread word of *their* new supergroup – a killer act named Scorpio – many of America's label heads swooped in for quick acquisitions.

Scorpio was, however, a prank – a wholly fictitious band that Anthony and Lane had concocted to test how high label heads would bid (sight unseen, ear unheard) – for such an act. At a B'nai B'rith dinner honoring Ahmet Ertegun, the Scorpio buzz captured the ears of hot signers like Asylum's David Geffen, Clive Davis, and Robert Stigwood, the manager of the Bee Gees and Eric Clapton who had his own RSO Records label affiliated to Atlantic. Master of ceremonies Joe Smith commented on Scorpio from the podium: "Not content with ripping off the bands they already have, Brian Lane and Dee Anthony are going to start ripping off this new band, Scorpio."

Doug Morris and Dick Vanderbilt sent their lawyer over to the Lane-Anthony table with an advance offer of $250,000 if their label, Big Tree (distributed by Atlantic), got Scorpio. Anthony rejected the deal money, politely implying it was too low. Ertegun insisted, in the weeks following, that Scorpio be on Atlantic. Contracts were actually drawn up by lawyers, despite no band-members' names being attached to the fictitious group. Signing pens were uncapped. Only as the pens hovered over contracts did the "managers" of "Scorpio" confess their deception to Ertegun. He thought the matter over, then commented dryly, "Hysterical." (Other versions of the story have a leading Warner executive marching to the Lane-Anthony table after news of Scorpio had started to spread around the room at the B'nai B'rith dinner and angrily complain that the band should have been offered to Warner first.)

The spate of mergers and acquisitions in the 1960s was little more than a trickle compared to the torrent of the 1990s and beyond. However, they reflected a re-evaluation of the music business, first by outside investors and then by record company executives themselves. Music was seen as a leisure time business that catered to the fast growing and increasingly affluent youth market that accounted for half of the population of the US and had a spending power far above that. As such it was a business to buy into. It was also a business in need of new capital to fund international expansion. By the end of the 1960s it was clear that much to the chagrin of melody-loving Columbia A&R supremo Mitch Miller rock'n'roll was more than a passing fad and that there was natural growth in the music business. I calculate that the retail value of the global sales of recorded music grew almost fourfold between 1960 and 1970, from $633m to $2.33bn. Such growth was impressive, but the amounts were still small.

But what if the amounts in question changed? Between 1970 and 1980 they rose fivefold, then in the 1980s came the CD bonanza, which lasted until 2000. It was the potential activity (and profits) that this represented that made the business doubly attractive to outsiders and investors in the 1980s and 1990s. Hence the decision by German media conglomerate Bertelsmann to extend its commitment to music, buying

RCA from General Electric for $300m in 1986 (*see* Chapter 5), Sony's purchase of the CBS Records group, which included the Columbia and Epic labels, in 1988 (*see* Chapter 11) and Seagram's sweeping up of first MCA and then PolyGram in 1998 (*see* Chapter 4). Bertelsmann's move was particularly noteworthy because, unlike itchy fingered US investors, the company was notoriously cautious and had strict financial rules that governed its investments, rules that would eventually lead to it withdrawing from recorded music.

Another trend that began in the 1960s was what might be called the stretching and reshaping of the industry itself. On the one hand, separate entities, like music publishers and record companies, were joining forces, while on the other, a plethora of new bodies started to appear, most notably production companies offering finished master deals to record companies and artist-owned labels needing infrastructure support. This swiftly led to the creation of a new level of executives to handle the new activities demanded of the majors as their revenues and scope expanded, including a raft of deal makers able to buy small, then mid-sized and finally large companies. The significance of these changes was less visible in the 1960s, beyond the idea that being a record company executive, which was no career for a right-headed person in the 1950s, was seen as "cool". As the years went on, despite periodic downturns in sales, from the 1970s on record executives were also far better paid, especially after the CD bonanza. The public face of the industry was the likes of über-cool Turk Ahmet Ertegun, Jamaican Chris Blackwell of the Cross & Blackwell dynasty, the founder of Island Records, and bearded, sweater-clad hippy entrepreneur Richard Branson, the founder of Virgin (and even on occasion the lesser known Mo Ostin). They were profiled and acknowledged in upscale magazine pieces. But alongside them a raft of far lesser known executives were also being well paid.

The record company executive, especially the dealmaker, had come of age. In each successive decade the number of chiefs expanded at a far greater rate than was required to look after the increased numbers of their various tribes. As the power and demands of superstars rose so did the demands of the executives they did business with, the executives finding themselves pushing at an open door as the corporations they worked for sought to keep them happy and in place. Hence the proliferation of stock options, bonuses and strategic offers to leading executives. Thus, for example, in 2003, after rejecting their $5bn offer for its music division, UMG, French conglomerate Vivendi considered it politic to offer the three key executives in question, Doug Morris, Lyor Cohen and Jimmy Iovine, a 7% stake in UMG at a preferential rate.

In part this was an indication of an industry that was shifting from seat-of-the-pants decision making to having Harvard MBAs as your assistants, but it also led to ideas of aggrandisement and high drama. Walter Yetnikoff, head of the CBS Records Group between 1975 and 1987, whose self-proclaimed motto was "Fuck Warner Bros.", explained how the bizarre bidding war that he mounted against Warner Bros. came about. In the course of the war CBS signed James Taylor from Warner Bros. (paying him a $2.5m advance and a guaranteed $1m per album) and pre-emptively signed prestige artists, including Paul McCartney and The Beach Boys, to prevent them from going to Warner Bros. Ostin in turn successfully won Paul Simon from CBS and pre-emptively signed the likes of Rod Stewart (who was given a 10 album deal at $2m per album) to prevent him from going to CBS.

In his autobiography, *Howling At The Moon*, one chapter of which is called 'Fuck The Bunny', Yetnikoff noted: "I [had] deep CBS money, and I was willing to spend it. I was intent on making noise. As a label honcho I needed an identity. Artists had images, and in this new era of corporate power so did execs. How would I gain [my image]? ... By knockout, that's how. By charging out of my corner like Raging Bull. By finding a way to shock my staff and the industry with the fact that Columbia Records was ready, willing, able and eager to win at any cost."

Yetnikoff prefaced this account of the war with Warner Bros. with the aside that: "With Warner movies and Warner music at his command, Ross was a smooth operator, a much beloved leader, who, unlike CBS, paid his underlings well." Yetnikoff's own salary would soon rise, but more significant was the cash washing around CBS and other major record companies. Yetnikoff again: "The mystique of the music business is that, though profits are huge, accounting is incomprehensible ... calculating profits requires decoding a system that defies normal scrutiny."

Commenting on this, analyst and former music industry executive David Kronemeyer noted: "Yetnikoff's use of the term 'profits' is imprecise; what he really means is 'free cash flow' generated by record company operations, which then can be deployed for other corporate purposes."

As WEA grew, money became more like Monopoly notes. When David Geffen (manager of Laura Nyro and Jackson Browne, who was also 'advising' the Eagles) started his own Asylum Records in 1970, he secured finance from Atlantic who distributed it. He struck a deal whereby at the end of the relationship he would get back ownership of the master recordings (this in contrast to Stax Records, who discovered late in the day that all their recordings that were released via Atlantic became Atlantic's property). The label was a success and Steve Ross, knowing the distribution agreement was coming to an end, offered to buy the company, $2m in cash and $5m in WCI stock. Geffen agreed and when the value of WCI stock fell to placate him Ross offered Geffen the job of running a combined Elektra-Asylum at a salary of $1m a year. As a bonus Geffen was to receive every five years 20% of the difference between $40, the value of the stock when Geffen sold Asylum, and its current price. Monopoly time.

And so WMG grew. During the period 1975–87, according to Kronemeyer, WEA had global revenues of $10.1bn compared to CBS' $13.9bn, but a return on sales of 12.2% compared to CBS' 7.9%, making WEA the more profitable. The parent company WCI made mistakes, overextending itself, buying the Atari computer company in 1976, only for the cash cow to turn into a cash hungry disaster. It also created and briefly co-owned MTV in partnership with American Express only to rapidly sell off it and Atari in 1984–85. But WEA continued to grow.

Warner took to the CD quicker than EMI and in the course of negotiations concerning its introduction, entered into preliminary discussions for a merger with Philips' PolyGram Records. That didn't come to pass, but when in 1987 Philips sold off PolyGram, WCI snapped up its publishing arm, Chappell Music, for $275m and merged it with its Warner Music publishing division. Then, in 1990, WCI merged with media giant Time Inc. The deal was called a merger but in effect Time Inc bought WCI for $14bn, creating Time Warner in what Time CEO Gerald Levin called at the time "a Transforming Transaction". For WCI the deal was also financially transforming: 50 WCI executives, film as well as music officers, received $680m between them in signing on fees and 20% of Time Warner's new stock was reserved for them at a fixed price of $38 a share.

Time Life's takeover of WCI began as a merger but was upped to a takeover when Paramount put in a bid for Time. Thus, the takeover became both a defence of Time's independence and an indication of the growing sense that a modern media company had to be wider than merely print-based, a view echoed across the Atlantic at Bertelsmann. And so Time Warner grew, becoming the largest media company in the world, with assets in excess of $20bn. WEA's music revenues in 1991 were in excess of $3bn, with operating profits of $550m, and by 1995 its domination of the USA was complete: that year WEA had a 26.1% market share, almost twice that of CBS, 13.9%, which was closely followed by PolyGram (13.5%), BMG (12.4%), EMI (9.8%) and MCA (9.7%).

However, the increased status that the move from Hollywood's cardboard mansions to New York's marbled floors brought increased visibility and a new set of problems. In 1992, a major controversy blew up over Ice-T's provocative gangsta rap single 'Cop Killer' from his *Body Count* album. The recording, which mentioned Rodney King, who had been beaten up by police in Los Angeles, was released just before the controversial acquittal of the officers charged with King's beating, which had led to the 1992 Los Angeles riots. In response police associations called for a boycott of Time Warner products, politicians, such as President George Bush, and would-be media censors, such as Tipper Gore, denounced Warner for releasing the track, Warner executives received death threats and stockholders threatened to sell their shares in the company. Ice-T later voluntarily reissued *Body Count* without 'Cop Killer' – replacing it with the equally vitriolic 'Freedom Of Speech' – but the fracas left Time Warner in a panic and in January

1993 it released Ice-T from his contract and returned the *Body Count* master tapes to him. While that solved Warner's presentational problems it gave UMG, to which it sold Interscope, the Warner label that had part financed Death Row Records on which *Body Count* had been released, a dominant market share in rap music, which then accounted for some 10% of recorded music sales in the US.

The company was also beset by a management crisis. At WEA the tensions long held at bay by Steve Ross' light hand on the tiller erupted after his death in 1992, resulting in one of the most public internal power struggles, which *The New York Times* described as "a virtual civil war" that led to a string of major executives leaving the company. Ostin believed in and paid for talent, both artists and executives; the new Warner Music Group chairman Robert Morgado, who had joined in the late 1980s, believed in cost-cutting and in his power as chairman being visible to all, most clearly in the new reporting structures he introduced.

First Bob Krasnow, the head of WEA's Elektra/Asylum/Nonesuch group, left, setting in motion a lawsuit by Elektra's most successful act of the period, Metallica, seeking a release from their contract and ownership of their master tapes on the basis that this had been promised by Krasnow and was now being denied them. Ostin then announced he would not renew his current contract and would leave when it expired at the end of 1994. Doug Morris, appointed President and Chief Operating Officer of WEA, settled with Metallica. Then, in October 1994, Morris and 11 other Warner executives in the words of the *L.A. Times* "staged an unprecedented insurrection that nearly paralyzed the world's largest record company". This led to Morgado being ousted and replaced by Home Box Office chairman Michael Fuchs. In the meantime Morris appointed "his men" to the leading positions within WEA, before being fired himself by Fuchs on the basis that he was "leading a campaign to destabilise Warner Music in an effort to seize control of the company". A relative calm returned with the appointment of Terry Semel and Robert Daly, the heads of Warner's film division, to oversee music too.

The story of the period, which is told in some detail in Stan Cornyn's *Exploding* and Fred Goodman's *Fortune's Fool*, is more than just an entertaining tale. Just as the furore surrounding 'Cop Killer' had been distasteful so the public bloodletting within Time Warner's music group following the death of Steve Ross was considered ungentlemanly at the very least. When I set up the newsletter *Music & Copyright* with the *Financial Times* in 1992, it was a quicker than expected success and the head of the *FT*'s newsletter division proposed a lunch in the *FT*'s dining room with invited industry figures, record company heads and suchlike, to celebrate and further promote in a convivial manner the aura of respectability the *FT* saw itself giving the industry. After the lunch on the way down in an elevator one of the *FT* directors muttered in my ear: "That went well. They didn't even throw the bread rolls around." The Warner Music executives had, twice. And henceforth Time Warner's interest in its music division fell.

Stan Cornyn again, in 2000:

On a trip to New York, I lunched with a Wall Street analyst, an acquaintance of mine. I'd called ahead, asking him to explain why, so suddenly, Warners was bums… My counsellor had brought to lunch a small pile of Time Warner's Annual Reports … He first showed me 1996's TW Annual Report, which talked a lot about the value of 'branding'. He explained that meant 'you put out more Superman CDs'. The Music Group appeared on page twelve, equivalent to finishing fifth in the Derby.

About Music, the report's writers had claimed 'outstanding achievements by Music Group artists were a bright spot in what was a difficult year *[visualize him punching his finger at the roman words]* throughout the music business. Adverse market conditions *were characterized by* ongoing weakness in the retail sector that is expected to continue through 1997. Warner Music Group has responded with a series of initiatives designed to increase efficiencies and reduce costs…*' 'Okay,' he told me, brushing crumbs off my cuff, 'now watch this!' He pulled out the next one: 1997's report. It showed Music moved back nine pages, to page 21, part of Daly and Semel's Entertainment group. Levin had been made to say that 'except for the Music Group, which continued to restructure in the face of internal and external challenges…' Later on, Daly was quoted: 'We had a weaker release schedule than in past years, partly because a number of our major stars pushed back their album release dates from '97 to '98. We always have* slippage, but rarely at the level we felt in 1997. Our catalogue sales were down, too, *which really speaks to an industry-wide problem, and we had a decline in our direct-marketing operations [Columbia House, half owned by Warner]. On top of that, we've had to deal with all the negatives that accrue from* flat markets, sluggish economies, *and currency fluctuation in various parts of the world. This mix made it a difficult year.*'

He nodded at me in a way I can only describe as shrewdly. While a waiter gave too much importance to decrumbing our table, my tutor, ready with an air of wisdom, found his next dog ears in 1998's report. 'Where's your Music now?' he asked.

Page 29, I saw, nestled inside Entertainment. He had underlined 'the continuing recovery of the US retail music business and a growing presence overseas, Warner Music Group regained its positive momentum… accounted for 23 of the year's 100 best-selling albums… share of US album sales was 19.8 percent.' I felt good, even if Music was finished off in just two skimpy columns. The report named no executives. Later in the book came a different story: 'Revenues decreased to $3.691 billion … EBITA decreased to $467 million from $653 million.' Uttering the phrase 'cappuccino Florentine', he nodded at the waiter and picked up his final report.

The one for 1999 seemed seriously short. Now, no division executives at all were pictured. Music was stuck back at page 29, but even the names Daly and Semel were gone, without explanation. Music was down to nine percent of TW's EBITA. In the back pages, an explanation went, 'While our Music business declined eight percent during the year, all of our other established businesses delivered solid, double-digit EBITA growth.'

My host looked over at me and exercised his eyebrows. 'When analysts meet with Jerry [Levin] now,' he said, 'music is not something he likes to talk about.' For five years, TW had been saying 'Wait till'. Back to the report, he pointed out where TW's Richard Parsons explained 'adverse economic conditions in Japan, Germany, and Brazil, three of the five major international markets' and where Jerry added 'some slippage' to that, because major performers — Madonna, Alanis, Jewel — had not shown. Or, as the report's next sentence quoted Jerry, 'Not enough of our big horses were out there.'

> *I asked my friend if he thought, under the circumstances, he could pay for lunch. He was a friend indeed.*
>
> *I saw it clearly. The continuing decline of the Warner Music Group's performance had handed Wall Street the yawns. An analyst at some Dutch financial conglom called Barings had written, 'Given that the entire music division represents only 10 percent of the company's [i.e. TW] cash flow, one would have to argue that the division is practically worthless.*

IFPI's figures for global music sales put this in more detail. After slow growth in the first half of the 1990s, far slower than in the 1980s, came first several flat years and then at the end of the decade the beginning of the decline in the global value of recorded music sales (*see table below*).

Retail value of global recorded music sales, 1991–2000 ($m)

Year	Retail value	percentage change
1991	27,476	–
1992	29,464	+7
1993	31,147	+5
1994	36,124	+16
1995	39,741	+10
1996	39,792	+0.3
1997	38,616	–3
1998	38,236	–1
1999	38,507	+0.8
2000	36,964	–4

Source: IFPI

Between 1995 and 2000 sales fell by 7%; in the same period the revenues of the Warner Music Group fell by almost 9% from $4,196m to $3,834m. All the majors were suffering to some degree, but WMG was the first to feel the immediate impact.

Cornyn again: "Daly's and Semel's contracts were to expire on the last day of the century. The July before, it came time to talk about the next term. Jerry Levin told them he wanted a next term, but on better conditions: that the music division be controlled by others; that their annual pay (said to be about $25 million each) be reined in; that they'd get fewer stock options; and that operations at Warner Bros., including private jets, round-the-clock nannies, and gifts of new Range Rovers to their executives – all that outdated, Steve Ross stuff – now lingering only in Burbank at WB and [Warner Brothers Records] would come to a halt. This was a new millennium on the way."

And so it happened, but once out of the bottle the genie could not be persuaded to return. Henceforth, while respect for the old guard of the record business, the Jerry Wexlers, rose and rose, it was the salaries of the generation of executives after them (and the monies spent on the likes of Boston Consulting) that reached the stratosphere. As the executives fled from WMG (and to a lesser extent from CBS) their habits and expectations coursed through the business. As deal-making became central to survival in the increasingly destabilised industry the certainties of the past grew ever more powerfully comforting. The universe had shrunk, but its one-time masters took no account of that. Unfortunately, as we shall see, they were no longer masters.

There was indeed a new millennium on the way. One of the reasons that Time Warner had started to distance itself from music was that it was about to redefine itself again. In its first public statement of 2000, on January 19, it announced it was merging with the Internet company AOL.

"Nothing will be the same again," said Jean-Marie Messier, CEO of Vivendi, "AOL and Time Warner are the first to understand that the new and the old economies must merge." The orthodox view at the time, expressed by a major shareholder in Seagram, soon to be entangled with Messier, was that "we are going to a world of vertically integrated companies where only the big survive". Edgar Bronfman, Jr. went one further: "We're going to get eaten alive here," he told John Borgia, Seagram's head of human resources, according to Nicholas Faith, author of *The Bronfmans: The Rise and Fall of the House of Seagram*. "Convergence" between every aspect of "content" and its "distribution" was the goal. A decade earlier Time Warner had been worried that being primarily print-based was too limiting in the fast-changing media landscape, now Levin was even more fearful of the seemingly unstoppable rise of the Internet companies, above all AOL. In retrospect, Levin was overly influenced by the analysts who talked up the dotcom bubble: when presenting the case for the merger he had Mary Meeker of Morgan Stanley, the analyst most closely associated with promoting the value of the Internet, address his executives and warn them that they had to act immediately. In 1995, Meeker and Chris DePuy at Morgan Stanley, published *The Internet Report*, which was quickly tagged as "the bible" for investors in the dotcom boom. In 2011, in an interview with the *Daily Telegraph*, Jeff Bewkes, the chairman and chief executive of Time Warner, described the merger with AOL as "the biggest mistake in corporate history", but at the time it was widely seen as a pre-emptive *tour de force*, giving TW first-mover advantage in a troubled media world.

At the same time as the agreed merger with AOL, TW, seeking a significant degree of cost-cutting in the physical world, approached EMI and proposed that the two might merge their two music companies. But this was never a priority for TW, as EMI was to discover.

Chapter 4

Would You Like To Dance? EMI And WMG

EMI was not the only hybrid company that had expanded its music interests. Hollandsche Decca Distributie, which was established in 1931 as the exclusive distributor of Decca product for all of the Netherlands and its colonies, was bought by Dutch electronics company Philips in 1942 on the basis that if one made gramophones it was sensible to make records as well.

Accordingly, Philips sought to expand its recording division, successfully merging it with Deutsche Grammophon in 1962 to form GPG. Jointly owned by Philips and German engineering conglomerate Siemens, GPG, renamed PolyGram in 1972, was the largest record company in continental Europe. In 1987, Philips, which with Sony was responsible for developing the CD in 1982 and more aware of the potential explosion of value in recorded music, bought the share of PolyGram held by Siemens and subsequently entered into a period of record company acquisition, buying Island in 1989, A&M in 1990 and Motown in 1993.

There then followed a change of management and philosophy at Philips in which the greater margins promised by synergy – here the potential match between various types of content creation, notably music and film, and the ownership of the manufacturing and distribution means of that content – were rejected in favour of efficiency and cost-management. The new board saw synergy as being fraught with too many problems when the major film and music repertoires were US-owned and the costs of building (or buying) into them were rising, but bringing little immediate success. Accordingly, in 1998 Philips sold PolyGram to drinks conglomerate Seagram, which merged it with its newly created Universal Music Group (UMG).

That wasn't meant to happen.

When, in 1996, Sir Colin Southgate said at Thorn EMI's last annual report meeting prior to the de-merger "this is likely to be my last annual report statement to you as chairman of Thorn EMI in its present form", he deliberately introduced the narrative that the newly de-merged EMI might be available for sale, speculating that the value of EMI Music (recorded and publishing) was about £5bn ($7.8bn) and that any buyer would have to "pay a premium on top of that". Southgate pointed to the manner in which EMI's recent acquisitions had allowed it to improve its profitability through economies of scale in manufacturing, distribution and administration in its recorded music division, noting that following the purchase of Virgin the staff there was cut by a third. (This last claim neatly bypassed the fact that the organisational problems caused by the different cultures of merging companies often outweighed the efficiencies promised by a merger or takeover, a fact that would become central in subsequent restructurings of the major record companies). In music publishing Southgate noted that the integration of SBK and EMI Music Publishing (EMI MP) had resulted in a 50% cut in staff numbers.

From the shareholders' perspective, the de-merger was a great success, with shares in the new EMI group rising sharply in the company's first week of trading to a high of £14.88 ($23.02). In contrast, the other half of Thorn EMI, the consumer goods rentals and rent-to-buy business Thorn, performed badly. Fears of slack consumer demand in the UK and US, its main markets, pushed down Thorn shares to a low of £6.04 on August 19, their first day of trading, before settling at around £6.19. This gave the de-merged group's two companies the distinction of being the best and worst performers respectively on the UK stock market FTSE 100 index on their debut.

At the shareholder meeting authorising the de-merger Sir Colin noted that there had been no serious bid for EMI, which now comprised the group's record labels, music publishing, HMV music stores and Dillons book shops. However, from now on the idea of a sale, particularly if it could include Southgate's "premium" that would generate further benefits to the shareholders, was always central to the evolving EMI story.

Pressures came from EMI's shareholders seeking to make good on their investment and from the market as general business concerns were increasingly applied to the record industry. Previously, when the industry had been below the radar of analysts, to be successful had been enough. Similarly, the industry was expected to be inhabited by a number of exotic, if not outrageous characters, figures such as Maurice Oberstein (then the head of CBS Records UK who almost always brought his dog Charlie along to meetings), rather than sober-suited businessmen. But once intellectual property was perceived to be of financial value and analysts became the indicators, if not the arbiters, of that value, record companies were expected to behave as traditional businesses. Initially some of the measures by which (publicly quoted) record companies were judged were crude, but relatively quickly, as the value of intellectual property was accepted, analysts became more sophisticated. As this happened, earlier unconsidered concerns – for example, that a company with an international reach should be "relatively" equally successful in all the geographical regions in which it operated, or that a company's releases pattern should be controllable, with a steady number of major releases being made available on a regular basis – came to the fore.

This new spotlight shone especially brightly on EMI, the only large publicly traded music company in the UK, which in 1998 became the willing subject of a takeover, the first it ever publicly acknowledged. After months of speculation EMI confirmed in April that it had received an approach for a "possible offer". At the time EMI did not disclose the identity of the interested party, but it soon became apparent that it was

Edgar Bronfman, Jr., who had previously created the Universal Music Group (UMG) following its purchase of MCA (and had opened talks with EMI a year earlier).

In 1994, Bronfman, the head of the Seagram company, who 10 years later would end up in control of WMG, began the process of diversification, moving the Bronfman family's assets from old style reliable commodities, nylon and drinks, into intellectual property, which he, and many others, saw as having greater potential for growth. Seagram bought a 14.5% stake in TW, opening the door to a possible takeover, but TW, viewing him as a threatening investor, did not welcome him. Bronfman eventually sold the shares at a profit, but it was not until his takeover of MCA, financed by the sale of Seagram's stock in Dupont, in 1995 that Bronfman won his spurs as an entertainment executive, simultaneously securing the first of a series of harsh judgments on his business sense. One *New York Times* article carried the headline *What Shiny Toys Money Can Buy*, and described MCA as Bronfman's "playground".

News of Bronfman's interest in EMI added 20% to the price of EMI shares, equivalent to almost £1bn ($1.67bn) in one day's trading. That said, EMI's failure to match its European success in the US and worries about its management structure and its reliance on the sales of a few key acts – these last two the key concerns of the analysts – were clearly problems for any sale.

Another issue, one that had been raised in earlier discussions with Bronfman and an issue that would be a constant in all subsequent merger/takeover attempts, was the future role of EMI's senior management. EMI wanted them to remain in place; Bronfman was less sure. More satisfactory was "the fit". UMG was seen as a natural partner for EMI because it has a significant presence in recorded music in the US (a 12% market share), but only a small, albeit fast-growing, international presence. Moreover, it had a publishing company that could be easily integrated into market leader EMI MP. A further, and far more complex, issue raised that would also become central to future mergers/takeovers was "the regulatory fit". At the time, based on 1997 figures, I calculated that a merged EMI-UMG would have an

18% global recorded music market share and a 25% share of the US album market, making it the largest music company in the world. Such market shares would have been expected to arouse the interests of US anti-trust authorities and the European Commission, as indeed they did in future mergers/takeovers.

A final feature of the EMI/UMG negotiations, which were also a feature of virtually all subsequent mergers/takeovers, was what might be called "the sick man of Europe syndrome". In 1998, despite having spun off its retail business to become a standalone music company that was increasingly judged on its financial and market share performance, EMI was still seen as both ripe for the picking and very willing to be plucked. Similarly, as the financially better placed company, UMG was able to simply walk away from the deal, a strategy other companies would often echo with regard to EMI.

One reason Bronfman was able to walk away from his putative deal with EMI is that he had another option: PolyGram. As noted above, PolyGram, in a similar fashion to EMI, but far more efficiently and expediently, had also expanded its music interests. Nonetheless, in great part due to the erratic nature of the recorded music industry and the high cost of entry into the film industry, Philips, PolyGram's owner, lost confidence in the potential that PolyGram represented, particularly as its CEO Alain Levy was trying to build PolyGram's film traction from the bottom up at great cost to Philips. The board, increasingly unhappy about this, decided to quit both film and music and PolyGram was put up for sale.

Bronfman switched targets on the simple basis that he wanted to buy a significantly sized European record company and that making a deal with Philips for PolyGram would be easier. UMG already had a strong US market share and was in the process of building up its international presence, but building was both costly and time consuming. Having committed himself to entertainment and its growth potential, Bronfman wanted to quickly expand his entertainment assets. Buying PolyGram gave him global market leadership in one fell swoop. And it was a far easier deal to conclude. Whereas EMI was seeking to profit from the sale, which required a higher price and negotiations dragging on in the hope of securing that, Philips, which wanted to quit the entertainment business, was a willing seller.

Making a deal easy to conclude would become central to subsequent mergers/takeovers, often creating a dilemma for EMI. Another feature of the UMG/PolyGram deal was that it introduced Doug Morris and Roger Ames to the world stage. As the head of the revitalised UMG, Morris would over the coming years become the source of stability for UMG that would allow it, through various executives, notably Zach Horowitz, to follow strategies that were rarely short term at times when a number of the company's competitors, including EMI, were repeatedly caught up in short-term concerns. Ames would become the first significant gun for hire of the modern record business, a roving executive who worked first with PolyGram, then WMG and finally EMI, in the latter years mostly in a shadowy role.

The deal concluded, UMG made it clear that, as the smaller music company outside the US, it needed to keep as many PolyGram executives as possible. Thus, senior PolyGram executives were offered leading roles in Europe, Latin America and Asia. At the same time, Bronfman once again declaring himself content oriented, sold a variety of assets, including its Tropicana drinks brand to Pepsi Co for $3.3bn, to help fund the purchase of PolyGram.

EMI took the view that UMG's change of heart was unfortunate but quickly retreated to the financial high ground, repeating that it would only sell itself at a price that would fully benefit its shareholders. The City demurred, taking the view that a standalone EMI was no longer viable. A report by Dresdner Kleinwort Benson (DKB) at the end of 1998 forecast that the company's falling US market share and increased piracy problems would mean that EMI's revenues would be flat and its profits would fall for some three years before returning to growth, before concluding that "the balance of probability weighs against a bid for EMI at present". When EMI published its annual results for the period 1999–2000, it performed better than DKB had predicted. Although sales rose by only 0.5% to £2.39bn ($3.55bn) – largely as a result of a 1.2% fall in recorded music sales to £2.03bn ($3.01bn) – operating profits rose 8% to £290m ($431m), EMI lost global market share, from 13.2% to

12.5%, according to the company. Another unsettling feature of EMI's sales – one that would continue into the future – was the company's over reliance on a few acts, such as Garth Brooks in the US and Hikaru Utada in Japan, for sales. Commenting on the interim figures six months to September 30, an analyst at ABN AMRO noted that Utada's sales alone were responsible for three percentage points of the company's Japanese market share.

But we're getting ahead of ourselves.

In March 1999, at the time of the annual report, Colin Southgate, for whom a sale of the company was the preferred option, was replaced by Eric Nicoli, for whom the sale or merger of the company was, in the eyes of most observers, the only option. Over the years – Nicoli was to remain at the helm of EMI in various roles until its sale in 2007 to Guy Hands' Terra Firma – Nicoli protested that the sale/merger of EMI was only one of several options that he considered, but the tortuous dance EMI made from one putative partner to the next suggested otherwise.

Interest in EMI as a potential partner did not take long to resurface. Its problems notwithstanding, EMI's significant market share outside of the US, its valuable back catalogue and leading music publishing market share made the standalone company an ongoing target for a wide range of companies seeking to expand their music interests. The first to offer itself as a partner was TW, which in January 2000 proposed the creation of a joint venture, WEMI, of WEA and EMI. (Actually the company would not be a partnership of equals; TW's WMG would have 50.1% and EMI a 49.9% share.) At the time, I calculated that the global market shares of BMG, SME and UMG were 10%, 18% and 22% respectively and had not changed significantly since the PolyGram takeover. On this basis I calculated that the new WEMI group would have a global market share of around 26% – IFPI later published the two companies' joint global market share at 25.7% in 2000 – and that in addition, the merged music publishing interests of WEMI would be even larger, at around 30%. According to figures released by WMG and EMI, WEMI had a *pro forma* turnover of $8.03bn for the year ending September 30, 1999, while according to their latest figures, UMG's revenues were $6.3bn (for the year ending June 30, 1999) and SME's revenues were $6.3bn (for the year ending March 31, 1999). In contrast the revenues of BMG were significantly smaller, at $4.6bn for the year ending June 30, 1999. This meant that WEMI would have both the largest recorded music and music publishing market share of any of the major international music companies and as such it attracted the interest of the regulatory authorities in both the US and Europe.

The deal between WMG and EMI was essentially defensive. In part it was seeking critical mass in the new digital marketplace, but the driving force behind it was the need for greater economies of scale in the troubled physical market. The CD bonanza was over. During the boom years, all the majors benefitted from increased revenues and profits, but in the more strained times of the late 1990s, although the still growing spend on leisure confirmed the continuing potential of the entertainment market. The problem for the majors was how to unlock that potential (and to get over the periodic dips in growth that might occur). Suddenly size mattered. EMI and WMG were not alone in such thinking. Thomas Middelhoff, CEO of BMGE's parent company Bertelsmann AG, just a week before the announcement of the proposed EMI–WMG merger, said that Bertelsmann planned to buy a major music company and was looking at both SME and EMI. In a speech given at the Bertelsmann Management conference in late 1998, Middelhoff succinctly, and even more aggressively, addressed the matter of size: "The position of the biggest media company is of no value, in and of itself. But in clearly defined market segments, market leadership is associated with disproportionately high profits."

Music was such a market segment and one, moreover, that was entering a period of fundamental transition. At the time, the key area identified, before record companies rediscovered their core activity as copyright creators, was the need to find increased manufacturing and distribution efficiencies in the physical market, while at the same time investing and making alliances in the new digital market. Indeed, the EMI–WMG joint venture documents identified these concerns as the starting point of the negotiations. Another feature of the talks was the savings that WEMI would represent, especially when seen in a historical perspective. Such talks would be a regular feature of all subsequent takeover/merger negotiations, with the figure of $400m quoted by WEMI as the annual cost saving being on the same scale as the $300m quoted by Seagram when it took over PolyGram.

Indeed, cost-cutting had become the main concern of the major record companies as the benefits from the shift to digital began to be outweighed by other changes in the marketplace. The process of consolidation and retrenchment was general, but the UK offers a good example of the process. As part of the need to position themselves for the predicted growth in e-commerce and respond to changes within the retail sector, the majors began reviewing their production and distribution (P&D) operations. Renewed concern with margins and economies of scale put pressure on the majors either to pull out of P&D or form joint ventures. The first stage of this was for the majors to move from national P&D towards regional solutions. In 1999, BMG, which had already ceased distributing its own product in Italy, signed a deal with sister company Bertelsmann Distribution Services (BDS), a general distribution company which handled product ranging from bibles to car parts, for the distribution of BMG product for three years from April 2000 in the UK. Separately, EMI, which held talks with BMG at the end of 1998 about the possibility of BMG acting as its P&D partner, acknowledged that it had been reviewing its P&D operations in Europe, while earlier in the year Sony and WMG inaugurated their long-planned UK P&D joint venture, the Entertainment Network (TEN), which replaced their individual UK distribution divisions. Based on 1998 figures from UK record industry association BPI, I then calculated TEN would distribute 23% of singles and 28% of albums sold in the UK in 1999. (In 2004, as the elimination of non-core activities took on an even grimmer urgency, TEN was sold to Canada-based independent manufacturer and distributor Cinram for an undisclosed sum.)

This effectively doubled the individual distributor market share of the partners and helps explain why BMG, which distributed 14% of singles and 11% of albums sold in the UK in 1998, decided to close down its UK distribution operation. Whereas independent distributors received a distribution fee for each title carried, the distribution of their own product represents a cost to the majors. In broad terms a market share of 20% or less made the majors' P&D costs onerous. This was particularly true of distribution. The shifts in retailing that had taken place in Europe over the last decade were a major contributor to this loss of P&D profit margin. The growing power of large music retailers, such as HMV, led to a new business model, whereby the chains accepted one-off huge deliveries of soundcarriers to a central warehouse and then distributed them to their own stores. In return they expected to pay less for the soundcarriers. (In later years as the physical market contracted further, chain retailers and even sophisticated retailers such as HMV collapsed).

Discounts became the norm. The UK offers a simple example of this. The entry of supermarkets into recorded music retailing in the UK in a significant manner in 1996 intensified the practice of discounting. Supermarkets, which according to UK trade association BPI in 2009 accounted for 23.6% of UK recorded music sales, successfully sought to pay less for soundcarriers just as they had successfully brought down the wholesale prices of a wide range of goods from baked beans to milk and electrical products. Like the major entertainment retailers they also had their own distribution systems. The net effect of these changes was that the amount of product passing through the majors' distribution systems fell, and while this was happening, the actual costs of physical distribution was rising. These commercial pressures increasingly applied to other territories around the world. In a number of markets, for example Australia and Malaysia, the majors set up joint distribution ventures. However, it was in the mature but complex markets of Europe and US that the pressures were the greatest. Ironically the one growth area within the distribution sector was fulfillment, the delivery of physical items that are ordered on the Internet. This involved the costly process of the delivery of small packets to a growing number of addresses and was mostly undertaken by independent companies, which benefit at the expense of High Street retailers. Thus in the UK, taking advantage of a tax loophole that VAT was not payable on goods valued at under £18, various small companies in the Channel Islands became the delivery partners of Amazon and the like, allowing the hybrid retailers to drastically undercut High Street prices for CDs and DVD. This loophole was finally closed in 2012, but long after its impact had led to the shuttering of various High Street stores. Elsewhere the digital distribution of recorded music grew apace, but the majors, for a variety of reasons (*see* Chapter 8), were unable to carve out a place for themselves in this arena akin to that which they had had in the physical marketplace.

A further pressure on the majors' P&D business came from the fact that they also had to prepare for the online era and digital distribution. This required significant investment that would not produce significant revenues in the immediate future and, even more importantly, a change of attitude in which previously highly valued practices and skills had to be jettisoned in favour of new, largely untested processes. As if this were not enough, as noted before, 2000 saw the end of the substantial and continued expansion in the value of the global recorded music market. The CD replacement factor had ended. At the same time, as recorded music became more widely available and a new set of retailers, well experienced in putting pressure on suppliers, entered the recorded music market, the strains on record companies' margins were intensified. One way of achieving economies of scale was expansion, broadening the content one owned and securing access to new markets. However, such expansion could be expensive and the investments risky.

It was in this complex situation that the EMI-WMG merger was announced. The issues were equally problematic for the regulators, who were asked to peer through a fog of competing analyses proffered by various interested parties and their lobbyists to come to a yea or nay decision. For them it was a voyage into uncharted waters. With this in mind, it is important to understand the differing concerns of the parties involved. In Europe, where the debate was most public, the EC's concern was with the matter of reduced competition – expressed most basically in the question "would the consumer suffer as a result of the merger?" In contrast, the interests of competitors, such as Walt Disney, were "would the merger make it more difficult for them to operate (profitably)". These interest were partially shared by the independents with the difference that their concerns, as expressed by their trade association IMPALA, were primarily those of smaller independents. Finally, although never an itemised concern of the competition directorate, which was examining the merger on behalf of the EC, above all there floated a concern with culture, as an economic activity: would this merger be in the interest of specifically European groups or would it speed up the Americanisation of European culture? This last issue would grow in the future, particularly as the EC moved from responding to proposed mergers and takeovers to taking the initiative and through a series of directives and recommendations outlining its preferred future for Europe.

At the same time that EMI and WEA, the music division of TW, agreed to merge their recorded music and music publishing interests to form the joint venture WEMI, TW announced that it intended merging with AOL, thus presenting the regulatory authorities with two (related) mergers to examine at the same time.

The conventional wisdom at the time had it that the two mergers were differently driven, the one, between WMI and WEA, being a defensive response to difficult market conditions and the other being an aggressive attempt to meld content and digital distribution to give AOL-TW a first-mover advantage. According to this narrative, when regulatory problems arose concerning WEMI its creation was sacrificed in the interest of securing the far more important (to TW) authorisation of the AOL-TW merger. Such a view is accurate, but from another perspective, the impact of the digital on the physical, the AOL-TW merger is more instructive than has generally been thought.

In particular, the merger threatened Bertelsmann, the parent company of BMG, which was significantly smaller than its competitors and a few months earlier had stated that it planned to buy a "leading music company" with the intention of taking advantage of market size.

The joint venture documents identified investing in and making alliances in the new online world as the starting point of the negotiations that on further examination led to the even more substantial agreement. However, in retrospect, such a view seemed to be offered primarily for public consumption. Although the problems posed by the coming online era were starting to be felt by the majors, most notably in the form of Napster, which had made the online sharing of music files an "easy to do activity", the focus of EMI and WMG was primarily on the physical world, where their combined recorded music market share, which I calculated at the time would be around 26%, making them the market leaders, ahead of UMG. Separately, the combined market shares of EMI MP and Warner Chappell would be over 50% in some European territories and around 30% globally.

World domination was a possibility.

Another major might seek to sweep up the world's significant independents, such as Zomba (which in 1999 was responsible for almost half of BMG's US market share), Japan's Avex or Germany's edel. However, the aggregate global share of the larger independents that operated in the international arena was significantly less than 10%, which was not enough to create a company with a 20 per cent plus share, and therefore have access to those "disproportionately high profits". Had the merger gone ahead, UMG would have remained the largest company in the US with a 28% share compared to WEMI's 25%, but in Europe, WEMI would have become the largest company with a 31% share compared to UMG's 25% share.

Announcing the proposed merger, both partners said they'd had talks with the relevant authorities and expected no problems because WEMI's market share of the recorded global music market, 25.7% on a *pro forma* basis in 2000 according to IFPI, was significantly less than 30%. Similarly, when the fact that the combined publishing market share of EMI Music Publishing and Warner Chappell was over 50% in some territories was raised, their response was that because publishers didn't set prices – mechanical and performing right rates are set independently of the copyright owners through negotiation between authors' societies and users – dominance within music publishing was expected to be treated by the regulators in a more relaxed fashion than other areas. At the same time, in view of the ease with which the Seagram purchase of PolyGram had been passed by the regulators, it was widely held that the creation of WEMI, a merger rather than a takeover, would be similarly nodded through.

This was not to be the case.

The US regulatory bodies hardly stirred themselves. That was not the case in Europe. Over the lengthy period of its investigation into the merger, the EC began to ask increasingly difficult questions relating to the possible creation of "a dominant market position or a strengthening of an already dominant position". This was laid out in a highly critical Statement of Objections (SoO) in September, 2000. The SoO found that the proposed joint venture would significantly reduce competition in the European Economic Area (EEA). It concluded: "The notified concentration [that WEMI represents] is incompatible with the common market and the functioning of the EEA agreement, since it would create a collective dominant position in the market for recorded music."

The report was even harsher on the music-publishing dimension of the proposed joint venture. With regard to that, it concluded that "the notified concentration would create a single dominant position in the markets for: 'Mechanical, performance and synchronisation rights throughout the EEA; the licensing of music rights for online music delivery; Online music; and Music software'."

The SoO was followed by a two day hearing at which EMI and TW representatives were offered the opportunity to rebut the EC's findings and introduce further evidence. At the hearing other interested parties were also given the opportunity to outline any objections they might have in greater detail. They included large multinational companies (for example, UMG), independent companies and their national and international trade associations, and authors' rights bodies. After subsequent informal discussions between EMI, which was leading the case for the joint venture, and the EC, the Commission noted that the parties offered no significant concessions that might alleviate its serious worries. In response EMI said it had addressed every issued raised by the Commission.

The SoO concentrated on the impact the creation of WEMI would have on three related markets: recorded music, music publishing and the developing online music market. Representatives of EMI and WMG argued that, although WEMI would be the largest record company in the world, it would not be able to unfairly exploit its market leadership. All that would happen, they argued, was that one company, WEMI, would replace another, UMG, as the global market leader but that the gap between them would be less than the existing gap between

UMG and second-place SME. Furthermore, they argued WEMI would not have uniform market leadership. As noted above, while it would be the leader in Europe it would be second-placed in the US after UMG. There were also some differences in dominance within Europe itself. At the time I calculated that WEMI would have been the 1999 market leader in seven European countries (Austria, 30% WEMI; 25.5% UMG), Denmark (47%; 17%), Germany (26%; 24.5%), Italy (33%; 28.5%), Spain (35%; 16%) Switzerland (26.5%; 24%) and the UK (31%; 25.4%), with UMG the market leader in France (34.2%; 25.3%) and the Netherlands (28.1%; 21.8%).

The WEMI partners also argued that the size of the potential new venture need not be an impediment to new players entering the market, or the growth of existing independents such as edel or Zomba, both of which had significantly increased their market shares in recent years. In response the SoO noted that the majors and the independents had markedly different characteristics, with the majors having global reach, vertical integration and being better diversified, while the independents were far more specialised and often relied on the majors to fulfill several functions for them. Additionally, while there was no bar to entry to the European recorded music market, the Commission noted that no independent had grown into a major. Rather, whenever one had reached a certain size, as in the case of Virgin, a major bought it. In effect, the EC argued that the independents did not compete with the majors, because to do so they would have to change strategy, build up a global presence, invest in distribution and compete for superstars. Rather, the EC suggested, the majors and the independents had a symbiotic relationship, with the majors setting the agenda.

The EC also noted that the structure of the European soundcarrier market was conducive to oligopolistic dominance as there was product homogeneity, standardised pricing, similar file, end-of-year and volume discounts with retailers, and significant commercial and structural links, such as joint deals on compilation albums and joint distribution deals within Europe. In both these last examples there has been increased co-operation between the majors. At the time there were some 40 compilation deals in Europe between the majors. Moreover, compilations, which then accounted for 18% of the majors' sales in the EEA, were more profitable than single artist albums.

The EC calculated that WEMI would own and/or administer 2m, or 33% of the estimated 6m music publishing copyrights in the world. WEMI accepted that it would be the largest music publisher in the world, but reiterated that publishers did not fix prices. According to WEMI's *pro forma* figures, WEMI would have an average 15% market share of the EU music publishing market. The spread of national market shares would be between 21% and 9%. The EC rejected these figures and the way in which they were formulated. On the basis of evidence supplied by the collection societies, the EC found that WEMI's market share would be much larger than 15%. Moreover, the WEMI calculations did not include the significant music publishing revenues from rights that are licensed directly by publishers, such as synchronisation. The licensing of compositions to film, television and advertising companies, synchronisation licensing, was done directly by music publishers. These revenues, which accounted for some 22% of the two companies' combined music publishing turnover, were not subject to rates set by the collection societies.

The EC made two further important distinctions: between music publishing market share and market control, and between the general market share a music publisher might have and the share of the synchronisation market, that a music publisher with deep back catalogue and Anglo-American repertoire might have. Because a high percentage of films, television programmes and advertisements are aimed at international markets their producers generally favour Anglo-American repertoire. On the basis of evidence placed before it, the EC calculated that WEMI had a *pro forma* share of the EEA music publishing market in revenues terms of between 30% and 40%, adding that WEMI's share would be three times more than the share of its next largest competitor in the EEA overall, and more than twice the size of the next largest competitor in any single EEA country. The report further argues that WEMI's control over the publishing market would be far greater than its actual market share. Publishers jointly hold many copyrights because many songs are co-written by authors represented by different publishers.

Although each publisher only receives the appropriate percentage of the revenues that a copyright generates, the permission of all the publishers of a work is required for its use. The EC argued that this had the effect of extending the control of large publishers over all the works they co-publish. This meant that in the significant areas of Anglo-American and catalogue repertoire, of which WEMI, according to the EC, has more than three times as many titles as any other publisher, its control might extend to over 50% of such repertoire. The report also noted that both Warner Chappell and EMI Music Publishing had strengthened their position in back catalogue, having acquired some 29 smaller publishers over the last three years.

WEMI's likely dominance of the far from transparent synchronisation market was of even greater concern for the EC. Synchronisation deals take place outside the tariff and regulatory structure that the collecting societies oversee with publishers setting synchronisation rates themselves in negotiations with film, television and advertising companies. The SoO noted that synchronisation deals entered into the US, where the major film and television companies are based, are normally extended to the EAA through international add-ons. The SoO thus concluded that WEMI would have "sufficient market strength to act independently of its competitors, users and ultimate consumers in setting the terms and conditions for the licensing of its synchronisation rights in the EEA Member States".

Several of WEMI's competitors suggested that in terms of copyrights owned and administered outright WEMI would have significantly more than 50% of the synchronisation market. At the Brussels hearing a representative from the Walt Disney company argued that Disney was fearful of being over-charged for the use of WEMI copyrights in its films. He also claimed that EMI MP's synchronisation rates were currently 10% higher than the market level and was fearful that that price increase would be made to the Warner Chappell catalogue, which included such writers as Cole Porter, Eric Clapton and members of the Red Hot Chili Peppers.

A further issue raised in the SoO was that WEMI "will have the possibility to bypass the collecting societies" and license the use of its works directly. EMI had initiated such moves in the past. For example, in 1996 EMI MP had threatened to withdraw the mechanical right from the collection societies to the Simply Red album *Life*, all of the songs on which it published. EMI set up its own mechanical rights agency, MRSE, to collect the mechanical royalties due it. Subsequently EMI MP disbanded MRSE when the threats it and the actions by other leading music publishers posed secured significant concessions from the European collection societies. At the Brussels hearing a representative of WEMI promised on behalf of EMI MPI and Warner Chappell not to withdraw from the collection society system.

The SoO also looked at the emerging digital market, an issue that would continue to trouble the Commission in the following years, particularly with regard to the slowness of its development in Europe compared to the US. The EC concluded that "the notified concentration would create a dominant position in the markets for online music delivery and music software". The SoO made specific reference to the proposed merger of AOL and Time Warner. The EC noted that AOL had signed a preferred content agreement with Bertelsmann, and that therefore it would be "highly unlikely that Bertelsmann would make its content available through any other Internet services company than AOL". On the assumption therefore that AOL-TW would have access to BMG's music catalogue as well as WEMI's, the EC calculated that AOL would have access to some 50% of music publishing copyrights, and probably even a higher percentage of sought-after Anglo-American repertoire, and thus be in a privileged position *vis a vis* possible competitors.

A further concern expressed in SoO was that AOL's Internet dominance, if matched with music content domination, could also lead to the dominance of its own proprietary music software, Winamp. In response, WEMI made a guarantee that it would give no preference to Winamp and make its content available on open standards.

Implicit in the SoO was the idea that the potential partners consider the disposal of various assets. The merger partners quickly began looking for things to sell. In the first set of concessions offered to the Commission the putative joint venture partners offered to sell selected record labels and music catalogues in Europe, to divest part of their European manufacturing and distribution businesses, and to end their participation in compilation joint ventures. This was in response to a further statement by the Commission that it intended to block the deal unless the parties offered concrete proposals of divestiture. This followed the growing concern of the Commission that mergers between companies such as EMI and WMG, which were already among the group of companies that had a collective dominance within a market, were inherently anti-competitive. Thus, whereas the Commission saw competition as being possible between five companies, it did not see it as probable between four. This was in marked contrast to the EC's earlier, much more relaxed, stance. In the 1990s the EC only blocked 13 of the 1,500 deals that it considered. In 2000 it blocked several mergers.

WMG and EMI identified four European countries where they had large combined *pro forma* soundcarrier market shares – Denmark, France, Greece and Spain – and offered to sell CMC (in Denmark), Pathe Marconi (France), Minos (Greece) and Dro (Spain). However, these were territories where WEMI's revenues were low on a *pro forma* basis – around $900m – and not particularly profitable, compared to, say the UK where its share would be over 30%. Moreover, the combined value of their recorded music markets at retail prices was $2,581m in 2000, which was significantly less than the value of the UK market at $2,829m. Observers suggested that the offer to withdraw from joint production and distribution (P&D) was also a minor concession. Cutting P&D costs in Europe was one of the starting points of the merger negotiations between WMG and EMI. EMI had already held discussions about rationalising this area of activities with most of its competitors and sold all or part of its German and Italian P&D operations in 1999. As the majors came to see themselves as copyright producers and exploiters, the production and distribution of physical soundcarriers was increasingly considered to be a costly non-core activity. Accordingly, EMI had already sought to either withdraw from distribution, through contracting out P&D to third parties, or looked for manufacturing and distribution efficiencies through joint ventures. A seemingly more significant concession was to withdraw from joint ventures with BMG,

SME or UMG in the creation of compilation albums in Europe. In the light of the EC's observation that such albums account for a growing share of soundcarrier sales in Europe and generate sizeable profits for the majors, this concession seemed significant. However, as the proposed WEMI joint venture would control some 25% of European recordings and would also be able to license recordings from independents, the new joint venture would have access to an estimated 45% of hit recordings for its own compilation albums, making the concession less important.

Despite a series of last-minute concessions, the merger collapsed in October. EMI and TW had offered to dispose of Virgin Records and Warner Chappell Music, in addition to the record companies and music catalogues they had already offered to sell, in order to gain regulatory approval for the merger from the EC. But this appeared to be too little too late, and when it became apparent that the EC was about to block the deal, TW and EMI withdrew their application. A further reason was that TW was concerned that problems with the EMI deal could endanger its parallel $120bn merger with AOL. In effect, TW sacrificed the smaller merger to ensure acceptance of the larger deal. Indeed, immediately after the WEMI merger was withdrawn, it was widely reported that the Commission would approve the AOL-TW deal within the month; it did.

The last-minute offer by EMI to sell Virgin Records in order to gain EC approval was hugely unpopular with EMI's institutional shareholders. As a result, EMI noted in its official statement that any future sales agreement would need EMI Group shareholder approval. It was subsequently reported in EMI's 2000–2001 annual report that the advisory fees associated with the merger cost EMI £42.9m ($65m).

Many reasons have been put forward for the collapse of the merger. Three stand out: the anxiety felt by TW at the prospect that the EMI-WMG deal might derail the AOL-TW merger; the greater knowledge the Commission had developed about the workings of the record business; and the disrespectful manner in which the merger was presented to the Commission. Often different reasons melded. Thus, representatives of TW often spoke on behalf of the AOL-TW merger and then as an afterthought segued into talk of EMI-WMG. Similarly, the expectation of success was so strong that the concessions came far too late, literally: the proposed Virgin and Warner Chappell sell-offs were made after the EC's official deadline and thus it was too late for them to be given due consideration and be market tested. In general the stereotypes attached to the various parties turned out to be accurate: the Americans were brash, the Brits too easily flummoxed and the Commission far more sophisticated than expected.

The response of the City and Wall Street to the end of the merger was immediate: the share price of EMI fell 5.6% to £5.28 ($7.81) valuing the company at £4.2bn ($6.2bn) compared with £5.5bn ($8.13bn) when the merger was announced. In contrast TW's share price rose 5%. The two companies said that the decision to halt the merger was temporary and that they were in talks with the Commission "to devise solutions that address the regulator's concerns while preserving the economic merits of the merger". Indeed WMG imposed a "no talks" with anyone else clause on EMI.

Nonetheless, within six weeks EMI had a new suitor: Bertelsmann.

Chapter 5

Bertelsmann Gets Itchy Feet

To understand Bertelsmann's more aggressive approach to the "disproportionately high profits" that a union with EMI might represent it is useful to look in more detail at the AOL-TW deal, which was approved within a month of the termination of the WEMI joint venture, and at Bertelsmann's very different strategy with regard to music.

Privately owned, and fiercely so, Bertelsmann began as a publisher and printer of mostly religious books in Germany in the nineteenth century. Re-founded after WW2 – the company had a chequered war history involving close co-operation with the Nazi party – by the mid-1960s it had grown into a media giant with book publishing interests, record club operations and the ownership of leading magazines through Gruner + Jahr. In 1959 it set up Ariola Records in Germany when it started having trouble getting licences from other record companies for its record club releases and in the 1970s it began its transformation into a multinational company, first expanding the reach of Ariola, establishing branch companies in Benelux, Spain, the UK and in 1975 the US, which was always the focus of Bertelsmann's expansion plans. It bought Bantam Books and later Random House, while at the same time it partnered with US media groups, including AOL and Time Warner, in Europe where through its ownership of RTL it became the largest private radio and television broadcaster.

Bertelsmann quickly found that the USA was a difficult market to fathom for a European-based company and, losing money, in 1979 bought Arista, the grouping of Columbia Pictures' recorded music assets (primarily Colpix, Colgems and Bell Records) that Clive Davis, the former head of CBS Records, had put together. Davis's signings included the highly successful Barry Manilow, as well as more left-field artists like Patti Smith, Gil Scott-Heron and Loudon Wainwright III. He also tempted such seasoned acts as the Grateful Dead, Lou Reed, Al Stewart and The Kinks to the label during the later 1970s. In 1983, RCA took a 50% stake in the expanded Arista company and in 1985 the jointly owned Ariola/RCA International company was established to oversee the recorded music interests of Bertelsmann and RCA. As part of the agreement each partner had the right to buy out the other if there was a change in ownership in either company. Thus in 1986, following General Electric's purchase of RCA, RCA sold its 50% interest in RCA/Ariola International and its separately owned record club to Bertelsmann for $330m and the company was renamed BMG. Bertelsmann was now a major recorded music player. In the year before the sale RCA, benefitting from the first ripples of the CD boom, saw its sales increase 4% to $622m and subsequently the newly expanded company soon had far greater success, with hits from hip hop artists, various boy bands and the likes of Whitney Houston, who was spotted and nurtured by Davis.

However, as the CD boom cooled, size and the Internet became crucial issues. The opportunities represented by the entertainment business were still there but how best to seize them? One of the concessions offered by WMG and EMI to the European Commission was that the joint venture would not give any preference to AOL's proprietary music delivery software Winamp. This concession was made in response to the SoO which, after noting that there soon would be an online music market, concluded: "The notified concentration would create a dominant position in the markets for online music delivery and software". However, digital was essentially a side issue with regard to

WEMI. In contrast, the AOL-TW merger was fundamentally about the digital future. Ultimately the deal, like Guy Hands' takeover of EMI, represented a huge miscalculation. Even as broadband was becoming the future Gerald Levin thought AOL, a dial-up success, could make Time Warner future proof, just as Guy Hands invested in EMI just before the financial crash, thus saddling Terra Firma with a debt burden it proved impossible to crawl out from beneath.* The merger, the largest in American business history, came about because Steve Case (head of AOL) and Gerald Levin (head of TW) both believed, for very different reasons, that the Internet, in Levin's words, had begun to "create unprecedented and instantaneous access to every form of media and to unleash immense possibilities for economic growth, human understanding and creative expression". For Levin the problem was how to transform TW for the digital age: "We were emerging from not just old media but from an analog world into a digital world, and philosophically people were beginning to understand that the digital world was a transformational universe." Case's problem was more mundane, but equally pressing. How to use AOL's high-priced stock – it was valued at twice as much as Time Warner with less than half the cash flow – to make a big acquisition, buy a more traditional company, and create a company of the future that would have both online and tangible assets.

The announcement of the deal was hailed as a momentous coming of age for the Internet and a triumph of the New Economy. That optimism crumbled fast: four months later the dotcom bubble began to burst, and online advertising began to slow down, making it impossible for AOL to meet the financial forecasts on which the deal was based. At the same time people started to move en masse to high-speed Internet access in preference to AOL's dial-up service. Subsequently, the merger unravelled with almost as much publicity as at the moment of its creation and the two companies parted. Financial irregularities were discovered

---

* For a brief but comprehensive review of the merger, based on extensive interviews with the participants, see *How the AOL-Time Warner Merger Went So Wrong*, by Tim Arango, *The New York Times*, January 11, 2010.

in AOL's accounts, which had to be re-stated, and AOL continued to under-perform, but even more critical was the mismatch of the business cultures of the two companies.

Richard Parsons, TW's president at the time, later offered a bleak view of the failure of the deal: "The business model sort of collapsed under us, and then finally this cultural matter. As I said, it was certainly beyond my abilities to figure out how to blend the old media and the new media culture. They were like different species, and in fact, they were species that were inherently at war."

Bertelsmann had no greater luck with its dramatic entry into the digital world, via Napster.

Napster's key offering, music for free, won it a huge and growing audience: at the start of October 1999 it had 150,000 registered users exchanging 3.5m files per day; by July 2000 it had 20m users. In between the two dates Napster survived bad press comments from a number of "non-mainstream" artists, most notably the thrash metal pioneers Metallica. Eminem charged "If you can afford a computer, you can afford to pay $16 for my CD." More problematic, and certainly not solvable by exchanging T-shirts, was the filing in summer 2000 of a preliminary injunction requesting that the Napster MP3 website be closed down by US record industry association RIAA and the National Music Publishers Association pending a judgment on the copyright infringement case brought against Napster by the RIAA.

Prior to the emergence of Napster the record industry had been more perplexed than threatened by the advent and fast-growing appeal of digital files. The RIAA's filing marked the beginning of the first of the three distinct strategies developed to cope with the Internet: a "do nothing" attitude, on the assumption that the record companies would find a way forward themselves and didn't need outside assistance, thank you; demanding often crippling advances from would-be digital distributors; and finally litigation.

EMI took the view that when making a digital deal it should generate as much as possible in terms of upfront fees and take a share in the companies seeking to license EMI repertoire. This attitude, which was most aggressively pursued by the EMI's (then) head of interactive media, Jay Samit, led to some start-up digital companies crashing on the basis of the overly onerous licence payments and equity agreements required by EMI. One reason EMI (and to a lesser extent other majors) adopted this strategy was a desire to make up for their failure to profit sufficiently from MTV's success. The music-only TV channel had developed a hugely successful business on the back of screening videos given to it for promotional purposes by the major record companies alongside advertisements, for which they (rather than the record companies) received revenues, for teen and twenty-something oriented products. The new breed of digital companies, which had no need for the manufacturing and distribution facilities controlled by the majors, threatened the status quo to an even greater degree. Change was good if it meant that suddenly boy bands, of which you had a few, were the in thing; it was less so when you lost control of your content to upstarts who suddenly knew more than you and had inklings of ideas as to how to reach the consumer/fan in a more attractive and interesting way. The new Internet upstarts were a threat.

Of all the majors EMI strove to present itself as being most open to the coming digital revolution on the basis that it was a standalone music company and therefore not susceptible to non-music concerns. Samit persuaded a very willing EMI board not to make simple licensing deals with the various dotcom companies that were focused on music but, in addition to high advances to partner with them, demand equity as part of the licensing arrangement, equity which EMI could sell when the companies went public. Interviewed by Brian Southall, a former press officer at EMI and subsequently a chronicler of the company, Samit said: "We did 120 deals and made $200m in profits for EMI and at one point we did a deal every nine days." Jeremy Silver, EMI's first ever vice president of interactive media, described one such deal in detail. Musicmaker, which offered users an *a la carte* service in which they could have favourite tracks burnt on to a CD and then mailed to them, was about to launch its IPO and was in need of repertoire. EMI offered it a licence for the majority of its recorded music catalogue (but not that of The Beatles, The Rolling Stones and a few others) in return for a significant equity stake in the company, reportedly 50%. EMI sold the stock on the first day of Musicmaker's IPO in early 2000, netting it $30m.

Good business in the short term, such deals were crippling for the start-ups, many of which soon collapsed under their debt burdens, making Internet companies in general increasingly wary. In the course of a meeting with Gerry Kearby of Liquid Audio, which produced a proprietary format that included encrypted locks on digital music files, Al Smith of SME admitted: "Look Kearby, my job is to keep you down. We don't ever want you to succeed." Later Kearby noted: "Some of them were more interested than others, there's no doubting about it. But they were, in effect, buggy whip manufacturers, trying to keep the auto at bay as long as they could." Another response to this situation was for Internet new starts to get their business up and running and then worry about licences.

Bertelsmann (then) had no such fears. The parent company of BMG, Bertelsmann in 2000 owned 16 e-commerce companies, including bol (bertelsmannonline), CDnow and 40% of bn (barnes&noble) and would later have enormous success with its investment in AOL Europe. These interests were held through Bertelsmann's e-commerce division, BeCG, which Bertelsmann (then) saw as the way to expand the Internet presence of its wide range of content.

In 2000, Bertelsmann expanded its Internet reach by concluding a deal with Napster, making it an initial loan of $60m to help develop a legitimate version of the service. The deal was made despite the threats, which were carried out, of the resignation of BMG president Michael Dornemann and CEO Strauss Zelnick. In effect, Bertelsmann was willing to sacrifice its "music experts" to get what it considered an advantage in the soon to arrive digital world marketplace in which the old terms of business – in particular the control of copyright – it gambled, would collapse. Distribution – not content creation – was to be the king. Reflecting this (short-lived) truth Bertelsmann was drastically restructured with BMG stripped of its management responsibility for storage, manufacture and record clubs, including BMG Direct and CDnow. This strategy proved to be equally short-lived. The Napster deal also proved very expensive. In 2008, Bertelsmann found itself paying out significant sums to rights holders because its investment in Napster was held to have assisted Napster to continue infringing copyrights.

Like the AOL-TW merger, Bertelsmann's Napster deal was an attempt at a radical restructuring of a content oriented corporation in response to the emergence of the Internet. But, as was the case for TW re: AOL, Bertelsmann found it difficult extracting value out of Napster. Bertelsmann had to both implement an in-house corporate reorganisation to make sense of Napster and work out a way to convert Napster into a secure fee-paying service. Addressing an industry conference, Andreas Schmidt, the CEO of Bertelsmann's e-commerce division BeCG, said that the company was holding "active talks" with the other majors about them joining the alliance. However, UMG, then developing its own service with SME, rejected the overtures, thus depriving any legitimate file-sharing service of the repertoire of the two largest record companies in the world. But that was a minor problem. Neither Schmidt nor Napster executives could explain how a pricing model of a file-sharing service might work, a problem subsequently faced by all peer-to-peer (P2P) services that attempted to go legal. In a nod to the future both Napster's founder, Shawn Fanning, and Schmidt hinted that maybe the record industry has been too rigid in its attitude to security, at the same time reiterating that tracking usage and compensating copyright producers was essential.

But if the Napster deal and the related restructurings of content exploitation on the Internet were fraught with difficulties, at least they seemed to point towards the future with an eye to securing Bertelsmann a prime position within it.

For a time at least.

The failure of the attempt to transform Napster into a legitimate service had dramatic results for Bertelsmann's Internet strategy. In November 2001, it closed down BeCG. As part of the restructuring, Andreas Schmidt left the company. The decision to invest in Napster, backed by Bertelsmann's CEO Thomas Middelhoff, had cost Bertelsmann all in all some $100m in soft loans and investments to little avail. The file-swapping service was closed down in mid-2001, largely because the other majors, all of which remained in dispute with Napster over copyright infringement, refused to license their repertoire to any "new" Napster. In 2001, the closest Napster came to a distribution deal with the majors was its agreement in principle (but never activated) to be a partner for MusicNet, the ill-fated online subscription service carrying repertoire from BMG, EMI and WMG that was soon to fail. BeCG had already been downgraded following the incorporation in May of online entertainment e-tailer BOL into Bertelsmann's book club business, while at the time of the closure of BeCG it was announced that its remaining operations, which include Bertelsmann's 36% stake in US-based online book retailer barnesandnoble.com and BeMusic, would be separately managed. The Internet, it seemed, was not the way to those "disproportionately high profits".

As these problems were mounting, Bertelsmann sought another route to those "disproportionately high profits" in the immediate present. The projected creation of WEMI had failed but to Bertelsmann and EMI (which by now was semi-publicly committed to finding a new owner or merger partner) the idea of a merger remained a good one. Hence in January 2001 Bertelsmann started negotiations to merge BMG with EMI.

Whereas the EMI-WMG proposal was both badly handled by the prospective partners and overshadowed by the bigger merger of TW and AOL, the new joint venture parties moved more judiciously. With the US regulators taking a relaxed attitude, the EC was the focus of Bertelsmann and EMI. Bertelsmann spoke with the EC at the same time as approaching EMI and both parties kept in close touch with the EC as their negotiations proceeded. Both immediately said that they were willing to dispose of assets to assuage EC concerns about market dominance. However, the assets put forward for divestiture were hardly major ones. EMI offered to dispose of small companies and labels such as Pathe Marconi (France) and Minos (Greece), and not to renew its licensing and manufacturing deal with Jive/Zomba. Jive/Zomba was licensed to EMI in France and Eastern Europe and EMI had a P&D deal with the company in several other European territories. The advantage of such a concession by EMI would be that it did not involve the disposal of any significant intellectual property assets. Bertelsmann said it would restructure its media holding so that its manufacturing division BMG Storage Media, which owned the Sonopress CD manufacturing factories, would no longer be part of BMG.

BMG and EMI found it easier than EMI-WMG to satisfy the EC regarding music publishing. The EC had calculated that in revenue terms WMG and EMI together had around a 30% music publishing market in 1999; BMG Music Publishing was the smallest of the major record company-owned publishers. At the time I estimated that the combined EMI MP and BMG MP market share would be 24%. This would make the proposed joint venture the largest music publisher, ahead of Warner Chappell with its 18% share, but smaller than the combined European market share of the independent music publishers at 30%.

Furthermore, whereas an EMI-Warner Chappell group would have had the ability to assert a degree of control over the publishing market far greater than its actual market share, a combined BMG-EMI music publishing group would not be so powerful. From this perspective, once the assumption that the appropriate concessions were made, it initially seemed likely that the EC would approve the merger of BMG and EMI.

BMG-EMI would have been a better-balanced company in terms of revenues by region than any of the other majors in the year 1999–2000. The balance of revenues from Europe and North America, which accounted for 36% and 44% respectively of the two companies' combined turnover, was far more in line with the breakdown of global soundcarrier sales (32%, Europe and 39%, North America) than those of either company alone. The two companies also fitted well. BMG, whose major acts include Britney Spears, 'N Sync, the Backstreet Boys (all Zomba signings), Whitney Houston, Kenny G and Elvis Presley, whose back catalogue continued to sell in quantity, was overly reliant on North America at 55% of its revenues while EMI was too reliant on Europe which accounted for 43% of its revenues in 1999–2000. Moreover, Bertelsmann's revenues from record clubs and manufacturing would not be part of the new grouping. Bertelsmann's annual record club revenues of around $600m derived mostly from North America. Eliminating this sum, BMG's revenue breakdown was 36% (Europe) and 41% (US), almost matching the global soundcarrier sales breakdown. Sonopress then was the third largest replicator of optical discs in the world. It had a 10% share of the US optical disc market, 12% in Europe and 50% in Latin America. BMG Storage Media had estimated revenues of $550m in 1999–2000. Subtracting $1,150m, the combined revenues of BMGE Storage Media and the record clubs, from BMG's total revenues, BMG's soundcarrier and music publishing revenues at $3.55bn were remarkably close to EMI's $3.54bn annual revenues. On top of this Bertelsmann's and EMI's shareholders looked favourably on the new proposal: the lowest valuation of the predicted premium placed on EMI's shares at 100p ($1.45) was higher than the $1.16 a share premium that TW offered as part of the failed EMI-WMG merger.

Based on BMG and EMI's combined 2000 market shares the new company would have a global market share of 23.1%, one percentage point more than its nearest competitor UMG (22.1%), but as with WEMI it would be the market leader in Europe but not in the US. While this would have satisfied Bertelsmann's declared aim of making BMG the biggest music company in the world, it also meant that the proposed deal would face similar regulatory problems to those which ended EMI's merger with WMG.

The failure of WEMI, understandably, made EMI cautious about commencing another set of negotiations that required the approval of the EC, and furthermore with a Commission that had an even more detailed knowledge of the record industry than it had 12 months earlier. The EC's prime concern was market dominance. The combined market share of BMG and EMI, which at 29.4% in 1999 was virtually the same as that of WEMI, was higher than that of WEMI in only two European territories (Germany and Netherlands, 30.5% and 25.8% respectively, compared to 26% and 21.8%). However, based on *pro forma* 1999 figures BMG/EMI had a combined market share in excess of 30% in five European territories, Denmark, Germany, Italy, Spain and the UK.

A new concern of the would-be partners was a growing uncertainty about the Commission's ever-widening agenda. In examining the EMI-WMG merger the Commission made a distinction between making mutual agreements (for example about prices, or about the division of the market) and abusing a position of power. Agreements, in which maximum prices are fixed, were allowed. However, minimum price-fixing agreements were forbidden on the basis that competition is expected to be conducive to efficiency and to benefit the consumer but when parties interfere with free competition by means of price-fixing, this was, in the main, disadvantageous to the consumer. Furthermore, if there were no price competition, the prices would, on average, be too high and, in addition, the incentive to renew the business and/or to produce more efficiently would be lacking. Accordingly, the similarity of the prices at which the majors offered their product to retailers was a concern of the Commission.

That concern became even stronger when in January 2001, the Commission announced that it had begun an investigation into possible price-fixing agreements in the European music industry, focusing on the relationship between the major international record companies and the major soundcarrier retailers: "The Commission ... is investigating the vertical relationship (or contracts) between CD manufacturers and retailers to establish whether the music majors are pursuing the same or similar retail price maintenance practices in Europe."

In April, European Competition Commissioner Mario Monti told the companies that their proposed deal would face a lengthy investigation. Reportedly BMG was willing to accept this, but EMI, which had gone through such an investigation once already to no avail, was unwilling to face another if there was a significant possibility that the merger would not be approved. Despite the basic strategy to try to sell the company as the best means of maximising shareholder value, EMI took the view that the EC would most likely block any merger/sale to one of the other major international record companies unless the EC's criteria for evaluating such a sale changed. Since the proposed EMI-WMG merger, the Commission had developed a far more sophisticated understanding of the European music industry that made it able to make crucial distinctions between what is beneficial for shareholders and what is beneficial for consumers. However, despite nods to the Internet – who remembers Winamp? – the Commissions concerns until very late in the game were directed towards the past, the physical market. As such, like Kuhn's perplexed scientists, they were caught ever-looking backwards while hoping for a benevolent future that they were powerless to prepare for or defend against.

In May, BMG and EMI called off their merger talks because they were unable to offer a proposal that had a "high likelihood of approval from anti-trust authorities". The central issue was their unwillingness to make sufficient divestitures to satisfy the EC. In retrospect the concessions offered seemed more like off-cuts than significant divestitures. Thus, there was no offer to dispose of Virgin (which EMI's shareholders had been unhappy with earlier). Instead, EMI offered to dispose of small companies and labels and reduce their P&D activities *(see above)*. However, at a time when P&D was increasingly considered by the majors to be a costly non-core activity, such promises were unlikely to find favour with the Commission. Indeed, in recent years the majors had either withdrawn from distribution in some countries or sought manufacturing and distribution efficiencies through joint ventures *(see above)*.

Following the termination of the merger proposal, EMI issued preliminary results for the year ending March 31, 2001. These showed that EMI's sales rose 12% and that group operating profit (excluding HMV and associates) rose 14%. EMI it seemed was doing OK and could survive the collapse of the merger. Bertelsmann made comments about seeking to buy up independents to bolster BMG, which with an 8.5% global market share in 2000, was the smallest of the majors, but it turned its attention briefly to the Internet. However, when the regulatory climate changed and the speed of the downturn in recorded sales increased, bringing about a wave of cost-cutting by the major record companies, Bertelsmann returned to acquisition and merger mode, striking quickly and forging a merger in 2004 with Sony, while EMI and WMG continued their unconsummated dalliance.

Chapter 6

Profit Warnings From EMI

Ken Berry (and his wife Nancy) joined EMI following its purchase of Virgin in 1992 for £560m ($868m). From the start there were doubts whether the different cultures of the two, one that had sacked the Sex Pistols and the other that had signed them and made money from them, could be held in check.

There was no love for EMI from the Virgin staff. Robert Sandall, writing in the *Daily Telegraph* in 2008 at the time of the Terra Firma takeover of EMI, recounted his days at Virgin:

I worked for Virgin Records, a wholly-owned subsidiary bought by EMI from Richard Branson in 1992. Four years after the acquisition, Virgin was in complete denial about its current status and was still being run as if it were an independent. When Virgin appointed me director of communications, it apparently bothered nobody that EMI Music already retained three other people with the same title.

Round at ours, EMI was spoken of, if at all, in the same dismissive tones as real commercial rivals such as Sony or Warner. Contact with the corporate HQ, only a couple of miles away in West London, was minimal, and we competed fiercely with the mothership whenever we got the chance.

I vividly remember the jubilation in the Virgin building when EMI's great white hope, Robbie Williams, failed to make number one with his first solo single, 'Freedom'. Our joy at the dismissal of a senior EMI manager following an onboard incident with a female flight attendant was unbounded. We swaggered outrageously in the year when, thanks to the soaraway Spice Girls, Virgin UK reported more profit than its EMI parent. With a roster that included the Chemical Brothers, the Verve and Daft Punk, in the late '90s we thought we were gods. We sneered when those cloth-eared fat cats at EMI signed a band we considered to be feeble Radiohead soundalikes called Coldplay.

In the course of the attempted EMI-Warner merger Berry, who in 1995 was appointed head of all music operations outside the US, was EMI's lead negotiator and also took upon himself the role of protecting Virgin from any concession EMI might contemplate. The appointment of Eric Nicoli, who was new to the music business, as chairman in 1999, thrust Berry and Marty Bandier, head of EMI Music Publishing, further into the spotlight, the one very willingly, the other reluctantly.

Bandier was known for his public exuberance – the regular advertisements for EMI MP in US trade magazine *Billboard* were double fold-out pages with the EMI MP staff in costume and Bandier at the centre, his cigar stretched across all three pages – but when speaking to the press, he was always far more willing to talk up the future of music publishing in general, but far more cautious when speaking on the record about EMI MP. Berry was far less cautious and often highlighted the divisions within the newly expanded EMI Music. However, in 1998 it was his wife Nancy, appointed vice chairman of Virgin Records America and vice chair of the Virgin Music Group Worldwide in 1997, who became headline news.

Briefly the Berrys rather than EMI became the story. There was a semi-public row about Berry's non-appointment as global head of EMI Music, but it was the ongoing stories of Nancy's wild spending on her special projects – 'Ken and Nancy's Rock 'n' roll Circus' was the headline of a lengthy feature on the pair in the *Wall Street Journal* – that added flame to the fire. Berry-type stories would resurface following the Terra Firma takeover when bills for "flowers" were questioned as being actually for drugs; at one point Guy Hands suggested the use of drug tests, then common in banking, on executives. (He was advised against it and took the advice.) The Berry-type stories erupted only occasionally, but throughout the decade EMI had a fixed place in the financial pages of the UK's (and sometimes the world's) newspapers, with stories in which speculation and rumours about rock'n'roll extravagance had as much space as the bare facts of the situation EMI found itself in.

One such issue was "prestige signings". The debate about big prestige signings took place at a time when they were considered to be both a mark of the success of a company – it had the money to make such a deal – and when the profits, those "disproportionately high profits", from several million plus sales of albums, which superstars were expected to deliver, were enormous. Thus, in the 1990s hundreds of millions of dollars were spent by record companies keen to sign, or re-sign, big names, such as Bruce Springsteen, Janet Jackson, ZZ Top and Prince, with varying degrees of success. In EMI's case, the pressure to make such a signing was even greater because, beyond Garth Brooks, a megastar in the US who sold fewer records outside it, Capitol had no stellar names.

The thinking behind the superstar concept was not new. Although some superstars were not profitable, they were always considered to be essential, as Warner Bros.' president Joe Smith explained in 1971: "I knew that our record company, if we do represent something in today's music, could not afford to let the Grateful Dead go, they are too much a fact of it, regardless of whether they meant a lot of profit for our company or a minor profit, they're too important for us to let them go somewhere else."

The Grateful Dead were primarily a live band whose touring revenues were among the biggest in the business, but they were considered crucial to the prestige, the image, of their record company. That image had its value in the company's relationship both with musicians and record-buyers. Having a highly respected artist on the label was considered more likely to persuade other artists to sign with the label. However, the cost of keeping the services of the Grateful Dead, even if it meant using up 20 miles of recording tape before an album came out, was relatively modest. By the 1990s, that was no longer the case and the "prestige element" was no longer considered important. In its place was a *mano a mano* attitude in which the price of "disproportionately high profits" was disproportionally high costs.

Hence, the controversy over the signing of Mariah Carey by EMI in 2000. Carey had sold 120m albums in the previous decade for Sony and seemed a good bet, a perfect way to reap more profits and attract new talent. Following strong urgings from the Berrys – the deal had to be agreed at board level – EMI agreed to pay Carey a £14.3m ($25m) advance for each album, £4.3m ($7.5m) for related music-video productions as part of the marketing of the albums and around £1m ($1.8m) to promote four singles. (Several other sets of figures have been published but all are at this level.) The first such album was *Glitter*. EMI hoped it would sell 20m copies worldwide, like her 1993 album *Music Box*. Around £7m ($12.2m) was spent marketing it worldwide. Released in September 2001, it sold 2m copies.

Such a failure might have been manageable in normal circumstances. But it came at an unfortunate time for EMI, although that didn't seem to be the case initially. The preliminary results for the year 2000–2001, published immediately after the collapse of the proposed merger with BMG, suggested that EMI was in good shape. The final results, published in May 2001, looked even better. EMI reported 12% higher revenues of £2.67bn ($3.79bn) and 11.7% higher EBITDA of £389.5m ($553.3m) for the year ending March 31. EBITDA, an acronym for earnings before interest, taxes, depreciation and amortisation, differs from the operating cash flow in a cash flow statement primarily by excluding payments for taxes or interest as well as changes in working capital. From the 1990s onwards it was increasingly used by entertainment groups on the basis that their tax liabilities and capital outlay were irregular and that, accordingly, operating profits alone did not reflect the performance of such a company. Some analysts were critical of the use of EBITDA.

Separately, EMI reported that its operating profit rose 14.4% to £332.5m ($472.4m). Coming at a time of a declining world music market – the retail value of sales in 2000 fell 4.4% to $36.97bn – these results suggested that, while EMI remained an attractive takeover target, it was doing well as a standalone company. However, part of EMI's growth stemmed from exchange rate fluctuations. According to EMI its global soundcarrier market share in the 12-month period rose 1.6 percentage points to 14.1% – IFPI put it at 13.6% – largely as a result of an improved US market share and strong sales in the UK and from classical music. However, that growth was over reliant on one title. The Beatles' *1* compilation album, the first such album of massive hits by the group to be released on a single CD, which sold some 23m units, was responsible for one-third of EMI's increased market share in the US (from 9% to 10.8%) and for almost half the increase in its global market share.

Sales at EMI Music Publishing (EMI MP) rose 10.4% to £390.7m ($555.1m) and operating profit rose 9.9% to £105m ($149.2m). EMI MP thus contributed 31.6% of EMI Group operating profits from 14.6% of the company's sales. The praise heaped on EMI MP was to be a feature of virtually all of EMI's subsequent annual reports. All areas of publishing revenue rose during the year, mechanicals by 8.4%, performance by 12.9% and synchronisation by 11.1%. The biggest sales increase was in the US (20%). That said, a geographical breakdown of EMI's sales and profits highlighted its general lack of success in the US. Thus, although North America accounted for 33% of revenues, it only accounted for 23% of operating profits whereas Europe (excluding the UK) accounted for 28% of sales and 34% of operating profits. The UK accounted for 12.7% and 13% respectively, Asia for 18% and 22.4%, and Other (Latin America and South Africa) for 7.8% and 7.4% respectively. Europe (including the UK) thus accounted for £1.1bn ($1.56bn), or 41% of EMI's 2000–2001 sales and 47% of operating profits.

The positive message of results was shattered within four months. In October 2001, EMI issued a profit warning. EMI was not alone: Time Warner and Sony also issued warnings, but EMI's was the most dramatic. The statements came in the wake of the September 11 terrorist attacks in the US, but they mostly reflected problems that had been identified before then, notably a downturn in consumer and advertising spending and a decline in soundcarrier sales. Two other major music companies said all was well. Vivendi Universal (VU), the parent company of UMG, said it was on track to meet its revenue and profit forecasts for the year, while Bertelsmann, after announcing record losses for the year to June 30, 2001 for BMG, predicted that BMG's profits and margins would rise to record levels in the current financial year. However, as the year wore on they too would turn to talk of problems rather than successes.

EMI said that its full year profits before tax in the 12 months to March 31, 2002 would be down 20%. It added that its Recorded Music division would report a loss in the six months to September 30, compared with a group operating profit of $58m ($84.5m) in the same period a year ago. After the trading statement the price of the company's shares plunged by over 35% to £2.14 ($3.11), its lowest level since 1988. EMI said sales and profits would fall primarily because of the slowdown of the US soundcarrier market. Another reason was the collapse of sales in Latin America. However, in 2000, Latin America, where EMI had a 16% market share in 2000, accounted for only 5% of world soundcarrier sales. Far more important was the US decline. Even if EMI's US market share held steady at around 10%, the 5% fall value of the US market (which represented 38% of world soundcarrier sales in 2000) in the first six months of 2001 meant a serious loss of revenues. In actual fact, the retail value of the US market only fell by 2.2% in 2001, but that presaged a period of decline, 10% in 2002 and 7.8% in 2003. One bright spot for EMI in North America was the successful introduction of the *Now* albums compilations of recent singles hits, which had been bestsellers in Europe and several other markets for many years, in 1998. *Now 6* and *Now 7* sold over 3m each in the US and all of the first 29 releases of the series sold over 1m units, small by the sales levels in Europe, but a new revenue strand.

In the past the various would-be merger partners had pointed to the savings that their mergers would bring; in its profit warning EMI said that it intended to make cost savings of £65m ($94.7m) which would necessitate making a restructuring provision of £100m ($145.7m). Henceforth, cost-cutting and restructuring would be a feature of all profit warnings and downturns in the market, merger proposal or not. EMI reported that it had already cut 100 jobs in Latin America following the

30% fall in soundcarrier sales there. EMI also said it would make further cutbacks and changes in its Recorded Music division, including the restructuring of under-performing labels and the consolidation of back-office functions in North America and Europe, having already merged Capitol and Priority Records in the US and laid off 80 staff. EMI also repeated an earlier statement that it expected to exit the production and distribution (P&D) of soundcarriers by the end of the year.

The low share price, which valued EMI at just £1.6bn ($2.33bn) – down from a high of £10bn ($14.57bn) in 1998 – inevitably renewed speculation that EMI might become the target of another takeover bid. In part to suggest that this was not to be the case and in great part to show Nicoli, who hitherto had been seen as overly passive, was a man of action, EMI fired Ken Berry and replaced him with Alain Levy, the former head of PolyGram.

Such management shuffles, particularly in the US, and concomitant cost-savings restructurings were to be a feature of the decade. A Frenchman, Levy joined CBS International (now SME) in New York in 1972 and a year later moved to the company's European headquarters in Paris. In 1976 he was appointed vice president of marketing in Europe and later also assumed the management of CBS Italy. In 1979 he became managing director of CBS France before in 1984 moving to Philips' music division PolyGram as CEO of its French operations, where he had successes with artist such as Serge Gainsbourg, Johnny Hallyday and Vanessa Paradis. In 1988 he moved to London to become executive vice president of PolyGram in charge of its worldwide pop and music publishing activities and in 1990 he moved to New York, adding to his direct responsibilities PolyGram's operations in the US. The following year he was appointed worldwide president and CEO of PolyGram where he led the company's expansion into the worldwide movie business with the establishment of PolyGram Filmed Entertainment. Initially successful as a productions source, the high cost of developing a distribution arm for the film company did not find favour with the board. Despite being responsible for the expansion of PolyGram's music interest in the US, buying Motown and Def Jam, Levy was unable to establish PolyGram as a forceful presence there and in 1998 Philips sold the company. Levy left to become another of what was to be a growing band of former high-level record company executives available for hire at a time when a central element of restructuring meant executives being moved like chess pieces. Levy, his relative failure in the US notwithstanding, seemed a natural choice for EMI.

The company said Berry left "by mutual agreement" – and a reported $5m payoff – but it was clear that EMI felt Berry had to be replaced in response to growing shareholder pressure to improve Recorded Music's performance, especially in North America. Significantly, Levy's one-year contract, although it was for a relatively modest amount, included a number of financial incentives, payable if he managed to increase the company's share price and profits. At the same time, David Munns, who had worked with Levy at PolyGram, was appointed vice chairman of EMI Recorded Music with special responsibility for global marketing and human resources. The immediate aim of the new team was to raise EMI's market share, which in North America had fallen from 10.5% in calendar 2000 to 10.1% in 2001 and would fall to 8.9% in 2002.

EMI's share price fell further on the news of Levy's appointment, suggesting that investors did not think a change in management was enough to restore profitability. However, Levy had one unassailable asset: he was an available experienced record company executive. One of the features of the record industry at the time was the merry-go-round of the executive turntable. In great part because of the cuts and restructurings, new appointees were often appointed to the higher levels of the industry, while for the same reason a number of high-level executives had their "one company" careers terminated early. Another career option for such executives was to become advisors and consultants to joint venture ensembles. Just as there were a number of veteran acts, such as the Rolling Stones, who took their back catalogue from company to company, so there emerged a number of high-placed executives who moved from company to company.

Never known as a cost-cutter, Levy, who had led PolyGram into film production and distribution at great cost, was charged with creating a leaner EMI. One of his first acts, as though firmly shutting the door on the past, was to end EMI's multi-album contract with Mariah Carey, paying her a $28m termination fee and allowing her to retain the signing-on fee she was paid. (Subsequently, Carey, who suffered a series of health problems while under contract to EMI, signed with UMG's Island label with great success. She released the best-selling album in the US in 2005, *The Emancipation Of Mimi,* and dramatically changed her image through appearances in independent films, before in 2012 further consolidating her position with the entertainment mainstream by taking the role of a judge on the *American Idol* talent show for a reported $18m.)

Following the fall in EMI's share price and the much reduced valuation – and therefore the acquisition price – of the company, there was renewed speculation that it would be available for sale. However, if EMI was reduced in value its activities were not, at least at the start of the 2000s, reduced in scope. Later, as we shall see, EMI would need to license its repertoire in some territories, even *in extremis* seeking to license its repertoire in North America, but in 2001, however troubled, the company had a worldwide reach and was active in all regions. Moreover, outside of the US, EMI was a relatively successful company.

EMI's profit warning came at a time when the company had been performing very well in some markets. For example, the company's album chart share for Europe in the first six months of 2001 was 22.4%, up from 15.3% in the same period of 2000, placing EMI second to UMG. In the UK, EMI's home market, in the first six months of 2001 the company improved its album market share to 17.4% (from 16.8%), making it the second largest behind UMG. EMI's biggest UK success was local superstar Robbie Williams. His third album *Sing When You're Winning* sold 4.3m units worldwide, 84% of those in Europe and most of those in the UK. However, EMI failed to break Williams in North America, despite concerted attempts to do so. Similarly, although she had some hits there, EMI was unable to break Kylie Minogue in the US. With Williams and Minogue, EMI was unable to transform local success into global success at the level achieved by Jive/Zomba's Britney Spears, UMG's Shania Twain or WMG's Madonna. A big hit in the US is profitable because of economies of scale, but global hit albums that sell 5m units or more worldwide are crucial to majors' profitability. EMI's last non-catalogue global superstar act had been the Spice Girls, which analysts calculated accounted for between 15% and 20% of EMI operating profits in 1998, but unlike, say, Madonna, they failed to sustain their initially promising career after managerial and personnel issues led to their disbandment and solo records by individual members of the group failed to bite.

When EMI published its six-month results to September 30 in December, they proved even worse than predicted in the October profit warning: sales fell 7% to £1.07bn ($1.5bn) and operating profit fell 60% to £69m ($97.2m). The decline came despite the continued success of EMI MP, which reported 4% higher sales of £200m ($281.7m) and a 5% higher operating profit (excluding New Media) of £51.2m ($72.1m). The overall fall was due to the poor performance of EMI Recorded Music where sales fell 9% to £867m ($1.22bn) and the division reported a loss of £8.1m ($11.4m). The company, which spent £15.1m ($21.3m) restructuring labels and other operations, the first of several such costs, also signalled the end of its dual label structure, meaning that Virgin, which hitherto had acted with relative independence, would lose that autonomy.

Little more than a month later, in February 2002, EMI issued its second profit warning within six months, predicting that its profits for the year ending March 31 would be £150m ($246m) and that there could be a net loss after one-off costs were included. The company in part attributed the expected losses to falling soundcarrier sales in Latin America and Asia, its own under-performance in the US and the delay of some album releases in Japan. Ironically, a couple of months later, EMI was awarded a Queen's Award for Enterprise for sales of UK repertoire overseas. In the warning EMI also noted adverse exchange rate fluctuations and one-off costs. These included an estimated combined payoff of $10m for the former head of EMI Recorded Music Ken Berry, Virgin executive Nancy Berry and chief financial officer (CFO) Tony Bates, and the termination of Mariah Carey's contract. The price of EMI shares fell 6% following the announcement.

The warning, allied to recent poor results reported by SME and WMG, was further confirmation that the decline in soundcarrier sales was affecting all the major international record companies to some degree. However, it was EMI, the only one of the five majors that was not part of a larger conglomerate, that was most affected.

The restructuring, indicated in broad brush strokes at the time of the six-month results, was given greater detail. The first tranche of Levy's management changes concerned Virgin. Ashley Newton and Ray Cooper, the British co-chairmen of Virgin North America, were replaced by outsider Matt Serletic, the producer of hits such as Santana's 'Smooth', as chairman and CEO, and EMI veteran Roy Lott, who was made president and CEO of Virgin North America. Levy has also made changes in the senior management of the EMI Group. Tony Bates, the group's CFO, was replaced by Roger Faxon, the CFO of EMI Music Publishing since 1999. Stuart Ells, with whom Levy worked at PolyGram, was recruited from Andrew Lloyd Webber's Really Useful Group theatre and music publishing company to be CFO of EMI Recorded Music.

At the same time Virgin North America was relocated to New York from Los Angeles and EMI announced that in future it would operate as two label groups worldwide, Capitol and Virgin, and that the EMI name would only be used for corporate and shared service activities and for the EMI Classics division. All back-office operations (sales, finance, IT, personnel and catalogue exploitation) were to be integrated and there would be only one managing director per country. This effectively ended the dual EMI-Virgin structure, which had operated in most markets since 1992, and was expected to immediately create significant costs savings. The name change was expected to help the company in North America: EMI had never been a well-known or successful brand there, whereas Capitol, which had been owned by EMI since 1955, was a well-respected name.

The new structure had the biggest consequences in Europe, where each territory had a single chief to replace the existing EMI and Virgin heads. Seeking to broaden the reason for some of the restructuring Levy noted that some of the company's difficulties were "a function of [general] music industry practices", adding that he was "committed to finding new ways to do business and to placing long-term sustainable development" at the top of the company's agenda. The unspoken thought here was that Levy wanted to improve functions such as cash management and investment in artists, offering them greater security without paying huge advances. This was a reflection of the fact that, although established acts were not selling in the numbers they used to, they continued to seek higher advances. While the majors in recent years publicly advised the need for smaller advances, generally one or other of them has always been willing to bid too high for that ever-so-necessary superstar act, as EMI was about to do in the case of Robbie Williams.

Levy's restructuring was one of the first cost-cutting exercises by a major to take on board external factors, such as the global growth in the sales of local repertoire that obliged record companies to maintain national offices worldwide and accordingly reduced their opportunities for cost-cutting. Levy also pointed to the higher number of releases and shorter artist careers and increased marketing costs at a time when only a few acts were profitable. For example, in the US, 1% of acts account for 75% of sales. Separately, Levy made the point that the restructuring represented a change in EMI's corporate culture. Acknowledging the contribution of EMI Music Publishing, which remained on course to report significantly higher revenues and profits for 2001–2002, Levy introduced a new mantra to the restructuring process that would be echoed by all the other majors in the course of the decade: EMI was a music company rather than a record company.

EMI said it would cut 1,789 jobs over the period 2002–2004, the equivalent of 20% of the current workforce, with most of the losses in Europe (34.5%) and North America (27.4%). The cuts translated into annual fixed cost savings of £98.5m ($140m) and a one-off exceptional cash cost of £110m ($156.5m), with additional exceptional charges of £130m ($189m) relating to asset write-offs – and writedown of loss-making businesses, such as the termination of the Mariah Carey contract. Given that all four other majors were also looking to cut costs, increase sales and grow their market share in a declining market, I and most analysts considered it difficult to see how EMI could outperform the other majors so as to automatically add percentage points to its market share and pounds to its revenues. Indeed, the only concrete example offered by Levy was one at the forefront of the minds of all the majors' CEOs: back catalogue. Levy suggested that increasing non-compilation catalogue sales (which I calculated at the time represented 25% of Recorded Music's revenues) by 10% would translate into extra revenues of £25m ($35.6m) a year and extra profits of £10m ($14.2m).

Another route to increased revenues is to buy them. With this in mind, in May EMI, which in April received a windfall from the increased value of HMV which it had spun off in 1998, bought UK-based independent Mute Records, which it already distributed in most large European markets, for £24m ($35.1m) and up to £19m ($27.8m) in performance-related payments. While the purchase didn't actually solve any of EMI's problems, it suggested that EMI was active and looking to work its way out of its troubles, rather than simply curl up and die. With the same aims, EMI also exercised its option to buy the share of the Jobete catalogue, the one-time music publishing division of Motown, that it did not already own.

As predicted in its February profit warning, EMI's revenues and profits fell for the year 2001–2002, though not quite as severely as expected. Revenues fell 8.5% to £2.44bn ($3.56bn) and operating profit (EBITA) fell 43% to £190.9m ($278.9m) producing a pre-tax loss of £152.8m ($223.2m). The fall in sales was attributable to the Recorded Music division where revenues fell by 11% to £2.03bn ($2.97bn). This fall was offset by continued growth at EMI Music Publishing (EMI MP) where sales rose 6.6% to £416.4m ($608.3m) and operating profit rose 2.7% to £107.8m ($157.5m). The contrast between the record division and EMI MP highlighted the problems that all the majors faced. The global trade value of soundcarrier sales had been in decline since 1999, falling from $38.5bn to $32.2bn in 2002, while the digital revolution had benefitted rather than just troubled music publishers, offering them new revenue streams, such as ringtones, as their mechanical revenues from soundcarrier sales started to fall.

Although a company's profitability does not necessarily depend either on higher sales or on a growing market, increasing sales is easier when the overall market is growing, leading to improved economies of scale and higher margins. In a declining market a company can only generate increased revenues at the expense of its competitors. This means higher spending on advertising, intense competition for proven artists, and, on the other hand, because all companies are facing falling sales, unprecedented moves, such as the setting up of joint sales and marketing ventures.

Cost-cutting seldom has the full impact hoped for by its iniators. By 2002, it was noticeable that the cost benefits of the merger of PolyGram and MCA (that led to the creation of UMG) had ended. All the majors' margins – operating profits as a percentage of sales – suffered. EMI's margin was only 5% in 2001–2002; its profit margins were over 20% at the height of CD replacement in the early 1990s. EMI said it was aiming for a profit margin of over 12% by 2005. Such talk became a regular feature of results announcements, where it was often tied to the belief that the digital revolution was imminent, bringing with it a return to profitability (but sadly not "disproportionate profits"). However, such talk was just that, talk. Year by year the digital revolution was creating a new recorded music industry, but one that increasingly looked like it would have to be smaller if it was to survive, let alone be profitable. Levy might point to the merger of labels and the closure, ahead of schedule, of EMI's UK manufacturing plant in Swindon. But, to a greater or lesser extent, all the majors were involved in restructuring activities, involving cost-cutting, placing greater emphasis on co-ordinated marketing campaigns, seeking to reduce payments to artists, and streamlining management practices. Why would EMI be more successful at these activities than other majors – particularly, as over the period 2001–2002, its global market share fell first to 13.1% and then to 12% in 2002?

The continued decline of global soundcarrier sales in 2002, down 7.2% after an 8.7% fall in 2001, threw serious doubt on the ability of EMI to meet the sales, profits and market share targets identified by the company earlier in the year. As noted earlier, EMI was the only publicly quoted standalone major music company. A recent history that included two merger attempts and well publicised management changes meant constant press coverage and a running commentary from the growing number of analysts who oversaw its performance. Further evidence of the high profile of EMI was the volatility of its share price. When in

September 2002, it fell to its lowest level since 1987 valuing EMI at £1.3bn ($2.1bn), the company was removed from the influential FTSE 100 index, which it had been on since 1931; it was ranked at 114 among UK quoted companies. At the same time, 2002 saw EMI reducing its reach, cutting its artist rosters by 25% and starting the integration in smaller markets, such as the Nordics and Benelux, of its branches.

EMI's falling market shares – in 2001 it lost market share in every region in the world except Australasia – came as the company had reached the halfway stage of the programme of cost-cutting and restructuring inaugurated by Levy. Nicoli responded with more talk: "shareholders could expect a 'substantial improvement' in operating performance in the year ahead" and there were "signs of a pick up" in Latin America and Asia – shades of Stan Cornyn's analyst friend indeed!

However, despite these cost-saving and money-raising initiatives, such as the sale of its stake in German music television channel Viva for €52.3m ($50.9m), EMI's targeted profit margin of over 12% by 2005 still seemed unlikely (and proved to be so). However speedily implemented, cost-saving measures always involve some expenditure and the real savings come in the future, a future, which EMI (and its competitors) were to find, was ever shifting. At the same time some things did not change substantially: while there was some degree of flexibility, the costs involved in marketing albums in a market that has declined by 10% are unlikely to be 10% lower even though the revenues generated by the same market share will be 10% less.

The integration of its Dutch and Belgian companies into a single Benelux branch marked the beginning of the second phase of EMI's restructuring programme, which included an overhaul of the company's European distribution network, the reconfiguration of its IT systems to create better financial reporting and forecasting structures, and the development of more effective marketing and promotional campaigns. However, although it put a lot of stress on cost-cutting and restructuring, EMI continued to acquire copyrights and even promised to increase its investment in A&R in the US, where EMI's ongoing low market share was having a serious impact on its overall sales. Tony Wadsworth, CEO of UK EMI, speaking to Brian Southall, highlighted what the lack of US repertoire meant to EMI. After noting that US repertoire accounted for around 45% of recorded music sales in the UK and slightly less than that around the world, he pointed out that, "If you are getting no US repertoire you are dealing in about 50% or 55% of the market, which means you have one hand tied behind your back." This meant that EMI "had a market share of UK music at times above 30% and a market share of non-UK music of about 4% or 5%, which is an imbalanced company". To help rectify this EMI recruited the experienced Phil Quartararo from WMG as executive vice president. The company also began preparing for the expected growth of the Chinese recorded music market, appointing former PolyGram and UMG Asian regional head Norman Cheng to a similar post at EMI, with special emphasis on Chinese-language repertoire.

EMI's performance in the six months to September 30, 2002, suggested that the company was overcoming its problems. Although sales fell 10% to £961.5m ($1.51bn) and its global market share fell, from 12.2% to 11.8%, EBITA almost doubled compared with the same period a year earlier, rising 83% to £79m ($124m). This represented a net profit before tax of £42.2m ($66.2m) compared to a loss of £2m ($3.1m) in the same period of 2001. The City was not convinced and EMI's share price fell sharply. This was for two reasons: the continued downturn in global recorded music sales, which would inevitably mean that EMI's revenues would fall, and the growth in operating profits was seen as a one-off, a testament to the cost savings instituted by Levy.

EMI had some real successes. These included the 4m-plus sales of Utada Hikaru's *Deep River*, the 3m-plus sales of Norah Jones *Come Away With Me* and the 2m-plus sales of Coldplay's *Rush Of Blood To The Head*. However, some big-selling albums were less profitable. Thus, although the Rolling Stones' compilation *Forty Licks* – the first such album to contain Stones hits from throughout their entire career – sold over 3m units, it was not particularly profitable for EMI because the marketing costs associated with it were very high. Moreover, EMI only had the rights to the album in Europe, so those costs were laid against a small sales base. This renewed emphasis on marketing was reflected in a further restructuring in the US to prioritise marketing by separating it from physical distribution. Such a concern was industry-wide. Earlier BMG had global restructured its operations worldwide to prioritise marketing, creating as it were a chute which meant "internationally oriented" releases could be controlled from the centre rather than the control being granted to the national companies. In the US, where the new division EMI Music Marketing (EMM) was first established, marketing, merchandising and promotion were made the responsibility of Phil Quartararo. EMI noted that the creation of EMM was made with the loss of fewer than 20 staff and without incurring any new costs or overheads. Based in Los Angeles, EMM's main remit was to increase EMI's efficiency by improving the flow of product between labels, retailers and consumers. EMI initially stressed that EMM would offer its six US label groups extra resources and would not assume any of the labels' existing marketing or promotion functions. However, it represented the first steps towards centralised marketing and indeed, to joint operations between the company's recorded music and music publishing divisions.

In addition to pursuing opportunities for selling music at non-traditional outlets, as well as bringing the development and marketing of DVD music videos under EMM's control, EMM's remit included expanding EMI's presence in the growing synchronisation market in the US through the creation of a central EMM negotiating team to license EMI recordings, compositions or acts to advertisements or film or television soundtracks. To make this team more effective than separate pitches from EMI labels and/or EMI Music Publishing (EMI MP), the head of EMM's strategic marketing unit was to spend one day a week in the offices of EMI MP. Other areas where EMI saw a role for EMM included merchandising agreements and promotions for soundcarrier/DVDs with large retailers, as EMI has previously done with cafe chain Starbucks, and national event promoters as well as artist appearance and other business opportunities. Thus began EMI's erratic journey to becoming an integrated "entertainment" company.

At the time, the inevitable comparisons between the two halves of EMI continued. As ever, EMI MP reported growth. Sales rose 1% to

£202.2m ($317.3m). This represented 21% of group revenues, while the 3% higher EBITA of £53.9m ($84.6m) represented 60% of EMI Group operating profits. This continued the disparity between the margins of the two divisions of the company, with EMI MP having a margin of 26% whereas that of EMI Music, the recorded music division, was 5%.

The City's qualms notwithstanding, by the end of 2002 EMI had a degree of swagger, as seen in its new deal with Alain Levy and, more dramatically, with Robbie Williams. Levy was awarded a new five-year contract with a base salary upped to £1m ($1.84m) from £700,400 ($1.29m) and his potential annual bonus was increased from two times salary to three times salary. Despite protests by some shareholders, Nicoli noted that it was performance-related and that most targets had been met in recent years. Deputy chairman John Gildersleeve declared the company's executive remuneration packages were "robust and appropriate".

That phrase could also be applied to EMI's new deal with the former Take That member Robbie Williams. EMI desperately wanted to retain Williams, who had sold some 20m albums for the company over a five-year period. His loss would have been a serious matter. At the same time there was the memory of the Mariah Carey disaster. To avoid that EMI and Williams' team contrived a new kind of all-rights deal, the first 360-degree deal to be made. Whereas in the past a record company had only benefitted from the recorded music sales of an artist, under 360-degree deals, which quickly became the norm for new signings despite resistance by managers and artists, the record company would benefit from other revenue strands available to an artist, such as merchandise and live performance. In return the record company was expected to expand the nature of its financial and promotional activities on behalf of the artist beyond promoting recorded music sales.

The financial details of Williams' four-album contract were unclear – most accounts suggest it was worth around £80m ($119m), £10m ($15m) as a signing-on fee, £15m ($22m) for the first album and £55m ($82m) for the remaining ones – but the structure was clear. Williams and EMI created a joint company owned 75% by the singer and 25% by EMI, into which all Williams' earnings, from record sales, sponsorship, live performance, etc, were placed to be drawn upon according to each parties' percentage of the company. Separately, at the conclusion of the contract Williams would take full ownership of his recordings, while a further clause, reflecting EMI's poor performance in the US where Williams was not a star, required a specific level of promotion on behalf of the first album under the deal, *Escapology*. That said, EMI made explicit that the success of the partnership with Williams was not contingent on US success. That was wise, for while the record, released in most countries in November 2002, sold 7.5m units worldwide, few of those sales were in the US where, released in April 2003, it peaked at a modest number 43 in the *Billboard* album charts. Williams' charm, such as it was, would fail to translate from Britain to America.

Another sign of a corner being turned was Norah Jones. If Williams failed in America, Jones was a huge success both there and globally. Her debut album, *Come Away With Me*, was the best-selling album of the year, eventually selling some 20m copies. Nonetheless, while that success demonstrated that EMI could break a US multi-million selling act globally, its US market share still fell, from 10.1% to 8.9% in 2002. EMI just couldn't break enough new acts in the US.

One of the benefits of being a standalone music company was that EMI was able to make decisions without concerning itself about the possible effects on other business divisions. As noted earlier, it was the most active in making deals with Internet start-ups and was the only one of the majors to licence repertoire to both Pressplay, in which it was a partner with BMG and WMG, and the competing SME-UMG venture Musicnet. However, Musicnet and Pressplay were short-lived attempts by the industry to control its Internet fate and few of the many Internet licensing deals EMI made were productive; many, such as Musicmaker, ended with the demise of the company in question. Far more significant for EMI and the industry as a whole – and imposed on it from outside rather than being nurtured from within – was the arrival of iTunes.

Chapter 7

Mostly Digital

It's hard not to parallel the trajectories of the Secure Digital Music Initiative (SDMI) and Napster. Both were short-lived but had long-lasting effects. The former brought digital rights management centre stage, while the latter brought a swathe of publicity to the idea of "music for free" and laid the foundations for P2P networks.

In December 1998 the majors established SDMI with the aim of creating a secure online system for the digital distribution of music. The move was made in response to the threat posed by the unregulated open MP3 standard. MP3 is a digital encoding format that uses a form of data compression designed to greatly reduce the amount of data required to represent the audio recording and still sound like a faithful reproduction of the original uncompressed audio for most listeners. Quickly established as the de facto standard of digital audio compression for the transfer and playback of music on digital audio players, from the second half of 1994 through the late 1990s, MP3 files began to spread on the Internet. In 1998, the Rio PMP300 digital audio player was launched, despite legal efforts by the US record industry trade association RIAA and international record industry trade association IFPI (both took the view that the MP3 format and the introduction of MP3 players enabled widespread Internet music piracy on the Internet).

The aim of SDMI was to establish a set of rules and technologies that would protect copyrighted music in all existing and emerging digital formats and create inter-operable products by harmonising different delivery methods and storage media, notably portable digital music players. The solution offered was control through encryption and for some time electronics and computer companies, such as Microsoft, Intel, Texas Instruments and Panasonic – but not Apple which did not join SDMI – as well as the five majors planned an encrypted future. The forum planned to develop such a system in time for the launch of portable players and Internet oriented devices by Christmas 1999. The tight schedule indicated that the majors accepted that the digital distribution and sale of music was inevitable, particularly in the wake of the growing success of MP3 as a format and the increasing availability of music in digital form on the Internet. That said, the SDMI forum was heavily technologically based. As such the whole process reeked of the idea that just as the CD had saved the record industry once so SDMI would do it again. Little time in SDMI meetings was given to the marketing and promotional possibilities that digital might offer content owners. Rather the concern was with setting limiting rules as to what technology companies could do. SDMI was also an expensive club to join, with the minimum membership fee set at $10,000 a year, rising to $50,000 for companies on the steering committee. The forum included the five majors, IFPI, the RIAA and representatives of independent record companies as well as music publisher and songwriter rights organisations, technology providers, music retailers and online distributors.

The SDMI forum initially seemed successful. In May 1999, UMG announced that in partnership with technology provider Intertrust, it would offer the secure digital delivery of (selected) music tracks for sale in the US later that year. These would be ahead of the creation of the SDMI standard, but would comply with it, when, as expected, it was agreed by all the SDMI partners. In the wake of this, a number of similar moves were announced. UMG announced an e-commerce venture between UMG and BMG, Microsoft launched a secure (SDMI compliant) music downloading and streaming software package and Sony announced an SDMI compliant portable player. In parallel, a number of best-selling acts, such as Alanis Morissette, the Beastie Boys, Public Enemy and Tom Petty, offered MP3 promotional downloads of upcoming recordings, sometimes with remarkable results. Prior to the download offer of two live tracks from Morissette's *Mirrorball* album on the BMG Arista label, orders for the album were modest: after the offer it became Arista's most ordered album.

As a promotional tool the Internet clearly made sense – and was beginning to be used as such. It also had economic possibilities, but quite what these were was difficult to determine. Yeasaying in unison were the many (self-appointed) analysts happy to sing the praises of the Internet, thus both boosting their own services and the possibilities of the growing number of Internet companies springing up, many of which centred on music. Music files were relatively small and their appeal relatively large. In the end SDMI was a dead end street, but it carried a lethal piece of baggage, a belief in digital rights management (DRM) which would act as a drag on the legitimate download market until it was finally rejected.

When Sony launched an SDMI compliant digital music player in the US in March 2000, the Music Clip, it played only copy-protected files, cost $300 and was a failure in the marketplace. Walter Mossberg, the highly influential reviewer of new gadgets for the *Wall Street Journal* noted "it treats users like potential criminals", initiating another theme of the decade.

Even more embarrassing were the final days of SDMI. In June 2000, the SDMI forum announced a digital rights standard that allowed record companies to inject inaudible watermarks into their copyrights which a digital player would only be able to play if it was able to detect them. Thus both player and content would be encrypted and the encryptions would be matched. The SDMI forum subsequently proudly offered a prize of $10,000 to anyone who could hack the system within three weeks. The prize was won by a computer scientist at Princeton University. He received the $10,000 on behalf of his team and promptly said he would publish his solution. The RIAA threatened to sue. That threat was not fulfilled, but litigation soon became the knee-jerk response of the industry.

Named after the nickname for his boyhood haircut, Shawn Fanning's Napster transformed searching for music into exchanging recorded music. By making *access* rather than the *ownership* that record companies had previously depended on the central element of music consumption, Napster laid the foundations for the P2P networks that would follow, Grokster, Kazaa, LimeWire, etc, and the social networking that developed around music and evolved into MySpace and Facebook. Napster wasn't alone: there were other similar online services, notably MP3.com, and soon a host of new ideas of ways to store and access music emerged. Useful accounts of many of these upstarts can be found in Knopper's *Appetite For Self-destruction* and John Alderman's *Sonic Boom*. But Napster set the ball rolling and along the way achieved a lasting place in popular culture, rather than merely a mention in history. In the video game *Grand Theft Auto IV* there's a spoof of Napster called Shitster featuring the Napster cat with fecal matter on its head instead of headphones, and the 2010 movie *Get Him To The Greek* riffs on a mythic moment in Napster's history when Russell Brand as Aldous Snow gets mad at Metallica drummer Lars Ulrich (playing himself) and yells at him, saying "Go sue Napster, you Danish twat!"

It goes without saying that the genesis of Napster came from without rather than within the record industry. What has been less commented on is just how deeply threatening Napster was. MTV was a company built on "stealing our copyrights" as one record company executive put it, but it didn't change the basic structure of the business beyond opening up a new promotional platform. Record companies have always had a fraught relationship with the retailers who sold their product to the public, but long established practices were in place and, while retailers carped about wholesale prices, at the end of the day they were in the same business as record companies: they made money selling records. Napster and its ilk didn't make money from music, but from offering access to music and in turn offering companies access to its users to whom they could advertise their wares. This difference would never really change. The P2P companies that replaced Napster did the same and when the legitimate market finally arrived it was dominated by Apple, a company that was focused on selling iPods, which were far more profitable for

Apple than music tracks. When Edward Lewis set up Decca Records in the UK in 1929, explaining his decision to add a record business to his gramophone company, he famously noted that if you sold razors it was stupid not to sell razor blades as well: Steve Jobs simply reversed the stratagem, offering music tracks to stimulate iPod sales.

Not only were Napster and the majors not in the same business, but Napster also challenged the careful divisions the industry had developed to its financial advantage. In the online world there was only minimal manufacturing and distribution – no record presses, cardboard boxes or trucks – but in the physical world these were controlled by the majors and treated as separate profit centres. As we have seen, EMI was initially reluctant to embrace the CD because it objected to the royalty Sony and Philips were demanding on each one made. The Warner Music Group had no such problems. According to Stan Cornyn, Warner merely made paying the CD royalty the responsibility of Warner's manufacturing/distribution division. The implication was that Warner then recouped that added cost by charging higher distribution fees to clients. Eventually the majors would retreat from both manufacturing and distribution as high-cost, non-core activities in a shrinking physical market, but only after it had become clear that an Internet-based music business was here to stay.

Music industry analyst Jim Griffin succinctly noted the perspective that "being in the product business" brought with it: "The motivation of those big companies is that they owned a lot of trucks, a lot of warehouses, and a lot of pressing plants. And furthermore, control over quantity and destiny of product is essential to running a product-based business. If you're in the product business you have to control the quantity and the destiny of the products you distribute, because if you don't, then the price falls to the marginal cost of delivery, and that can be pretty savage."

Griffin might have mentioned another reason that record companies were (and continue to be) concerned with the physical. Even today in the fast shrinking physical market, *physical is more profitable than digital*. This is because physical is primarily (CD) albums and digital is single tracks, and albums, bundles of tracks marketed as a single unit, generate more revenue and profit than singles. At the dawn of the digital age the general view of analysts and forecasters was that as physical sales faltered so, when the record companies finally accepted the inevitability of the digital revolution, digital sales would take their place, eventually overtaking them and compensating for the loss of revenue from physical sales by a new, less costly, digital revenue stream. To some extent the first part of this has happened, albeit at a far slower pace, but such digital compensation has been far less that initially predicted. Despite the overall unit growth of digital sales, the digital compensation factor has failed to kick in either in revenue terms or, even more significantly, in profit terms.

The annual result of Vivendi-owned UMG, which breaks out its revenue in some detail, is helpful here. Excluding music publishing, UMG has three revenue streams related to recorded music: physical, digital and licensing and artist services (*see table below*).

UMG: Recorded music revenues by source in 2010

	€m	$m	% change on 2009	% of total
Physical sales	2,128	2,837	−10.3	59.5
Digital sales	1,033	1,377	+7.7	28.9
Licensing & other	415	533	−0.3	11.6
Total	**3,576**	**4,747**	**−4.6**	**100.0**

Source: Vivendi.

Of these physical and digital are the major sources of UMG's recorded music overall revenues, accounting for 60% and 29% respectively of UMG's recorded music revenues. Although it is difficult to disentangle the profits that accrue to these revenue streams one thing is clear: the profits on a CD (or digital) album are significantly greater than on a single track download (or physical single). The table below details the breakdown of sales by digital (single track and album downloads) and physical album sales in the US over the period 2006–2010. The figures in brackets are the percentage changes on the previous year.

US: Recorded music sales by format, 2006–2010 (units m)

Year	Digital tracks	Digital albums	Physical albums
2006	582	31	557
2007	844 (+45)	50 (+53)	451 (−19)
2008	1,070 (+27)	66 (+32)	363 (−20)
2009	1,159 (+8)	76 (+8)	298 (−18)
2010	1,172 (+1)	86 (+13)	237 (−19)

Source: Nielsen SoundScan.

The table shows that physical album sales, mostly of CDs, declined at a faster rate than overall digital sales grew. Moreover, the most profitable area of digital recorded music sales, albums, only accounted for 36% of the overall album market and the rate of their growth was slowing down. In effect this means that the profits from online and mobile activities are unlikely to ever match the losses in profits from the continuing decline of the CD album market: it would seem that the digital compensation scenario has ended, producing reduced revenues and even greater reductions in profits.

It's doubtful that the issue of the level of profits that online sales might represent was uppermost in the minds of record executives as they pondered whether to upset the treasured and familiar applecart of the past and peer into the unknown that might be good for them or might be better for the new entrants to the music market clamouring at their door. But the analysts who fuelled the first dotcom boom and bust with their rosy predictions of a future in which the once omnipresent CD storage rack had no place saw huge profits in digital music.

Consider stock market analyst Sanford C Bernstein's *Assessing the Potential of the Internet on the Music Industry*, which was published in 2000. Assuming that the (then) current retail price was maintained, *Assessing the Potential* calculated a record company stood to make an operating profit of $7.61 on the sale of a CD via digital distribution. This compared to a profit of $2.19 on a hybrid sale (an album ordered via the Internet but delivered physically) or $1.66 on a CD sold at a traditional bricks and mortar store. From this perspective, *Assessing the Potential* predicted that the net impact of the Internet would be extra profits of $180m a year to the US record industry by 2003, rising to some $500m if a non-MP3 industry standard emerged and piracy was reduced. Bernstein was simply wrong: Internet sales were predominately of less profitable single tracks. Or consider the predictions of Forrester Research concerning online soundcarrier sales in the US between 1999 and 2003. According to Forrester, by 2003 only 50% of US soundcarrier sales by volume would be physical and would fall from then onwards. In actual fact in 2010, according to Nielsen SoundScan physical recorded music sales still accounted for just over 50% in the US.

As the digital future drew nearer and record companies started to commit to it, however reluctantly, a realistic awareness of the probable level of profits from digital sales became a growing concern. From this perspective, the attitude of the majority of the record company executives – litigate and wait and see rather than give up the certainties of the past – seemed, for a while at least, a sensible attitude. The evidence concerning those who jumped early into digital, such as Time Warner and its ill-fated merger with AOL, and the ever growing number of collapsing Internet music-related start-ups didn't bode well.

And yet digital clearly was the future.

In its first iteration between June 1999 and July 2001, Napster allowed people to easily share their MP3 files with others. By February 2001 Napster had some 26.4m users worldwide. Ironically, its fast growth was in great part due to the copyright infringement lawsuit raised against it by US record trade association RIAA in December 1999. On the day the lawsuit was started Napster had 50,000 subscribers; by the end of the month it had 150,000. The lawsuit alleged that Napster's users were directly infringing the plaintiffs' copyrights and that Napster was liable for both contributory and vicarious infringement of the plaintiffs' copyrights. Napster lost the case and lost a subsequent appeal, even though it was recognised that its technology was capable of commercially significant legitimate uses. It also failed to comply with an injunction ordering it to block access to "infringing material" and shut down in July 2001.

Mostly Digital

On September 1, Napster agreed to pay copyright owners a $26m settlement for past, unauthorised uses of music, as well as an advance against future licensing royalties of $10m for the use of digital tracks by its planned subscription service Napster Mk2, which never launched because of difficulties in securing licences from the majors, and in May 2002 German media group Bertelsmann bought Napster for $85m.

Seen as one of the first acceptances by an established media company that file-sharing represents a business opportunity for rights holders, as we saw in Chapter 5, Bertelsmann's move (like that of Time Warner's earlier) was a failure. The deal would also prove expensive. It immediately cost Bertelsmann some $100m in loans to keep Napster afloat and subsequently several millions in damages when various rights owners later successfully sued Bertelsmann, claiming that by keeping Napster alive it had helped it continue to infringe their copyrights.

The plan had been to create a membership-based file-sharing service that would both preserve the Napster experience and to properly recompense all the rights holders involved. When such a service was created – it never was – Bertelsmann said BMG would drop its legal action against Napster. The general reaction to the proposed restructuring of Napster was one of puzzlement rather than hostility. How was it to be done? How were users used to getting tracks for free to be persuaded to pay for them?

Online research service Webnoize (which was itself an early dotcom bubble victim: it closed down in December 2001) suggested, on the basis of a survey of Napster users, that 70% of current users would be willing to pay $15 a month to subscribe to the Napster Mk2. Taking that as a basis and assuming that actually only 50% of Napster's 20m US users would be willing to pay $10 a month, in 2000, I calculated that Napster Mk2 would have potential annual revenues of $2.4bn. This was at a time when, according to IFPI, the trade value of the total recorded music market in the US was $8.3bn. On the basis of the US market shares of the majors in 1999 and the assumption that they would receive 50% of Napster's revenues, this would generate annual revenues of approximately $160m for BMG, $110m for EMI, $175m for SME, $385m for UMG and $180m for WMG. Similarly, assuming that Napster divided its revenues equally between the two partners, BMG could receive a further $600m a year. Assuming that most of these subscription revenues would be complementary to traditional CD sales, and given that placing files on the service involved minimal overheads, the new revenue stream must have looked attractive to the majors. Of course the figures were pie in the sky. No previously free service has to date managed to re-invent itself as a viable commercial service. Indeed, the subsequent history of Napster, which we will brush into on occasion, sees it valued as an icon rather than as a business.

If the revenue figures for the new Napster seemed highly speculative, the user figures for the old Napster were decidedly impressive. The lurking suspicions of record company executives remained; digital might destroy the foundations of the business they knew, but it was real and pretending it didn't exist wouldn't make it go away. Even litigation wouldn't make it go away. The RIAA took a contrary view. It started suing individuals and services.

Following its lawsuit against Napster, the RIAA initiated suits against similar services, including Aimster (in 2002), Grokster (2003) and LimeWire (2006), achieving legal success with the last two, but not significantly affecting the level of file-sharing. Those actions ruffled no feathers but the RIAA's suits against universities and individuals, "the record industry suing of its own customers" as the process was commonly called, were greeted with the same level of ridicule and antagonism as the lawsuit raised by American authors' society ASCAP against the US Girl Guides for copyright infringement by singing the copyrighted song 'Happy Birthday' in public, as they commonly did around campfires and in meetings when a member had a birthday, without a licence. The RIAA's lawsuits began in 2003 and ended in 2008 when it accepted that the strategy had failed. The RIAA first targeted universities. In August 2003, it raised some 900 federal subpoenas against ISPs and universities compelling them to identify the real names and mailing addresses for users on their networks known only by their nicknames. At the same time RIAA was getting the approval of about 75 new subpoena applications a day. Obtaining the subpoenas represented the first step in the RIAA's contentious plan to file civil lawsuits against Internet users who shared music files without authorisation and came just weeks after a US appeal court ruling requiring Internet providers to identify ISP subscribers suspected of illegally sharing music and film files online. In some cases, the subpoenas cited as few as five tracks as "representative recordings" of music files available for downloading from these users. The RIAA, which had previously indicated its lawyers would only target Internet users who offered substantial numbers of files, declined to say how many tracks a given user would need to have shared in order to face a lawsuit. The RIAA was filing so many subpoenas that the US District Court in Washington had to reassign employees to help process the extra paperwork.

Not all universities accepted the subpoenas unreservedly. Representatives of MIT and Boston College said they were required under the Family Education Rights and Privacy Act to notify students before they released personal information such as names and addresses, and that they had been advised that the subpoenas were not in compliance with court rules concerning the proper venue for such a filing. The RIAA sought information from Boston College about three students who shared music using Kazaa, while in a subpoena addressed to MIT, it was seeking the name, address, and phone number of a student who downloaded at least five songs, including Radiohead's 'Idioteque' and Dave Matthews Band's 'Ants Marching'. In each subpoena, the RIAA provided a Kazaa screen name, an Internet Protocol, or IP, address, and a list of tracks it said were shared from the location identified. Service providers were then asked to release the names of the users whose computers were associated with the addresses.

By November 2003, the RIAA had filed three rounds of lawsuits against individuals. That month it issued 41 new lawsuits and sent 90 lawsuit notification letters to alleged illegal file-sharers in the US. This followed the sending of 308 lawsuit notification letters and the filing of 341 lawsuits in September. Some of the lawsuits were successful: the RIAA reached settlements with 220 file-sharers, and 1,054 former file-sharers submitted affidavits for the RIAA's *Clean Slate* programme, under which the RIAA offered individual file sharers amnesty for past infringements, "on the condition that they refrain from future infringement". However they remained a public relations failure: the American Civil Liberties Union (ACLU) filed a motion in a federal district court in Greensboro, North Carolina, to overturn a subpoena issued by the RIAA seeking personal information on a student at the University of North Carolina. The RIAA alleged that the student used a university computer connection to make nine copyrighted songs available for download on the Internet. ACLU argued that the RIAA was violating the student's constitutional rights to privacy and anonymous use of the Internet. The RIAA also engaged in the practice of "spoofing", deliberately flooding P2P networks with "junk music". This was discovered when computer software and src codes along with emails were stolen from MediaDefender. Its software was designed to facilitate "interdiction" on all the then known peer-to-peer file-sharing networks, while the emails made it clear that both P2P network monitoring and interdiction were undertaken by MediaDefender.

Clearly the rising levels of music piracy had an impact on the fortunes of those who depended financially on the sale of recorded music. That said, piracy is best seen as a key element of the backdrop to the new world the industry found itself in, rather than the reason for its problems. Accordingly, in this account I will only occasionally nod in the direction of piracy.

One factor affecting the decision making of record company executives was the proliferation of portable digital devices. All featured DRM but enough came from electronics companies with a reputation to make their arrival at the market significant. New music players, like new formats, could have a positive effect on recorded music sales: the Sony Walkman had extended the life of the cassette significantly. In the course of 2000 it became clear that individual companies had individual solutions and saw the digital era as a means of extending their market presence – a move that of all the companies only Apple would make successfully.

Sony developed its own secure digital download system, MagicGate, and announced plans to market a proprietary download copyright protected portable device player, including the ill-fated Magic Clip. Several other companies announced similar products, each with their own clever tricks, notably Microsoft, which claimed its MS Audio 4.0 was secure, that files in the format took up half the space of MP3 files and downloads could be made twice as quickly. Microsoft also claimed that MS Audio 4.0 was better than MP3. Other similar products include AT&T's subsidiary a2b, which launched new free software, the a2b music Player 2.0, which it claimed had a 25% faster download speed than MP3 and offered streaming based around RealNetworks' Real Player G2. The spate of product announcements, particularly those from Sony and Microsoft, leaders in their respective fields, confirmed that consumer electronics companies and technology providers realised it was important to enter the Internet digital delivery market quickly. Although such devices were all created with DRM in mind, this was an irritation for electronics companies and led to an ongoing and deep-seated friction between record companies and technology providers. Record companies sold repertoire; technology companies sold devices, which were appealing to consumers because you could play music on them at your convenience; but DRM was not to the consumer's convenience.

Nonetheless, maybe something could be worked out.

In 2001, UMG and SME announced they intended to launch an online music subscription service, Duet (later renamed Pressplay). RealNetworks, EMI, Bertelsmann and AOL Time Warner announced a competing service, MusicNet. Initially, Pressplay would just offer a streaming service, with downloads and portability being added later. However that portability would be limited by DRM software being embedded in all the tracks made available, which would consist solely of recordings from UMG and SME. The back-end technology for the service was supplied by MP3.com, which UMG's parent company Vivendi bought in May for $370m. (In contrast to EMI, which as a matter of course sought equity and high upfront fees as part of its licensing agreements, UMG licensed less of its repertoire but bought companies when it lacked the relevant expertise; earlier in the year Vivendi bought eMusic, which had a working subscription service.)

Even as the lawsuit against Napster was going on, MusicNet concluded a licensing arrangement with Napster Mk2, giving its subscribers access through RealPlayer software to MusicNet partners' repertoire in addition to the repertoire of a number of independents for a further subscription fee. From the start, it was clear that in contrast to the P2P networks where everything was available, the repertoire available via MusicNet and Pressplay was too limited. As if that were not enough, Napster Mk2 was more cumbersome. MusicNet and Pressplay were even worse, winning joint ninth place in *PC World*'s list of the "25 Worst Tech Products of All Time".

A further problem quickly emerged: the regulators. In August, the US Department of Justice (DOJ) announced it was to begin an investigation into both MusicNet and Pressplay. This led to a lengthy court case, which was still active in 2012. When the regulators examined the acquisition by Seagram of PolyGram in 1999 to form UMG there was only light scrutiny and no concessions were demanded. That changed when the EC looked into the proposed mergers of EMI and WMG and later BMG and EMI. Serious concessions were sought which led to the parties calling off the mergers. Similarly, the US Federal Trade Commission (FTC) and the EC sought and obtained significant concessions before approving the merger of AOL and Time Warner.

This new attitude signalled not only a belated realisation of the economic importance of the cultural industries, but also the growing power of the consumer lobby, and more aggressive lobbying by smaller companies and interest groups that stood to lose from more industry consolidation. The newfound interest of the regulators in the music industry also meant they became far more knowledgeable about it and thus more able to understand previously opaque industry practices. In the US in 2000, following a two-year investigation into the majors' Minimum Advertised Price programme, the FTC found the five major record companies guilty of "horizontal collusion" with certain retailers. The state attorney generals of 43 US states filed suits against the major international record companies, their distribution subsidiaries and retailers alleging that majors' distributors and retailers colluded to fix CD retail prices at an artificially high point. The court rejected a motion by the major record companies and several retailers, including

Tower Records, Trans World Entertainment and the Musicland chain, which had argued that the plaintiffs' price-fixing allegations were vague. Significantly the FTC looked at the structure of prices rather than the prices themselves. This was in marked contrast to the 1994 UK Monopolies and Mergers Commission report into CD pricing, which merely compared retail prices throughout the world.

The majors responded to the stricter regulatory environment by extending their lobbying activities and hiring people familiar with the regulatory process. In January 2001, Bertelsmann hired Joe Klein, previously the assistant attorney general in charge of the antitrust division of the DOJ, the first such appointment for a record company. This marked the beginning of serious lobbying by the industry. According to the Center for Responsive Politics, based on data collected from the United States Secretary of the Senate Office of Public Records (SOPR), the recorded music industry and the RIAA had spent over $90m in lobbying efforts in the US between 2000 and 2009. The industry spent $4m in lobbying in 2000, a figure which rose significantly to $17.5m in 2009. The industry has also actively lobbied officials of the World Intellectual Property Organization (WIPO) and affiliated organisations, although data indicating how much it spent for these groups is not readily available. In an online posting in 2011 the newsletter *Intellectual Property Watch* noted that "The sum spent on lobbying efforts to enforce copyright protections reflects an effort to thwart file-sharing that is more ambitious in scale compared to other media industry groups in the United States. The motion picture industry, for example, spent less than half of what the music industry invested in lobbying during the 2000–2010 period." The RIAA and record companies also spent over $50m in legal fees on the lawsuit campaign intended to frustrate illegal file-sharing, according to tax filings and estimates by attorneys involved in the litigation. As the industry moved from filing lawsuits against alleged individual copyright infringers to seeking increased copyright protection legislation, that lobbying has been spread even wider. As we shall see, the interest of the regulators in the music industry would play out over the first decade of the 21st century in a wide variety of ways.

However clunky they were, the arrival of MusicNet and Pressplay brought the possibility of a commercially viable market for the online distribution of recorded music further forward. That was advanced again when MusicNet and Pressplay announced the cross licensing of the repertoire available to them and that tracks could be burned onto a CD or downloaded onto a portable storage device. This meant that subscribers to either of the services had access to thousands – at this time record companies were only making limited selections of their repertoire available digitally – of tracks from all five major international record companies. The deal and others concluded around the same time suggested that the online market as it slowly emerged would be centred on downloads rather than subscription.

Despite the fact that neither the technological nor the licensing infrastructure which would enable an online music market to develop was in place, 2001/2002 saw a return to the bullish predictions of the previous couple of years. Thus, said the analysts, digital downloads would soon represent as much as 25% of the value of soundcarrier sale and even piracy was going to be conquered. This enthusiasm spread to the record companies. At the presentation of EMI's six-month results in November 2002 the company predicted that piracy would have fallen to "acceptable" levels within two years and confirmed the global roll-out of copy-protected CDs. Separately, Sony and Philips bought DRM company Intertrust for $453m, while copy-protection technology providers Midbar and TTR were bought by US-based technology company Macrovision for an undisclosed sum. According to Larry Kenswil, then head of UMG's online music division eLabs, "Legitimate online music consumption is about to explode."

Among the other deals, addition to the MusicNet-Pressplay cross-licensing agreement, were EMI's download licensing of "tens of thousands" of tracks with independent companies, including Roxio, Liquid Audio and Streamwaves. Separately, UMG licensed over 40,000 tracks, including hits by Eminem as well as back catalogue recordings, to Liquid Audio, all of which could be burnt to CD and transferred to secure portable devices. Liquid Audio would distribute the recordings via its network of 30 website partners for *a la carte* downloads at $0.99

per track or $9.99 for a whole album. Consumers were able to preview and purchase music tracks in both the Liquid Audio and Windows Media formats. Under a revised agreement with WMG, MusicNet users in the US could choose from nearly 40,000 WMG tracks, be able to buy the tracks online, download them to a PC or secure portable device, and burn them to a CD-R. In addition to the deals with the five majors and Zomba, MusicNet and PressPlay agreed streaming, download and burning licences with a host of independent labels. The services also started to gain visibility with potential users. This was particularly important for Pressplay, which was marketed to consumers through relationships with MP3.com, MSN Music Pressplay Connect, Roxio, Sony Music Club and Yahoo!. I note these developments to both show that progress (of a sort) was being made and just how minor these initiatives were.

MusicNet and Pressplay represented an attempt by the majors to control the digital music environment. The regulators remained worried about the degree of control they were seeking. Circuit Judge Robert Katzmann in January 2010, ruled against the earlier dismissal of the complaint alleging anti-trust violations of the Sherman Act against Bertelsmann AG, EMI Group, Sony Corp, Time Warner Inc, Vivendi SA, the Warner Music Group Corp and their various affiliates involved in MusicNet and Pressplay. He ruled that the plaintiffs' allegations were "sufficient to plausibly suggest" a conspiracy to fix prices, adding that both the joint ventures themselves and the RIAA, the trade group of the US record industry, which was dominated by the five majors concerned, could have "provided a forum and means through which defendants could communicate about pricing, terms and restrictions".

After noting that MusicNet and Pressplay controlled more than 80% of digital music sold to US purchasers, the judge went on to describe the workings of the services: "To obtain Internet Music from all major record labels, a consumer initially would have had to subscribe to both MusicNet and Pressplay, at a cost of approximately $240 per year. Both services required consumers to agree to unpopular Digital Rights Management terms ('DRMs'). For example, Pressplay prohibited consumers from copying more than two songs from any particular artist onto a CD each month. Music purchased from MusicNet and Pressplay would often 'expire' unless repurchased: A MusicNet consumer would need to repurchase music each year and a Pressplay consumer who unsubscribed would immediately lose access to all of the music he or she had purchased. MusicNet and Pressplay also did not allow consumers to transfer songs from their computers to portable digital music players like the iPod."

The judge noted that that one industry commentator had observed that MusicNet and Pressplay did not offer reasonable prices, and a prominent computer industry magazine concluded that "nobody in their right mind will want to use" these services, adding that, "some form of agreement among defendants would have been needed to render the enterprises profitable". In effect the allegation was that the majors had entered into some form of restrictive licence agreements.

What was needed was a group in sympathy, to a degree, with record companies – because it, like the record companies, made its money by selling recorded music and, also like the record companies, was threatened by the new breed of online music services. Enter US recorded music retailers. In response to the continued fall in physical sales of recorded music in the US (and the growing number of specialist music retailers closing down) six US retailers created Echo, a joint venture company to sell music downloads online, in February 2001. The Echo project involved Best Buy, Virgin Entertainment, Tower Records, Trans World Entertainment, Hastings Entertainment and Wherehouse Entertainment. Each of the six retail partners took an equal share in the company giving them a combined controlling stake. In direct competition with MusicNet and Pressplay as well as independent download services such as Rhapsody, Echo planned to offer paid-for downloads, either under the Echo brand or the partners' individual brands. A mark of the urgency with which the retailers had set up the venture is that at the time of the announcement Echo had not signed a licensing deal with any of the five majors and had not decided which delivery technology or systems it would use. As well as offering downloads, Echo promised an ambitious membership scheme offering consumers a wide range of in-store and online content and special deals while giving Echo's owners information about its members' patterns of consumption.

However, in June, 2004, Echo abandoned its plans, saying that mounting development costs, many rivals offering cheap services and smaller-than-hoped-for online sales in general had led the retailers to end funding for the project. Echo was not the only online music store to disappear. In May 2003, SME and UMG sold Pressplay to US-based CD burning software company Roxio, which earlier in the year had bought Napster for $12.5m in cash and 3.9m shares of Roxio. As part of the deal, which valued Pressplay at $39.5m, Roxio acquired Pressplay's distribution infrastructure and its catalogue licensing deals with all five majors. Roxio said it aimed to re-launch Napster as a legitimate online music service, using Pressplay as the foundation.

Although nothing was said at the time, the sale of Pressplay and the demise of Echo were direct results of the hugely successful launch of Apple's iTunes online music store in April 2003. At the time of Echo's closure, a co-founder and investor, Alex Bernstein, noted that Apple's music sales were "insignificant".

In the next chapter we shall see just how "insignificant" Apple turned out to be.

Chapter 8

A Revolution In Retailing

The aim of "the beautiful agreement" of 1907 was to ensure that the two signatories had as great a degree of control as possible over the fast developing record industry. The world was divided into two and each party agreed not to sell records in the other's market. At the same time each granted guaranteed and exclusive access to the other to the repertoire they recorded, thereby making it more difficult for others to enter the market.

For the first half of the twentieth century the agreement more or less worked. New record companies did establish themselves, mostly through concentrating on new music genres and local repertoires and by making use of technological improvements, such as the introduction of the magnetic tape recorder (which much reduced the cost of making recordings and thus the cost of entry to the industry). However, over the years the effectiveness of the agreement significantly lessened and instead of being a firm partnership between two parties the sense of the agreement morphed into an "us and them" statement, with the international record companies being the "us" and the new breed of independent record companies being the "them". What they had in common was that both groups were dependent on the sales of recorded music for the majority of their revenues. That changed in the last quarter of the century, as a new breed of "thems" arrived. The most successful of these was Apple, a company that had no connection with the music industry, beyond a long-running dispute with the Beatles' Apple Corps over its name, until 2001 when it introduced the iPod. By 2010, this late entrant was the world's largest retailer of recorded music and a setter of conditions to the record industry rather than a devoted follower of the diktats of puzzled Kuhnian record company executives.

In this chapter I want to follow a number of related strands: the changing role of the single, the arrival of mass merchandisers into music retailing, the price wars that followed the introduction of the Minimum Advertised Price (MAP) and the unbundling that took place after the establishment of a legitimate online music market for recorded music. These developments took place first and in their purest form in the US. Europe also saw the emergence of mass merchandisers and supermarkets as key retailers. As in the US, they upped and downsized the shelf space given to music as they too caught the Internet bug and/or sought to wield the power they had become accustomed to over their other suppliers. More dramatic in the UK was the widespread closure of both specialist and general chains, such as Virgin and Woolworth's.

This threat even extended in 2011 to HMV, for so long lauded as the most sophisticated entertainment retailer in Europe. Under fierce competition from Amazon and feeling the impact of the contraction of physical sales, it was widely predicted to fall into bankruptcy, especially when it started a widespread store closure plan in 2011. Then in January 2012, after a series of profit warnings, a consortium of record and film companies forged a deal with the crisis-stricken retailer under which HMV would hand 2.5% of its equity to its major film and music suppliers in the form of warrants. At the same time it agreed to a change in the terms of business with the consortium companies, which included Disney, EMI, SME, UMG, Universal Pictures and Warner Brothers, under which they would retain ownership of any stock sold to HMV if the retailer went into administration. As part of the deal, HMV, which previously had given increased shelf space to video games and related products, agreed to refocus its product mix, expanding the shelf space given to film and music product by some 15%. HMV identified vinyl, which in recent years has been the most profitable music format for both suppliers and retailers, as a format it would give greater shelf space to. One aim of the agreement, which was reported to run for three years, was to guarantee a significant presence on the UK High Street of physical music and film product. From this perspective the support offered HMV by the music and film companies was yet another indication that, the digital revolution notwithstanding, because physical product carried higher margins, any reduction of its availability was to be bitterly fought. However, the strategy failed and in January 2013 HMV went into administration after poor sales over Christmas.

This struggle was a global one, but for reasons of brevity and clarity, I will concentrate on the US in this chapter. Some of the actions detailed below were set in motion by the industry itself and some by general changes in the pattern of consumption: all were reshaped and given new significance by the arrival of iTunes in 2003 and the power it brought Apple.

The first of these was the changing status and character of the single, which by the end of the century had become far less important and profitable than the album in its physical form. In 1984 some 125m singles were sold in the US and 6m CD albums. Twenty years later the balance was reversed, with sales of 40m singles and 943m CD albums. In the intervening years several new formats, including the cassingle, MiniDisc, DAT albums and DualDisc, and packages, such as Sound & Vision and Ear Books, were introduced, but the dominant formats remained the album and the single, with the latter mutating first to a CD and then single track download in recent years.

Introduced in 1983, the Compact Disc was, as its name implies, small and neat, and it was also user friendly in that individual tracks could be located and played automatically. Despite questions over whether the depth of sound was as rich as vinyl, its benefits overcame its flaws and, not surprisingly, it became a significant format in 1984, when sales in the US rocketed from 6m to 150m units.

Until the early 1990s the CD and the single had little impact on each other. CD album sales grew as CD player ownership increased,

A Revolution In Retailing

leading to the repurchasing of LPs, mostly catalogue items, in the CD format. The determining factor as to whether the single market either shrank or grew was largely a matter of repertoire. Disco and pop, for example, were singles genres, whereas rock and jazz were album genres. However, in the 1990s two events took place which yoked together the fate of the physical single and CD album. The first was gradual disengagement of the industry from the single and the second was the entry of mass merchandisers into the retailing of recorded music. Both had unforeseen consequences.

As noted before, albums are inherently more profitable than singles for record companies. Indeed, for the first few years as the album replacement syndrome kicked in, the industry gave little thought to singles. Then in 1988, with 1.6m of singles sold in the US in the CD format, the CD started on its path to become the dominant singles format as well as the dominant album format: in 1992 CDs at 408m units outsold all other album formats in the US and in 1997 the CD single with sales of 66.7m units outsold all other singles formats. As the majors began to turn their attention to CD singles they soon noted that the cost of their manufacture and distribution was virtually the same as that of CD albums. And so began the long process of withdrawal from the physical singles market. In his survey of the US record market in 1999, *Billboard* columnist Ed Christman pointed out that singles sales at 83.6m units fell 23.8% from the 109.7m units of the previous year, adding: "Industry observers say the rapid decline in singles sales is due to reluctance on the part of the major record companies to release singles. Many label executives believe singles sales cannibalise album sales, and their companies either don't issue singles or, if they do, cut them out once a song becomes a hit, with the hope that fans will buy the album instead. Retailers, however, argue that a low-priced music configuration is essential if the industry wants to encourage young consumers to buy music."

A similar decline in the sale of singles took place in the UK. The editors of the BPI *Statistical Handbook 2002* in their survey of 2001 suggested one reason was the growth of file-sharing. But the editors further noted that "Singles fell 10% in 2001... The factors contributing to this have been the eroding price differential between singles and albums [and] the increasing speed with which singles are appearing on compilation albums". The *Now! That's What I Call Music* series, the leading compilation series, first appeared in the UK in 1983 and in 1998 in the US, where it had a similar impact on the sale of physical singles. In the US they more than halved in units sales between 1988 and 2000, from 87.8m to 40.3m units.

Over the course of the 1990s the record companies, after briefly trying to make the single more profitable by raising its price (on the basis that it was now a *CD* single), turned their back on the format. In effect the single became a promotional tool for the album. Thus, a track was given to radio stations and if it showed potential as a hit a single was released and then quickly deleted if it became a real hit for fear it might negatively impact on the sales of the album. Consumers could still get single tracks (and albums) from the likes of Napster, which opened for business in June 1999, but, until the advent of the legitimate market that iTunes represented, the majors gave up on the single.

Another reason for this was that the majors had other, more pressing, concerns in the 1990s. On the retail front two significant things happened in America (and later throughout the world). Electronics companies and mass merchandisers (notably Wal-Mart) added recorded music to the lines they carried. Best Buy, which began as the Sound of Music record store in St Paul, Minnesota in 1966, transformed itself in the 1980s into an electronics chain, with discounting its key strategy, and subsequently expanded its product lines to include recorded music. Although it was active in music sponsorship for a while, sponsoring Stevie Nicks' *Enchanted* 1998 tour, for example, for Best Buy recorded music was always a loss leader. Another such retailer (which closed in 2009) was Circuit City. The attraction of music for companies like these and the other electronics chains that started to stock music was the increased footfall music could bring. At the same time they saw a synergy between selling CD players and CDs. Just as CD players were cool, unlike gramophones and older style Hi-Fis, so CDs were new and modern, not old and fuddy duddy like vinyl albums.

A Revolution In Retailing

Coolness was not a concern for the other new entrants into recorded music retailing. Part of the retailing revolution of the 1980s and 1990s was the rise of the hypermarket and out of town mass merchandiser. The classic example was Wal-Mart, which entered music retailing to extend its product lines and, like the electronics stores, to increase its general footfall. Another new type of retailer was the hybrid store, such as Amazon, from which one ordered CDs online and had them delivered by post. And then there was Apple, another new entrant to the business, and the other online stores that followed in its wake. The success of these four groups, albeit relatively short-lived for some of their number, was phenomenal, as the table below shows.

The Top 10 music retailers in the US in January 2008 (%)	
Apple	19
Wal-Mart	15
Best Buy	13
Amazon	6
Target	6
FYE/Coconuts	3
Borders	3
Barnes & Noble	2
Circuit City	2
Rhapsody	1
Others	28

Source: NPD

None of these were traditional music retailers, mom & pop stores or specialist chains – there was no Tower, Virgin Megastore, Trans World Entertainment. The table below details the changes in recorded music retailing over recent years.

Recorded music sales in the US by outlet types, 1993–2008 (%)

	1993	1996	2000	2004	2008
Record stores	56.2	49.9	42.4	32.5	30.0
Mass merchandisers	26.1	31.5	40.6	53.8	28.4
Internet	–	–	3.2	5.9	14.6
Downloads	–	–	–	4.0	13.5
Other	17.7	18.6	13.8	3.8	13.5

Source: RIAA

By 2010, the changes were even more marked with, according to Nielsen SoundScan, chain and independent stores having less than a 30% market share, hardly much more than that of digital download stores (26%).

Music retailing had changed dramatically and not for the better from the majors' perspective. If the relationship between traditional music retailers and record companies was uneasy, at least they both depended on selling recorded music. This was not the case with Apple, Best Buy or Wal-Mart. Nor was it the case with other entrants to the music business such as the coffee chain Starbucks. In 2008, as the economy contracted, Starbucks began scaling back its ambitions to make it a must-go destination by turning itself into an entertainment hub, but a few years earlier it had entered the music industry with a bang. In 2005 it started to offer customers selected CD albums in its stores and in 2007 established a joint venture record company, Hear Music, with the Concord Music Group, releasing albums by Paul McCartney (after he left EMI) and others. At the time it secured decent discounts from record companies, who saw it offering them niche market opportunities unavailable elsewhere but as the recession started to bite and Starbucks' coffee sales started to slip, after expanding its CD offerings to some 20 titles in selected stores and selling some 4m CDs a year, the chain retrenched, handing over control of Hear to Concord, and re-inventing itself as a social networking location.

To see how Apple and the others achieved this market dominance, how a coffee chain became briefly a significant retailer, and how the record industry lost control over the retailing of its product, particularly its pricing, we need to go back to 1994 when the store wars began. A similar shift took place in Europe. In 1998, according to various retail surveys, the supermarkets' share of recorded music sales in national markets in Europe ranged from 10% to 20%. As such, like their American cousins, they developed an enormous leverage on the record companies when seeking discounts, which they used to bring down CD album prices and to compete more aggressively with traditional specialist music stores.

While US soundcarrier sales grew by 8% in 1994, the amount of retail space devoted to recorded music rose by over 20%. Major specialist retail groups such as Musicland, Blockbuster and Tower continued to expand, while remaining under strong pressure from consumer electronics chains selling CDs as loss leaders. The largest of these chains was Best Buy, which operated 200 stores in 26 states and planned to open a further 80 outlets in 1995. In 1994 Best Buy was selling new release CDs with a list price of $16 for under $10 and other full-price CDs for under $12. Other consumer electronics chains, such as Good Guys and Circuit City, also entered the record market. The response of the larger specialist chains was twofold: competition, which made discounting almost universal in large and medium-sized stores, and consolidation and closure. In 1995, the share of soundcarrier sales taken by specialist music stores continued to fall under pressure from discount chains (and from mail order companies, including record clubs). According to the National Association of Recording Merchandisers (NARM), over one-quarter of smaller specialists had lower sales in 1994 than in 1993. Typical of the bankruptcies was that of Wherehouse. The 400-store chain had sales of almost $500m but losses of $162m in 1994. Wherehouse declared itself bankrupt in 1995 with debts to record companies of about $40m. Some specialist stores continued to expand. However, while sales grew, it, and alongside it a growing a number of chains, started to report losses. Over the period 1994–6 more than 1,000 independent stores closed and a dozen or so chains filed for Chapter 11 protection, thus allowing them to continue trading and reorganise their debts.

One reaction of the smaller stores to their ever falling share of recorded music sales was to start selling used CDs, a strategy that would be taken up by larger stores, such as Trans World, by the end of the decade. In 1999 the value of the used CD market in the US was $254m, according to US trade group NARM. The aim was to revitalise the used CD market and discard its bargain bin image by addressing one important and often neglected characteristic of the CD: if used reasonably it is unbreakable and difficult to corrupt. In marked contrast to either vinyl soundcarriers or cassettes, both of which suffer notable deterioration of quality (and therefore value) through usage, CDs can have a long life.

Selling used CDs and discounting were anathema to record companies who wanted to sell new CD albums at list price. Taking the view that they might lose whatever influence they had over the specialist stores – stores moreover that had the deepest inventory and so made more music available to consumers – the majors responded with the Minimum Advertised Price (MAP) programme with the aim of keeping prices high, making discounting more difficult and helping traditional retailers, which had also started to cut prices. Under MAP, retailers were offered advertising support in return for maintaining prices at an agreed level. The threat was that if a retailer refused to maintain prices, either openly or covertly, a record company might stop doing business with it. However, for non-specialist retailers for whom music was more important in footfall than in revenue terms, this threat was an irritation at most in view of the volume they represented.

The resulting price war between the new entrants and traditional music retailers led to retail prices of under $10 for some hit CDs and high profile bankruptcies in the specialist sector as music retailing became unprofitable for many companies. In response the majors threatened to end outlets' access to the co-operative advertising funds that they had hitherto supplied to stores if they sold CDs below the MAP set price. Used for local advertising of new releases and promotions, the MAP money had become very important to the smaller stores as their customers fled to Circuit City and the larger chains. The threat seemed to work. The average price for a CD album had fallen from $10.41 in

A Revolution In Retailing

1994 to $8.97 in 1995, but in May 1996, *Billboard* reported that the prices of hit CDs at discount chains rose to $11.99.

On the basis that this price rise was not in the consumers' interest, the Federal Trade Commission (FTC) promptly began an investigation. That was concluded in 2000 when, while admitting nothing, the US distribution subsidiaries of the five major international record companies reached a settlement with the FTC. The FTC concluded that, as a result of MAP, US consumers had paid an additional $480m for soundcarriers over three years. The FTC found that by instituting their MAP policies the majors had violated US anti-trust laws in two respects: firstly they constituted "horizontal collusion among the distributors" and secondly "each individual [MAP] arrangement constituted an unreasonable vertical restraint of trade under the rule of reason". Under the terms of the settlements with the FTC, the majors were prohibited from linking the co-operative advertising funds they offered music retailers to the retail prices charged for soundcarriers for a period of seven years (under previous co-operative advertising deals record companies and record stores shared the cost of advertising). The agreements also prohibited the companies from terminating a relationship with any given retailer based on the price that retailer charged for soundcarriers. The FTC alleged that the majors had required retailers to advertise CDs at or above the MAP set by the distribution company in exchange for substantial co-operative advertising payments. According to the FTC, the majors withheld advertising support from retailers that did not comply with the MAP programmes. These restrictions applied to all advertising including radio, television, newspapers, and in-store displays, even to advertising funded entirely by the retailer. Thus, large retailers could lose millions of dollars if they failed to follow the MAP restrictions.

The FTC added that in future it would "view with great scepticism" co-operative advertising programmes that effectively eliminated dealers' ability to sell product at a discount and that it would consider as unlawful any arrangement between a manufacturer and its dealers that included an explicit or implied agreement on minimum price or price levels – even if adopted by a manufacturer that lacks substantial market power. The FTC alleged that the MAP programmes "achieved their unlawful objective" in that the price war ended soon after MAP was introduced and the price of CDs rose thereafter. In early 1997, despite stable market conditions and a decline in manufacturing and distribution costs, the majors increased their wholesale prices, which US retailers passed on to consumers. The FTC suggested that the majors were able to impose this increase because they had a combined distributor market share of about 85% in the US.

A few years later UMG, the largest of the majors and therefore the company with most to lose if physical album sales continued to decline, embraced price reduction as a means of stimulating sales, reducing the price of the majority of its frontline product by 24% to $9.09, thus allowing retailers to sell them at $9.99. The Jump Start programme, which was introduced in autumn 2003, marked a change of strategy for UMG (and eventually the other majors, each of which produced their own version). Previously, the majors had supported the specialist chains and smaller stores through co-operative advertising if they accepted the terms of the MAP programme. Jump Start saw the leading major in the US seeing that its commercial interests lay with the big (mainly non-specialist) national chains and that this outweighed its long tradition of working closely with independent specialists.

Jump Start was similar to the new terms Best Buy and other non-specialist stores were able to secure with SME, UMG and WMG earlier in 2003 for catalogue titles. Those agreements were on a title-by-title basis but, at the time, all the retailers granted them noted that they would have preferred a deal covering the entire back catalogues of the majors in question. Jump Start allowed for that. Where in the past the majors responded angrily to decisions by retailers to commit more space to DVDs and video games, Jump Start accepted that a mature physical recorded music market had arrived and addressed the problems it posed for general large-sized entertainment retailers as well as record companies: in effect Jump Start saw one major accepting that to ensure retailers would agree to continue to carry high-value items including catalogue titles, it would have to accept lower margins on the items in question.

UMG accepted as a consequence of Jump Start that more specialist retailers would be likely to cease trading, but considered the guarantee of lower trade prices and reduced administration costs a benefit worth securing. Jump Start encouraged the electronics stores and mass merchandisers, which had been selling CDs as loss leaders, to see them as a significant revenue stream, and therefore maintain and/or increase their commitment to recorded music in a similar fashion to hypermarket chains such as Carrefour and Leclerc in continental Europe which treat soundcarriers as a critical part of the product mix they offer consumers. The programme was a success for a period of time, but as physical album sales continued to decline mass merchandisers inevitably reduced the shelf space given to recorded music.

In 2000, 706m CD albums were sold in the US and UMG had a US album market share of 28% representing sales of 198m albums; in 2009, although its increased market share rose to 30.2%, it sold less than half the number of albums, 89m. This represented a huge loss of economies of scale. Nonetheless UMG remained committed to the Jump Start idea, re-launching in a slightly different guise as Velocity in 2010.

When UMG introduced Jump Start a number of academics offered analyses of the scheme. In *Manage for Profit, Not for Market Share: A Guide to Greater Profits in Highly Contested Markets,* Frank F. Bilstein, Frank Luby and Hermann Simon argued that Jump Start's price cutting was a drastic mistake. Their account of Jump Start confirms the gap that often occurs between practical market knowledge and theory. Thus, they argued that the reductions in suggested retail prices, combined with a less steep reduction in wholesale prices, could cause retailers to shift shelf space away from CDs to other products, which was already happening because CDs were selling less than before. Indeed, Wal-Mart had already planned to reduce the space it devoted to music by 15% because of slow sales and low profits. Separately, *Manage for Profit* argued that, in moving its marketing dollars away from in-store promotions and towards advertising directly to consumers, UMG might accelerate the demise of smaller and specialty chains. But this too was already happening, for reasons other than mere price.

Manage for Profit presents the US CD market in isolation, in which one move, reducing the price of a CD, is all that is examined. UMG's decision, which after a degree of finessing seems to have worked, if only for a period, reflected sales trends in which specialist retailers, from the perspective of a major record company, were no longer as important as before and the fact that mass merchandisers wanted new reasons (i.e. lower wholesale prices) to continue to stock CDs at similar levels, albeit at levels that would inevitably be reduced in response to ongoing changes in the patterns of consumption. [A good counter example of this is the success – yes they had some successes – the majors had with variable pricing at iTunes. Overall the sales of higher priced individual digital tracks fell following the introduction of variable pricing, but the margins on them rose, because the profit on a higher priced track is greater than the lost sales, since digital tracks remain (to date) compelling and a significant number of consumers have been willing to pay that higher price. In such a situation, price rises are sensible because people want digital tracks. In the physical CD album market, which has been in decline for a wide range of reasons, price cutting and price rises for the all-embracing re-packaging in which albums are extended through the addition of extra material have been ways to lengthen the life of physical product].

Another survey, *EMI Group, PLC CD Pricing in the Recorded Music Industry*, took as its central question whether or not EMI should follow UMG in reducing its wholesale prices for CD albums. The report noted that whereas before the introduction of Jump Start UMG spent $4.7m on co-operative advertising (with mostly specialist stores), EMI spent only $0.7m and as such its savings would be considerably less. Accordingly, *Pricing in the Recorded Music Industry* recommended that EMI only decrease some of the wholesale prices on selected physical product and concentrate instead on seeking "to create a new market based on Internet and focus on the regions, such as Asia and Japan, where it had a larger market share", a recipe that sounds rather like Ahmet Ertegun's famous reply when asked by the TW board how he planned to make Atlantic more profitable, but without the laconic irony: "sell more records".

UMG was also active in support of the physical market in Europe. In July 2006, after nine months of market testing, UMG announced a significant revamping of its physical CD album price structure. Under the new scheme UMG releases came in three formats: the limited-edition Deluxe package for major artist album releases including a bonus CD or DVD, the Standard release for all new albums with the Super Jewel Box, and the Basic package for older albums in a slide-pack cardboard CD case with minimum packaging. UMG recommended that Deluxe releases be priced at €19.99 ($25.56), Standard at €14.99 ($19.17) and Basic releases at €9.99 ($12.77).

The period saw sporadic attempts by retailers, large and small, to secure better terms from the majors or, like the ill-fated Echo, to find a way to move online. In 2000, NARM filed a lawsuit on behalf of its members against SME, alleging that SME was illegally seeking to direct consumers to online retail locations which it owned. NARM was seeking an end to SME's insistence that stores stock enhanced CDs containing hyperlinks directing consumers to SME sites, which include part-owned online retailer CDnow. NARM added that because SME's US market share was so high – 16.3% of albums in 1999 – retailers could not refuse to carry the enhanced CDs if they wanted to remain in business. The root of the dispute was the increased competition between retailers and the majors for a greater share of the retail margin on each soundcarrier sale in the first year of the decline of the value of recorded music sales (by 1.5%). This was to become a permanent feature of the first decade of the 21st century and was accompanied by a continuous fall in the share of recorded music sales taken by specialist music stores and chains.

One retailer that the majors could not hope to dictate to was Wal-Mart. Sales at Wal-Mart accounted for 20% of the majors' revenues; music accounted for a mere 2% of Wal-Mart's revenues. Accordingly, the mass merchandiser generally got its way in negotiations with the majors. Wal-Mart crept up on the music business to become the most powerful force in record retailing. The end of MAP largely ended the use of discounting as a means to greater sales, but as its competitors floundered – an estimated 1,200 record stores closed in 2002–2004, according to market-research firm Almighty Institute of Music Retail – Wal-Mart prospered. Wal-Mart also changed the rules of retail. The average outlet in the Tower Records chain, which declared itself bankrupt in 2004, stocked around 60,000 titles; an average Wal-Mart stocked about 5,000 CDs, leaving little shelf space for independent labels or catalogue items, which were more profitable to record companies. Wal-Mart was also choosy about what it stocked. As a "family" store, it often refused to carry CDs with cover art or lyrics deemed overtly sexual or dealing with topics such as abortion, homosexuality or Satanism. Where the content was, by Wal-Mart's standards, dubious the company demanded and got "sanitised" versions of the offending title. Thus, an angel and devil on the cover of a John Cougar Mellencamp album were airbrushed out and Nirvana changed a song title from 'Rape Me' to 'Waif Me' for the Wal-Mart version.

As recorded music sales continued to fall in the US so Wal-Mart's power grew and the company moved from discounting albums as loss leaders to asking record companies to fund the discounts by reducing the wholesale price. When in 2003 it asked record companies to increase the number of titles they made available for its selection of albums priced at $9.72, the majors complied, the threat being that Wal-Mart would reduce the shelf space it gave to music and increase what it gave to DVDs and games if it didn't get the required price reduction. Eventually, as physical sales fell further, Wal-Mart would reduce the space allocated to CDs anyway. In the shrinking music market Wal-Mart sought exclusives to ensure that it got far closer to 100% (rather than 20%) of the sales of a given title. Titles sold exclusively at Wal-Mart included releases by AC/DC, Garth Brooks, Journey and, most notably, the Eagles, whose *Long Road Out Of Eden* sold 3.5m units in 2007 in the US. This led to the bizarre sight of other retailers buying copies at Wal-Mart to sell at a loss in their own stores.

The volume of product going through Wal-Mart eroded most of the leverage the majors might seek to apply to it. Another factor was that whereas traditional music retailers took advertising money from the labels to push new releases in local papers, Wal-Mart didn't depend on such advertising. It hardly ever advertised locally, preferring to use national campaigns in which it promoted its own low-price policy rather than the artist, except when it had a special release.

A Revolution In Retailing

As we come to the present day, the story is one of how the majors in the US, and to a lesser extent around the world, lost control of the physical retailing of their product to a number of new entrants to the music business. For these retailers music was merely a part of their commercial activities rather than central to them. Accordingly, they could seek and achieve greater discounts from record companies, thus reducing the margins of the most profitable items for them, back-catalogue product, and cut back on the space they allocated recorded music when sales started to drop. Around them small and large retailers closed down, producing a retail environment in which finding, let alone buying, a CD was difficult enough. The majors had tried to keep prices (and their margins) high and failed. They tried the same in the digital market and failed there too.

Chapter 9

Digital Problems Galore

The principal reason for the decline of physical sales that continued in the US, and reached double digit falls between 2006 and 2010, was the growth of the digital market for recorded music. A commercial market that hardly existed before the advent of iTunes, by 2011 it accounted for 51% of US recorded music sales by value. In the wake of the success of iTunes various companies followed suit, including Wal-Mart, which even discounted the tracks it sold online, offering them at 88¢ compared to the 99¢ charged by iTunes. By 2011 there were some 400 online music stores worldwide, with the most important of iTunes' competitors being Amazon's MP3 online store. However, iTunes reigned supreme. By 2010, it accounted for 70% of all recorded music digital sales in the US and its overall market share had risen to 28%. Wal-Mart's market share, which stemmed primarily from physical sales, fell to 12% and in 2011, it closed its online store. This confirmed that price, the key to Wal-Mart's high level of physical sales, wasn't the most important thing when it came to music downloads. Once upon a time, Wal-Mart was seen as an "iTunes-killer" with its deeply discounted MP3s, but it turned out that discounts meant little compared to the seamless iPod and iPhone integration with iTunes, the superior iTunes user interface, and the tether created by stored credit cards.

Digital Problems Galore

iTunes wasn't developed to save the record industry, but to transform Apple's iPod, launched in 2001, from its status as a cute gizmo for Apple lovers into a must-have mainstream product. Initially the entry of Apple's iTunes was welcomed by the industry, but soon record companies found that just as they had been unable to control the new bricks and mortar entrants to the market so they couldn't control Apple. Even worse, as the digital market grew, it became clear that single tracks, the least profitable item of the majors' products, were the mainstay of this new market. To understand the industry's failure to tame iTunes and make it do its bidding, it is necessary to go back to iTunes' launch in April 2003.

Sources differ as to whether the 99¢ price of a download was the idea of Steve Jobs or came from within the record industry during the course of Apple's negotiations with the majors for the necessary licences to launch iTunes. Of that price record companies were to receive 67¢ and Apple 22¢ of each download sale. Certainly from the start there was opposition within sections of the industry, initially not merely to the price being the same across the board, but to the actual 99¢ price itself. Most of this opposition came from the people within the distribution arms of the companies, executives who dealt with profit and cost margins on a daily basis. That said, the record companies went into the first iTunes licensing arrangements with their eyes open. Doug Morris, then head of UMG, the world's largest record company, which was the second of the majors (after WMG) to licence iTunes, succinctly noted: "I don't think we're going to make a lot of money, but [Jobs] is going to sell a lot of iPods."

iTunes seemed to be the last hope for the majors. The P2P networks were growing and physical record sales were still falling. The previous would-be industry champion, Pressplay, was widely considered as clunky and consumer-unfriendly. Indeed, a month after the launch of iTunes, Pressplay would be sold to Roxio who would use it as the basis of their re-launch of Napster as a legitimate online service. Apart from the success of iTunes and others in selling music to Internet customers and making a legitimate service "cool", it provided the record industry with proof that a legitimate online market was developing. This became increasingly important as a means of persuading governments to take action against the proliferating P2P websites. The first successes in this war against P2P came two years after iTunes had arrived.

Later, in 2005, the Federal Court of Australia would rule that Kazaa's owners had knowingly allowed users illegally to swap copyrighted music recordings and in the same year the US Supreme Court would rule that Grokster's P2P file-sharing software also encouraged the infringement of copyright. In those cases the key question asked was whether Kazaa or Grokster contributed to copyright infringement for their own benefit. In both cases they were found to have done so. Judge Murray Wilcox of the Sydney Federal Court ruled that the companies and individuals associated with Kazaa knowingly facilitated and profited from the copyright infringements that their software made possible. He ruled that Sharman, the owner of Kazaa, authorised copyright infringement by Kazaa users, failed to take measures to stop such infringements, and actively encouraged copyright infringement through its *Join the Revolution* campaign, although it clearly had the power to prevent, or at least substantially reduce, the incidence of copyright file-sharing over the network. This ruling was in step with the Supreme Court's Grokster ruling that "one who distributes a device with the object of promoting its use to infringe copyright, as shown by clear expression or other affirmative steps taken to foster infringement, is liable for the resulting acts of infringement by third parties".

Thus, the Supreme Court ruled against Grokster because the company "took active steps to encourage infringement". At the same time the Supreme Court was equally concerned to precisely define inducement: "Mere knowledge of infringing potential or of actual infringing uses would not be enough here to subject a distributor to liability ... Nor would ordinary acts incident to product distribution, such as offering customers technical support or product updates, support liability in themselves. The inducement rule, instead, premises liability on purposeful, culpable expression and conduct, and thus does nothing to compromise legitimate commerce or discourage innovation having a lawful promise." Both decisions received lots of publicity and were claimed as victories for rights owners, but neither ruling, nor a similar

Digital Problems Galore

one in 2011 against LimeWire, had a real impact on P2P file-sharing, which continued to grow. More significant were the lengthy battles with Russian online service AllofMP3.com and Chinese search engine Baidu, which are described in Chapter 16.

In Europe, the issue of piracy took a different turn with the emergence of a political party whose main plank was the abolition of copyright. The Swedish Piratpartiet was founded in 2006 and other parties soon sprang up in Austria, Denmark, Finland, Germany, Ireland, the Netherlands, Poland and Spain. The Piratpartiet remained marginal but it won seats in the European Parliamentary elections and became part of the political process, making representations to the regulatory authorities when copyright reform was being debated. And in January 2011 an activist of the Tunisian Pirate Party, Slim Amamou, was appointed Secretary of State of Youth and Sport in the Tunisian government. On occasion, matters piratical took upon a farcical character, as in the media circus that surrounded the trial in 2009 of The Pirate Bay, a file-sharing service that was charged with copyright infringement in Sweden. At the trial *Wired*'s reporter had to buy a seat in the public gallery of the Stockholm courtroom from a ticket tout for $60. But if piracy achieved a political voice, particularly in Europe, the work of industry lobbyists and the growing realisation of legislators that piracy was a problem for any industry based on intellectual property rights brought the record industry better access to the ears of governments around the world. Thus, the end of the decade saw a plethora of "three-strike" laws, under which an Internet user would have his Internet connection terminated or reduced if he did not cease infringing copyright through file-sharing after two warnings, enacted, often in contentious circumstances and certainly with controversial consequences (*see* Chapter 16).

However, to gets its complaints about piracy to be taken seriously by governments the record industry needed to show a real commitment to online music services and that such services were commercially viable. That's where iTunes came in. Things started out very well for all concerned. Launched in the US on April 28, 2003, and only available on Mac computers, the iTunes store sold more than 1m downloads in its first week, which was the target set for the first month of operation. In week two it sold another million downloads and when in October a Windows version of iTunes was launched, another million downloads were sold in three days. The service garnered wide publicity and was welcomed by commentators and users alike for its stylish and easy to use interface with the iPod.

Following its launch in the US, Apple established online stores in Europe and quickly became the dominant online music store with a global market share for downloads of over 75%. With growth came problems. In March 2005, French consumers association Union Fédérale des Consommateurs-Que Chosir filed lawsuits against Apple and Sony, alleging that the proprietary DRM systems used by the two companies to prevent tracks bought from their own online music shops being played on other manufacturers' players, limited consumer choice. A move was made to make interoperability a requirement of DRM technologies by the lower house of the French Parliament in 2006, but the upper house rejected the provisions. Similarly, attempts were made to require that Apple and Sony share their FairPlay and ATRAC3 file formats with other portable player manufacturers. However, lawyers successfully argued that it would be unfair for either Apple or Sony to be made to share what they considered commercially sensitive information with competitors. Nonetheless, the regulators in Europe and competitors continued to attack the closed element of the iPod and iTunes systems. This problem was solved when in 2007 Jobs called for an end to the use of DRM altogether which would inevitably lead to full interoperability between all digital players. There was an immediate response to Jobs plea. Breaking ranks, EMI announced that it would sell DRM-free downloads thus confirming that contrary to the hopes of rights owners, the legitimate DRM protected online market was neither large enough, nor growing fast enough, to compensate for the precipitous, and continuing, fall of physical recorded music sales. At the announcement, at which Jobs was present – he called the move "the next big step forward in the digital music revolution". EMI also said that its DRM-free tracks would be exclusively available from Apple for a period, introducing the first of many promotions made by Apple and Amazon seeking to drive customers to themselves.

If the end of DRM helped Jobs with a tricky situation, it (briefly) offered EMI a potential revenue increase. After issuing its second profit warning in six months and having dismissed its CEO Alain Levy, the company clearly had a need to stimulate digital sales. One way was to abandon DRM, which EMI had tested with earlier releases by Norah Jones ('Thinking About You') and Lily Allen ('Littlest Things') among others. In support of this, EMI noted that in a survey of digital consumers by research group Indicare, 84% said that they agreed fully or somewhat with the statement that "it is important to be able to transfer files between devices", something that was not possible with tracks bought from iTunes. Eliminating DRM allowed for this. This finding was echoed in the performance of UK-based online music provider, Wippit, which sold tracks in both (protected) WMA and (unprotected) MP3 formats. According to Wippit, where a track was available in both formats, sales of the MP3 track outweighed sales of the WMA file by a factor of five to one. (Despite being a pioneer in the digital music market, Wippit never gained the traction necessary to compete with Apple and Amazon and closed in 2008.)

While EMI's decision brought the end of the imposition of DRM on all online legitimate downloads altogether closer, it also highlighted the lack of unity between the majors and their ongoing displeasure with Jobs, once seen as the industry's saviour. It also suggested the depth of the problems EMI was facing. According to *Business Week*, one major record company executive bitterly opined that Apple's motivation had little to do with compatibility and was more about selling iPods and fighting off the complaints of European regulators, adding that "to shake off regulators in Europe [Jobs went] after the weakest, most desperate music company to help him promote DRM-free".

Jobs had need of an ally to help fight off the European Commission. By 2007 more complaints had been laid against Apple, for not making iTunes available across Europe and for charging different prices in different territories. The EC's anti-trust investigation into Apple's iTunes music service was ended in 2008 after Apple promised that within six months it would lower its UK pricing to the level that already applied in 16 other European countries. Apple explained that it paid higher wholesale prices in the UK for online rights, and that it would reconsider its relationship in the UK with record companies that did not extend pan-European pricing to the UK. In their concluding report, EC officials noted they had found no agreement between Apple and the record companies regarding the organisation of the iTunes Store in Europe. The record companies were treated harshly. In her concluding remarks European Commissioner Neelie Kroes abruptly and pointedly returned to the music business, noting that "if a solution to the problems we face today is not found, then the music industry can hardly complain if regulators or enforcers step in".

By the end of the decade Apple was seen as an ally of the EC in the campaign to speed up Internet-based commerce in Europe, moving from being taken to task to being asked to join the Roundtable on the Online Distribution of Music. The shift was a significant one, reflecting the Commission's view that Apple and Google (also a Roundtable member) were the future and that the record companies were old-fashioned, the past. Once masters of all they surveyed they were reduced to being "content providers"; the content was hugely important but UMG *et al* only provided it, and inefficiently at that. The new perspective of the regulators was to make content providers (and copyright administrators, such as the collection societies) more efficient. The Roundtable, which included leading music publishers, collection societies, representatives of consumer groups and digital retailers, was established by the Commission to outline the general principles that could underpin the online distribution of music in the future and would, hopefully, lead to improved online music opportunities for European consumers.

If Apple modified several of its practices in its dealings with the regulators, it mostly acted from a position of strength in its dealings with record companies. Knopper offers a typical example of this in Coldplay's 2002 smash *A Rush Of Blood To The Head* which was supposed to sell for $13 on iTunes, but one particular day an EMI distribution executive alerted [Ted] Cohen [then a new media executive with EMI] that it was going for $11.88. The distribution rep called Apple. "OK," the Apple contact responded, "you want us to take it down?" The distribution rep was stunned. "Welcome to the world of Apple," Cohen told him. "If you don't like it, they'll stop selling your music."

That strength was deep-seated. In 2009, Apple finally agreed to variable prices for downloads at its iTunes store: 69¢, 99¢ and $1.29. According to a report in *The New York Times*, after this was agreed in principle, the negotiations moved onto when the new price points would come into play. Sony Music chairman Rolf Schmidt-Holtz had a heated Christmas Eve phone call from Steve Jobs. Schmidt-Holtz wanted variable pricing to go into effect directly, the immediate post-Christmas weeks being the time of the greatest sales of downloads as new iPod owners set about filling their playthings. Jobs wanted the new prices to go into effect in the spring. They did.

Doug Morris was right about iPod sales. In February 2010, Apple noted that in the seven years since the introduction of iTunes it had sold 10bn downloads. That represented approximately $7bn in revenues for the record industry as a whole. Since the introduction of the iPod in 2001 Apple sold 220m iPods, each with a profit margin of around 50%. That represented revenues for Apple of some $40bn and profits of some $20bn. Or, to put it another way, whereas the value of recorded music sales fell by over 30% from $25.4bn to $17.2bn between 2000 to 2010, in the same period the value of Apple, for which the iPod accounted for around 30% of its revenues, grew so dramatically that in 2012 its market capitalisation overtook that of Exxon Mobil to make it the most valuable company in the US. In other words, Apple was the Wal-Mart of the Internet.

Apple's success, in the manner of MTV at its start, was based on access to the copyrights of record companies – it was iTunes that sent sales of the iPod rocketing. The day after iTunes opened for business, Apple launched three new versions of the iPod. Before iTunes, the iPod was merely one portable music player among many, albeit it a cool one. After iTunes the iPod and its army of variant versions was *the one*. Later, record companies would seek and get a fee from the sale of every Microsoft Zune player in addition to any licensing fees, but the player, which Microsoft would no longer support after 2011, never had the same level of sales as the iPod and the revenues it generated for record companies at $1 per player were minimal.

As well as hijacking control of the pricing of downloads, iTunes also further eroded the revenues of the record companies' most profitable format: the album.

The revenue splits for single download and physical album sales

	Single download (¢)	Album ($)
Retail price	99	15
Record company's gross revenue	65	11
Record company's direct costs	40	5
Record company's overhead	13	2
Record company's profit	12	4
Record company's margin	12%	36%

The table above details the broad breakdown of the costs and revenues of a single track download and a physical album sale in 2006–2007. I have constructed it from various revenue and cost breakdowns published in *Billboard, Music & Copyright, theviewfromtheboundary* and made by analysts. It assumes a price of 99¢ per download – the standard iTunes price – a wholesale price of $11 per physical album, and that the artist in question is a medium level star, rather than a superstar. The record company's share of the download price is 65¢, with iTunes taking 34¢ while its share of the wholesale price to the physical retailer is $11. From those sums the company has to pay out marketing, promotion and distribution costs as well as artists and composer royalties relating directly to that title. These are 40¢ and $5 respectively. A record company also has non-product specific costs, such as salaries, travel, rental, etc, which significant-sized companies, such as a major, charge at around 20% of their gross revenues. These are 13¢ and $2 respectively. This leaves a record company with a profit of 12¢ from a single track download and $4 from a physical album sale and margins of 12% and 36% respectively. In other words the margin is three times as great from the sale of an album as from the sale of a single track download. A million single track downloads generate profits of $120,000, while 100,000 albums (which represent around 1m tracks) represent profits of $400,000 and a million album sales produces profits of $4m. These figures are approximate of course, but they indicate the low level of profitability of single track downloads as opposed to albums. Confirmation of this comes from Danny Goldberg, a former Chairman and CEO of Warner Bros. Records and, from 1993 to 1994, President of Atlantic Records. He notes in his book, *Bumping into Geniuses*, of Hootie & the Blowfish, which he describes as an "inexpensive signing", that their debut album *Cracked Rear View* (1994) "eventually sold more than 14m records, generating around $75m in profit for Warner Music". On a wholesale price of $11 that is a margin of 49%.

One reason the profits on *Cracked Rear View* were higher was that the album was distributed by Atlantic as well as released by it. The distribution division of a major is set up as an independent economic entity. Thus, it seeks to make a profit on the albums it distributes. (This is one reason UMG, which has the largest physical sales of the majors, and accordingly the largest distribution pipe, is particularly active in bidding to distribute albums for third parties, such as the Eagles' *Long Road Out Of Eden*.) On the conservative assumption that Warner Music made a profit of around a dollar on the distribution of *Cracked Rear View*, WMG's total profits on the album would have been, as Goldberg asserts, in the range of $70m.

Equally important for the majors, the large margins on physical album sales gave them some wriggle room. Danny Goldberg again: "When I was at Mercury Records, we agreed to give Shania Twain an increase in her royalty rate in the range of 40% if she would deliver *Come On Over* in time for a fourth-quarter release in 1997. Shania had a weak deal despite having sold 10m copies of her previous album, *The Woman In Me*. The boost in royalty rate was conditional upon Shania finishing her work quickly; she did, and the Q4 ... release of *Come On Over* [which eventually sold over 29m units worldwide] significantly propped up the PolyGram numbers for 1997. And in the process, the renegotiated rate... earned Twain at least an extra $10m."

Such practices weren't new. In 1983 David Bowie's *Let's Dance* album produced three hit singles for EMI. To persuade Bowie to deliver his next album, *Tonight*, before the end of EMI's 1983–4 financial year the company paid Bowie an extra-contractual advance of $1m. In a similar fashion, after Tina Turner's 1984 album *Private Dancer* was a surprise hit, selling over 10m copies, Capitol paid her an extra-contractual advance of $1m to deliver her next record, *Break Every Rule*, before the end of EMI's 1985–6 fiscal year. Neither *Tonight* nor *Break Every Rule* were particularly successful, in comparison to their immediate predecessors.

When, as was the case with Garth Brooks in the 1990s, you were responsible for some 60% of Capitol's profits and 90% of EMI's profits in North America, the decade in which he sold 60m albums, virtually all of them in North America, it was the artist not the record company that negotiated from strength. According to Brooks in conversation with Bruce Feiler in *Dreaming out Loud*, when he was first signed to Capitol's Nashville-based label he had a conventional recording contract. After the success of his first two albums, he renegotiated the royalty rate up to 15%, with escalations based on future anticipated net sales. After his continued huge success, he sought a further increase in royalties, final ownership of his master recordings and yearly guaranteed payments among other things. Jimmy Bowen, then head of Capitol Nashville, turned Brooks down on the basis that it would leave him no money to sign other acts. Determined, Brooks went to Jim Fifield, the then head of EMI worldwide and in 1993 secured a new deal that was hugely favorable to him. Brooks set up a company, Pearl Records, to which he granted the ownership of his Capitol recordings, which had been financed by Capitol. These were then licensed by Pearl to Capitol, which carried the burden of all the marketing and promotion costs. After these costs were deducted from the revenues Brooks took 58% of the profits. The killer clauses were that the deal was retroactive, covering the 25m or so records already sold, and that at the end of the agreement Brooks was granted ownership of all the master recordings.

Digital Problems Galore

Reportedly, the value of the contract to Brooks, before he retired (for the first time) and quit Capitol, was around $300m.

EMI was willing to agree, under duress, of course, to such a contract, which on a pro rata basis was better than that of The Beatles, because although Brooks was big in country music and country music was big in North America, his (and country music's) appeal was limited elsewhere. On a pro rata basis, he was less successful than The Beatles and EMI was sharing with Brooks more of less. This equation explains why huge global acts, equally concerned to maximise their earning potential, are less immediately demanding. A case in point is U2, whose *360°* world tour became the most successful ever in 2011, grossing in excess of the $554m generated by the Rolling Stones' *Bigger Bang* tour between 2005 and 2007, according to US trade paper *Billboard*. Under their contract with UMG, after an agreed period of time the ownership of a U2 album is transferred to a separate company, jointly owned by UMG and U2, which then receives the revenues generated and divides the profits, after costs (some of which are performer and composer royalties due to U2) have been deducted.

Companies with a range of assets could make even broader concessions. When CBS was struggling with WEA for US market supremacy (*see* Chapter 3), it decided that Paul McCartney should be on the label. Knowing that McCartney was building up his music publishing business, CBS offered him as a sweetener, in addition to $20m for five albums, the Frank Loesser song catalogue which it owned (which included the likes of 'Praise The Lord And Pass The Ammunition' and 'Baby It's Cold Outside') . McCartney signed with CBS.

The wriggle room large margins create also allows record companies to make deals with retailers as well, to discount a little extra for a bigger order or the better placement of a title in-store, a practice that became a regular feature of the new releases of superstar acts. Such opportunities disappeared when CD sales collapsed. What took their place, but with less dollars available, was single-track download discounts.

In her essay *Bye-Bye Bundles* Harvard Business School Associate Professor Anita Elberse tracked what happened to music sales as more people took to the digital purchasing of music. Looking at the recorded music sales of some 200 artists in the US between January 2005 and April 2007, Elberse found that people were buying more music than they used to, but because more were buying online, they were buying singles and/or single tracks from albums instead of full albums and that the revenue from the additional purchases didn't compensate for the revenue lost on the albums they hadn't bought. The table below details the various growth and decline rates of the single track download, album download and physical album sales.

US: Recorded music sales by format, 2006–2011 (units m)

Year	Digital tracks	Digital albums	Physical albums
2006	582	31	557
2007	844 (+45)	50 (+53)	451 (–19)
2008	1,070 (+27)	66 (+32)	363 (–20)
2009	1,159 (+8)	76 (+8)	298 (–18)
2010	1,172 (+1)	86 (+13)	237 (–19)
2011	1,271 (+8)	103 (+19)	223 (–6)

Source: Nielsen SoundScan. The figures in brackets are the percentage changes on the previous year.

In percentage terms, Elberse calculated that for every one percent increase in users who move to the online buying of music, there was a six percent fall in album sales. This meant that the average weekly sales of a "mixed bundle" (an album and its singles sold through all channels) fell from just under $13,000 in early 2005, when digital accounted for around 2.5% of recorded music sales, to about $8,500 in early 2007, when digital accounted for 9%. Despite selling an increased amount of single track downloads, record companies were making less than half as much on an album and its tracks, because digital gave more people the option to choose the single rather than buying the album to get the single. Large numbers of consumers chose that option.

In the past, record companies had watched the record industry grow from a singles business to an albums business, a process given further impetus by the 1960s album culture in which, after *Sgt Pepper's Lonely Hearts Club Band*, many acts, such as Pink Floyd and the Grateful Dead, made albums not singles. Then, after the album bonanza of the CD revolution, as we saw earlier, just as record companies forsook the single in search of the greater profits the album represented, a new set of retailers set about reducing the costs to them of albums and consequently the profits to record companies. The arrival of iTunes and subsequently Amazon MP3 (the only other online music service to achieve mainstream status) invigorated the single track market while depressing the price of digital albums compared to physical albums. In effect iTunes "unbundled" the album into a series of individual tracks and in doing so reduced the revenues (and profits) generated by mixed bundles.

Elberse's conclusion is bleak: "Revenues for mixed bundles substantially decrease as music becomes increasingly consumed digitally. Although the demand for individual songs is growing at a faster rate than the demand for albums is declining, the dollar amounts gained through new song sales remain far below the level needed to offset the revenues lost due to lower album sales. According to my estimations, a drop of approximately one-third of the average weekly mixed-bundle sales are directly attributable to increased digital music downloading activity from January 2005 to April 2007, which confirms recent concerns about the recorded music business: The unbundling of music online poses a significant risk to record labels, which, over time, will probably experience further erosion of revenues."

One such area of erosion was the releases by major acts. Elberse shows that established acts were the least affected by the unbundling process and record companies were accordingly able to charge higher prices without a serious decline in sales volumes. The industry responded to this by releasing very expensive multi-disc back catalogue items by heritage acts. That included a wealth of unreleased material and memorabilia, a trend which exploded in 2011, when curated works by the likes of The Beach Boys and Pink Floyd were released in a myriad of physical versions, some costing in the region of £100. However, many of these acts have either left record companies for other partners (Madonna with concert promoter Live Nation), started looking after their own affairs (Eagles, Radiohead) or moved their repertoire from one record company to another in search of more favourable terms (The Rolling Stones, Queen), so further decreasing the majors' profit margins.

Another issue is what people put on their iPods. The CD revolution brought massive replacement sales of catalogue titles that consumers already owned on vinyl or on cassette. The iPod revolution brought no such bonanza. According to calculations by US-based Jupiter Research in 2008, less than 5% of the recordings stored on digital players were actually bought from legitimate online stores. Most were either ripped from CDs or downloaded from unauthorised P2P services. As UMG chairman and CEO Doug Morris, blunt as ever, put it: "These devices are just repositories for stolen music."

Unlike Apple's iTunes which was largely created for the benefit of iPod buyers and hence as well as being an online store was a facility that allowed users to rip (their) CDs to their iPods, Amazon's online music store, Amazon MP3, was an online store pure and simple. It was as easy to use, allowed you to automatically store your downloads on your iTunes library or your Windows Media library and like the other sections of the Amazon store was highly price conscious, offering a range of prices and discounts that either it would fund or could be funded as a marketing exercise by a record company. The result was deep, continuing and ever-changing discounting, such as its Friday Five and Daily Deal programmes in the US. Running for a week, Friday Five offers a selection of five albums, which are a mix of current hits and catalogue titles, such as *The Essential Frank Sinatra* and Linkin Park's *Minutes To Midnight*, for $5, while the Daily Deal programme offered one-day deals on selected albums by such acts as Madonna, Coldplay and Weezer for between $2 and $4.

There is a premium as well as discount element to Amazon's variable pricing scenario. Amazon MP3 charges more than its average price for certain tracks. For example, for a period one track from Coldplay's *Viva La Vida Or Death And All His Friends*, then the best-selling album on Amazon MP3 US, cost $1.94, while the rest cost $0.89. This was consistent with the marketing policy of the record companies to use variable pricing to increase volume on slow-selling titles and to seek maximum profits from best-selling tracks and albums, a strategy they had established for physical product, but one denied them in the digital marketplace by iTunes. Accordingly, the majors welcomed the price war that broke out in the second half of 2010 between Amazon and iTunes. For example, Amazon priced Arcade Fire's *The Suburbs* at $3.99, helping generate first-week sales of 156,000 (of which 97,000 were digital, according to Nielsen SoundScan) and a number one debut on the *Billboard 200* chart. Subsequently, Amazon repeated the strategy with Kanye West's *My Beautiful Dark Twisted Fantasy* at $3.99. Amazon's success brought protests and a new wave of "exclusives" from iTunes and delight from record companies, seeking leverage over market leader iTunes.

The launch of iTunes in April 2003 marked the beginning of a commercially viable legitimate online market. A little more than a year later telco T-Mobile launched its Mobile Jukebox music service, announcing the beginning of a market for mobile recorded music. Ringtones had produced as new revenue for music publishers; maybe master tones, full recordings rather than just the tune, could become a new revenue strand for record companies. Or maybe there was life in subscription services. The problem for the majors was how to take advantage of the fast-developing but still problematic digital opportunities, which hitherto they had been fighting against, before the collapse of the physical movement left them no room to manoeuvre. So despite, all the worries notwithstanding, being convinced that there was a digital future, the majors returned to matters physical, cost-cutting and consolidation.

Chapter 10

The Conglomerates Think Again About The Music Business

If by the turn of the century it was clear that digital was the future of recorded music, the majors were focused on a more immediate matter, a decline in sales that looked to be a trend rather than a mere blip. Digital sales might be growing, albeit at a slower rate than forecast, but the downturn of the physical market and the smaller profits it generated were more pressing matters. The trade value of recorded music sales fell 1% to $254bn in 2000. That 1% fall was repeated in 2001 and then in 2002 the rate of decline increased to 7% marking the beginning of a permanent physical decline in the sales of recorded music, that at the time I termed the "slippery CD slope". The majors' immediate response was more cost-cutting and restructuring. To this was added merger mania and as the final solution, sell-offs, a process further intensified by the difficulties experienced by the parent companies of several of the majors following a period of over optimistic expansion.

Just as EMI de-merged from Thorn in 1996 to liberate the value of its music interests, so in the 1980s and 1990s, confident of the higher level of profitability that the CD would bring to copyright owners, Philips allowed its subsidiary PolyGram to expand its recorded music portfolio.

The Conglomerates Think Again About The Music Business

By 1999, with Alain Levy, then CEO of PolyGram, pressurising Philips to expand further (and more expensively) into film, to compete with Hollywood, entertainment suddenly looked like being an expensive business for the cautious Philips. Accordingly, in a *volte face* Philips sold PolyGram to MCA taking the corporate decision that music (and film) was overly risky and did not bring with it significant advantages for an electronics-based corporation.

In contrast, Sony, which like Philips had extended its recorded music interests, buying the CBS Records group in 1987 for $2bn, continued expanding its entertainment interests, buying Columbia Pictures for $3.4bn in 1989. Of all the corporate groups with intellectual property interests, Sony was the most wedded to the concept of synergy between software (music and film) and hardware (televisions and audio equipment). That synergy was sometimes difficult to achieve in practice, as we have seen during the SDMI saga when Sony's hardware divisions sought the greater ease of use of new technologies, while its music division fought for more protection. As a result, Sony was sometimes unbalanced, and certainly some of the results of the company's Janus-like position, such as the clunky Music Clip portable player, showed that. Nonetheless the ties that bound remained stronger than the tensions. Thus, although in 2002 Sony saw the revenues of its music division SME fall 1% to $5.3bn and its operating profits of the previous year turn into a loss of $72m, there were no rumours of a sale of SME. Most of SME's loss was due to increased restructuring costs, including a charge of $190m used to close a CD manufacturing facility in the US, the consolidation of distribution centres outside the US, label consolidation and other cost-cutting measures. The restructuring included the replacement of SME CEO and Chairman Tommy Mottola by Andrew Lack. Mottola's severance package was some $40m, while the restructuring charge was up from $70m in the previous year and involved the loss of 1,400 jobs worldwide.

The two conglomerates that had most committed themselves to the digital future were AOL Time Warner (which in 2003 abandoned AOL as part of its name) and Bertelsmann. Having grasped the digital nettle prematurely, by 2002 Bertelsmann was widely reported to be considering withdrawing from the recorded music market. Matters were made worse when Bertelsmann was forced to buy Zomba from Clive Calder when he exercised his "put" option. Bertelsmann's BMG had owned 25% of Zomba's music publishing business since 1991 and 20% of its recording business since 1996. As part of the 1996 deal BMG was required to buy the remaining shares before December 31, 2002 if Calder exercised his put option. In June 2002, Calder exercised the option and in November BMG Entertainment, on behalf of the parent company Bertelsmann, agreed to purchase Zomba for $2.74bn, the highest price ever paid by a major for an independent. Sales of Zomba acts Britney Spears, the Backstreet Boys, 'N Sync and others helped increase BMG's worldwide market share from 8.1% in 2001 to 10.9% in 2002. That said, the acquisition price valued Zomba, which as an independent had a global market share of less than 3%, at more than the stock market valuation of EMI, which was less than $2bn.

More problematically, the Zomba deal meant the greater involvement of Bertelsmann in recorded music at a time when soundcarrier sales were in decline and Bertelsmann wanted to expand its television interests and protect itself from the possibility of going public. BMG's 2002 revenues fell 9% to €2.7bn ($2.9bn) and operating EBITA for the year was €125m ($135m) compared to a loss of €79m ($85.3) the previous year. While the return to profitability fulfilled BMG's recent predictions, observers noted that the contributory factors, such as the acquisition of Zomba and the cost savings from corporate restructuring, were unrepeatable. This would become a continuing problem for all the majors over the next few years as cost-cutting and restructuring became commonplace. Moreover, BMG's profits represented a low return on sales of 4.6%, compared with UMG's 8.9% and WMG's 11.5%. One reason was that, in contrast to the other majors, Bertelsmann did not include manufacturing revenues in BMG accounts as its CD manufacturing belonged to a different division of Bertelsmann. These revenues, often significant – according to some reports they accounted for 20% of WMG's 2002 operating profits – would soon also be eliminated from other majors' accounts as they quit manufacturing, seeing it as a "non-core" activity. Before the fall in physical sales became a trend rather than an irritating blip, manufacturing had been a significant profit centre for the majors.

By the early months of 2003, Bertelsmann hardly denied that it was contemplating a BMG-less future. The speculation that BMG had been in merger discussions with both EMI and WMG was hardly nipped in the bud when Bertelsmann's CEO Gunter Thielen opted for the double negative, saying that the company did not intend to sell BMG, but could not refuse a good offer for the division. The company's finance director added that Bertelsmann would "not put in a lot of cash to strengthen the music business". The combination of declining soundcarrier sales, the high cost of the Zomba acquisition plus the potential costs of settlements of the lawsuits concerning Bertelsmann's investment in Napster looked set to leave BMG highly exposed. Bertelsmann's debt rose from under $1.1bn to $2.9bn in 2002 and the company, with falling revenues, prepared to sell assets.

The financial cost of AOL TW's momentous mistake was that for 2002 the company reported a $99bn loss, the greatest corporate loss to that date. It attributed the loss to $100bn in non-recurring charges, virtually all from a writedown of the goodwill from the merger in 2000 following a revaluation of the AOL portion of the company. This was caused by the simultaneous bursting of the dotcom bubble, the discovery of financial irregularities at AOL, and the realisation that AOL's Internet model – dial-up connections – was the past and that there were no real synergies between AOL and Time Warner. Not unexpectedly WMG outperformed its parent company. Sales in 2002 rose 4% to $4.2bn, while its operating profit (EBITDA) increased 5% to $348m. The company also reported a 5.5% increase in fourth quarter sales to $1.3bn and a 25% rise in EBITDA to $188m, the fourth consecutive quarter that WMG had increased both its revenues and EBITDA, making it an even more attractive sales option for a corporation in need of cash.

Another corporation looking to sell assets was Vivendi Universal (VU), which was created in 2000 through the merger of Vivendi's media, transport and utilities interests and the Canal+ television network and the acquisition of UMG from Seagram. Edgar Bronfman sold UMG to Vivendi on the basis that being the world's largest record company did not by itself give UMG enough power and influence in either a digital future or a physical present in which single entertainment strands were becoming increasingly intertwined. In Jean-Marie Messier of Vivendi he found a gambler's version of himself, someone rushing to build an empire at any cost. The cost arrived in 2002 when VU's losses rocketed to €23.3bn ($25.2bn). In response VU set about selling assets, raising €7bn ($7.6bn) from disposals in 2003 to reduce its debts of €12bn ($13bn). UMG was regularly mentioned as possibly being available for sale. However, in view of the ongoing slippery CD slope, which led to low valuations being placed on record companies, the new board of VU considered that a sale in 2002/2003 would be unlikely to achieve UMG's true value. When rumours of a possible sale of UMG first circulated, the price tag was estimated at between $4bn and $5bn, less than half the price VU paid for it. As 2002 wore on and rumours of the sale of this or that major became commonplace, even getting $4bn was considered unlikely. Accordingly VU decided not to sell, despite UMG's relatively poor performance. In 2002, it reported a 4% fall in sales and a 23% fall in operating profits and parent company VU predicted flat revenues and a further fall in operating profits in 2003.

It was against this backdrop that EMI reported its 2002–2003 results in May. Keenly anticipated, they followed indications from first half year results that EMI was mounting a recovery and that maybe Levy's plan to increase market share was more than merely hopeful. That hope was dashed – EMI market share fell from 13% to 12.2% in 2002 – as was the rise in revenues that the first half figures predicted. However, against the odds, EMI reported a return to net profitability. Even though sales fell 11% to £2.18bn ($3.54bn), it reported a 33% increase in operating profits to £254m ($412.7m) with an operating margin of 11.5%, the highest of the majors.

EMI noted that a great part of this improvement came from the 1,900 job cuts, reducing the artist roster and other restructuring moves which it said would lead to savings of £100m ($162.5m) over the period 2001–2004, with almost £89m ($130m) of that in 2002–2003. Recorded music's sales fell 12.6% to £1.77bn ($2.88bn). However, its operating profit rose 81% to £150.5m ($244.5m) producing an operating margin of 8.5%, compared to 4.1% in 2001–2002. The essential structure of the company hadn't changed: Music publishing remained smaller but more profitable. Recorded music accounted for 82% of Group revenues but only 59% of operating profits, but that performance was improving. EMI's senior management emphasised that EMI was seeking to build profitable market share, not to buy it at any cost. They highlighted the US where, although its market share in the 12-month period fell to 10.1% from 10.4%, the division reported a profit for the first time in five years.

Suddenly it seemed that EMI might be in a position of strength, that being independent was a viable alternative to life within a corporate shield and that profitability was not dependent upon size, as Thomas Middelhoff had famously declared. Small might yet be beautiful. So began the strange game in which EMI spokespersons directed journalists to such a view, while also noting that the logic behind the merger/sale forever under discussion with WMG also made so much sense. After all, the mission chairman Eric Nicoli chose to accept when he was appointed was to secure "shareholder value". As global soundcarrier sales started to decline, the previously close relationship between size and profitability looked to have been broken. Size surely mattered as economies of scale and high sales led to large profits. But no, there was very little relationship between sales, profitability and size, as measured by market share in 2002. Despite its increased market share, UMG's sales and profitability fell in 2002, while EMI's operating profits rose despite a fall in sales and market share. BMG also reported lower sales but higher operating profits, while WMG, with a marginal increase in market share (from 11.8% to 11.9%), saw both its profits and sales rise. EMI, whose global share dropped the most, from 13% to 12%, had the highest profit margin.

In retrospect, the profitability of EMI *et al* was less a matter of size and more one of timing. The prime reason for the increased profits of BMG, EMI and WMG in 2002 was that they were getting the benefits of earlier cost-cutting exercises. UMG, which had greatly benefitted from economies of scale and cost reductions following the 1999 takeover of PolyGram, saw those benefits end in 2002. SME, which only inaugurated a set of cost-cutting and restructuring measures at the turn of the century, had yet seen the direct economic benefits of them by 2002–2003.

What the sudden interest in size highlighted was a real difference between the majors. In effect there were two tiers of majors, UMG and the others, with UMG having a market share that was some 10 percentage points larger than its nearest rival and the three other majors having market shares that fluctuated between 11% and 14%. This power shift followed the creation of UMG in 1998 (*see table below*).

The market shares of the majors, 2002–2003 (%)

	2002	*2003*
BMG	10.9	11.9
EMI	12.2	13.4
SME	13.8	13.2
UMG	25.4	23.5
WMG	11.8	12.7
Independents	25.9	25.3

Source: IFPI

By 2003, it was clear that cost-cutting and mergers would be a constant feature of the record industry, whatever form it took. Press speculation linking all five majors to some form of outright sale or merger at the start of 2003 was followed in the second quarter by reports that different combinations of two of BMG, EMI and WMG, all of which had similar market shares, had held talks about merging all or significant parts of their operations. The implication was that a merger of two of these small majors – with BMG and WMG identified as the keenest would-be partners – would bring the required critical mass and allow for further restructuring and cost-cutting, thus delivering increased profits in a declining market. For overstretched corporations with their own problems, such mergers/sales represented either a useful financial injection or a further distancing of themselves from what was looking increasingly like a failing commercial activity.

Alongside all the talk of mergers there was a widespread assumption that only one would be permitted by competition authorities, thus leaving the remaining smaller major unable to undergo any comprehensive restructuring beyond simple internal cost-cutting and divestments. The first to go public were Bertelsmann and AOL TW, the two corporate groups wanting to reduce their exposure to the music market. In the same week in May that VU categorically stated that it had abandoned its plans to sell UMG for the foreseeable future, Bertelsmann and AOL TW announced that they had begun a 60-day period of exclusive talks concerning the merger of their music divisions.

The merger of BMG and WMG would give the new entity a *pro forma* global market share of 22.7%, making it the second largest record company after UMG with its 25.4% market share. As part of the deal AOL TW was widely expected to dispose of its music publishing group Warner Chappell, which was the second largest music publisher in 2002 with sales of a little over $500m, while Bertelsmann excluded its music publishing operations from the deal. Thus there would be no music publishing issues for the regulators. Previously, some observers, noting the positive reception of iTunes, had described VU's decision not to sell UMG as a vote of confidence in the music business. The proposed merger of BMG and WMG, which involved the creation of a 50:50 joint venture and no cash payment, was an indication of increased caution rather than confidence. The move put further pressure on EMI, which had previously held merger talks with both companies.

In July, AOL TW and Bertelsmann agreed to extend their negotiations. It seemed that the two groups, one privately owned the other publicly traded, were having problems at valuing their respective businesses and agreeing on a management structure for the joint venture. Nonetheless, representatives of Bertelsmann approached the European Commission to test the regulatory waters, while lawyers from AOL TW met with US regulators to assess their reaction. The expectation was that the authorities would allow the merger and several speculative articles in the trade and business media outlined new reporting structures and new jobs for various senior BMG and WMG executives in the new merged company. Much of this comment was concerned with a supposed struggle for power between the two partners over which would have most control. This was a theme that would be repeated as each new merger was announced.

The BMG–WMG merger plan solved the critical size issue, putting the joint venture within three percentage points of UMG while saving something in the region of $400m a year through the integration of back-office activities and cuts in staffing levels. The two corporations had already reduced the non-core activities of their music divisions. As part of its latest corporate reorganisation Bertelsmann had removed its replication and manufacturing operations, which mainly comprised the Sonopress optical disc manufacturer, from BMG and placed it in a new division, while in 2003, AOL TW agreed the sale of its North American DVD and CD manufacturing, printing, packaging, physical distribution and merchandising business to Cinram International for $1.05bn. The purchase was not a successful investment for Cinram: in June 2012, the company reported losses of $88m on revenues of $8000.9m and filed for bankruptcy protection in preparation for the sale of all its assets and operations to investment group Najafi Companies.

By entering into merger negotiations, Bertelsmann appeared to have conceded that it wouldn't be able to build BMG into a large and profitable major and instead was concerned to protect its other business interests. Even if the proposed joint venture would not immediately lead to greater profitability, it offered the possibilities of greater economies of scale, increased market share, and improved access to new repertoire.

The two parties in the proposed joint venture fitted together well. BMG had a large roster of black and urban music, an area where WMG had been unsuccessful in recent years. In contrast WMG had several big country and rock acts on its roster and successful local artists in such key markets as Brazil, Mexico and Spain. The sources of the two companies' revenues were also complementary: some 55% of WMG revenues came from outside North America, while 55% of BMG's revenues come from North America. From this perspective, taking into account the divestments that the regulatory authorities were likely to require in order to approve the merger, it would seem relatively easy for the parent companies to reconfigure BMG and WMG so that their book value was virtually the same, thus creating a 50/50 joint venture.

The most vocal opposition to the merger came not from the other majors – although EMI reportedly made an outright purchase offer for WMG before the discussion period ended – but from the independent record companies of Europe. Their argument was that the joint venture would have a 25.5% market share in Europe in 2003, and with UMG, which had a 25.6% European share, the companies would dominate the European soundcarrier market. At the time, I calculated that the joint venture and UMG's combined share would be less than 40% in only two of the large and medium-sized markets in 2002, Portugal and Sweden. In four, Austria, Denmark, the Netherlands and Norway, the combined shares would be between 40% and 45% and in another four, Belgium, Spain, Switzerland and the UK (the largest soundcarrier market in Europe), between 45% and 50%. Finally BMG and UMG would have had a combined market share of over 50% in the major markets of France, Germany and Italy. This level of market dominance, however sympathetic a view the EC might take of the economic problems facing the industry, was cited as a reason to refuse to approve the merger by IMPALA, the trade association of the European independent music companies.

In the past such objections might have had little effect. However, after the lengthy hearings at the EC into the attempted merger of EMI and WMG and the briefer discussions concerning BMG and EMI, the EC officials had developed a more sophisticated understanding of the workings of the record industry. At the same time the cultural and employment issues (in which mergers meant job losses not job creation) involved had become more important. Nevertheless, seen from the outside, it looked as if the objections raised by IMPALA could be overcome. From the start, Bertelsmann and AOL TW had indicated that they were willing to make concessions. However, it transpired they were not as willing to make concessions to each other. An earlier proposed sale of AOL TW's book division to Bertelsmann for some $400m had fallen apart leaving a degree of ill-feeling between the two. That falling out was over price and it was disagreements about price that brought about the downfall of the proposed joint venture. In September, Time Warner (TW, which had reverted to its original name) and Bertelsmann said they were not extending their (already extended) exclusive negotiations.

And so a new horse race began.

The last week of September 2003, saw the most intense bout of merger speculation in the history of the record industry. In seven days there were both confirmed and unconfirmed reports of merger negotiations between various combinations of all the major international record companies. The week began with the news that TW and Bertelsmann disagreed over the valuations of their respective recorded music companies. EMI promptly announced that it had entered into "preliminary discussions" with TW concerning a transaction regarding their recorded music interests. As the only one of the majors without a parent company with interests outside, EMI was the most vulnerable to (perceived) shifts in the music business, even when it was not directly involved. The announcement of UMG's Jump Start programme in the US resulted in an immediate fall in the EMI share price as did the announcement of the Sony BMG deal. This was despite the fact that the day before EMI announced that it had raised enough funds to make a $1.6–$1.7bn cash and shares offer for 75% of WMG.

As if in response, it was then reported that Bertelsmann was still in discussions with TW. This was followed very shortly by unconfirmed reports that Bertelsmann was about to begin exploratory talks with Sony regarding the sale of BMG to Sony. In quick succession Bertelsmann dismissed these reports as "speculation" and ratings agency Standard & Poor's issued a negative report on EMI's credit worthiness, thus raising doubts on its ability to raise the $1bn it offered TW in cash for a majority share of WMG. Lastly, IMPALA, the European trade association of independent music companies, said it would oppose any merger of the majors because the new entity would have unacceptable market dominance.

The dramatic end to the Bertelsmann-TW joint venture over the issue of price led to intense media speculation as to the future manoeuvrings of the majors, with most of the conjecture carrying a decided touch of desperation. Thus, it was suggested that TW entertained discussions with EMI in order to apply pressure to Bertelsmann and so get it to agree to TW's valuations of BMG and so pay the $100m that Bertelsmann had hitherto been unwilling to agree to as part of the BMG-WMG deal. Similarly, it was suggested that Bertelsmann did not explicitly deny reports regarding talks with Sony in order to put pressure on TW by implying that it had other options.

The week's events displayed a level of brinksmanship akin to gambling. However, the core issues underpinning them were very serious for the industry as a whole and particularly for EMI, which of all the players looked the loneliest. By 2003, it was becoming clearer that in revenue terms it was unlikely that online sales would ever compensate for the continuing fall of physical sales. In the 1990s the forecasts for online sales were rosy. By 2003, these estimates had fallen steeply. Informa Media's *Music on the Internet* forecast the global value of online recorded music sales might reach $3.9bn in 2008, while US-based research group Jupiter lowered its forecasts for the sale of music online for the third time. Its latest prediction was that Internet sales at $3.3bn would account for just over 25% of US recorded music spending by 2008. (In actual fact they were $2bn and accounted for 39% of recorded music sales, so strong was the decline of physical sales.) Reality was entering the prediction business. At the same time, as we have seen, the fast-developing online market brought with it lower profits than those available from the fast contracting physical market.

The acceptance that the record industry was in long-term decline (at least in terms of the sales of physical product) was a key reason behind the desire of Bertelsmann and TW to reduce their exposure to its problems. Both companies were also under strong pressure to reduce their levels of debt. Hence the cash payment sought by TW as part of any BMG-WMG merger and the reluctance of Bertelsmann to part with any money. At the same time, the proposed BMG-WMG merger represented a form of insurance, in which Bertelsmann and TW would be able to benefit from any turnaround in the recorded music business.

The steep fall in the perceived value of major record companies is seen in a comparison of the prices paid for PolyGram ($10bn) in 1998 and for Zomba in 2002 ($2.74bn) to that offered by EMI for 75% of WMG in 2003, $1.6bn in cash and shares. Values were falling fast and EMI, as we have seen, did not have the luxury of time. The pressure on EMI further intensified when, in October, 2004, hardly a month after the breakdown of negotiations between BMG and WMG, Sony and Bertelsmann announced that they had agreed to form a jointly owned (50:50) recorded music company to be called Sony BMG. In the manner of MCA's decision to buy PolyGram when negotiations with EMI, its original choice of partner, turned difficult, Bertelsmann simply switched its target partner from WMG to Sony. The move took observers by surprise. Most industry observers had been focused on the ongoing negotiations between EMI and WMG.

The proposed joint venture gave a new urgency to deal-making, making it a race between the two groups to get their deal authorised first. If approved by the US and European regulatory authorities the Sony BMG deal would make it highly unlikely for WMG and EMI to be able to form any sort of competing joint venture and vice versa. The impact was deepest on EMI. One effect of the Sony-BMG deal, if it went ahead, would be to make it far more likely that WMG's parent company TW would sell its music division outright to a concern without any significant music industry holdings, such as the consortium led by Edgar Bronfman, Jr. Such a sale might produce less money marginally, but it would pose no regulatory problems.

The proposed merger of SME and BMG did not include the two companies' music publishing divisions or distribution and manufacturing operations. Separately, Sony's Japanese music affiliate, SMEJ, was excluded from the deal, for a mixture of economic reasons and matters of national pride. The exclusion of SMEJ made sense in terms of both the valuation of SME and the operational independence of SMEJ from SME. In the third quarter of 2003, SMEJ had accounted for 26% of SME's sales and virtually all of SME's profits. SMEJ's music publishing company was separate from SME's publishing company Sony/ATV and, although its substantial non-music activities had been spun off, it still operated in a completely different way to Western record companies, mostly under its own management. In contrast, BMG's relatively unsuccessful Japanese subsidiary, BMG Funhouse, reported to BMG's Asia-Pacific management. The exclusion of SMEJ also helped with the valuation problems.

In their last financial years (2002) SME and BMG had revenues of $5.3bn and $2.9bn respectively. That means that excluding the revenues of SMEJ ($1.bn), SME was 28% bigger than BMG. However, SME reported an annual operating loss of $72m while BMG reported operating profits of $135m. Furthermore, since those results BMG had enjoyed a period of great chart success, especially in the US, whereas SME has continued to lose money. Nonetheless, even stripping out SME's non-recorded music activities, and including the $100m in Sony debt that the joint venture was proposing to take on, the valuation seemed generous to BMG; and it was over valuation that Bertelsmann and TW had fallen out.

Bertelsmann's previous conversations with the EC concerning its earlier proposed joint venture with WMG left it feeling confident that the regulators would look on its new merger proposals favourably. Separately, lawyers and observers noted that several EC refusals to authorise to mergers had been overruled in the past 18 months. Moreover, a general climate was emerging that given the state of the industry, the EC would be more likely to approve a merger of two majors than it had been in 2000. That said, the independent record companies said they would oppose *any* merger. A further problem, one that emerged in the failed EMI-WMG merger of 2000, was that the level of divestiture the regulators might insist on in order to meet market share requirements could make it harder for the merged company to achieve sufficient cost savings.

While neither merger seemed a sure thing, that the regulators would approve both was highly unlikely. The first problem was size and market share, as noted above. The second strategic issue was the more problematic one of market dominance and consolidation. Would the reduction in the number of major record companies from five to four or even three reduce the choices available to artists and consumers, particularly in North America, Europe and Australasia where the dominance of the majors was greatest? Was the co-operation between the majors with regard, for example, to compilation albums of recent hits (which accounted for some 20% of soundcarrier sales) overly close?

For the four majors the more immediate question was how could they successfully bring about their mergers or purchases. For one man the question was could he get back a seat at the top table?

Chapter 11

The Rise And Fall Of Sony BMG

Time was running out for Edgar Bronfman, Jr. He had swapped the drinks business for the record business, only to lose control of Universal. He needed some success.

Bronfman's transformation of his family firm Seagram from a serious money-making drinks company to an exciting but troubled entertainment company had won him no plaudits for financial savvy. His critics said he had exchanged jewels for bling and then done the same again when he sold Universal to Vivendi in search, *a la* Middelhoff, of size at all cost, but to the further dilution of the family's wealth. Even worse, it then transpired that the safe hands of Jean-Marie Messier were not at all safe as he embarked on a whirlwind of spending that brought Vivendi Universal (VU) to its knees and resulted in the need to sell assets that nearly included UMG. The verdict of *The New York Times* was harsh: "His reputation as a financial steward has been the butt of jokes ever since he sold his family's liquor empire, Seagram, to Vivendi in 2000, only to watch the whole thing nearly implode."

On his own Bronfman essayed a couple of solo investments, including one in British luxury goods company Asprey & Garrard, which lost him over $100m, before VU's need for cash made Universal Studios available for sale. Bronfman put together a consortium to bid for it in conjunction with television network Cablevision, which would have given the studio its own outlet for its films. The bid failed, but his presence in the auction won VU – of which the Seagram family was still a major shareholder – a higher price for its film operations and some respect from the financial community. Part of the consortium was private equity firm Boston-based Thomas H. Lee Partners, whose earlier bid for Warner's manufacturing division had also failed. More significantly, in Scott Sperling, the managing director of Thomas H. Lee, Bronfman found someone who, like him, believed in the music business. While readying the bid for Universal Studios, Sperling was also preparing to invest in two music management companies, Irving Azoff's Front Line Management and Jeff Kwatinetz's The Firm, with the idea of merging them. The proposed merger never took place, but the attempt secured for Thomas H. Lee the services of Azoff and Kwatinetz as advisors for a time, making it one of the few equity investment groups with access to a real working knowledge of the music business.

To most outside observers, the record business was in a mess in 2003. Sales were down, the revenues of the major players were falling and the margins were low. However to private equity firms, this was not a disaster but an opportunity. And it was private equity firms that were to be the key players in the bizarre game of Monopoly that the record industry became in the second half of the first decade of the 21st century. Moreover, falling interest rates, new lending standards and related regulatory changes meant that money, which had been hard to come by in the 1990s, was easily available to investors. In 2000, a record amount of $160bn was available to private equity firms looking for troubled companies to buy at discount, give them a spit and polish (or rather cut and trim) and sell at a profit. Bronfman and Sperling took that view and were successful; a few years later Guy Hands would follow suit but with disastrous results.

Knowing that EMI was in the middle of due diligence of its bid for WMG, but aware that the increasing likelihood of a speedy conclusion to the Sony-Bertelsmann negotiations was making WMG anxious, Bronfman and Sperling decided to bid for the whole group (which EMI couldn't because adding EMI Music Publishing and Warner Chappell together would never be accepted by the regulators). The consortium thus gave TW the possibility of exiting the music business with one deal. In late October, TW said Bronfman could bid, but must do by November 20, the day the TW board was to review EMI's offer.

On November 18, the consortium, which comprised Bronfman (with a 12% share), Thomas H. Lee Partners (49%) and Bain Capital, another investor in Front Line, (39%), submitted its bid of $2.6bn to TW. TW then announced that it had entered into exclusive negotiations to sell its music interests to Bronfman's consortium and within days EMI withdrew its bid. On news of the agreement between Bronfman and TW, the price of EMI's shares fell. They fell again on news that EMI had withdrawn its offer. On November 24 the deal was concluded.

Roger Ames, then the chairman of Warner Music, explained why: "I thought it crazy to go to the EU with two deals in front of it. If you're Time Warner why take the risk? If you decide to exit, do you care if Bronfman is giving you $200m less? The answer is no."

Bronfman as CEO and chairman of the reconstructed Warner Music Group was back at the top table, while Nicoli was, again, left alone at the altar.

The success of the consortium bid was good news for Sony and Bertelsmann, making it more likely that the Sony-BMG merger would be approved by regulators now facing just one merger approval request. However, as in the past over Napster, the deal led to considerable disruption within Bertelsmann. This began when the chairman of the company's supervisory board, Gerd Schulte-Hillen, resigned after voting against the proposed merger. The long drawn-out saga of the merger – involving investigation, approval, appeal, annulment re-investigation and a final re-approval, lasting from 2004 to 2007 – was extremely illuminating. It highlighted both the changing concerns of the regulators and the growing power of industry bodies, such as IMPALA, who were given an added edge as the Commission's priorities changed.

On the table were competition issues but surrounding them were larger political matters. Mergers and takeovers inevitably involved job losses – analysts calculated some 2,000 jobs would be lost by the creation of Sony BMG, generating annual savings of $350m – while support for small and medium business enterprises, the constituency of IMPALA, meant job creation. The Sony BMG saga also underlined the importance of corporate culture: it was not the regulators but the BMG and SME executives (and Bertelsmann's changing priorities) that brought down Sony BMG. Tasked with forging unity, they created an atmosphere of uncertainty and management tension that eventually led to Bertelsmann selling its 50% share to Sony.

Things started well. Within a few weeks of the initial announcement, Bertelsmann and Sony announced on December 12 that they had signed a binding agreement to form a joint venture of the majority of their recorded music interests. Its chairman was to be BMG chairman and CEO Rolf Schmidt-Holtz and its CEO SME's chairman and CEO Andrew Lack. At the time, observers noted that the two executives, who had been recruited from the television sector to cut costs and restructure their parent companies' respective music businesses, appeared to have been able to negotiate the joint venture so swiftly in part because neither had ingrained music business preconceptions. This was not true of the second tier of management at either company.

With manufacturing and distribution and music publishing excluded from the merger, the key issue was market share and its implications. In 2003, SME and BMG had a combined total US album market share of 29.2%, compared to UMG's 28.1%, giving the two a combined share of 57.3%. The combined shares were even greater in current albums, with SME and BMG at 30.9% and UMG at 28.9%, giving a total of 59.8%. If UMG and Sony BMG were to retain that level of success in the US – as they did in 2004 – this would mean that about 60% of distribution in the US music market was controlled by two companies, something no regulator was likely to welcome. Another problem was that the Federal Trade Commission (FTC), not the Department of Justice (DOJ), was to oversee the merger application. The FTC was reportedly less favourably disposed than the DOJ to industry consolidation.

But the main problem was Europe where Sony BMG and UMG controlled over 50% of the recorded music market. Here the joint venture faced concerted opposition from IMPALA, which was concerned about the negative impact that the merger would have across the whole value chain, from record companies and artists to composers, writers, publishers, artists' managers, retailers, collecting societies, users and consumers. Largely as a result of the objections raised by IMPALA, members of the EC competition authority went to the MIDEM trade fair in Cannes in January 2004 to meet music industry executives. IMPALA also hosted a press conference at MIDEM where it raised the issues of cultural diversity and market dominance, issues that had been given high priority by the EC with reference to the European television and film industries.

IMPALA further noted that, although the European recorded music market had worsened since 2000, structurally little had changed since then, adding that "already excessive levels of concentration, product homogenisation and other supply problems have had a large part to play [in changing market conditions] and they won't be cured by further concentration" and that, given its previous market assessment in 2000, the EC "would have to rewrite competition rules to get this deal through". The EC, which had earlier sent a detailed 40-point questionnaire to all interested parties, said in February that it would launch a detailed Phase Two inquiry to investigate "whether the deal might create or strengthen a collective dominant position between the remaining four major record companies". It added that it would examine "the extent to which the vertically-integrated structure of both Sony and Bertelsmann could raise competition concerns".

Those who responded to the questionnaire included EMI, UMG, Apple, several European entertainment retail chains, IMPALA and several collection societies and music publishers. Vertical integration was a key concern. A number raised the issue of the television talent show *Pop Idol* in which Bertelsmann had an interest and the synergies the company had developed around the franchise. These ranged from soundcarrier sales and music publishing revenues to broadcasting and related advertising revenues of broadcaster RTL, which was 90%

owned by Bertelsmann. The general anxiety was that RTL, Europe's leading media group with over 20 television channels and almost 30 radio stations, might look more favourably on proposed deals from Sony BMG than from other record companies, and that Sony BMG, because of its size, would be able to secure more favourable deals from third parties, such as broadcasters or retailers. The best-selling singles of 2003, in both the US and Germany (BMG's home territory), were related to television talent shows, while in the UK the second best-selling single of the year was by Gareth Gates, who was a runner-up on *Pop Idol*. In 2002 and 2003 the global sales of all singles associated with television music talent shows comprised 40m units (or about 1% of world singles sales). At the time, I calculated that album sales associated with such shows accounted for some 12m units (or about 0.3% of world album sales) and that the value of sales of soundcarriers and music videos associated with the *Pop Idol* format in Germany, the UK and US totalled some $170m over the same period.

The *Pop Idol* synergies were based on market dominance that stemmed from ownership and the control of rights. Such dominance could also be bought, as in the allegations of a pay-for-play deal between UMG and Germany's Viva music television channel, which echoed that uncovered in the US (*see* Chapter 5). UMG reportedly paid Viva a set fee of around $20,000 per video broadcast plus a share of the royalties on the sales of relevant CDs of around 24¢ per copy in exchange for Viva playing specified videos by new UMG acts. This was described as being only viable because UMG, with a 27% German chart share, could guarantee Viva videos from a wide range of acts. With an even greater combined market share Sony BMG would be in an even more powerful position than UMG. Other respondents voiced worries about Sony's planned online music service Connect, which some suggested might favour Sony BMG product, while WMG raised concerns that Sony BMG could unfairly exploit links to its parent companies in areas such as television rights and music publishing.

In May, the EC issued a far more rigorous than expected Statement of Objections (SoO) centring on issues of price collusion, collective dominance, especially of the developing online music market, and the effect on music publishing of the joint venture. In response Sony said "We plan on working closely with the European Commission over the next few weeks to respond to the concerns raised by the Statement of Objections." Separately Bertelsmann said that it remained confident it could demonstrate "in addressing the [EC's] remaining concerns, that the merger will not impede competition".

The EC's main unease regarding the merger was that it created a situation in which two companies, Sony BMG and UMG, would dominate the recorded music market to the extent that there would be more opportunities for "tacit price collusion". Based on 2003 market shares, the merged Sony BMG was the second biggest record company in the world with a 25.1% market share, just ahead of UMG's 23.5%. These two companies would thus control around half of the recorded music market both globally and in Europe. They have a combined 48.6% global market share and a combined 50.2% market share in Europe.

Most of the 51-page SoO document was taken up with discussion of pricing. Giving the example of a recent Led Zeppelin compilation album *Early Days And Latter Days* (WMG) and Eminem's *The Eminem Show* (UMG), the EC suggested that it would expect the former album, aimed at older, more prosperous consumers, to be more expensive than one aimed at teenagers. However, both were very similarly priced. Using this and other examples the EC suggested there was tacit collusion on CD album pricing between the majors, and cited this as evidence of collective dominance. The central argument concerning prices was that "the net average real prices of *all majors* [my emphasis] moved in parallel within a range that can be considered as a tunnel... and [that this] is likely to be the result of co-ordinated behaviour and not of effective competition". In its SoO the EC added "there are efficient and deterrent mechanisms in place which reduce, and are likely to continue to reduce significantly, any incentive to deviate from the common pricing policy". In response the two companies argued that their discount terms were not shared with other majors and offered the EC data about the wholesale prices of a wide range of individual titles that in their view showed that the average prices highlighted by the EC were not reflective of industry practices.

The key example of tacit collusion offered by the EC's SoO was that of compilation albums, which (then) accounted for some 25% of album sales in Europe and more often than not were joint ventures between two or more majors. Noting that, through a variety of sources, the majors knew the various promotional discounts given by their competitors to retailers, the EC reported that the majors had the ability to exclude a given record company (major or independent) that deviated from "parallel pricing from the conclusion of joint new [CD album compilation] ventures, or could even terminate some of the existing joint ventures". As proof of this it was noted that there were proportionately fewer tracks on compilation albums by artists signed to independent labels than might be expected from the overall market share of the independents.

Moreover, in both Europe and the US there was a lengthy history of alleged collusion between the majors regarding CD pricing. In Europe most investigations, such as that by the EC into CD and DVD pricing and an investigation by the UK Office of Fair Trading, were cursory and found these allegations to be groundless. However, in October 1997, following a year-long investigation, Italy's anti-trust authority fined the five majors $4.3m for "procedures that can be qualified as a mutual understanding" when the majors, as a group, had encouraged supermarkets to stock CDs by offering them preferential terms. In the US, in 2000 the majors and a number of large entertainment retailers agreed to end a number of practices, which were part of the Minimum Advertised Price programme, that were described by the FTC as price-fixing (*see* Chapter 8), although the majors did not admit liability. In a separate case, concerning the release of a Three Tenors album in the US, UMG and WMG were found to have colluded in setting prices.

The Commission's investigation of price-fixing was centred on the past, primarily the sale of physical albums, and came at a time when in both the physical and digital worlds the majors in the US ran into the likes of Wal-Mart and Apple, powerful trading partners able to demand that the majors accept their terms. In Europe, however, no physical or digital retailer had that power and accordingly the majors were able to maintain a greater degree of control over price for a little longer.

In Europe, the EC suggested that there already was "passive dominance" by the majors in setting the price range of CDs and a similarly broad acceptance by the major entertainment retailers of those prices and the various discounts offered to them. Several observers noted that this relationship required further investigation, while the EC's preliminary SoO report suggested that such collusion might further increase if only two record companies (UMG and Sony BMG) dominated the market in most regions.

Such collective dominance, which the EC claimed would "be even easier to monitor and to sustain as the number of [major] players would be reduced from five to four", would be particularly detrimental to the independent sector. In what was described by some observers as raising the spectre of job losses and playing the card of cultural diversity at the same time, Sony and Bertelsmann argued that the proposed Sony-BMG joint venture was a "response to long-term change in the economic viability of the recorded music industry" and that it would enable "the creation of a focused recorded music business which can sustain higher levels of investment in A&R than would otherwise be possible, thereby safeguarding and promoting cultural diversity in Europe". Separately the trade press saw a flood of articles and interviews in which it was argued that unless the merger was allowed, either or both of the companies in question might quit the record business, so important were the cost savings the merger represented at a time of falling revenues. Rather curtly, the Commission noted that the majors had responded to the decline in recorded music sales not by price reductions but by maintaining high price levels, which they had only been able to do through their ability to preserve "a remarkable stickiness of prices over the years in the [face] of a changing market environment".

The independents' problems in the face of ongoing global consolidation in the music industry was borne out when their combined global market share fell from 25.9% in 2002 to 25.3% in 2003 and their share in Europe, which had been 22.6% in 1999, fell from 20.8% in 2002 to 19.4% in 2003. In contrast to the majors – which the EC described as being international, vertically integrated and having significant financial assets – the independents were pictured as more focused on A&R and having limited possibilities of expansion. The Commission cited the example of the leading Spanish independent record company Vale Music. Its 21% market share in 2002 was mainly due to the marketing tie-ins with the television talent show *Operación Triunfo*. Recordings linked to the show accounted for 65% of Vale's sales in 2002. In 2003, following the declining popularity of the show, Vale's market share fell to 11.5%. The combined share of Spain's independents fell correspondingly, from 36.4% in 2002 to 26.6% in 2003. This strong level of dependence on highly variable local trends and niche markets was typical in the independent sector in Europe. When, for example, German independent record company edel attempted to transfer its growing regional market share into a significant international presence it failed, and was only able to return to profitability by selling labels and publishing catalogues and repositioning itself in large part as a service provider for other independents. The reason no independent had become a major in recent years was that none had the resources to move into all the majors' areas of activity and range of businesses. Moreover, large, well-resourced independent competitors, such as DreamWorks and Zomba, were eventually taken over by the majors.

At this time the *New York Post* claimed that Bertelsmann offered to sell its music publishing division if that would help secure approval of the joint venture. Soon after the joint venture was authorised, Bertelsmann did precisely this, confirming some observers' view that, while the proposed merger was in part motivated by a general concern to cut costs, Bertelsmann's ultimate aim was to withdraw from the music business altogether. Whereas Bertelsmann's previous CEO Thomas Middelhoff sought to expand the company's music interests, both online and offline, its current management curtailed rather than expanded its music ventures, in favour of expanding its television holding and increasing the television synergies represented by the *Pop Idol* franchise. Bertelsmann's later creation, BMG Rights Management (BMG RM), a partnership with private equity company KKR, reflected not a change of heart *vis a vis* music but a desire to create a new rights business in the music sector that carried with it none of the baggage of its past music business activities. As we have seen, the majors had moved from describing themselves as *record* companies to music companies. BMG RM, a company that exploited and administered rather than created rights, represented a further step away from the past.

Sony's position was more complex and more to do with the present. Although the bulk of its revenues were generated by consumer electronics, it owned a wide range of content, ranging from film to music. Music represented only 7.5% of group revenues in 2002–2003, but it provided 19% of Sony Corp's $951m operating profits. In part because of its history – the company invented the Walkman and co-owned the CD patent – Sony continued to stress the advantages of synergy between its content and technological holdings. Thus, despite technological setbacks – such as the Music Clip portable music player and the Pressplay online subscription service – Sony continued to invest in the online music market, for example through its Sony Connect online music service.

Sony Connect was raised by the EC, which concluded that there was evidence of "a co-ordinated strategy of the major record companies as regards the development of the legal online music market". Concerns regarding preferential access to any AOL music service had been critical in the EC's ruling against the proposed EMI-WMG merger in 2000. In the Sony BMG case the EC stated that Sony had a "strategy to increase the sales of [Sony's] portable music players by offering a downloading service adapted to the format of the specific player", in this case Sony's ATRAC system and its proprietary DRM system Open MagicGate. The EC further noted that there was evidence that Sony "already applies a very restrictive licensing policy, including high royalty rates that do not seem to be cost based". This echoed the view of EMI, in its submission to the EC, that Sony Connect would be able to make lower royalty payments to Sony BMG acts than to other artists, to the detriment of other record companies.

The issues of tacit collusion and collective dominance are inevitably raised by regulatory authorities facing, across a wide range of industries, a process of greater concentration as the key players turn their attention from national and regional markets to the global marketplace. This process generally accelerates in a declining market, as companies seek mergers to better protect threatened profit margins. The music industry, however, was in a more complex situation. Although the physical recorded music market was in decline, it was also undergoing a period of transformation. Indeed, while the EC could be described as being composed of Kuhnian scientists caught in mid-paradigm, unable to know what to ground the future on, it was clearly seeking to ensure that the practices of the physical market (such as price collusion) and the responses to the decline of the market (mergers) should not simply be transferred to the emerging online market, the problems and opportunities of which it saw as being radically different to those of the offline market. At the same time, many of the Commission's concerns were overly theoretical as a response to such a fast changing market. Such a concern was price. In the US, as we have seen, the majors were unable to control the retailing of their goods either online or offline, despite making serious and sustained attempts to do so. Within a few years the situation changed again with physical entertainment retailers collapsing left, right and centre in the US and elsewhere, not because of price collusion between the majors but because of the move by consumers from consumption to access. This process has continually accelerated every year since, leaving record companies to play catch up while online services expand their offerings to the cloud and beyond, dragging the record companies behind them still hoping that somewhere in the mix there might be a magic business plan that reinvigorated digital profits to the extent that they match the lost profits on physical sales. Cloud storage is a model of networked online storage where an individual's content, music files, for example, is stored on his behalf outside his own device, be it computer or portable player, and accessed only when required. Thus, cloud storage frees consumers of the need to keep such content on their own devices. The promise of such storage quickly became an offer made by the various competing online services, notably Apple and Amazon. The trouble the cloud represented for record companies was that it didn't stimulate sales but merely helped consumers archive tracks they had already bought or ripped from CDs. From this perspective it wasn't a new revenue stream, merely another diminishment of their already limited control of the usage of their product.

The grand old men of the modern record business: Nesuhi Ertegun (centre), President of Atlantic Records, with Vice Presidents Jerry Wexler (left) and Ahmet Ertegun. BURTON BERINSKY/TIMEPIX/TIME LIFE PICTURES/GETTY IMAGES

Len Blatvanik, the man who bought WMG but lost EMI.
RICK MAIMAN/BLOOMBERG VIA GETTY IMAGES

Lyor Cohen, Chairman and CEO, Recorded Music Warner Music Group, the man who slashed and burnt at WMG yet managed to re-energize the company. CINDY ORD/GETTY IMAGES

Guy Hands, founder of Terra Firma Capital Partners Ltd., who claimed he was tricked into paying $6.7 billion for the EMI Group by Citigroup Inc. He sued and lost and then lost EMI.
LOUIS LANZANO/BLOOMBERG VIA GETTY IMAGES

The dynamic duo: David Munns and Alain Levy during their brief period in command at embattled EMI.
DIMITRIOS KAMBOURIS/WIREIMAGE

Napster CEO Hank Barry, Andreas Schmidt, President and CEO of Bertelsmann eCommerce Group, Thomas Middelhoff, Bertelsmann Chairman and CEO, and Napster founder Shawn Fanning in 2000 when Bertelsmann sought growth through an alliance with Napster. The strategy failed. CHRIS HONDROS/NEWSMAKERS

Warner Bros Records executive Mo Ostin, the quiet genius. FRANK MICELOTTA/GETTY IMAGES

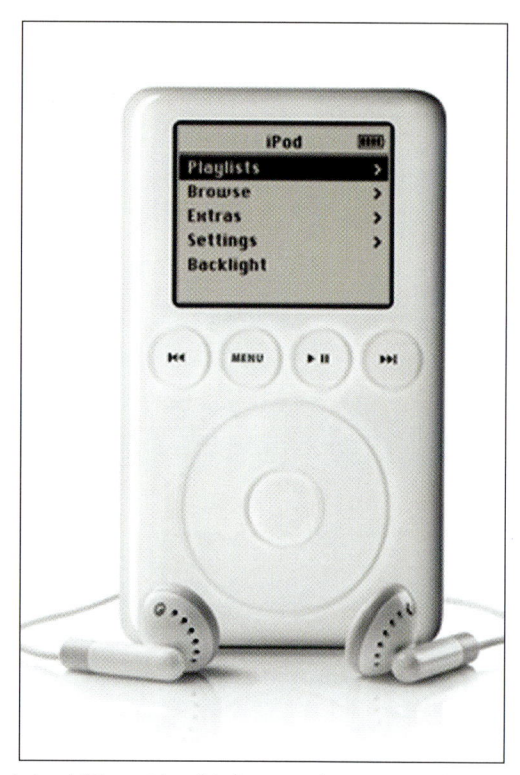

Thomas Middelhoff, Bertelsmann Chairman and CEO, who famously declared, "The position of the biggest media company is of no value in and of itself. But in clearly defined market segments, market leadership is associated with disproportionately high profits."
CHRIS HONDROS/NEWSMAKERS Right: Apple's iPod, the catalyst for change. APPLE COMPUTER/GETTY IMAGES

Edgar Bronfman Jr., the almost man of the record business.
HUBERT BOESL/DPA/CORBIS

Jeff Bezos of Amazon, iTunes's only serious competitor.
JOE KLAMAR/AFP/GETTYIMAGES

Lucian Grainge, chairman and chief executive officer of UMG (left) and Roger Faxon, chief executive officer of EMI (centre), react as Edgar Bronfman Jr., director of Warner Music Group Corp., argues at the Senate Judiciary sub-committee hearing that Universal's proposed takeover of EMI should not be allowed. JONATHAN ERNST/BLOOMBERG VIA GETTY IMAGES

Founder and Chairman of Beggars Group Ltd. Martin Mills (left) and President and CEO of Public Knowledge Gigi Sohn argue that the takeover of EMI by UMG is not in the consumers' interests. ALEX WONG/GETTY IMAGES

"No really, it's up to you." Radiohead introduce their own version of variable pricing of their album *In Rainbows*. DAVID BRABYN/CORBIS

Martin Bandier, CEO and Chairman of EMI Music Publishing. REUTERS/CORBIS

Doug Morris, the head of UMG who jumped ship to head-up SME, with Neil Portnow, president of the National Academy of Recording Arts and Sciences. GREGG DEGUIRE/FILMMAGIC

Chairman of EMI Group Eric Nicoli (left), the man who finally sold the company, and Roger Faxon, its last CEO as an independent company. DAVE M. BENETT/GETTY IMAGES

Sam Walton, the founder of Wal-Mart, once the largest retailer of CDs in the US. LOUIE PSIHOYOS/CORBIS

The Winner, Lucian Grainge, head of UMG. REX FEATURES

Steve Jobs, the man behind the iPhone, iPad and other devices that turned Apple Inc. into one of the world's most powerful companies. BRUNET/ZUMA PRESS/CORBIS

At the closed hearing that followed the publication of the SoO, Bertelsmann and Sony sought to convince the Commission that its overall fears were groundless. In this they were given help by the "devil's advocate" panel, the EC internal panel given the task of challenging the SoO, which concluded that the alleged tacit collusion on CD album prices was unproven. In a press release issued by Bertelsmann, the oral hearings were described as being "constructive" and "Bertelsmann and Sony [were] confident that their presentations on the business environment of the music industry and the nature of music as a cultural product [were] understood".

In July 2004, both the US and European regulators ruled in favour of the merger. Before, there had been five majors, now there were to be four. But what kind of a music company would Sony BMG be? The key question raised by the merger was whether it was a backward or forward-looking move. Was it created to take advantage of the digital future that was fast becoming a reality or was it merely a cost-cutting exercise seeking to extend the time frame of the physical market and its higher margins?

The economies of scale created by the joint venture were obvious: less staff would be needed to bring product to the market, thus cutting the per unit costs of A&R, marketing, promotion and back-office administration. At the same time it was argued that having a bigger market share would make it easier to attract and market top talent and secure advantageous deals with suppliers, retailers and other companies, such as MTV. In this new world Sony BMG was now challenging UMG for pole position. From being two companies with half the market share of UMG, Sony BMG had become a serious challenger to UMG, leaving EMI and WMG as the mini-majors.

In the years immediately following the creation of UMG, the logic of building profitability through market domination seemed unassailable. The various mergers attempted by BMG, EMI and WMG since 2000 sought to repeat the success of that deal, but they were essentially backward looking, seeking to protect performance in a physical marketplace that was slipping away but still more profitable than the digital one that was evolving, but which the majors had no control over. If the immediate years after 2000 saw a growing number of executives became Kuhnian sceptics and begin to reject the primacy of the physical past in favour of a yet ill-defined digital future, their financial overseers were only willing to talk the talk; from their perspective the walk remained the physical. Each year digital revenues grew and each year the bean counters saw that digital profits did not grow at the same speed while physical sales retained their higher margins, even as the amounts fell.

It was these conditions that overshadowed the creation of Sony BMG. Soon after his appointment, EMI's CEO Alain Levy redefined EMI as a "music company", one that creates and exploits intellectual property rights, rather than makes, distributes and sells pieces of plastic. This new view, increasingly shared by EMI's competitors, meant a withdrawal or partial withdrawal from non-core activities, such as manufacturing and distribution. What was meant by non-core activities had expanded in recent years. Thus, in June 2004, UMG, Warner Music Group and software developer and systems operator Exigen formed EquaTrax which was designed to lower the operational costs of the administration of royalty payments while the number of royalty due transactions rose as the digital use of music exploded. From this perspective, the creation of Sony BMG seems backward-looking in that the economies of scale that the new company was seeking to achieve lay largely in areas from which it would eventually withdraw. Sony BMG said it would generate some $300–350m in cost savings, largely by selling and closing offices and cutting some 2,000 jobs, or around 20% of the new company's workforce, mostly in marketing, sales, middle level management and back-office functions.

A further problem was that Sony and Bertelsmann had very different perspectives. Sony was a company that manufactured consumer electronic goods and the function of its film and music divisions was to provide content for its consumer products. Bertelsmann had always been a content producer and distributor. Another divisive issue was management. There were several high-ranking executives and artists at both SME and BMG who found it hard to work with or for certain people at Sony BMG. This first came to light at the beginning of 2006 when it was announced that the chief executive and chairman of Sony

BMG would change positions. Rolf Schmidt-Holtz, a Bertelsmann executive, took overall management control of Sony BMG while Sony's Andrew Lack, the chief executive of Sony BMG, was appointed chairman and given the task of overseeing public policy strategies and the company's small film unit. Reportedly Bertelsmann earlier in 2005 had made it clear that it did not want to extend Lack's contract when it came up for renewal in March 2006. One reason was that Lack did not name a replacement for former BMG executive Michael Smellie when he resigned as chief operating officer in November, leaving Bertelsmann with no senior executive at Sony BMG. (Under the terms of the merger Sony named the Sony BMG CEO until 2009 with Bertelsmann unable to exercise any veto over these decisions until August 2006). This echoed the battles within EMI when Ken Berry treated Virgin as a separate fiefdom and EMI the enemy (*see* Chapter 4) and the wrangles between the label divisions at Warner after the death of Steve Ross (*see* Chapter 3). Another complaint lodged against Lack was his $100m renewal of Bruce Springsteen's recording contract, which Bertelsmann reportedly considered to be misjudged in view of Springsteen's declining sales.

These problems were further exacerbated by the company's poor performance in its early days when it lost market share and reported a loss. Sony BMG's revenues were $936m in the three months ending September 30, 2005 and the company recorded a net loss of $60m, $43m of which was attributable to restructuring costs. At the time of the merger, Sony and BMG's joint market share was calculated to be over 25%. Once the merger was in place that share fell to below 20%, only returning to that level following Sony's buying Bertelsmann's 50% share in Sony BMG in 2008.

As well as being disappointed with Sony BMG's lower than expected market performance, Bertelsmann from the start was in two minds about it music interests. Immediately after making its deal with Sony, Bertelsmann bought the US music club Columbia House, which had revenues of some $800m in 2004, from private equity firm Blackstone and minority shareholders WMG and Sony BMG, and folded it into its US-based CD and DVD club BMG Direct. Three years later

Bertelsmann sold BMG Direct, which in 2007 had losses of $558m on sales of $1.1bn, to Najafi Companies, the Phoenix-based private equity firm. As early as spring 2006 rumours were circulating that Bertelsmann planned to dispose of all its music interests because it wanted to expand elsewhere and still remain a private company. This required it to raise the funds to buy out the 25.1% held in Bertelsmann held by Groupe Bruxelles Lambert, which had announced that it intended to go public which would force Bertelsmann to do the same. Bertelsmann delayed selling its 50% stake in Sony BMG until July 2008, when after opening preliminary negotiations with several private equity groups it sold it to Sony for some $950m. This followed Bertelsmann's sale of its music publishing operation in 2007 to Vivendi, which immediately set about combining it with its existing publishing group UMPG. That transaction also required the approval of the European Commission, but that investigation went far more smoothly. The deal also marked a new pragmatism. Vivendi guaranteed Bertelsmann that it would pay the agreed price whatever ruling came down from the EC (*see below*). One reason for this was the melodramatic end to the Sony BMG merger.

After the approval of the Sony BMG merger, IMPALA appealed to the European First Court of Justice (CFI) alleging that it was anti-competitive. To the surprise of most observers, in July 2007 the CFI annulled the EC's approval and Bertelsmann and Sony were given seven days to reapply for EC approval of their plans for the joint venture. Separately, the EC was given two months to appeal the decision of the CFI. The CFI's judgment was particularly harsh on the EC's investigation into the proposed merger, calling it "cursory" and noting that the EC made "manifest errors of assessment" in its representation of the evidence put before it. For several months, at least, the future of Sony BMG, which was proving to be to be an uneasy partnership, was made even more problematic.

One immediate effect of the CFI's ruling, delivered on the day of EMI's annual meeting, was that it made it extremely unlikely that a takeover of EMI by WMG, or of WMG by EMI, which the two had been attempting, could be achieved. On news of the CFI's ruling the share prices of EMI and WMG, which had been rising in anticipation of a takeover, fell by 9% and 17% respectively. There had been some surprise at the EC's decision, bearing in mind the strongly critical tone of the preliminary SoO issued by the Commission.

One reason for the contrast between this and the EC's final decision was the political climate at the time. In the course of 2002, the CFI overturned three EC decisions to prevent mergers between travel companies AirTours (now MyTravel) and First Choice, electrical equipment manufacturers Legrand and Schneider and between US telecoms giants Sprint and WorldCom. In all those cases the EC was criticised for being too aggressive. The EC's decision in the Sony BMG case, which the CFI found as lacking in rigour, was widely seen as a response to this criticism. In marked contrast to its reading of the proposed merger between EMI and WMG in 2000, the EC did not contest the view put forward by both Bertelsmann and Sony that unless they were allowed to merge their recorded music interests then they would have to reconsider their investment in recorded music and that the merger was a necessary step in support of the European Union's determination to support "cultural diversity".

Both these concerns were (only briefly) addressed in the CFI's judgment, nor were they seen as central. The CFI in its ruling returned to the facts discovered by the EC, which formed the basis of its SoO, which indicated at point 81 that "the Commission considers that there is sufficient evidence that majors are aware of each other's commercial terms". What is more, it follows from the SoO that that is not so much an assessment by the Commission, that might be modified, but, rather, a finding of fact resulting from its investigation. Point 92 of the SoO states that "information obtained from retailers indicates that not only are majors aware of each other's list prices but they are also aware of each other's discounts and commercial practices. Some major retailers in France, the United Kingdom and Germany have communicated to the Commission that they believe that the majors are well aware of each other['s] commercial terms". Likewise, explanatory note 54 to the SoO reports that retailers declared that the "majors are fairly well acquainted with the range of discounts that their competitors gave. It is widely known that the discounts on commercial operations granted by the recording companies are known by the majors['] commercial teams. A customer declared [that] the majors knew each other's discounts within 0.5%–1%."

The CFI contrasted these (and many other) facts discovered by the Commission and reported in its SoO concerning the pricing policies of the majors with the presentation of such facts in its decision: "The Commission has not found sufficient evidence that, by monitoring retail prices or by contacts with retailers, the majors have overcome in the past the deficits as regards the transparency of discounts, in particular campaign discounts as described for the five larger Member States. Clearly, such vague assertions, which fail to provide the slightest detail of, in particular, the nature of campaign discounts, the circumstances in which such discounts might be applied, their degree of opacity, their size or their impact on price transparency, cannot support to the requisite legal standard the finding that the market is not sufficiently transparent to allow a collective dominant position."

Despite this damning account of their original authorisation of the merger, in 2008, the Commission re-approved the creation of Sony BMG.

The EC's second investigation was unprecedented in terms of its diligence and attention to detail – the published version of the report runs to over 300 pages. It took into account the substantial growth of the digital market since 2004. The EC questioned the major international record companies, many independents and the leading digital services. It also examined some 10m transactions throughout the EU during a five-year period seeking evidence of price collusion and evidence that the merger would create or strengthen a "collective dominant position" in the digital or physical distribution of recorded music in Europe. The key question facing the EC was whether a reduction in the number of majors from five to four would "facilitate co-ordination" by creating a situation where it would be easier for companies to reach a mutual understanding on how to deal with competitors and customers, for example by fixing prices in a market, reducing the buying power of customers, or by diminishing competition through withholding content from some digital services. On the basis of these criteria the EC again approved the merger.

This was seen by some as a defeat for IMPALA. However, the appeal process gave IMPALA a platform, which the trade body would subsequently use to great effect. One argument raised against the merger was that it would increase concentration in the online market so that barriers to entry for smaller companies would be increased. The success of Merlin, the global online licensing rights agency acting on behalf of the independents, which became fully operational in April 2008, diminished the importance of this argument. Merlin was largely funded by WMG as part of a private agreement with IMPALA that the independent labels body would not object to the merger WMG was attempting with EMI in 2006 (*see* Chapter 11). Merlin signed up more than 12,000 independent record companies in its first month of full operation, including the largest independents in Europe, the UK and US.

IMPALA also gave greater weight to cultural arguments. This encouraged the European Parliament, if not the EC, to raise cultural questions as well as economic matters with regard to the music industry, particularly emphasising the plight of independent companies as an endangered species. IMPALA to date has failed to persuade the EC to introduce new competition rules which recognise the specificities of culture and the crucial role of economic diversity in music. However, such a concern has coloured what previously was a purely economic debate. Noting that the independents produce over 80% of all music released in Europe and are responsible for over half the jobs in that business sector, IMPALA has further argued that accepting the cultural element is essential for the EC to deliver its Lisbon Agenda, which includes unlocking the economic potential of culture and support for small and medium-sized businesses as a top priority because they are recognised as "drivers of growth, job creation and innovation". The Lisbon Agenda was an action and development plan devised in 2000 by the European Council in 200 with the aim of making the EU "the most competitive and dynamic knowledge-based economy in the world capable of sustainable economic growth with more and better jobs and greater social cohesion", by 2010. (By 2010, most of its goals had not been met.)

Although, cultural concerns are not part of the remit of the competition unit of the EC, there is widespread evidence that such arguments are finding greater favour in Europe and that intervention rather than merely responding to changes proffered by commercial groups is required. Concern about the slow pace of development of a pan-European online music market had been a minor feature of the EC's response to the Sony BMG merger, but subsequently this became a major theme of its policy pronouncements on music and other cultural industries. This shift was seismic, generating a regulatory environment in which intervention from the Commission and other European bodies to speed up the development of a European digital revolution, through cross border licensing, greater transparency in the administration of copyrights, and the creation of useful tools, such as a global repertoire database, was considered essential.

These changes in the priorities of the EC were seen clearly in the investigation and approval of Vivendi's purchase of BMG Music Publishing (BMG MP). When Bertelsmann put BMG MP up for sale in August 2006, most observers expected that an investment group would be the buyer because the rejection of the Sony BMG merger by the CFI had occurred only a month earlier. With this in mind, Bertelsmann invited bids from a mix of publishers too small to excite regulatory attention and investment groups.

However, in contrast to TW's sale of WMG, where TW chose the lower bid from the Bronfman consortium with no regulatory issues attached over a higher one from EMI with a lengthy investigation by the regulators (*see* Chapter 10), Bertelsmann chose the higher but more regulator-unfriendly bid from French media group Vivendi, the parent company of UMG and Universal Music Publishing (UMPG), which offered €1.63bn ($2.09bn). The sweetener was that Bertelsmann would get the money even if the EC rejected the purchase. The price represented a multiple of almost 10 of BMG MP's net publisher's share (NPS) of €170m ($213m) in 2005. The deal meant that, as well as UMG being the leader in recorded music sales, the expanded UMPG would also be the market leader with a 25% share of the $4.25bn global music publishing market. At the time I calculated that the combined revenues of UMPG ($510m) and BMG MP ($552.5m) were $1.06bn in 2005. According to Bertelsmann, which released its first half 2006 accounts on the same day that it reported its acceptance of Vivendi's bid, in the first six months of 2006 BMG MP had sales of €183m ($243.3m), which was almost the same as that of UMPG in the same period.

The US Federal Trade Commission and Department of Justice, after a light review of the case, had no objections to the takeover. Following the conclusion of its preliminary investigations, the EC decided to conduct a second, more detailed review. This tougher approach was rehearsed in a press release: "The Commission's initial market investigation indicates that the proposed merger would raise serious doubts as regards adverse effects on competition in an already concentrated music publishing market." The press release also indicated that the EC was broadening its investigation: "The Commission will investigate whether the leading position of Universal and the further concentration of the market structure would be likely to have a negative impact on fees for publishing rights or on the conditions for songwriters in the EEA or in individual Member States. In assessing the effects of the merger, the Commission will take into account the role and position of the collecting societies."

Prior to the EC's preliminary review, under the direct instructions of Neelie Kroes and Philip Lowe, the competition commissioner and director general responsible for mergers, the EC team investigating the takeover took the unusual step of meeting with a number of parties who objected to the proposed merger. Among these was IMPALA, which had successfully challenged the creation of Sony BMG. The first questionnaire sent out by the Commission was unusually detailed and was widely circulated among those opposed to the deal. IMPALA immediately signalled that it would raise objections to Vivendi's purchase of BMG MP because the sale would further damage competition in recorded music, strengthen existing collective dominance in publishing, and prejudice collecting societies and the online licensing and synchronisation markets. The response of Vivendi and Bertelsmann was the usual one, that the recorded music and music publishing markets were radically different and that issues raised with regard to recorded music were not relevant to music publishing. Vivendi and Bertelsmann rejected the charge of collective dominance, arguing that within the music publishing sector it was the collecting societies rather than music publishers that set most prices in negotiation with end users. They accepted that the new company would have a large European music publishing market share – I calculated it at around 22% – but argued that would be less able to influence prices than a record company with a comparable market share. They also noted that, because the cost of entry into music publishing was far lower than that of entry into the recorded music business, the merger would not inhibit any expansion of music publishing in Europe via new entrants to the market.

Vivendi received approval from the EC to buy BMG MP from Bertelsmann and to combine it with Vivendi-owned UMPG with a few divestitures agreed by Vivendi. The catalogues to be divested included Zomba UK, 19 Music, 19 Songs, BBC Music Publishing and Rondor UK as well as an EEA licence for the catalogue of Zomba US. The total value of these, which at the time I calculated at around €100m ($130m), only represented 6% of the purchase price of BMG MP.

The conclusion of the Sony BMG merger and Vivendi's purchase of BMG MP ended the involvement of the EC in the music industry as a retroactive adjudicator of business decisions. The next stage in the development of the modern music business would be shaped by new concerns and different players. The European regulators would be involved but their newfound role would be to be proactive and so directly shape the digital landscape that was the new environment of the modern music business. Accordingly, they prodded, poked and recommended, but to little avail, while the money men took centre stage. To see how this happened we need to go back and watch the last attempt(s) of EMI and WMG to make political sense of the economic sense that virtually all observers saw in their union.

Chapter 12

WMG, The Bronfman Era

The Bronfman consortium's takeover of WMG in 2004 was an immediate financial success. Within three months, with the help of Warner's former CEO Roger Ames, Bronfman sold some $700m of bonds to investors. This meant that over half of the $1.25bn the consortium had invested was repaid. An equally quickly mounted initial public offering (IPO) – the first sale of stock by a company to the public – pushed the consortium into profit. Historically the deal was also hugely influential. The language and promises of WMG's new owners both confirmed that digital was the future and foreshadowed a period in which, the declining sales of recorded music notwithstanding, venture capitalists replaced media conglomerates as the bodies keenest to snap up music companies.

The deal was widely seen as a bargain with Time Warner bested because it was in need of cash and didn't understand the value of what it was selling. The plaudits went mostly to the consortium and Scott Sperling in particular. Bronfman was depicted as having fallen lucky. He was not expected to be a long-term CEO. Even Sperling in an interview with *The New York Times*, while noting that Bronfman had on occasion been ill treated by the media, made it clear that his power at WMG would be tightly supervised: "The deal with Edgar is, he does a good job or someone else comes in who does a good job."

A more measured and understanding view of Bronfman was offered by Andrew Ross Sorkin, the creator in 2001 of DealBook, one of the first online financial newsletters. His DealBook memo of March 4, 2008, written after the consortium had, wrongly in Sorkin's opinion, rejected the sale of WMG to EMI in 2007 well captured Bronfman's predicament as a businessman, outlining the quandary that has faced Bronfman at every stage of his career. It's worth quoting at some length:

For a brief, shining moment, Edgar Bronfman Jnr. had redeemed himself.

It was 2006, and Mr. Bronfman, the bearded scion of the Seagrams, seemed to have successfully reinvented himself as a music mogul after nearly losing his family's fortune. It looked as if he had actually turned around Warner Music, which he had bought from Time Warner with a group of private equity firms.

Warner Music had gone public, and its stock had nearly doubled. Mr. Bronfman had managed to cut $250 million in annual expenses at the company. His private equity partners had doubled their money. And EMI, the British record company, had put a bid on the table for Warner Music.

Mr. Bronfman's critics, and there are legions of them, were stunned.

It was a classic comeback story – and all the more astounding because Mr. Bronfman had lost so big by selling Seagram, his family's liquor-cum-entertainment company, to Vivendi in 2000. That deal went down as one of the worst mergers in history.

And the Seagram sale wasn't Mr. Bronfman's first multibillion-dollar mistake. Many criticized his decision to sell the company's $9 billion stake in Dupont to buy the entertainment giant MCA in the mid-1990s. He earned a reputation as a star-struck rich kid who made one bad deal after another. New York magazine famously called him 'possibly the stupidest person in the media business.' Ouch.

Now, though, this return-to-glory tale has taken a regrettable twist. Have you seen Warner Music stock's lately? It pains me to tell you that it is trading at about $6 a share, less than half of its I.P.O. price…

Warner Music's stock aside, Mr. Bronfman's deal is actually a huge success. Or at least that is the judgment of the smart money that backed him. Mr. Bronfman and his private equity partners have gotten their original investment back and are now playing with house money. They're up some 130 percent – not bad for a company in a dying industry. (Note to Time Warner: No matter how you rationalize it, you sold the business cheap.) ....

His big mistake was not to accept EMI's bid. Even here, though, the situation is more complicated than is often portrayed.

While at $28.50 a share – at one point the offer was worth $31 a share – the deal seems like a no-brainer, the fact that the EMI bid was partly in stock created a lot of risk. There was a high probability that EMI's stock might tank – and that Mr. Bronfman would find himself in the same situation as he was in with the Vivendi deal. Indeed, that is exactly what happened: EMI's stock tanked before getting scooped up by Guy Hands, the private equity mogul, who everyone agrees wildly overpaid for it.

Warner Music's board did not help. Behind the scenes, the board is run by Scott Sperling, an aggressive silver-haired managing director at Thomas H. Lee Partners who is a board member and put the original deal together. Mr. Sperling and others convinced themselves that Warner Music was worth more and, barring a deal at a higher price, that Warner should be the one taking over EMI, not the other way around.

Sorkin (and others) could have been even more critical of Bronfman and the consortium much earlier. Unbeknownst to them, even before the deal to buy Warner was completed, in February 2004, EMI made the Bronfman consortium an offer of more than $3bn in cash and stock for the company. The offer was refused for two prime reasons: the WMG board considered EMI's shares price was highly vulnerable and that EMI could not raise a cash-only bid. Another reason was a management clash. Although EMI offered Bronfman the post of CEO of the expanded company, Bronfman was wary of working with Alain Levy, with whom he had experienced difficulties in the course of the UMG-PolyGram takeover.

Anyway, for Bronfman, winning WMG was only part of the battle. It brought some praise, but running WMG successfully would bring redemption. Luckily for Bronfman, although eight of the 13 members of which were Thomas H. Paine appointees making Sperling the key strategic decision-maker, the board as a whole thought WMG was worth more than was on offer and turned down EMI so giving Bronfman his chance to be CEO of WMG.

Bronfman's first task was implementing the cuts that the consortium thought necessary. This involved putting into practice the cuts the past management had prepared and making a greater reduction in WMG's international operations than previously intended. All in all some 1,000 staff (around 20% of the workforce) were let go and 30% of the acts signed to the various WMG labels had their contracts terminated. Separately, the three-label configuration – Warner, Atlantic and Elektra – was ended and Elektra folded into Atlantic. The man appointed to implement this restructuring as chairman and CEO of WMG recorded music US was Lyor Cohen with whom Bronfman had worked at UMG where Cohen ran Def Jam. The havoc wrought by Cohen at WMG, which one executive described as being akin to the arrival of the Visigoths at Rome, was thoroughgoing. (The changes he brought about are entertainingly told in some detail in *Fortune's Fool*.) The sackings and appointments were as much to do with changing the guard as with simple cost-cutting. A new prince had arrived and the fiefdoms were re-arranged to honour him, past loyalty being rewarded and those with allegiances to the other past princes being passed over and/or let go.

Cohen made Atlantic his base and henceforth most of WMG's successes, be they gestural or real, would be associated with the label. Thus, as WMG sang ever more loudly from the digital hymn sheet, it was Atlantic that WMG signalled had the sweetest voice. WMG didn't normally break out the performances of its individual labels, but it announced that in the three months ending September 30, 2008, Atlantic was the first US label to report that over 50% (51%) of its sales came from digital sources. Similarly, Cohen was the man identified within WMG as the person responsible for making the 360-degree deal an integral part of WMG philosophy.

The 360-degree contract was part of the transformative process of moving from a record company to a music company. In the past record companies had signed up the recording (and sometimes publishing) rights of artists, thus limiting themselves to the revenues earned from recorded music-related sales and performances. Under a 360-degree deal, which was pioneered in the Western world by EMI with its groundbreaking Robbie Williams deal but was already widespread in Asia, the company took a percentage of all the artists' revenue streams, notably merchandising and touring. All the majors made such deals but WMG presented itself as having made the most progress with the concept and Cohen, a former manager, tour promoter and agent as well as record company head, was the man who made it happen. According to the story that has become part of company folklore, a year or so after he joined WMG, Cohen took his 12-year-old son to a sold out Madison Square concert, only to have to confess to his son who thought it so cool that he, Lyor Cohen, was making all this money for WMG, that actually WMG got nothing from the ticket or T-shirt sales of the acts they signed.

And so began the 360-degree deal for WMG, with Cohen making it company policy that 20% of Atlantic signings would be 360-degree deals. By 2010 non-recording revenues accounted for around 8% of WMG revenues and the company claimed that around 80% of the company's active signings were on a 360-degree deal. As this revenue stream grew WMG commissioned a study to calculate what it would have made if past superstar acts, such as Green Day, had started with 360-degree deals: 160% more, according to Cohen. That said, at the same time acts like the Eagles were happily discovering that if they did it all by themselves, merely paying a company to press and distribute their CDs, as they did with *Long Road Out Of Eden*, they made far in excess of 160% more.

Cohen was highly praised by his fellow WMG executives for devising the now-standard record industry strategy of making new releases available at a reduced price for the first week to boost sales of high priority albums. The strategy was doubly important: it increased the potential sales of physical product in the all-important first week, which would set the parameters for future sales, while at the same time it reduced the number of units needed to ensure healthy first-week sales, thus reducing the future inventory problems that over-pressings inevitably created. Before such a reduction was applied to high-profile releases the shipment formula of the majors called for shipping three units to retailers on the expectation that one would be sold and scanned in the first week. After the price reduction policy was initiated and quickly followed by all the majors, the ratio fell to under 2-to-1 and led to a more efficient inventory replenishment system.

As ever, however, there were unforeseen consequences.

The stratagem only worked if the price reduction was controlled by the record company. If the album in question was extra high priority for both the record company and another player the result could be dramatic but at increased, rather than decreased cost to the record company. This was the case with Lady Gaga's 2011 album *Born This Way*. The CD version of the album sold 449,000 units of the 2.1m shipped in the first week, which represented a 21.4% sell-through. Second-week sales were at 174,000 units (136,000 CDs), or 27.8% sell-through. UMG, determined to make big splash had shipped 4.7m units, rather than the conventional 2m, for each first-week scan. What dented UMG's success was the decision by Amazon to sell downloads of *Born This Way* for 99¢ for two days only, at a cost to itself of $3.3m. Having paid $8.40 per digital album, Amazon lost $7.41 on each of the 443,000 scans during the two-day sale, but put itself on the map as a digital music merchant, in a way that the same amount of money spent on traditional advertising could never have done. The 99¢ pricing brought Amazon mainstream media news aplenty and huge sales for Lady Gaga: the album sold 1.1 million units, 662,000 digital and 449,000 physical, in its debut week ending May 29, 2011, according to Nielsen SoundScan. However, if UMG had known in advance of Amazon's plan, it would almost certainly have cut back on the initial CD allotment, which created a serious inventory burden for itself. The move also marked a shift in power between digital and physical retailers, with the higher profits that physical generated per unit of physical sales leading to record companies willing to play the game of price reduction with CD stores and being outwitted by a digital retailer in search of exposure.

While Cohen was responsible for the day to day makeover of WMG, and as such largely responsible for the company's increased market share and return to a reputation for good management, Bronfman presented himself as being the company's visionary. If the arrival of iTunes, for all the unforeseen consequences it would bring with it, marked the general acceptance of the majors that digital was going to be an important part of the future, Bronfman's arrival at WMG marked the final realisation of the once puzzled Kuhnian executives that digital was the future. From the WMG's IPO onwards Bronfman highlighted the company's digital performance and the potential it represented. Others, notably EMI, would sing from the same hymn sheet, but it was WMG that most closely associated itself with matters digital. It did this so successfully that when in 2011 WMG was sold to Len Blavatnik's Access Industries, the first press release Access issued noted with regard to the digital world that, "Warner is the most progressive of the majors in this area in the US market and combining their expertise with Access' interests and knowledge in this area would be extremely beneficial to both companies". Another area that Bronfman highlighted, again one which EMI would also stress, especially in the days of Terra Firma, was music publishing, which was presented as the steady side of the coin compared to the other face, the riskier record business.

Bronfman renamed WMG's Los Angeles headquarters in honour of Mo Ostin, but the Ostin era of big spending was over. Or was it?

Recorded music sales were falling not rising and pay cuts might have seemed more appropriate than bonuses. That was not the Bronfman way. While Bronfman presented himself primarily as an investor, someone who would benefit when the company did well, as he certainly did with the IPO, to spread that commitment further he rejected the trimmings of salary and perks of the past regime. From the start he put in place generous profit participation programmes for senior executives. Immediately after the takeover the leading five executives of the new management team of WMG were paid bonuses that totalled $16.1m. Bronfman might not be Steve Ross but he could dispense largesse with the best of them.

Given the economic climate and the company's continued losses despite its increased performance this led to some bizarre conjunctions. At a time when record companies, WMG included, were spending less money to market artists, cutting the costs of promotional videos and reducing the support previously given to publicity tours when a new album was released, senior executive bonuses were rising. In 2010, Cohen was granted a bonus of $3.5m on top of his salary of $3m. Earlier, in 2007 Cohen had received $4.7m in salary and bonuses and in the summer of 2008 he sold $6.8m worth of WMG shares granted him, which had the effect of depressing the share price. He reportedly sold the shares to fund the purchase of a house in the Hamptons, leading financial analyst Richard Greenfield of Fulcrum Global Partners to note, "While WMG continues to reduce staff and scale back compensation for its employee base, its senior management continues to carry on as if the music industry was in its heyday." Other CEOs received similar levels of compensation. In 2005, for example, Doug Morris of UMG received $14.6m in salary and bonuses. Such levels of pay were similar to those in other industries, but the sense that those working at the heights of the record industry in particular required a significantly high remuneration was reflected in the compensation package of Cary Sherman CEO of the RIAA. In 2009, RIAA, which had revenues of a little over $50m, paid Sherman $3.2m, according to *CEO Update* the US based trade publication for association executives, making him the best-paid trade association CEO in the US.

These salaries were the price that the professionalisation of the record business brought about. The legendary record men of the 1950s and 1960s were "music men" who made seat of the pants decisions. Riding the teenage wave, they transformed a welter of once separate styles of music (country, blues, pop, etc) into a generic product in which blues, country, reggae and suchlike were tributaries rather than isolated islands. However, although the "music men" laid a key part of the foundations of the modern entertainment industry, they were not well paid for their efforts. The classic example of this was the belated understanding by the one-time owners of Atlantic that they had undervalued their company when they sold it in 1967. The response of Ahmet Ertegun, as we have seen, was to seek a seriously high compensation package when he went to work for Warner, becoming both a record man and a corporate exec. This was easily granted.

One reason was the natural growth of the industry from the 1950s on, a growth further fuelled by the CD boom, as noted earlier. But there was a deeper reason. As entertainment became a business, so music, be it squawks emitting from a boom box, pop at its silliest or rock at its most pretentious, was seen to be intellectual property and to have real value as such. Such a value needed a different kind of administration and a different set of executives. Thus, it was that the new would-be moguls came to sit at the feet of Ahmet Ertegun to learn the old ways of doing business, to touch the hem of his garment as it were, while seeking inflated salaries for themselves, just as their bosses started regularly hiring MBAs and making use of the likes of the Boston Consulting Group to advise them on how to run the new business. The record industry had taken to heart the unofficial motto of renowned management consultancy group McKinsey, "Everything can be measured and what can be measured can be managed". It was a far cry from the seats of pants philosophy.

Part of the transformation was the need for new skills. Not only were large international corporations – Bertelsmann, Philips, Time Warner, Vivendi – moving in and out of the record industry, but within it mergers and acquisitions and a whole set of new deals were to be made, requiring new executives with new skill sets. As the career of David Geffen demonstrated it was still possible to start out in the mail room at the William Morris agency, but having an MBA was no hindrance. Part of this process was a growing respect for money. As previously noted (*see* Chapter 1) the response of record companies to the flood of cash that the CD boom produced was to keep as much of it as possible. Rather than sharing it with artists or investors it was shared within the majors by the key executives. Once their salaries and perks had risen so dramatically, they could not fall. Hence Cohen's comment in a video interview with *Forbes* magazine in May 2011. Asked to justify the seeking of additional rights from artists in 360-degree deals, he said that WMG needed the extra cash to retain "the very finest, most seasoned, most creative, thoughtful, transformative" executives to run the company. Wayne Russo, one-time P2P player turned commentator, in his blog raised the point made earlier by Greenfield that Cohen was talking about executives who had lost hundreds of millions of dollars for the company.

At a time of contraction, such salaries and bonuses seemed over the top. When an outsider, such as Terra Firma, entered the industry, an early reaction was surprise at the levels of remuneration within the industry. Lord Birt, the chairman of Maltby Capital, the vehicle through which Terra Firma bought EMI, made this evident in his annual review for the year ending 31 March, 2008:

> *Music industry senior executive salaries have traditionally exceeded norms in the wider media, telecommunications and entertainment industry and EMI Music was no exception. EMI Music executive salaries were historically very high, with some individual executives being paid at the very top of their peer group in UK companies. At the same time, contracts at EMI Music were often fixed over unusually long periods and guaranteed its executives generous benefits. EMI Music paid some functional roles salaries at double market rates or more, while paying more junior staff closer to average salaries. At the same time, EMI Music was overstaffed at these junior levels and lacked suitably qualified middle management.*

In the wake of the banking collapse of 2008, questions were raised about the levels of compensation of banking executives, particularly with regard to their bonus structures. The same questions can be asked of record company executives, especially with reference to the different treatment meted out to the small and large investors, an issue that was raised following the sale of WMG to Access Industries (*see* Chapter 14). More problematic has been the impact of high salaries on the decision-making process of record company executives. As I've said earlier the Bronfman consortium takeover of WMG marked the final acceptance that digital was the future. But in the lengthy period before then, most companies were staffed by doubting Kuhnian executives, who, despite the clear loss of profits that the retail and digital revolutions represented, resolutely turned their faces to the past (and high salaries) rather than to an uncertain future and the possibility that a new wave of executives with Internet oriented skills might supplant them. In effect, the loss of control of their product by record companies that the digital era represented resulted in a bizarre scenario in which companies offered increasingly complex and lucrative compensation packages to executives who could do little but arrange the deckchairs on the *Titanic*. The executives could cut, promote, energise and restructure but the key players were outside the record companies. There was no way back to the heady days of calling the shots. The CD revolution had brought significant profits but it hadn't resulted in a reciprocating structural change in the majors. The advent of iTunes had brought relief to the majors, creating as it did a commercially viable online market for recorded music. At the same time it signalled the transfer of control of the distribution and transmission of recorded tracks to companies which the industry had marginal influence over, bar refusing a licence. Henceforth the major announcements of new offerings of recorded music would be from the likes of Amazon, Apple, Google, Pandora and Spotify, not from the majors.

The structure of compensation packages can have a direct impact on company policies. In the 1970s and early 1980s the business plans of the national branches of the majors, although different in many ways from company to company, were structured around bonus packages for their leading executives, based on simple financial performance. Thus, the more revenues generated from the least expenditure the greater the bonus. Spending A&R money on local signings reduced the potential bonuses available and, accordingly, most of the heads of the national branches of the majors concentrated on marketing international rather than national repertoire in their markets. This held back the signing of domestic acts at a period when national repertoire was taking an increasing percentage of sales.

The Bronfman consortium's first financial report showed increased revenues for the 10 months ending September 30, 2004. (The unusual reporting period was caused by a change in WMG's financial year-end from November 30 to September 30.) The 10-month period covered three months prior to Time Warner's sale of WMG and the seven months thereafter. Year on year revenues rose 2.5% to $2.54m, while operating profit rose to $7m from an operating loss of $197m in the same 10 months of 2002–2003.

In the 10-month period, WMG reported that sales at its recorded music division rose 1% to $2.6bn generating an operating profit of $7m. US sales, which were down 3% to $977m, accounted for 47% of WMG's recorded music revenues, while international sales rose 5% to $1.09bn. The period also saw recorded music benefitting from past cost-cutting actions, including $143m in savings made before the consortium bought the company from Time Warner. WMG noted that its restructuring programme was "ahead of schedule" with a total cost of $225–250m (less than the predicted $310m) leading to $250m of recurring annual cost savings by 2005. The company also reported lower manufacturing costs resulting from the company paying Cinram market rates rather than the higher intercompany rates it paid when manufacturing was treated as a separate profit centre. (Canada-based Cinram had bought WMG's manufacturing operations from TW in mid-2003.)

The revenues of the music publishing division Warner Chappell rose 8% to $505m, representing about 20% of WMG's total revenues. On this basis, at the time I calculated that, excluding corporate expenses, Warner Chappell accounted for a little over 80% of WMG's operating profits and that pro rata the 10-month revenues indicated 12-month revenues of some $600m. In subsequent financial reports WMG would focus on synchronisation revenues from the use of Warner Chappell copyrights in film, television and commercials and were not dependent on the sales of recordings. In the three months ending March 31, 2011, the last quarter before WMG's sale to Access Industries, synchronisation revenues at $31m accounted for some 23% of Warner Chappell's total revenues. In comparison in financial year 2009, synchronisation accounted for 17% of Warner Chappell's revenues and 16% and 13% in 2008 and 2007 respectively. In 2004 WMG also sold most of its print division, Warner Bros. Publications, which printed and distributed sheet music, books and educational materials, folios, orchestrations and arrangements, to US-based Alfred Publishing. Although a steady source of funds, printed music was the 19th century past of publishing and a non-core business; synchronisation was the 21st century future – the Warner Chappell mantra.

Having bought WMG, the consortium next set out to get back the rest of the money spent in acquiring it. There was a private placement of $700m of high yield bonds in December 2004, the proceeds of which were returned to the original investors. In March 2005, WMG filed papers with the US Securities and Exchange Commission (SEC) announcing its intentions to make an initial public offering (IPO) in the US of $750m its common stock. The IPO offering valued WMG at over $4bn compared to the $2.6bn paid to Time Warner in 2004. This was despite WMG's faltering market share in 2004. According to IFPI, WMG's market share fell in all regions of the world giving it a global share of 11.3% compared to 12.5% in 2003. One reason for the fall was that its new owners acted quickly to cut costs. At the time several observers, surprised by the speed and depth of the cost-cutting programme, said that the cuts would be to the long-term detriment of the group.

The IPO was widely criticised as being a "quick flip", the term used on Wall Street to describe private investor groups that seek to too rapidly realise their investment in a company. At the same time leading music industry executives and recording artists expressed disquiet with the management of WMG and the motives for the IPO. However these worries and the continuing fall in recorded music sales in 2005 fell on deaf ears. The success of iTunes, the boost in physical sales in the US for most of 2004 and clear evidence of significant cost-cutting by WMG won the approval of Wall Street. Well, rather the partial approval. As the May 2005 date of the IPO approached, a number of US securities firms balked at the asking price – Fulcrum Global Partners said the price range of between $22 and $24 was "too high", suggesting that $20 or less was needed to achieve a minimum 12-month return of 15%. Investment bankers also expressed disquiet at the prospect of the original members of the consortium issuing shares in the company, in effect selling stock to make money for themselves while the IPO proposals placed no incentive on the WMG management team to perform better. WMG's senior executives duly benefitted from the sale of shares in the group, with only $7m of the monies received via the IPO being identified as being used for "general corporate purposes".

However, the speed with which institutional investors took up the offering of bonds demonstrated that WMG's ability to cut costs was well received in the investment community. In retrospect, that confidence was clearly misplaced, but at the time owners and investors alike believed that cost-cutting and restructuring – hence the mantra of EMI plus WMG means profits – could transform losses into profits. Some might talk of smoke and mirrors or the three-card trick, but from the moment of the consortium's purchase of WMG and its successful floatation, venture capitalists started to look on music companies with renewed interest. Such a belief seems almost beyond reason, more akin to religion, but it remained powerful enough to survive the disaster of Terra Firma's ill-timed purchase of EMI and produced the successful sale of WMG in 2011 that went a long way to handing Bronfman a new reputation as a canny businessman rather than a squanderer of family funds.

The concern over WMG's quick flip was not restricted to the investment community. The rap-rock band Linkin Park sought to be released from its WMG recording contract because WMG was unable to live up to its fiduciary responsibility to adequately market and promote the band. The group also played the bonus card. Their management issued a statement noting that, "The new owners of the Warner Music Group will be reaping a windfall of $1.4bn from their $2.6bn purchase a mere 18 months ago if their planned IPO moves forward. Linkin Park, their biggest act, will get nothing."

The intervention of Linkin Park, who by 2005 had sold some 35m albums worldwide, came at a time when artists, especially in the US, were starting to present themselves as an organised body and regularly make public interventions in debates affecting their interests. This led to them working both with the major record companies, as in the Grokster case, sometimes through the lobby group the Recording Artists Coalition and sometimes in opposition to the majors, as when they lobbied for changes to California contract law, for more transparent record company accounting practices, or against record companies treating master recordings as works made for hire. The WMG IPO was another such issue. Speaking to *The New York Times* about the forthcoming IPO, music industry attorney Peter Paterno, who represented artists including

Dr. Dre, Pearl Jam and WMG act Metallica, noted, "It's becoming more and more apparent that this is nothing more than a financial play for the investors. It's not about the music or the employees; it's about a return for private equity investors." Separately, rappers Ludacris and Jay-Z, both of whom were offered contracts by WMG, decided to renew their deals with UMG's Def Jam label. The actions taken by a record company's leading acts can have a direct impact on it. Earlier in 2005 EMI issued a profit warning because two expected best-selling new albums, by Coldplay and Gorillaz, would be delayed. EMI's share price fell as a result.

This mistrust of WMG was not only held by artists' representatives. In September 2005, Christian label Integrity decided not to renew its distribution agreement with WMG's Word division. Also, Concord, the company that in 2004 released the Ray Charles album *Genius Loves Company*, which sold 1.9m units in the US alone, refused WMG's offer of a distribution deal. According to reports at the time, WMG's perceived lack of commitment in these labels' repertoire contributed to their decisions to seek other partners. Jeremy Weiner, president of Integrity, when interviewed by *The New York Times* about the consortium and WMG made the point succinctly: "They're very smart money guys, but for us at the end of the day we need someone who really cares about the records we're putting out, not the amount of volume or the price of their shares."

WMG was not alone in pursuing cost-cutting. In response to the downturn in sales, which exposed the heavy cost structure of all of the major international record companies, all the majors instituted second and third rounds of cost-cutting and as a result improved their return on sales. For example, UMG reported that the company's revenues rose 0.4% to €4,993m ($6.49bn) in 2004 compared to 2003 and that operating profits for the year rose almost fivefold to €338m ($439.4m). Two reasons put forward by UMG's parent company, France-based Vivendi Universal, for the improved profitability were lower marketing expenses and the success of the company's cost-cutting programme.

Despite its cost-cutting programme and the high level of media hype – spin doctoring was now an essential part of company presentations of self – WMG did not outperform the recorded music market in 2004. It global share fell from 12.5% to 11.3% and in its all-important home market WMG's market share fell from 15.8% to 14.2%. The company had only five of 100 of the best-selling albums worldwide, with Green Day's *American Idiot*, at number 11, the only one in the Top 20. Of the 14 territories surveyed by *Music & Copyright* in 2004, WMG only increased its market share in two, Brazil and Taiwan. In the five largest markets, US, Japan, UK, Germany and France, which collectively accounted for 74% of the value of recorded music sales in 2004, WMG's market share fell.

WMG's new owners had predicted that there would be some decline in the company's global market share for the first 12 to 18 months after the purchase, as the artist roster was cut and uncertainty delayed key album releases. However, the decline in WMG's US album sales in 2004 was greater than the company expected. In the US WMG released or distributed only five of the 70 albums that sold over 1m units in 2004. The decline continued into 2005 when in the first quarter WMG's total album market share in the US fell from 15.3% to 14.9%, while its current album market share fell one percentage point to 12.8%. But this was the low point: from 2006 onwards WMG's US market share bounced along at around 20%.

Matters digital were seen in a glowing light by investors in 2005. This was a card WMG played to the full. In its IPO prospectus, WMG argued that, if it could successfully control the costs of the manufacture and sale of physical product, it would benefit from the predicted growth in the digital music markets. It further claimed that, because they eliminate a wide range of fixed costs, such as packaging and transport, online and mobile sales are inherently more profitable than physical sales. While this, as we have seen (*see* Chapter 9), was dubious, it reflected the early thinking about the digital sector. At the time of the IPO, digital accounted for a small percentage of recorded music sales, 2% in the case of EMI, 4% of UMG's total revenues. By 2010 digital sales would account for 32% of WMG's total revenues.

WMG showed would-be investors in its IPO a range of forecasts for digital and mobile sales (*see table below*).

Low and High forecasts of the value of online and mobile music sales in 2004 and 2008 ($m)

	2004	*2008*	*% change*
Retail value of US digital downloads and subscriptions			
Low forecast	169	901	+533
High forecast	308	4,572	+1,384
Retail value of international digital downloads and subscriptions			
Low forecast	33	631	+85
High forecast	65	2,433	+7,273
Total value of digital downloads and subscriptions			
Low forecast	202	1,701	+742
High forecast	373	7,005	+1,778
Retail value of US mobile music revenues			
Low forecast	122	790	+548
High forecast	316	1,402	+343
Retail value of international mobile music revenues			
Low forecast	3,461	3,914	+13
High forecast	5,227	8,049	+54
Total value of mobile music revenues			
Low forecast	3,583	4,704	+31
High forecast	5,543	9,451	+71

Source: Baskerville/Informa, IDC, Strategy Analytics

These figures were highly optimistic, with even the low estimated total for all digital recorded music sales of $6,450m being almost twice the actual digital sales in 2008 of $3,784m, and the high estimate being over five times the actual value. WMG also highlighted the extra popularity and profitability of catalogue download sales and the strength of its catalogue sales, which accounted for 40% of WMG sales in the physical market in the US in 2003 and 61% of its digital sales. WMG claimed that its market share of digital music downloads in the US in 2004 was higher than its overall recorded music album market share. However, the essence of the argument presented by WMG to investors was equally applicable to other majors. WMG argued that digital was the future of the industry and that accordingly an investment in WMG was an investment in the future, thus side-stepping the question as to whether over the years WMG digital performance would be superior to its performance in the physical market. Other companies, notably EMI, attempted this three-card trick but WMG played the card most elegantly.

The IPO prospectus also kept open the possibility of a merger with EMI, which would bubble once more to the surface just before Terra Firma made its fateful swoop on EMI in 2008. In its filing with the Security and Exchange Commission WMG noted, as part of its overview of the recorded music industry, that the similarly sized UMG and Sony BMG groups dwarf the smaller players of EMI and WMG and that it might "enter into a strategic alliance with companies involved in businesses similar or complementary to ours".

Acknowledging the slack demand for its IPO, WMG cut the price to $17 a share, below a planned range of $22 to $24. With 32.6m shares on sale, this put the company's initial market capitalisation at some $2.4bn, not counting debt, compared to the earlier price range which valued the company in the region of $4bn. Nonetheless this meant that the Bronfman consortium, which had already got back the money it invested in WMG through a combination of dividend payments and proceeds from bond issues, turned a profit on the IPO: the consortium members received a special $141.5m cash dividend (part of which was shared with 10 leading WMG executives) and $73m in "management termination fees".

Although Led Zeppelin guitarist Jimmy Page entertained the New York Stock Exchange with 'Whole Lotta Love' at its opening on May 10, the day of the IPO, WMG stock fell to $16.40 on the first day of trading. WMG had only partly convinced Wall Street of the inherent value of the digital future. However, its performance in the course of 2005 won it praise from analysts and saw its stock price rise to just under

$17 in the summer, closing at $18.87 on the publication of its results for the year ending September 30, 2005.

Revenues for the year rose 2% to $3.5bn and operating profit increased to $84m. Digital revenues rose fourfold to $157m (of which 73% came from the US), accounting for 4.5% of WMG's total sales. Recorded music sales rose 2% to $2.9bn, including $137m digital sales, 5% of the total. Most of this, $105m, was generated in the US, accounting for 7% of WMG's US recorded music revenues. However, Warner Chappell's digital revenues at $20m only accounted for 3% of its total sales.

One of the questions raised at the time of the IPO was whether the consortium was in for the long haul or merely out to make a quick million or so. The cost-cutting and payments made to the consortium members suggested the latter but as 2005 wore on WMG began to invest in the future, suggesting that the consortium was not simply seeking quick profits. Bronfman bought Festival Mushroom Records (FMR) of Australia, whose back catalogue included recordings by Kylie Minogue and Olivia Newton-John, from Rupert Murdoch's News International and subsequently the Ryko Corporation, an independent, integrated music and entertainment company from an investment group led by JP Morgan Partners for $67.5m. The purchase of Ryko, like that of FMR, suggested that the restructuring period at WMG was over and that the company was starting on a cost-conscious process of expansion. At the same time Bronfman was taking care of the usual items of record industry business. Thus, he sorted out the company's relationship with Madonna, whose *Confessions On A Dance Floor* was one of the company's bestsellers in 2005, sealing the conclusion of the dispute with the gift of a diamond necklace. Earlier, WMG became the second major international record company – the first was Sony BMG – to acknowledge and halt all payola to radio stations and their employees. New York Attorney General Eliot Spitzer's investigation of pay-for-airplay between recording companies and radio businesses forced a settlement out of WMG, including an Assurance of Discontinuance under which the company admitted to improper conduct, agreed to fully disclose all items of value provided to radio stations, and to provide $5m for music education through the Rockefeller Philanthropy Advisors to New York State.

All the while Bronfman and his executives set about trying to re-invent the music business — one of the chapters of Fred Goodman's book about WMG is called 'The "Try Anything" Company' — setting up Cordless as a digital-only label run by a returning Jac Holzman and re-starting Asylum as an incubator label with the idea of testing the popularity of indie bands with the option of later signing them. However, while continuing to experiment with the new opportunities that the online world offered, WMG was particularly concerned to maximise the potential of online sales from established acts. It was very active in seeking increased online sales of "bundled" product — complete albums, often plus additional product — as opposed to single tracks from albums. Bundling addressed the issue of the low profitability of individual download tracks by charging more. Premium bundles, which contain album-only bonus content including videos, liner notes, lyrics, bonus tracks, artist interviews, concert tickets and behind-the-scenes footage cost between 20% and 80% more than the standard $9.99 digital album. WMG reported that some 75% of the sales of *Confessions On A Dance Floor* via iTunes came from album bundle purchases. Such bundles, called Premium Tracks on the iTunes online music store, then comprised only a very small percentage of iTunes sales overall. In view of the potentially greater profits for all concerned, WMG entered into discussions with a wide range of online and mobile operators and distributors as to how they could increase the percentage of bundled rather than unbundled product they offer consumers. WMG also was very aggressive in using online and mobile media to generate offline sales. The classic example of this is *Confessions On A Dance Floor*, which was primarily marketed via ringtone, streaming, making the single available early to those who pre-ordered the digital album and offered as a rich bundle, rather than via traditional radio promotion. The result, despite little advance radio play, was Madonna's biggest album in recent years, selling over 7m worldwide and generating a minimum of $100m for WMG.

WMG claimed it had significant success with such promotions in the US. It claimed that it had a far greater share of such sales via iTunes, compared to the other majors in the period May 2005 to mid-February 2006. However, that first-mover advantage was soon lost. As mega bundling became the name of the game, with the release of the likes of "immersion" sets of Pink Floyd albums and suchlike, all physical offerings at high prices, it was back catalogue that mattered.

Despite its growing US market share, as a global player WMG remained small. Its 2005 global market share of 12.8% was precisely half that of UMG's 25.6% and even less than EMI's 13.6%. WMG couldn't grow 13 percentage points of market share, but it needed to be bigger. Then in May the phone rang: it was EMI's Eric Nicoli with a proposition.

Chapter 13

EMI Finds Independence Lonely

Even though it lost WMG to the Bronfman consortium, at the end of 2003 EMI looked to be in decent shape. It was the second largest of the majors, with a 13.4% global market share. It still remained over reliant on its home market: sales in the UK and Ireland accounted for 14.5% of sales and 21.5% of operating profit in 2003–2004, whereas the UK and Ireland accounted for 10.4% of global recorded music sales in 2003. However, EMI had started to remedy its long-standing structural problem in North America. The region accounted for 31.7% of sales and 39.8% of operating profit in 2003–2004. EMI only increased its North American market share by 0.5 of a percentage point in 2003–2004, but the company claimed that it had been profitable in the US for two years, following years of losses, and that North America's near 40% contribution to operating profits in 2003–2004 was up from 27% the previous year. EMI pointed to the restructuring of its US operations, ending the separate management of Virgin, reductions in staff and roster levels, and reduced promotional costs, notably on television. At the same time, after years of poor A&R in America, it had signed internationally successful acts there, most conspicuously Norah Jones, while at the same time it was having US success with UK signings such as Coldpay. Separately, the company said that although Robbie Williams meant nothing in the US he was hugely profitable in Europe. In response critics said that in essence all EMI had done was have a few hits, and from a few acts, and that no real infrastructural transformation had been made.

This over reliance on a few acts was demonstrated in February 2005 when it issued its third profit warning in three years: the reason, the failure of Coldplay and Gorillaz to complete their new albums on schedule despite, it was rumoured, being offered financial incentives to deliver the albums as planned. Nonetheless EMI remained optimistic: "While this rescheduling and recent softness [EMI's sales in the last three months of 2004 had been less than expected] is disappointing, it does not change my views of the improving health of the global recorded music industry," said CEO Alain Levy.

Levy's optimism was matched by that of the City. A Deutsche Bank report on the music industry that focused on EMI published in April 2005, just before EMI's annual results, noted:

We believe that the global music industry is about to enter a new growth phase. While we expect further negative value growth of physical format sales going forward, downloads and mobile master tone sales open up incremental and sizeable revenue streams for the industry and will be the main drivers of growth going forward. We forecast that EMI's top line in recorded music (RM) will grow 1.2% in FY2006 and 3.0% in FY2007 as CD sales declines bottom out in key markets, Music DVD's continue to post solid growth rates, and digital sales see triple-digit growth rates.

Recently released IFPI figures show that the industry is close to reaching the bottom with a value decline of only −1.4% which follows three years of decline in global music revenues from 2001–03 of 9%, 7% and 7.5% respectively. IFPI expects a bottoming out of the market for 2005, underpinning our view that the industry has reached the bottom and is poised for a new growth stage. We forecast 3% FY2005-10 CAGR for EMI's recorded music division.

Deutsche Bank saw the driver of this recovery as the MP3 player:

The strong take-up of MP3 players and subsequent emergence of viable business models for legal music downloads represents an inflection point for the industry. Incremental download revenues will in our view be a key driver in terms of helping to put recorded music revenue growth back into the black beyond 2005.

Downloaded music sales have taken off since Apple's launch of iTunes, its online music portal in 2003. The main driver of the immediate success of iTunes was the phenomenal take-up of the iPod hardware and other portable MP3 players. Since its launch in 2001, Apple has sold more than 10m iPods of which 4.6m in Q404 alone. This implies an almost doubling of the installed player base in the last reported quarter alone where 4.6m newly shipped units in Q404 compare with an accumulated total at the end of Q304 of 5.7m.

The dramatic increase in the installed MP3 player base has fed through to download sales. Driven by the increased iPod penetration, Apple has so far sold a total 300m songs via its iTunes download retail websites in North America and Europe. In 2004 in the US alone, 131m single tracks have been sold and the current run-rate for January- February 2005 sales is running at around 200% y-o-y growth.

Accordingly, Deutsche Bank upgraded its recommendation for EMI stock to "buy". This meant that from the 13 analysts who rated EMI's shares over the past 12 months EMI had seven buy recommendations, three "holds" and three "sell" recommendations. As such the Deutsche Bank report mirrored the return to cautious optimism of the period.

These predictions turned out to be mistaken: the decline in recorded music sales did not end, rather the rate of decline increased. Moreover, the report was too generalised, relying too much on the mantra of "music publishing is good business" and "the worst is over for the recorded music business". Deutsche Bank paid too little attention to the issue of size and its implications for EMI and gave too much credence to the claim by EMI that it could outperform the market, an assertion also regularly made by WMG. EMI itself was more cautious. Despite its relatively solid performance in the period 2004–2006, the disparity in mass between it and UMG and now Sony BMG gave added urgency to the issue of size, an issue that couldn't be solved by organic growth or restructuring. In May 2006, EMI made a cash and shares bid of $4.2bn for WMG. At the time I calculated that a combined EMI-WMG would have a global market share of around 25%, compared to UMG's 25.6%, making it the second largest recorded music group in the world ahead of Sony BMG. EMI's share price rose on news of the bid and fell when it was rejected.

While WMG reported a loss of $7m for the three months ending March 31, despite higher revenues, EMI announced an increase in revenues and operating profits for the year ending March 31, 2006, declaring that both its recorded music division and its music publishing division outperformed the market. However, the press conference called to present EMI's results was far from festive. The conference was dominated by talk of the bid for WMG: "The industrial logic is compelling and the synergies would unlock considerable additional value," said Nicoli. Bronfman agreed with the proviso that he would be the buyer and so made an offer for EMI. Thus began a summer bidding war with each company making counter offers to the other.

Then on July 13 the European Court of First Instance ruled against the EC's approval of the formation of Sony BMG. Suddenly, it no longer seemed feasible that the Commission would approve the takeover of EMI by WMG or vice versa, however compelling the industrial logic might be. Nonetheless, over the course of 2006–2007 that logic became particularly compelling for EMI. If 2005–2006 had been a positive year for the company, 2006–2007 certainly wasn't.

The change in EMI's fortunes was announced, as usual, with a profit warning. In October 2006, EMI said that it expected its revenues for the six months ending September 30 would fall in constant currency terms by 3%. This followed other disturbing news. In September, after speaking to the European Commission, WMG revived its bid for EMI. Bronfman told selected EMI shareholders that it was WMG's view that, despite the FCI's ruling, the EC would again approve the Sony BMG merger (which it did) and was also likely to authorise the merger of the recorded music interests of EMI and WMG if such a merger was presented to it.

This was followed by reports that Martin Bandier, the head of EMI MP, who was due to retire in 18 months and had set in motion a handing over process that ensured continuity, was to leave the company immediately. Even worse he was rumoured to be going to WMG's publishing division Warner Chappell. News of such a move by the executive primarily responsible for building EMI MP into the world's leading music publisher that consistently produced profits for the EMI Group, was deeply unsettling for EMI's shareholders. Bandier's departure – he eventually left in April 2007, taking the top job at Sony/ATV – meant the end of stable management at EMI MP and a new level of anxiety for investors: would other key men or acts leave? Moreover, coming so soon after the sale of BMG MP to UMGP it brought renewed speculation as to the value of music publishing and what companies might become available for sale, bringing yet another area of unease to EMI's investors. Bandier's move was further confirmation that in the new record industry world it was a select band of executives that were the Pelés and Magic Johnsons. Talent could be always found, after all it was just content, but knowing how to find that talent was seen as an extraordinary gift, as Jon Landau, Bruce Springsteen's manager noted in a *New York Times* profile of Doug Morris after he quit UMG to become CEO of SME in 2001: "He is a master at attracting and developing executive talent... No one is better at picking the people who pick the hit artists."

When EMI's actual six-month figures were released they were worse than predicted. Group revenues fell 4.1% to £867.9m ($1.62bn) and operating profits fell by 27.7% to £62.7m ($117.2m). EMI blamed this failure on the overall fall in the value of recorded music in the period, notably by 6.1% in the US, its release schedule, which was heavily weighted to major releases in the second half of EMI's financial year and a £9m ($16.8m) fraud at its Brazilian branch. EMI further noted first half sales suffered from a tough comparison with the previous year when EMI benefitted from global sales of Coldplay's *X&Y*, which sold 7.5m units worldwide in the six-month period, and Gorillaz' *Demon Days*, which sold 3.4m units. Group digital revenues rose by 68% in constant currency to £73.7m ($137.8m) and accounted for 8.5% of group sales. As a percentage, this was lower than that of market leader UMG whose digital sales accounted for 10.5% of overall revenues in the first nine months of 2006. Digital sales may be growing overall, but EMI's rate of digital growth was not outperforming the market.

EMI's problems attracted the attention suitors outside the music industry. At the end of November EMI confirmed that it had received a "preliminary approach", which might lead to an offer being made for the company. EMI declined to name the bidder but press investigation soon revealed that it was private equity company Permira and that other venture capital groups, such as Goldman Sachs, KKR (which would later partner Bertelsmann in BMG RM) and Apollo Management, had also expressed interest in EMI. Private equity groups smelt trouble and saw potential profits. EMI received and rejected an offer from Permira, which valued EMI at some £2.5bn ($4.9bn). The language of bids and counter bids from WMG had been about "commercial logic". There was no such logic when private equity entered the picture. The WMG scenario since its successful acquisition by the Bronfman consortium offered a picture in which long-term plans had a place but, without an Edgar Bronfman seeking redemption, private equity firms were more akin to vultures settling on a dying corpse than medics offering a kiss of life. Their growing interest suggested that EMI was in truth the sick man of the record industry.

This was made dramatically evident when at the start of 2007 I calculated the market shares of the majors: EMI with 12.8% was now the smallest of the majors and for the first time had a smaller market share than WMG, which was 13.8%. EMI had lost ground in its all-important home market. In the UK, EMI Music's share of album sales fell 2.3 percentage points in 2006, to 17.9%, according to the trade publication *Music Week*. The fall in recorded music sales was general. The best-selling album in the first week in January 2007 in the US was the *Dreamgirls* soundtrack, which sold only 66,000 units, the lowest sales of a number one album since SoundScan began reporting music sales in 1991. (A mark of the increase in the rate of decline of physical sales was that in the first week of January 2011, Taylor Swift topped the charts with a new low, *Speak Now*, which sold only 52,000 units.) The fall might have been general but it was EMI, with decidedly disappointing sales in the crucial holiday shopping period, that suffered the most.

At the same time there was growing discontent within both the company and the investment community. In the US Lyor Cohen had slashed and burnt at WMG and yet managed to re-energise the company to the extent that its market share grew. Bronfman, had managed to present it as the most digital-friendly of majors. In contrast, EMI's posturing, the brief ray of warm sunshine from Deutsche Bank apart, was treated as such. There was a growing sense among analysts and investors that executives trained in the traditional business of selling physical product were not prepared for the digital era and that such companies were in need of an overhaul. WMG played the three-card trick well: UMG as the market leader was needed by the new digital entrepreneurs, Sony BMG was in poor shape because of merger problems but would overcome those by virtue of its size, but EMI at the start of 2007 had the appearance of a busted flush.

Desperate times called for desperate measures. On January 11, accompanied by the regulation profit warning, EMI dismissed Alain Levy and his vice chairman David Munns. Controversially EMI announced that Eric Nicoli, who had been executive chairman of the EMI Group since October 1999, would become group CEO and take direct responsibility for managing EMI Music. Nicoli, dubbed "the biscuit man" – a former executive of United Biscuits he reportedly "invented" the Yorkie chocolate bar – had no experience of the music industry when he was appointed chairman in 1999 and in 2007 had no operational experience of running a record company. In view of the dilemma EMI found itself in in 2007, Nicoli was widely presented in the press as the man who had failed to sell EMI and Levy and Munns as the pair who had failed to re-invent it. One had to go and Nicoli's sacking of the pair was widely presented as an act of job security rather than a grand strategy. Indeed, the time for grand strategies was over. Charged with selling EMI to generate shareholder value, Nicoli's new job was to prepare for the dismemberment of the company. Henceforth, EMI was little but a lonely swimmer in the waters around Amity waiting for the shark.

In the next trading update, EMI identified the Christmas period as being "below prior expectations... in terms of revenues and profits".

However its half year results and the profits warning that preceded them, showed that EMI Music's problems had started far earlier than Christmas. The demise of leading entertainment retailer Tower in the US and the collapse of Music Zone in the UK confirmed that the overall recorded music retail environment was more than simply difficult in 2006. In the US EMI sold 60m albums (compared to 64.2m in 2005). This represented a fall in album market share, from 10.4% to 10.2%, and a loss of some $45m in revenues.

The solution was another new restructuring scheme with virtually all the cost projected savings to come from the recorded music division. Most of the proposed changes, such as the outsourcing of EMI's distribution and administration activities, were now standard industry cost-cutting practice. However, two changes would have far deeper significance. One involved finding "revenue and cost synergies between recorded music and music publishing" so that in a number of territories EMI Music and EMI MP would be combined and that the scope of each would be accordingly limited. Even more problematic was the plan to reduce "exposure to territories and business areas in which... superior, secure returns [cannot] be generated". This led to EMI Music's withdrawal from some markets in Asia and Latin America. In the beginning restructuring and cost-cutting had meant quitting "non-core" activities (manufacturing and distribution), culling the roster, pulling together the back-office operations of the company's label divisions and reducing executive numbers. Now EMI was contemplating reducing the very scope of the company, withdrawing from markets and opting for a narrower global focus. The net result of the restructuring statement was to further lower the perceived value of the company.

One remedy for a condition of desperation is to call on an equally desperate partner for help. While never as desperate as EMI, Apple was troubled by the mounting attacks from regulators in Europe and its competitors on the closed element of the iPod and iTunes systems, which meant that tracks purchased from iTunes could only be played on iPods. Rejecting the solution to make its 'FairPlay' DRM system available to all, in February 2007 Apple's Steve Jobs called for an end to the use of DRM and for full interoperability between all digital players. To be successful Jobs' proposal needed a copyright owner to agree. For the majors DRM, whether it was one format oriented or generic, was essential. In response to this in a rare open letter, *Thoughts on Music*, posted on Apple's website, Jobs urged record companies to abandon DRM technologies. After noting that Apple had been forced to create a digital rights management system to get repertoire for the iTunes store, Jobs detailed three futures: Apple and the rest of the online music distributors could continue down a DRM path; Apple could license the FairPlay technology to others; or record companies could be persuaded to license music without DRM technology. Apple favoured the third option: "Imagine a world where every online store sells DRM-free music encoded in open licensable formats. In such a world, any player can play music purchased from any store, and any store can sell music which is playable on all players. This is clearly the best alternative for consumers, and Apple would embrace it in a heartbeat."

With a view to the industry's concern about P2P piracy he added: "Why would the big four music companies agree to let Apple and others distribute their music without using DRM systems to protect it? The simplest answer is because DRMs haven't worked, and may never work, to halt music piracy."

Competing digital music services reacted positively but the response of content owners and their representatives was less so. The RIAA said that, "Apple's offer to license FairPlay to other technology companies is a welcome breakthrough and would be a real victory for fans, artists and labels. There have been many services seeking a licence for the Apple DRM. This would enable the interoperability that we have been urging for a very long time." However, it remained silent on the idea of making music available without DRM. Bronfman, the industry cheerleader for the digital revolution went further, noting that the call to drop DRM was "without logic or merit" adding that WMG "will not abandon DRM"; it did.

Taking Apple's shilling, seeking credence as the leading music industry digital player and above all desperate to present itself as a viable modern music company worthy of purchase, in April 2007 EMI broke ranks and announced that it would sell DRM-free downloads. The end of DRM helped Jobs solve a tricky political situation; it offered EMI at best a temporary respite. EMI presented itself as the key mover in the decision to end DRM on all online downloads, which soon took place, but others saw EMI's breaking ranks as merely highlighting the depth of the problems EMI was facing.

Whatever, the dam was broken and while EMI was (briefly) held responsible for breaking ranks it soon became apparent that individually majors were in discussions with both established (Apple) and new players, notably Amazon, which announced it would launch a digital music store in May 2007 (but only if the tracks were DRM-free) in response to the new situation created by the Apple-EMI agreement. The Apple-EMI agreement effectively ended DRM's power as a control tool and confirmed iTunes as the leading online retailer, with Amazon its only significant global competitor. In the wake of the iTunes deal, EMI agreed to sell selected repertoire from its catalogue in the open MP3 format through MTV, Napster and RealNetworks. And, notwithstanding the initial rejection of Jobs' proposal by the RIAA and WMG, the majors soon concluded DRM-free deals with Apple and others.

The ending of DRM was the price of achieving interoperability, which in turn would bring about the variable pricing that the majors saw as the key to fully stimulate the online music market. Such a move would not have been possible a few years earlier when a recovery in physical recorded music sales still seemed feasible. But by 2007, DRM, like SDMI before it, had become an embarrassment.

However, if the Apple-EMI agreement moved matters digital further forward, beyond briefly shining a friendly spotlight on EMI, it did little of substance for the troubled company, coming as it did among a welter of offers to buy it. EMI's aim was to present itself as forward-looking, as it were wresting the digital crown from WMG, but many saw it as a further sign of weakness. The failed attempts by EMI to either sell off its recorded music division or to raise money from its music publishing arm in order to make it less attractive to would-be bidders only further highlighted EMI's weaknesses.

Offers came thick and fast. There was a further bid for EMI by WMG and news of potential bids from private equity and investment groups, including One Equity Partners and Fortress Investment. WMG's new bid was planned with the regulatory authorities very much in mind. In an attempt to appease in advance both European regulators and IMPALA, the European trade association of independent record companies, WMG concluded an agreement with IMPALA at the same time as its bid for EMI. In return for IMPALA providing "full and complete support" for its bid, WMG, should it succeed in buying EMI, agreed "to enhance competition and market access" for the independents. And whatever the outcome of its bid, it agreed to provide financial assistance for the creation of Merlin, the online aggregator that the independents were struggling to establish.

IMPALA's decision to seek commercial concessions rather than merely seek to occupy the moral high ground lost it some gravitas and some members. Leading UK independent Ministry of Sound (MOS) resigned from the UK arm of IMPALA, AIM, on the grounds that it hadn't been consulted on the IMPALA/WMG agreement and "the ongoing consolidation of the major music industry has impacted negatively upon our music business in every way". At the same time nobody knew what impact IMPALA's change of heart would have on the EC, particularly at a time when the Commission was re-examining the creation of Sony BMG and investigating Vivendi's proposed purchase of Bertelsmann's music publishing division. EMI said in a terse formal note to WMG that its response to the takeover bid would be determined by the price offered and the regulatory issue. From this moment on the private equity companies had the inside track.

The crunch came at the press conference to announce its annual results for the year ending March 31, 2007. A year earlier EMI had been the predator reiterating its desire to acquire WMG, but now it accepted that it was the victim and announced that it was recommending an offer for the company from UK investment group Terra Firma, led by the high-profile Guy Hands, a man whose profile would rise even higher over the course of his short ownership of EMI.

Terra Firma's bid valued EMI at £3.2bn ($5.9bn) including debt. Other consortia put together by private equity companies immediately indicated they would not make counter-offers. WMG was the most likely company to make a higher offer than Terra Firma's offer of 265p ($4.91) a share, but for EMI, WMG's side deal with IMPALA notwithstanding, the regulatory issues were a deal breaker. A few years earlier Time Warner had rejected a (higher) bid from EMI for WEA because of uncertainty about clearing regulatory hurdles. In 2007 EMI took a similar view and opted for Terra Firma rather than WMG.

In common with the other majors EMI had learnt to live with the uncertainties and difficulties of a market in decline; such uncertainty was increased a thousand fold with the entry of Terra Firma into the picture. If timing is all, Guy Hands and Terra Firma started their dance with EMI with crutches needed from the off. With Terra Firma EMI moved from the problems of collapsing CD sales to a collapse of the financial system in which debt, previously the engine of expansion and growth, became a drag on economic activity of virtually any kind. And so EMI entered a period when however well (or badly) it performed in its own little market its fate would be determined by events and issues completely outside its control and would end in a court case in which a private equity investor, a man whose skill lay in seeing opportunities, would sue his financing partner on the basis that it had mislead him.

The tension surrounding the purchase started to shimmer in the very process of its completion. The deal took longer to conclude than expected. Terra Firma announced the agreed takeover in May, but it was not completed until the end of July, principally because Citigroup, Terra Firma's financial backer, demanded 90% shareholder approval before it would commit more than £2bn ($1.86bn). The delay led to mounting speculation that the EMI takeover could become a victim of the fallout from the US sub-prime mortgage crisis. Terra Firma survived that hurdle and was granted a final extension by the City of London Takeover Panel, but at the same time, it emerged that Citigroup would not agree to a waiver if Terra Firma came close to securing as much as 80% shareholder approval. Such inflexibility was unusual and offered further indication of just how jittery finance houses had become faced with the prospect of syndicating debt to other banks in a market that was becoming ever more volatile. Finally, on August 1, Terra Firma reported that it had received valid acceptances of 90.27% per cent of EMI shares. Eric Nicoli had finally sold EMI. The price was lower than desired, but the deal was done.

EMI was now Guy Hands' problem, as he made clear in the statement he issued as Nicoli stepped down as CEO: "Terra Firma's success is founded upon the real commitment it makes to the businesses in which it invests ... The new management structure will allow EMI to benefit from Terra Firma's experience in strategically transforming businesses and driving operational change. The initial focus will be to maximise the value of the significant assets in EMI's publishing business and to realise the digital opportunity in recorded music. We will invest in the business to ensure that it grows both organically and by acquisition. The goal is for EMI to be the world's most innovative and consumer-focused music company and the best home for musical talent."

Chapter 14

Transforming EMI: The Hands Era, Part One

Before his problems with Citigroup exploded and struggling to retain control of ownership of EMI in the face of its ever imminent insolvency became *the* issue, Guy Hands had a brief period of calm in which to look at what he had bought and to contemplate how to bring it to profitability. His first port of call was EMI's annual results for 2006–2007, which were published in June, shortly after the takeover was agreed but just before it was completed. As expected, the results were not pleasant reading.

Of the company's two divisions, EMI MP fared far better. It reported a 4.4% fall in revenues to £401.3m ($743.3m), but a marginal rise in profits to £105.6m ($199.6m). Although EMI MP's revenues only accounted for 23% of EMI Group's revenues, its operating profits accounted for 70% of group operating profits. Digital revenues rose by 28% to £25.3m ($46.9m), however, phono-mechanical royalties, the revenue stream most dependent on the sale of recorded music, fell by 6.7%, while performance revenues increased by 10.1% and synchronisation rose by 5.6%. EMI also reported that its profit ratio for EMI MP was 26.3%, compared to the 3.3% of the record division and 8.6% for the EMI Group overall.

EMI Music's operating profits had fallen precipitously by 69%, to £44.9m ($84.7m). In the report accompanying its results EMI acknowledged that digital sales were not increasing at a fast enough rate to compensate for the decline of physical sales. This was in contrast to previous presentations by EMI (and WMG) in which digital music sales were trumpeted as taking the place of lost physical sales. In fact at around 6% of total sales, EMI's digital revenues were lower than the 11% for the industry as a whole. EMI was under-performing rather than outperforming the market.

Hands took this in his stride. On September 17, the day before EMI was to be delisted from the Stock Exchange after over 70 years as a leading public company, he sent the EMI staff a memo, the first of many, all of which were leaked – *see* Appendix 1 for the collection – in which he professed himself relaxed by the difficulties the annual results highlighted:

Dear colleague,
Last Friday, I was on a panel on embracing change at the UK's annual major convention on broadcasting at which all the industry's major players were represented and which received some press coverage.

I made the point that Terra Firma's biggest successes over the years had been when we had bought those businesses in need of the most change and in sectors facing the biggest challenges and that EMI fits that model perfectly. I went on to say that Terra Firma's model transforms companies that have been in the past poorly managed and have lost their direction and EMI had to date not disappointed in its potential for transformation. However, this is not just an EMI issue as the recorded music industry as a whole has not positioned itself well for the changing environment over the last ten years and has failed to anticipate or adapt to the new market place.

With regard to EMI specifically, I believe that there has been too much management focus over the last seven years on a potential merger with Warner and on a continuous cost-cutting programme which has failed to deliver a new business model and sadly has led to the loss of many talented people from the business. Terra Firma has inherited EMI past management's business plan which is currently being executed. However our future focus is to develop a plan that ensures that EMI's Recorded Music business, as an independent company (i.e. without a merger with Warner), can best serve its artists, the music industry, its customers and employees. Put simply, focusing alone on the production of multi-million selling albums cannot produce a sustainable business model. In developing the business plan for EMI Recorded Music, we intend initially to look at these areas:

* The relationship between EMI and its artists and what contractual relationship best serves those artists
* Digitalization and how EMI's recorded music business can embrace and benefit from it
* How EMI can be the most efficient partner in recorded music for artists who are likely to sell less than 200,000 copies of their albums
* How EMI can develop a closer and more valuable relationship with its customers
* What services and products EMI should be developing and delivering to its artists and customers
* How EMI can provide multi-million selling artists with a top quality service internationally.

In short, how EMI can be big enough to serve anyone but small enough to truly care.

So far, we have not spent a huge amount of time on analyzing what might be done with EMI's publishing business. As I said at the broadcaster's convention, "If it ain't broke, don't fix it". However, Roger Faxon has a number of new initiatives which he is intending to roll out to ensure that EMI Publishing will continue to grow and prosper which Terra Firma supports.

In the near term, I am embarking on a roadshow over the next month in which I intend to meet as many of EMI's employees as possible. At those meetings, I will be happy to answer your questions. Additionally, feel free to email me in confidence on … any ideas as to how we can make the business work better to the benefit of EMI, its staff and its artists.

In spite of a lack of clear direction and an extremely challenging market, EMI's artists and employees have delivered a huge number of successes in recent years and have much to be proud of. I continue to be impressed by your commitment and creativity and would simply ask that you continue to be focused on the work you are doing for EMI and its artists. Terra Firma's commitment to EMI is total and we have invested more financially, both personally as individuals and as an organization, in EMI than any other company in our history. We are absolutely committed to making EMI the world's most innovative and consumer-focused music company and the best home for musical talent. I look forward to working with you in order to achieve just that.

Guy Hands
Chairman

This memo introduced the philosophy, outlined in more detail in the subsequent *AnnualReview*, that would underpin Hands' attempt to transform EMI into a Terra Firma model company. It also represented the first time the internal workings of a record company and the record business as a whole were exposed to public scrutiny. More immediately, the memo and Hands' first few meetings with "the talent" introduced his braggadocio – "EMI had to date not disappointed in its potential for transformation" – and the chalk and cheese scenario. In this, Hands presented himself as an upstart not concerned with the strange rules and practices rife in the music industry, while EMI's executives and the representatives of "the talent" were presented as living in an already deflating bubble with little sense of reality. This antagonism faded as Hands stood back from direct involvement in EMI, but the Hands' would-be transformation scenario only ever sputtered into life. With the arrival of the credit crunch, just after Terra Firma's purchase of EMI, making the deal one of the worst timed investments ever and leaving EMI with debts to Citigroup (which had been unable to sell on its loans), Terra Firma's stewardship of EMI quickly turned into a farce. Along with the debt was a punishing schedule of repayments which meant that, if EMI were to default it would fall into Citigroup's hands leaving Terra Firma with immense losses. The endgame was particularly surreal with Hands, a self-styled ace venture capitalist and sniffer out of bargains, seeking (and failing to get) financial relief through the courts, alleging that he had been tricked into buying EMI. He lost the court case and within a month on a technicality EMI was declared insolvent and was swept up by Citigroup

To help consider why "the recorded music industry as a whole has not positioned itself well for the changing environment over the last ten years and has failed to anticipate or adapt to the new market place" Hands and his Terra Firma executives might have looked at current surveys of the record industry. In May and June 2007, three such were published, each painting very different pictures and making decidedly contradictory forecasts of the future. Below I collate the predictions of the surveys by eMarketer, Enders Analysis and PricewaterhouseCoopers (PwC), and the actual figures for 2010 as reported by IFPI.

The trade value of recorded music sales in 2010, forecasts and actual ($m)

Format	Ender Analysis	eMarketer	PwC	IFPI
Digital	6.9	12.9	20.0	7.2
Physical	15.0	22.2	19.1	16.2
Total	21.9	35.1	39.1	23.4

Source: eMarketer, Enders Analysis, PwC and IFPI.

Sector surveys have a wide array of functions, depending on the drive behind their construction and their intended audience. Thus, the PwC survey of the music industry was part of a larger survey, *Global Entertainment and Media Outlook 2007–2011*. Its eighth annual survey published in 2007 was intended as a calling card to possible clients and a demonstration to the world at large that PwC was a reliable and authoritative source of financial guidance. However, that guidance was general, offering formula-driven analysis conducted at some distance from the belly of the beast. Accordingly, its authors had a greater tendency to believe in or at least accept the views, of its subjects. Such a position led inevitably to a degree of optimism, even if expressed in terms of "the problems are not insurmountable". Other surveys have a more specific function: to talk up a specific sector. The classic example of this is the series of analysts comments, each rushing to outdo each other, that talked up the digital musical economy to such a level that they helped trigger the first dotcom collapse. eMarketer's 2007 survey, *Global Music*, was such a survey with the difference that, the company's name notwithstanding, the hidden value it uncovered was the value of live music. Enders Analysis, which had its origins in an in-house industry research body, was the closest to the industry in terms of knowledge and the most sceptical of the industry's oft-stated optimism about the problems it faced. Not surprisingly, Enders' future forecasts in *Recorded Music and Music Publishing* were the most conservative of the three reports and, as the table above shows, the closest to the actual figures published by IFPI.

If the heart of would-be industry transformer Hands was momentarily warmed by the eMarketer and PwC reports, *Recorded Music and Music Publishing* confirmed his initial sense that "the recorded music industry as a whole has not positioned itself well for the changing environment over the last ten years and has failed to anticipate or adapt to the new market place" without offering any way out of the maze. The Enders report predicted that the trade value of global recorded music sales in 2010 would be $21.9bn, of which physical sales would account for $15bn (68.5%) and digital sales $6.9bn. Although it did not state that in terms of profitability digital sales, mostly single tracks, were inherently less profitable than physical sales, which were mostly of CD albums, the report noted that digital recorded music sales, the growth rate of which was already in decline in 2007, would not compensate for the fall in physical sales. In some detail the report looked at the growth of online piracy; the complicated impact on physical sales of legitimate online sales; the contraction of specialised retailers and the consolidation of entertainment retail; the decline in the retail price of physical CDs; the declining sales of "hit albums"; the contraction of the majors who had cut staff and exited from manufacturing and other non-core activities in response to the fall in their revenues; and the mistakes of the majors in opting for litigation rather than monetisation.

These are issues that have been treated at length earlier in this book, but for a record executive, let alone an outsider who had just bought the world's fourth largest music company, such a view in 2007 made for uncomfortable reading, particularly as *Recorded Music and Music Publishing* also edged towards the idea of a Kuhnian paradigm shift, noting "The software, hardware and communication technologies of the Internet age have had a disruptive impact on traditional forms of music consumption in a more far reaching way than analysts could have predicted a decade ago."

When the Bronfman consortium bought WMG, it had in Scott Sperling a venture capitalist au fait with the music business and in Edgar Jr. an executive with industry experience. Terra Firma had no such expertise. Past successes of Terra Firma had included German motorway stations where the venture capitalist mantra, buy cheap, examine, change and sell at a profit, had worked well. After buying the stations Terra Firma learnt from a survey that Germans felt that the hygiene standards of the stations were below par. The stations were cleaned up and sold at a profit. Similarly, after buying the Odeon chain of cinemas, Terra Firma swiftly realised that it was in the popcorn business, not the film business, and restructured priorities accordingly. Hence Hands' September 17 memo: "Terra Firma's model transforms companies that have been in the past poorly managed and have lost their direction." To this Hands added "EMI had to date not disappointed in its potential for transformation". The problem facing Terra Firma was that transformation indicated here, the impact of the digital world, was not something Terra Firma was at all knowledgeable about. Transforming a record company demanded more than just cleaning the toilets.

Sadly, neither Hands nor John Birt, the former head of the BBC appointed chairman and blue sky thinker of Maltby, the financial vehicle through which Terra Firma bought EMI, looked significantly beyond re-arranging the deckchairs on their own little *Titanic*. Restructuring and cost-cutting – a 1,500 reduction in the workforce was announced in January 2008 – not blue sky visions, formed the horizon for Terra Firma's take on EMI. Thus, fiefdoms were reshaped, non-industry veterans appointed to high positions and cuts were intensified, but little deep restructuring was attempted. The loss of control and the low margins that the digital revolution represented were hardly addressed. That and the dismissive attitude to industry "truths" meant the restructurings were superficial.

Terra Firma had no deep understanding of the significance of the etiquette required to handle "the talent", one that was decidedly different to that of other industries. In the music industry stars were stars and success was success but the two concepts were only intermittently related. Thus, a star, such as Paul McCartney, could have less than expected sales but still would be a star whose views were influential. The economics behind such scenarios were radically different from assessing the potential sales of a product line in Boots the chemist. (The stories about the confrontations between Hands and the talent were also fun for the financial press, which jumped at the idea of stories that could be illustrated with pictures of rock stars rather than sombrely suited businessmen for a change.) The disjuncture was highlighted in a *Financial Times* editorial of August 30: "Nobody really expected the new bosses to appoint a board consisting of Robbie Williams, Sir Simon Rattle and The Spice Girls, but the record company's new executives – a former ICI senior vice president of finance, a management consultant and a lawyer – could hardly be greyer. In case the message that change is in the air is lost on employees, one of the trio has taken the ominous title of 'director of business transformation'." But even this wry witticism missed the point. The music business is dependent on A&R, on finding and keeping artists who sell product in large quantities. In the 2000s, it was no longer possible to sign and keep acts like Randy Newman or the Grateful Dead (as WMG did in the 1960s) even though they sold in moderate quantities because they attracted other acts to the label like a magnet. The finding, signing and management of talent was a far more sophisticated business than Terra Firma's brusque demands and EMI's poverty allowed for. The result was that EMI haemorrhaged artists, in particular artists whose back catalogue sales produced considerable revenues for the company.

So striking was the disconnect between Hands and the people he was addressing that his memos were memorably parodied by *The Sunday Times* (January 6, 2008):

Dear Mr Jagger

I write to you as a last resort, having failed to get a sensible answer to my requests from other members of your group. As I'm sure you are aware, it is vital to the running of any modern business that employees accurately fill in their timesheets. Unfortunately, when I contacted your colleague Mr Richards to find out why he hadn't filled out any of his timesheets for 2006, his reply was, "What's 2006?" As for Mr Watts, sending back a timesheet with "Five years playing drums. Forty years hanging about" scrawled across it does not meet the standards of detail and accuracy that our group needs to function. When I pointed out to Mr Wood that if we didn't have accurately returned timesheets, then for all we knew he might have spent the past three decades playing snooker in a drunken haze, he merely laughed. I trust that you will be able not only to fill in your own timesheets, but to chivvy your colleagues into doing the same.

Yours, etc

To: Kate Bush
From: Head of Album Scheduling
Re: Productivity
Dear Ms Bush
As you will have seen in the recently circulated training DVD "EMI and You: Working Together (A Bit Harder)", we expect our artists to produce an album every two years. Given the 12-year gap that preceded Aerial, *I'm sure you've already realised that to keep up your average, we are expecting six albums from you in the next 12-month period. Please let me know if you anticipate any problems with this. On a related matter, that song on* Aerial, *Mrs Bartolozzi, about the woman who cleans the whole house thoroughly and puts all the clothes in the washing machine – you know the one: "It took hours and hours to scrub it out" – is it based on a real person? If so, could you ask her to send in her CV?*

Many thanks

As Hands drew further back from day to day involvement in EMI fewer gaffes were made, but they always remained a possibility as when desperate to raise money to pay to Citigroup, in 2010 EMI briefly proposed selling off Abbey Road studios. News of the proposed sale brought about an astonishing outpouring of public emotion with the UK's National Trust being called on to mount a campaign to save the iconic studios for the nation. "It's not often that the public spontaneously suggests that we should acquire a famous building," said a National Trust spokesman. "However, Abbey Road recording studios appear to be very dear to the nation's heart – to the extent that we will take soundings as to whether a campaign is desirable or even feasible." From one perspective, the closure and sale of Abbey Road made commercial sense: studios were no longer core facilities for record companies when recordings could be made piecemeal and virtually anywhere as the costs of recording technology had fallen. Indeed EMI had closed Olympic Studio in 2009 as part of a cost-cutting measure. Abbey Road was different. It was iconic, the home of The Beatles, the name of a Beatles album. Anyway, the money garnered would hardly dent EMI's loss of £1.8bn in 2009. EMI quickly changed tack and, in a complete reversal, in 2011 in celebration of the Abbey Road's 80th birthday, EMI MP co-published a board game based on the studio which fittingly, in the era of exclusives, was initially available only online from UK supermarket Tesco.

Hands' emails and meetings with the EMI staff and artists representatives all made it clear that Terra Firma demanded from EMI "a fundamental change in the way we do business". The initial response to this was largely hostile. Radiohead, which had sold some 25m albums for EMI, left the company in acrimonious circumstances when negotiations broke down over ownership of the Radiohead masters and digital royalties. The first problem, which turned up increasingly in artist-record company negotiations (for example, Garth Brooks) generally was solved to the benefit of the artist on the basis that it was better to retain successful artists than lose them. (A second issue was soon to become an ongoing thorn in the side of the record industry as acts which had had a degree of commercial success in the past, such as the Allman Brothers, Whitesnake and Cheap Trick, sued record companies on the basis that royalties from digital sales should be calculated as licence revenues, which are greater than the royalties due from physical sales, *see* Chapter 17). The rejection of Radiohead's demands turned out to be a disaster for EMI both in terms of press coverage and lost revenues. In 2007, after fulfilling their six-album contract with EMI, Radiohead noted ironically, "We have no record contract as such ... What we would like is the old EMI back again, the nice genteel arms manufacturers who treated music [as] a nice side project who weren't too bothered about the shareholders. Ah well, not much chance of that ..." adding in a later interview "[We] like the people at our record company, but the time is at hand when you have to ask why anyone needs one. And, yes, it probably would give us some perverse pleasure to say 'Fuck you' to this decaying business model."

Radiohead soon demonstrated that they had no need for EMI. Released as a download on October 10, *In Rainbows*, was described by *The New York Times* as "the most audacious experiment in years". Packaged as a zip file, the 10 album tracks were encoded as 160kbits/DRM-free MP3 files. Prior to download, the buyer was prompted to type in the price they were willing to pay and to enter their credit card details. Three months later, the download was made unavailable and replaced with a limited made-to-order "discbox", available online, containing the album on CD and two 12" heavyweight 45rpm vinyl records with artwork and lyric booklets. The box also included a second enhanced CD with eight additional tracks, as well as digital photos and artwork. The overall set, packaged in a hardcover book with a slipcase, was priced at £40 ($80), and also included the MP3 download. In December the original album was released in conventional CD format around the world on a variety of independent labels.

According to an Internet survey conducted by *Record of the Day* of 3,000 people, about one-third of people who downloaded the album paid nothing, with the average price paid being £4 ($8). In October 2008, a report from Warner Chappell, Radiohead's music publisher which had helped facilitate the process, revealed that although many people paid nothing for the download, pre-release sales were greater (and more profitable for the band) than the total revenues from sales of the band's previous album, *Hail To The Thief*, and that *In Rainbows* had sold 3m copies (including digital and physical format sales) since the album's physical release. The discbox also sold 100,000 copies. In the week of its retail release, *In Rainbows* went straight to number one on the UK album chart, with first-week sales of 44,602 copies and it topped the US charts in the second week of its release. The strategy won the band press acclaim as a brave, and successful, pointer to the future. It was Radiohead, rather than EMI, that made "a fundamental change in the way we do business".

Hands responded with a memo:

> *Dear all*
> RADIOHEAD
> *As you know, Radiohead, a band with whom we have enjoyed a long and productive history, have decided to release their new album, In* Rainbows, *directly to consumers via their own web-site. They have also allowed fans to download the digital album at a price to be set by the consumer. While some recorded music executives and other firms have expressed shock and dismay at this development, it should have come as no surprise. In a digital world, it was inevitable that a band with the necessary financial resources and consumer recognition to be able to distribute their music directly to their fans would do so. Radiohead is one of the most iconic, original and successful bands in the world, and one of the few with a fan base large and devoted enough to support the costs of such an initiative.*
>
> *However, whilst most bands, including many successful names, will not be able to – or want to – follow in their footsteps, there are some important lessons to be learnt which support our analysis of what needs to change in the recorded music business model and which many of you have touched on in your letters and emails to us since Terra Firma bought EMI.*

EMI consequently took the Radiohead strategy to heart, to some extent at least. In October 2007, in association with the Cliff Richard Organisation, EMI announced "an innovative pricing model" to mark the release of Richard's latest album *Love, The Album.* The scheme allowed fans to pre-order the album, which included special bonus material, from the website lovecliffrichard.com, ahead of its November release with the twist that as more orders were placed the price of the album would fall. The maximum the consumer was charged was £7.99 ($15.98), with the figure dropping down to a potential minimum of £3.99 ($7.98). On release of the album all consumers were asked to pay the same, lowest price. EMI released no sales figures for the album and did not mount any further schemes of this type. In September 2011 the album was available from Amazon for £4.47.

Few artists followed Radiohead directly but other ways of doing business without the majors were developing on an almost daily basis. The Eagles could go it alone in their own way, Madonna could swap WMG for Live Nation and a host of acts, such as the Arctic Monkeys or Mumford & Sons, could kick-start their careers through touring and the Internet and find success through independent record companies without the need of a long-term commitment to a major.

Such a trend was catching. In 2007, Paul McCartney quit EMI. In an interview with *The Times*, he complained that the company had become too bureaucratic – and how he had "dreaded going to see them. Everybody at EMI had become part of the furniture. I'd be a couch; Coldplay are an armchair. And Robbie Williams, I dread to think what he was. But the most important thing was, I'd felt [the people at EMI] had become really very boring, you know?" He also complained about the long marketing lead times demanded by EMI, the so-called process of "setting up a record" in an attempt to enhance sales, recalling that John Lennon was able to force EMI to release 'Instant Karma' a week after he had written it in 1970. McCartney's strictures were primarily aimed at the Nicoli-era of EMI, but the loss of McCartney to Starbucks-owned start-up record label Hear Music, which released *Memory Almost Full*, cost Hands' EMI 1m CD album sales. Subsequently McCartney withdrew his Wings and solo back catalogue from EMI.

The uncertainties surrounding EMI, which accelerated in 2009–2010, led to other artists leaving, notably the Rolling Stones and Queen, acts whose back catalogues were highly profitable for the company. Both left for UMG which made better offers and marketing promises. A mark of UMG's achievement with such catalogues was that even though the Stones' 1972 album *Exile On Main St.* had been re-issued and re-mastered by EMI in 1994, UMG was able to issue a new re-mastering of *Exile on Main St.* in a deluxe package in May 2010 to enormous success.

It was the first re-issued album to top the UK charts and it re-entered the US charts at number two, selling 76,000 during the first week. The departure of these classic acts came just after EMI had reorganised its music division to prioritise back catalogue. The importance of back catalogue for EMI was emphasised in 2009 when re-mastered Beatles box sets sold more than 2.25m albums in the first five days of release in North America, UK and Japan. This made the group the fourth most successful in the US in 2009. Because of the high royalties the Beatles' lawyers negotiated when the group finally allowed EMI in 1987 to release their music on CDs, the profit margins on Beatle product is very low for EMI, but the margins on Pink Floyd, the second best-selling UK group after The Beatles, and Queen are higher. Moreover, like that of The Rolling Stones, both catalogues are deep and successful: the Floyd, whose *Dark Side Of The Moon* was still in the *Billboard* Top 200 chart in 2010, signed to EMI in 1967, while Queen joined EMI in 1972.

When Pink Floyd brought a lawsuit against EMI in 2010 it was widely expected that they would follow The Rolling Stones *et al*. Pink Floyd claimed that there had been an underpayment of royalties and argued that EMI had no right to sell their songs except as part of full albums. According to the group, tracks such as 'Money' and 'Another Brick In The Wall' could not be "unbundled" from the albums on which they appear. Robert Howe, the group's lawyer, at a London High Court hearing noted that Pink Floyd's renegotiated 1999 contract "expressly prohibits" EMI from selling songs "out of context". Nonetheless, EMI permitted "individual tracks to be downloaded online and ... [therefore allow] albums not to be sold in their original configuration". EMI rejected this, arguing that the restriction relates only to physical product, in part because "In 1999, when [the contract] was negotiated, iTunes didn't even exist." Pink Floyd won the court case, but decided on the basis of a new offer made to them by EMI, an offer very much skewed in their favour, to stay with EMI. Pink Floyd's decision to stay with EMI was a solitary and expensive victory for the company.

Terra Firma also ran into press difficulties when it sought to reduce its pension fund commitments in July 2008. This led to the EMI pension trustees asking the UK pensions regulator to conduct an independent review after which the dispute was settled in favour of the trustees. Receiving less publicity outside the trade press, in 2008 EMI threatened to leave IFPI, the trade association that represents the recording industry worldwide, unless it agreed to implement cost-saving measures that would reduce the membership fees paid to IFPI by EMI (and the other majors). EMI sought similar reductions in fees paid to national IFPI groups. In the end, IFPI's membership fees were adjusted downwards and no defections took place.

However, simply raising the issue exposed the financial pressures EMI (and the other majors) were facing. It would seem that EMI, which had broken rank over the issue of DRM, no longer saw the point of being part of IFPI dominated by the old-fashioned companies.

Hands spoke of a transformation needed for the record business as a whole, but his prime concern was EMI. At a meeting with staff, artists and managers in January 2008 he sang the simple song of restructuring, cost-cutting, reducing the roster and staff, and simplifying the organisational configuration of the company. This won him some breathing space and to some extent mollified the artistic community that in the early months of 2008 found renewed hope and possibilities in the "new" EMI. In early November EMI Music's newly appointed chief executive Elio Leoni-Sceti announced a restructuring of recorded music into three business units: new music, catalogue and music services. The appointment of Leoni-Sceti in July 2008 signalled a double change for EMI. Firstly, Guy Hands stepped down as CEO which meant fewer memos and public irruptions (that is until the lawsuit against Citigroup). Secondly, while previous executive shuffles had meant one record company executive being replaced by another, Leoni-Sceti was an outsider. He came from a consumer products group, Reckitt Benckiser, where he had been responsible for the company's marketing until taking over its European operations. His appointment, which followed the enforced departure of UK head Tony Wadsworth, a man much respected within the UK music business, seemed to suggest a shake-up of the close-knit world of the music industry. In retrospect this and a raft of similar appointments had little lasting impact. They talked the talk – consumer awareness, marketing, focus — and oversaw a (surprising) return to success but despite the talk they hardly walked the digital walk.

Just as EMI had over-egged its digital commitment and expertise compared to the other majors so its newfound sense of "the importance of the consumer and the market" was in reality only new to EMI. A central part of the restructuring of all the majors was the prioritising of the marketing of international repertoire. Indeed one of the ironies of the Hands era was that, while the debt incurred in buying EMI eventually led to Terra Firma losing EMI, the record division during the period did rather well, turning in a profit through content creation, notably with the likes of new acts such as Katy Perry and Lady Antebellum and established brands such as Coldplay. Following the mantra of Ahmet Ertegun, EMI managed to "sell more records". However, such were its debts that it could never sell enough. Freed of those debts, when Citigroup took control of EMI in 2011, EMI's success was real and produced real profits, notably through the well managed triumph of Katy Perry's *Teenage Dreams* album and associated singles.

In November, Maltby Capital, the financial vehicle used by Terra Firma group to buy EMI, issued an *Annual Review* (AR) covering the year to March 31, 2008. The AR was a devastating account of the sins committed by EMI prior to Terra Firma's purchase (and by implication the "Spanish practices" that it implied were endemic to the music business), while the financial picture it detailed explained the need for restructuring. However, even though it was one of the first public liftings of the bonnet of a record company, the examination offered was far from a full service. The AR was largely limited to the physical marketplace, seeing the online world as little more than an extension of the physical.

EMI Group had losses in the year of £757m ($1.5bn) compared to losses of £287m ($574m) in the previous year. EMI's revenues fell by 17% in the same period to £1.46bn ($2.92bn). In 2007, EMI lost market share in the leading five national music markets, which accounted for 74% of recorded music sales that year. In the same period EMI also saw its global market share decline by almost two percentage points to 10.9%. An indication of the scale of EMI's losses in 2007–2008 can be seen by comparing its performance with that of the other majors. Over the same period, Sony BMG recorded a 4% decline in revenues to $3.93bn but a 111% rise in net profits to $178m, while for the year ending December 31, 2007, UMG reported that its net profits fell by 16.1% to €624m ($918m) on sales of €4.87bn ($7.27bn), down 1.7% compared to 2006, representing a profit margin of 12% compared to a margin of 15% the previous year. (The difference in the accounting period of WMG, the company closest in size to EMI, makes a comparison unrealistic.) Things were not going well for the majors.

Meanwhile, in an email to EMI staff, Hands tried to accentuate the positive and reported that in April-June, the three months following its gloomy annual results, EMI Music both increased its revenues and made a profit. Recorded Music's sales rose 61% to £288.1m ($572.9m) and transformed a loss of £45.1m ($90.2m) into an EBITDA gain of £59.2m ($117.7m). Terra Firma did not release figures for EMI MP, but since in the first three months of 2008 it was the leading music publisher in the US and the UK, it is highly likely that EMI MP also performed well financially.

However, the AR barely touched on EMI's financial performance. Maltby's chairman, Lord Birt, in an accompanying letter made it clear that the function and scope of the AR was different to that of most annual reports: "I would like to say at the outset that this report is not a typical company report. Listed company reports tend to minimise challenges and highlight successes in order to manage their reputations in the marketplace. Readers of this report, therefore, may well be struck by the forthright presentation of problems and the absence of rosy assurances about the future."

The AR had several functions. Firstly, it aimed to be positive about Terra Firma's longer than expected ownership of EMI. The downturn in the financial markets made its sale impossible. Citigroup hadn't been able to sell on loans to Terra Firma and bidders for EMI were scarce on the ground. From this perspective the aim of the AR was to say the past was hell, but the future was Terra Firma. Initially that approach was well received. In November 2007, despite the credit squeeze in the world's financial markets, Terra Firma raised £250m ($490m) in new equity. Investors took a positive view of the planned restructuring. Although the new funds, the largest amount ever raised by Terra Firma in a one company investment, diluted the equity of Terra Firma, they enabled it to finance the job cuts in back office and administration. The new funds also helped to strengthen EMI's balance sheet as it prepared to pay interest on the £2bn ($3.9bn) loan facility with Citigroup.

In retrospect the AR also admitted that the presentations made to investors by Terra Firma earlier that year contained a strong element of Cloud Cuckoo Land. Leaked memos as reported by the *New York Post* at the time, showed that Terra Firma was telling prospective partners they could nearly quadruple their money in the struggling international record company and publishing group within five years through a mix of cost savings, improved digital revenues, strategic acquisitions and the development of new revenue streams. Terra Firma's investor presentations were made in the same week that the share price of WMG fell (from a high of $27) to under $9 and were recommended to be offered for sale at $7.50 by stock market analyst Richard Greenfield. According to the *New York Post*, EMI's expansion plans included buying independent record companies for which Terra Firma had set up a fund of $100m which it would double if it attracted outside investment in EMI. This too was Cloud Cuckoo Land logic. As a basis for strategic acquisitions, such a figure was tiny. Live Nation, which set itself in competition with EMI and the other majors in seeking to reformulate itself as a 360-degree music company and had already secured Madonna's recording rights, earlier in the month bought the Signatures merchandising company for $79m. $100m would not buy you a significant-sized record or music publishing company in 2008.

Although the AR observed that "EMI cannot be turned around overnight", it suggested that the steps already taken by the new management at EMI would solve the majority of the problems identified. July, brought more good news, notably increased sales and improved profits in the three months to June.

The AR also sought to emphasise the clean break between the old regime at EMI and the new management installed by Terra Firma, to indicate the priorities of the newly engineered EMI and to show its success by comparison with the failure of the old EMI. Lord Birt emphasised this last point at the conclusion of his introduction to the report: "The numbers presented here today tell you clearly that this is the first year in the radical turnaround of a company culture, a business model and perhaps even a market. It will not be a quick fix. Nevertheless, we expect to be in line with targets by the half year period. We are on track to address the company fundamentals and to reverse the decline in profitability even before we move ahead with a new strategy to address the music market today. We are in the process of taking EMI back to business basics: understanding customers, sourcing an excellent product, finding the right channels to market, and packaging and marketing music in an appealing way."

Birt was hugely critical of past attempts to address EMI's problems: EMI – and much of the industry and its commentators – saw declining music industry fortunes as primarily a market issue. Falling CD sales and piracy had eroded revenues from its core product so quickly and so severely that the resulting losses could not be offset even by the continuing good performance of EMI Music Publishing. In its public statements, EMI highlighted piracy and a generally adverse market as the reasons for its difficulties, while its strategy was particularly focused on external solutions such as anti-piracy legislation or a merger.

While it was right for EMI to address these external market issues and to pursue legal or regulatory solutions, analysis quickly revealed that it had also failed to tackle equally important problems in its own business. "It is not easy or palatable for any organisation, particularly a listed company, to critically and openly evaluate itself. The pressure on management teams to unveil strategic solutions at short notice – without really facing up to internal problems that may be the root cause of failing profitability – is intense. For outsiders with access to only published reports & accounts, many of which are opaque, the information necessary to get to the root causes of problems is often simply unavailable. By acquiring EMI and taking it private, we have had the time to understand those root causes; and the insight obtained has enabled us to establish a sound foundation for the Group's new strategy."

The market was, of course, a major factor in EMI's recent decline. But close involvement with the company over the past year had exposed how internal factors within EMI Music had significantly eroded the Group's profitability.

Firstly, EMI Music had a culture where high expenditure at odds with the challenges it faced was widely accepted. This meant the company accepted as normal costs that should have been substantially cut back.

Secondly, EMI Music's traditional way of working with artists – highly successful in the days of booming CD sales and a significantly simpler and less fragmented market – had become less fit for purpose. As a result, EMI Music's creative performance, as well as its financial performance, had begun to slide.

Thirdly, the company's internal reporting, while data-rich, focused on traditional measures which could tell the company little about the major changes in its marketplace as they evolved. It provided insufficient information for fundamental metrics – such as artist profitability.

This last point, which obscures as much as it reveals about EMI's past performance, is a good example of the limited vision Terra Firma brought to the repositioning of EMI. EMI was clearly unaware of the "the major changes [taking place] in its market place" – the digital revolution and its unforeseen consequences. When Jay Samit had been head of EMI's interactive business division, EMI went beyond the disdain most of the majors had for digital start-ups. Instead it concluded a large number of deals with the start-ups, but not primarily to help create a legitimate digital music sector from which it and they would benefit, but rather to secure cash advances and equity for the necessary licences to make their businesses legitimate. The overly onerous licence payments and equity agreements required by EMI resulted in a number of such start-ups failing (*see* Chapter 5). Such a misjudgment is a perfect example of the Kuhnian scientist presented with intriguing ideas that challenged past business practices and deciding that the past was more familiar and easier to deal with. Terra Firma's new vision for EMI, made long after digital with its contradictory mix of opportunities and problems, was clearly that the future hardly figured in Birt's thinking. His concern was EMI's lack of information about "artist profitability", a key piece of financial knowledge but hardly a core element of "the major changes [taking place] in its market place". In support of this the AR notes that "EMI Music has not made the most of its top 250 artists. Catalogue sales of these artists varies widely: while EMI Music has successfully worked with some artists so that their new releases also trigger sales of their catalogue work, with other artists it has much weaker working relationships and has only driven limited sales."

The body of the report offered another example of EMI's failure to come to grips with the real changes taking place in its marketplace. Noting that sales of recorded music were increasingly taking place at mass merchandisers and supermarkets rather than at specialised stores, the AR condemned the past management of EMI Music for not re-aligning its marketing plans to take account of this change: "EMI Music... lost touch with a customer base that had undergone significant change as the digital revolution gathered pace and the market fragmented. Research conducted since the acquisition of EMI shows that a number of clear customer segments have emerged in recent years, each of which has a distinctive buying behaviour. This research indicates that persuading these groups of customers, many of whom are at least partly disaffected, requires marketing individually to each segment, something EMI Music was not set up to do."

As I have previously demonstrated, individual record companies could do little to confront such changes. In the US, the MAP strategy failed and Wal Mart, even though it was able to secure large discounts and the exclusive right to sell certain albums, reduced the shelf space for music when the sales volume slipped.

It's surprising that Terra Firma's research didn't highlight non-traditional sales (digital and hybrid CD sales at the likes of iTunes and Amazon). By mid-year 2011 these accounted for 42% of the 155.6m albums sold in the US, more than any other retail strand. In the UK in the same period sales of digital albums in the three years since 2008 rose from 10% of album sales to 24% according to UK trade body BPI.

If the legitimate digital market was hard to assess in 2008, the appeal of digital music was easy to see. According to research group ipoque, P2P file-sharing, of which the majority was music, accounted for over

50% of Internet traffic, with other research bodies putting it as high as 80%. Attempts to monetise P2P had failed regularly, but the demand for digital music it signalled was real. From this perspective Terra Firma, like the past regime, could be equally accused of focusing "on the historical business and not on the future".

If the record companies as a whole had been slow to see that in the wake of their previously general control of their repertoire, their power was largely limited to the licensing of their copyrights for sale or use by others, EMI's weaknesses, and its over-long pursuit of a fairy tale-like union with WMG had fatefully blinded it. Thus, it danced to Steve Jobs' tune, making DRM-free tracks available when "asked". However, when it came to new and possibly game-changing digital business opportunities it was not EMI but the market leader, repertoire rich UMG, that companies came to. Such plans could fail, as in Nokia's Comes With Music service for its mobile phone subscribers, but as digital became the new mantra for the record industry, it wasn't a future EMI had planned for.

Rather EMI was playing catch up with the past, and in a fuddled way. Back to the AR: "Recent years have seen the emergence of new wholesale music customers, such as Tesco, and global customers like Nokia or Apple, who are best served by global marketing. However, EMI Music had a primarily regional structure. This could lead to duplication of research and marketing efforts across regions and did not provide motivation to individual geographies to put global EMI marketing priorities ahead of local objectives."

A concomitant of signing superstars was that to make the most from them required sophisticated marketing (and distribution) strategies to unfold around their releases. The aim was to start with a bang – hence the first-week discounts pioneered by Lyor Cohen at WMG – and then market and market to extract the greatest possible sale because after the first million the margins on subsequent sales grew exponentially. Most of the majors had such marketing stratagems in place. EMI, which until Coldplay had no currently active superstars, didn't. This changed following the success of the campaign for *Viva La Vida*, which was critically well received as both a campaign and album as well as being a significant commercial success. Subsequently EMI would have similar success with Katy Perry, especially her second album, *Teenage Dreams*. This ski slope approach in which a superstar's album was launched with a global marketing strategy already in place merely required efficient compliance by each national branch company.

But not all acts were superstars, many were national or regional stars and the number of these was growing according to IFPI statistics. In Asia local acts had always dominated recorded music sales, but as the table below shows between 2002 and 2008 the appeal of local repertoire grew considerably across continental Europe, with all the major territories, bar France, seeing greater revenues coming from local acts.

Domestic repertoire as a percentage of total recorded music sales by value, 2002–2008

	2002	2008
France	59	57
Germany	45	52
Italy	47	52
Spain	38	40
Russia	60	72

Source: IFPI

To fully exploit the popularity of such acts, record companies needed sophisticated national and regional marketing as well as global marketing strategies. Some French, German and Spanish acts had potential regional sales outside their own national markets, but many, like Italian signings, had limited international appeal. Superstars were hugely costly to sign and market but the rewards were equally huge. Domestic acts cost less to sign and market but the revenues they generated were far smaller. In this delicate balancing act, EMI, like WMG before it, chose to stress the global and cut back on the local, because of EMI's poverty and the higher cost margins of local signings. UMG, also facing the problem of declining sales, but sheltered by its parent company, Vivendi, and by its size, took a contrary view seeing local acts as being potential superstars. Accordingly it presented itself as being both A&R driven, looking for local acts with global potential to sign around the world, and as a lean, smart machine able to send the likes of U2, Eminem and Kanye West down the ski slope to global success.

EMI's poverty, in investment terms, also severely limited its expansion into other areas of the music business. The company sought and made 360-degree deals with most of its new signings, but while UMG, WMG and SME bought concert promotion companies around Europe, EMI, despite its brave talk of being an all-round music company, did not. The company also failed to invest in its core businesses. When Spectrum Equity Investors and Crossroads Media brought music publishing company Bug Music to market in 2010, just before Hands' Citigroup problems became deeply serious, EMI was one of the larger publishers that tried to buy Bug. The bid failed, but what was notable was that EMI MP alone couldn't afford the $250m price tag. Its bid involved separate financing from Terra Firma's investors, to whom Hands was to turn repeatedly that year. In 2011 Bug Music was sold to BMG RM, the most acquisitive music company of the decade.

When the AR spoke of costs it did so to damn the past regime: "[Its] approach to travel and expense policies was more than generous. Recent investigation showed EMI Music to be the fourth largest spender on a well-known taxi firm in London, with a bill of over £700,000 [$1.4m] in the last year. This was only slightly less than the bills of three investment banks, with 8–10 times more staff than EMI Music."

Returns in EMI Music over the last few years fluctuated considerably – averaging around 20% in the financial years ending March 2007 and 2008. However, sales noticeably trended higher in the period leading up to each half year and full year results, causing sales in the subsequent periods to be depressed by returns. When the market for physical CDs worsened in Q1 2007/08, the gap between sales and actual sales net of returns widened significantly. In April and May 2007, there were returns of close to 50% of gross sales.

This last was an issue that EMI successfully addressed, according to a memo from Guy Hands in June 2008: "A year ago, returns in quarter one totalled 42% of our gross physical sales. In the last three months we have reduced the returns to less than 16% of gross sales."

Having trashed the past, Birt, in the AR's conclusion, suggested that EMI has been radically overhauled, things were in motion and a new EMI was about to emerge that would be profitable:

We have dwelled on these historical issues to make the extent of the task ahead of us plain to our stakeholders. However, this in no way alters the fact of the substantial potential that can be released from EMI's considerable assets over time. Indeed, we have already tackled many of the practices that lay behind EMI's financial difficulties and have made significant progress against the restructuring goals set out at acquisition.

In particular: We have got costs under control, and introduced compensation policies in line with general business norms. We are on track to achieve Year 1 target run-rate headcount cuts of 1,500 and headcount and other savings of between £85 million and £100 million. Further cost savings will be achieved, keeping us on track for our target of £200 million savings overall.

We have put a new organisational structure in place, addressing the problems of geographical silos and promoting best practices and global cost saving and standardisation. We have introduced business discipline, ensuring that decisions are economically rational and that profitability and return on investment are front of mind.

We have appointed a strong and talented new senior team in EMI Music. Individuals with experience in digital and consumer markets that EMI particularly lacked – and strong creative A&R track records – are already reshaping the company's culture, introducing new dynamism and commercial rigour...

We are in the process of taking EMI back to business basics: understanding customers, sourcing an excellent product, finding the right channels to market, and packaging and marketing music in an appealing way. These basics will take us a long way. Keeping close to today's demanding customers, while thinking constantly of artist profitability, will concentrate EMI on finding outstanding new music, and fresh, imaginative ways of getting it to listeners. This is the only way we can succeed for our artists and all our stakeholders.

It will take time to build a new EMI fully equipped to meet the radical challenges of a wholly new and different modern media and entertainment environment. However, we expect our first half results to demonstrate that EMI Music has begun its journey to recovery. The task of restoring this business's creative vibrancy and commercial vitality – while making even more of the Publishing business – is underway.

Lord Birt, Chairman, Maltby Capital Ltd.

In truth there was no major overhaul nor rethink of what a modern record company might be, just restructuring and cost-cutting with a canny eye on previous excesses. The amazing thing is that despite the turmoil of the executive changes – a turmoil made even greater by the short stays of many of the new executives in their posts – a successful EMI, albeit still debt-burdened, emerged.

Chapter 15

Battling Citigroup: The Hands Era, Part Two

The first signs of a commercial renaissance at EMI was the huge success of Coldplay's fourth album, *Viva La Vida Or Death And All His Friends*, which, with sales of 6.8m, according to IFPI, was the best-selling album of 2008. Another 2008 success for EMI was Katy Perry who in 2010–2011 would dominate the US charts. Perry's success, which was followed by US hits in 2010 for Lady Antebellum and in 2011 for country acts Luke Bryan and Eric Church, who transformed themselves from minor stars to near superstars, brought a temporary end to EMI's failure to find talent in America. EMI also had fairly predictable success with The Beatles whose recordings were finally made available on iTunes at the end of 2010. This represented a pleasant back catalogue bonus for EMI: in 2009, 39 years after breaking up, The Beatles sold the third-highest number of albums, 3.3m copies, of any act in the US.

EMI's success with The Beatles was to be expected. Coldplay's success was the more significant. It was global, proving that EMI could manage international ski slope marketing and it was innovative. Not groundbreaking, but a demonstration that EMI could reconfigure past marketing schemes for the digital age. The campaign began with

Coldplay giving away a free MP3 of 'Violet Hill', the first single off the album. This had 2m downloads, generated press coverage worldwide and extended Coldplay's fan database, almost overnight, by 300,000 people (to get the free download consumers had to give their email and physical addresses and allow "Coldplay" to email them once a month). Separately, the group entered into cross promotions with radio stations and iTunes and started their world tour in support of the album with two free shows. The title track, 'Viva La Vida', was released exclusively on iTunes and became the group's first US and UK number one based on download sales alone. Towards the end of the tour the band recorded a live album, *LeftRightLeftRight*, which, released on 15 May, 2009, was given away at the remaining concerts of the *Viva La Vida* tour and made available free at the band's website.

The key to the success of the *Viva La Vida* campaign was Coldplay's consumer database, which grew dramatically through the giveaways. Previously it had been record stores that knew the customer. The Internet offered the possibility of getting closer to fans, but iTunes and Amazon kept their customer information to themselves. It was largely acts rather than record labels that forged closer ties with fans.

The most dramatic example of this was Radiohead's "pay what you want" *In Rainbows* campaign, mounted after EMI failed to agree new terms with the group. Other, smaller groups also sought to revive and extend their careers by building on their relationship with their fans. An earlier, innovative example of this was progressive rock band Marillion, also a one-time EMI group. Before it left EMI by mutual consent in 1995, the group had dabbled in fan sponsorship, raising via the Internet some $60,000 to fund a US tour. After a brief stay with Castle Records, accessing and energising the band's fanbase through the Internet became the new business model for Marillion.

In November 2000 Steve Hogarth, the band's lead singer, outlined their predicament to London's *Evening Standard*: "We'd come to the end of our record deal and there were various indie labels interested in us. But we didn't feel comfortable with any of them. We're a band with a big fanbase, but the problem is that, as a result, no-one has an incentive to market us. Record labels know they could spend a fiver on promoting our album and our fans would still go and buy it if they had to find it under a stone. And we knew what would happen if we signed to an indie label. They'd do nothing, sell the album to the fanbase and put the money in the bank."

As an alternative, the band decided to try the (then) radical experiment by asking fans to help fund the recording of a new album by pre-ordering it before recording even started. The result was over 12,000 pre-orders, which raised enough money to record and release *Anoraknophobia* in 2001, with "thank yous" to the fans who had pre-ordered the album printed on the booklet notes. EMI distributed the album but Marillion retain all the rights in the recording. Marillion worked their fanbase for subsequent releases with increasing degrees of sophistication, always granting the fans exclusive offers, such as a two-CD version of the 2004 album *Marbles* that was only available at the band's website. The culmination (to date) of this strategy was the release of *Happiness Is The Road* in October 2008. A double album, it once more featured a pre-order "deluxe edition" and a more straightforward regular release. In September, Marillion pre-released their album via P2P networks themselves. When they tried to play the downloaded files, users were shown a video from the band offering various options, to purchase the album at a user-defined price or receive selected DRM-free files for free, in exchange for an email address. In the video the band explained that they did not support piracy, but they realised that their music would inevitably be shared in this manner anyway, and wanted to engage with P2P users and make the best of a bad situation. This was probably one of the few examples of the monetisation of P2P networks, a dream that the majors indulged in regularly to little avail when a P2P network, shuttered by law, attempted to operate legitimately only to discover that it had lost its fanbase.

As the first decade of the 21st century moved on a website became de rigueur for acts, new and established, and particularly for vintage acts. Thus, for example, The Blues Band, which had evolved from Manfred Mann (and would regularly devolve back into Manfred Mann for touring purposes) had a website that alerted fans of its activities. In this, the band was just one of many finding a life outside a major or even small record company. Such a DIY strategy was embraced by the very successful (Eagles, Radiohead), to the modestly successful (where it leaned heavily on touring) and the barely successful (where it was a would-be door-opener to greater triumphs). The one party for whom it worked less well were (non-specialised) record companies. People largely bought U2 records not UMG records. There were moments when a record label had real charisma and appeal in itself – Motown in the 1960s and Island in the 1970s, for example – but largely it was artists that people believed in. Currently all record companies and their associated labels have websites that offer information about upcoming releases and suchlike. But they lack the oomph, enthusiasm and the possibility of personal contact that make artist websites, such as Marrillion's, so sticky.

In an attempt to rectify this, at the end of 2008 EMI set up EMI.com, a website offering audio and video content direct to consumers. Although the website competed with third-party services that sold content to consumers, such as iTunes and MySpace Music, EMI's primary motive was to discover how consumers behaved in the digital environment. The direct-to-consumer website gathered data on fans in order to improve EMI's talent acquisition policy and marketing and promotional services. The new website, which was given its own portal, rather than be part of the existing EMI corporate website, followed the appointments of Douglas Merrill, formerly of Google, to oversee EMI's digital operations, and of Cory Ondrejka, an executive associated with the virtual world and social networking website Second Life. The mantra at EMI was "the consumer is king". Such appointments, like that of Elio Leoni-Sceti, were proof of Hands' desire to hire executives from a range of consumer oriented industries, as opposed to music industry specialists. The experiment, bold or not, failed. All three executives left EMI after a short stay in which their restructurings were little more than new letterheads on EMI's stationery. Similarly the EMI.com website, which was roundly condemned as clunky beyond belief, was short-lived.

Nonetheless, the would-be new EMI continued to see the way forward as requiring a radically different type of record company whose future revenue streams would be dramatically different in the future, with the value of physical sales falling by almost half between 2009 and 2013 (*see table below*).

EMI Music revenues by segment as a percentage of total revenues predicted in 2009 and 2013 (%)

	2009	*2013*	*% change*
Physical sales	65	39	−40
Digital sales	20	30	+50
Neighbouring rights	6	8	+33
Non-recorded revenues	1	10	+900
Synch, licensing and brand partnerships	8	13	+62

Source: company accounts

In support of this transition of the company's revenue mix away from physical sales, which EMI predicted would account for less than half of EMI Music's sales in 2013, the company pointed to a variety of new ways of consuming recorded music, from "singing" T-shirts and toothbrushes, to video games such as *Guitar Hero*. EMI Music's prediction of its neighbouring rights revenue growth was realistic. However, whereas the cost of collecting those revenues was low, because an existing infrastructure is largely in place, the costs of collecting brand royalties and artist's royalties from touring and merchandising are considerably higher. And even The Beatles couldn't guarantee success. *The Beatles: Rock Band* garnered huge publicity on release in 2009 alongside new, re-mastered compact disc versions of The Beatles' albums. With the Support of Apple, The Beatles and EMI, *The Beatles: Rock Band* sold more than half a million units in a month in the US, but sales slowed down considerably as game players lost interest in the rhythm game genre. In truth, in contrast to the other majors, EMI invested little in outside activities and while Hands and his team talked much of transforming EMI, when it finally slipped from Hands' grasp it was little different from when he bought it.

But it was more successful, on the surface at least, as the table below shows.

EMI: Revenues and Operating Profits, 2008–2010

	2008–2009 Value (£m)	% change	2009–2010 Value (£m)	2009–2010 Value ($m)	% change
EMI Group					
Revenues	1,569	+7.6	1,651	2,578.7	+5.2
Operating profits	293	+78.7	334	521.9	+14.0
EMI Music					
Revenues	1,101	+4.0	1,173	1,832.8	+6.5
Operating profits	160	+220.0	184	287.5	+15.0
EMI Music Publishing					
Revenues	468	n/a	478	746.9	+2.1
Operating profits	133	+19.0	150	234.4	+12.8

Source: Maltby Capital

These results represented a considerable recovery since EMI's years of losses and profit warnings. However, Guy Hands didn't benefit from EMI's success: he lost £1.75bn of his investors' money, and £200m of his own.

The reason for this lay in the (mis)timing of Terra Firma's purchase of EMI, which landed EMI with an unsupportable debt burden. The £4.2bn ($6.6bn) deal was the last big European buy-out to be completed before the credit crunch that heralded the start of the global financial crisis. Later, in 2010, Guy Hands wryly noted that his private equity group would have "looked liked geniuses" had it not bought EMI Group. The deal was concluded in August 2007, a few weeks before Lehman Brothers went under, unleashing the credit crunch, which made raising money for acquisitions much more difficult. The crisis in global credit markets left Citigroup with the difficult problem of disposing of some $43bn of leveraged-buyout loans. Not included in the attempted disposal was the $4bn provided for the purchase of EMI. That debt was not considered marketable due to continuing investor anxiety over EMI's future.

When the Bronfman consortium bought WMG in 2003 for $2.6bn, the general consensus was that the upsurge in digital sales and a new management might, even could, transform the fortunes of WMG. With this in mind, the consortium moved quickly to restructure: they bought on a Monday, announced a cost-cutting plan on a Tuesday and within a month claimed a reduction of $250m in annualised costs. Such optimism quickly evaporated, leading to a collapse in the share price of WMG. It went from $17 when Bronfman took the company public to around $27 at its height, but then quickly fell to below $10 before it eventually settled at $7 when the company was sold in 2011. However, the optimistic atmosphere continued long enough for debt incurred by the lead investors to be sold on. In contrast, Citigroup's failure to sell on its debt meant that instead of a myriad of small investors EMI had one large, very powerful and anxious investor that would be very active in overseeing the investment debt.

Once the smell of crisis arrived Citigroup started to take a decidedly cautious approach to its investment. Even before the transaction closed, it had tightened the terms of its £2.5bn loan. Citigroup set in place separate quarterly covenants on EMI's recorded music and music publishing divisions, requiring of them a specified level of performance relative to the company's overall debt to be able to cover the interest payments on the loan. If these covenants were not met, Citigroup had the option of taking control of EMI, which set in motion a growing hostility between lender and borrower that eventually turned into the farce of the lawsuit raised by Guy Hands.

In the period September 2008 to June 2009, EMI's music division failed three covenant tests while EMI Music Publishing passed the tests each time. The failures required Terra Firma to top up its investment in EMI. Thus, in March 2009, Terra Firma invested a further £28m ($47.2m) into EMI to prevent it from breaching debt covenants.

Separately, in 2009, Terra Firma wrote down the value of its investment in EMI by 90%. This followed an earlier writedown of half of its investments, primarily EMI, on the grounds of a permanent impairment in [their] "value". In early 2009 Citigroup rejected Terra Firma's offer to inject £300m ($506m) into EMI if it would reduce its debt by a similar amount. In November, it rejected a similar offering involving the sum of £1bn ($1.69bn) in EMI in exchange for Citigroup foregoing a similar proportion of its £2.5bn ($4bn) loan to Terra Firma. Citigroup explained its position simply, noting that by writing off the debt, it would reduce its share in the company if EMI became profitable.

Terra Firma's response to this rebuff was to seek outside investment. In the course of 2009 it approached pension funds, insurance companies and foreign banks seeking fresh investment to ensure that EMI would not default on interest repayments to Citigroup. When these failed, in December, in what was widely seen as an act of desperation, Guy Hands sued Citigroup, seeking £1.5bn ($2.14bn). His suit alleged that Citigroup committed fraud in the course of Terra Firma's purchase of EMI by making various specific misrepresentations at crucial points in the takeover negotiations. The central allegation was that Citigroup had lied about whether or not there were other bidders for EMI. At the same time, Terra Firma approached the 159 investors in its Terra Firma Capital Partners III fund asking them to invest a further £105m ($162m) to enable it to meet its forthcoming covenant agreements with Citigroup. To satisfy the investors that they would not be pouring good money away, Terra Firma demanded that EMI put together a new business plan focused on immediate savings. Terra Firma raised the money in May 2010 with just over 75% of investors voting in favour.

Terra Firma promised investors, who had seen the value of their original stakes written down by 90%, that they would see a recovery in EMI's fortunes. It added that it was investing a further £58m ($89m) and presented a new business plan from Charles Allen, who had just been parachuted in to replace Elio Leoni-Sceti as the new executive chairman of the group's recorded music division. The Allen plan offered more job cuts, possible asset sales and further attempts at outsourcing. Extraordinarily, it promised investors a 58% return on any money they put into EMI, raising the question of how EMI could suddenly change gear and outperform the market. In late April EMI made a U-turn, withdrawing that offer in favour of simply seeking $105m ($162m) from its original investors and raising extra money through asset sales and/or licensing agreements as per the Allen plan.

Terra Firma gained the necessary agreement of 75% of its investors for its rescue plan. However, according to *The Times*, one of Terra Firma's 200 plus investors said that he was not in favour of injecting new money into the project, while an adviser to another investor was reported as saying: "It took us 45 minutes to find flaws in the EMI business plan. From a financial perspective this is a no-brainer. You walk away."

Terra Firma's fundraising success was only a temporary solution: The company faced similar payments later in 2010 and in 2011 and the new funding arrangements only gave Terra Firma until the end of March 2011 to put in place a turnaround plan for EMI. A Citigroup spokesperson compounded the difficulties facing EMI when he made it brutally clear what would happen if Terra Firma had defaulted and what lay in store in the event of any future defaults: "After 14th of June, we don't want to be landed with this for more than a week, we want a quick sale." At the same time, Citigroup started to become proactive. It appointed a restructuring adviser in case it had to take control of EMI and instructed PricewaterhouseCoopers to act as the administrator of EMI in the unlikely event that Citigroup decided to take control by putting the company into administration.

Terra Firma's approach to EMI from 2010 onwards was one of damage limitation. There was no more planning for the future. According to press reports, one significant investor said that he and others were unsure as to whether to put more money in "unless we are well informed about the likely outcome of the legal case", while a second noted that since the lawsuit against Citigroup had been raised he had only received "limited" information from Terra Firma about how things stood. A further problem for Terra Firma was that the £105m only gave it breathing space – future covenants were looming large and in 2014 the entire debt was due.

As if in preparation for this, in 2008, Terra Firma had started to look at a number of opportunities to reduce its financial outgoings. These included minor matters, such as the cost of its membership of IFPI, which was a general concern of the majors (*see* Chapter 14), and larger problems, specific to EMI, such as its pension commitments, which it challenged to no avail. When Terra Firma bought EMI in 2007, it immediately sought to reduce the company's pension responsibilities, leading to a dispute in which the chairman of the EMI pension trustees was removed by Terra Firma and the trustees appealed to the Pensions Regulator. According to an analysis carried out for *The Sunday Times* by Lane Clark & Peacock (LC&P), by 2010 the pension deficit had since grown to £250m ($384m). The Pension Regulator ruled that EMI had to make more money available to cover EMI's pension deficit, money that came from post-tax profits and, as such, was at the expense of the investors.

At the same time, Terra Firma started to significantly reduce its managerial involvement in the company. It had seconded some 40 of its executives to EMI after the takeover. After Hands stepped away from day-to-day control of the music division in late 2009, the company withdrew some 10 of its executives who had been sent in to help run EMI on a day-to-day basis.

Then in 2010, following the resignation of Elio Leoni-Sceti and a further tranche of Terra Firma appointed-in executives, as the financial situation grew increasingly desperate, Terra Firma threw caution to the wind, attempting the sell-off of Abbey Road studios, to huge public outcry, and the much more significant move to license EMI's repertoire to another major in North America. However, the talks, which were most advanced with SME and UMG, foundered on pressures of time – EMI's need for funds was immediate – and were further hampered by the rather more compelling matter that any licensing arrangement would have to be approved by Citigroup, whose long-term interests were clearly different to those of Terra Firma and EMI's shareholders. A further problem was quite what EMI would bring to the table. Would back catalogue superstars, such as The Beatles, want split representation around the world? Would big stars want other companies to know the full details of their EMI contracts, considering they might want to move? Furthermore, closing down its North American operations would represent a significant diminution of EMI's stature, a cost hard to evaluate but a serious one. Add the retreat from Japan and/or Latin America to this and, EMI RM would in effect be reduced to a "large indie" only active in Europe.

In an October 2009 memo to Hands, Leoni-Sceti had said that uncertainty about EMI's stability had caused the company to lose distribution deals that would have generated income of $13m a year. In an interview with UK trade paper *Music Week*, he added that "Not only are artists and artists' managers raising concerns but morale within the company has reached a low point." At the same time EMI was haemorrhaging back catalogue acts.

In June 2010, Maltby announced a new structure for EMI with former head of EMI MP Roger Faxon appointed CEO of both its recorded music and music publishing divisions. At the same time EMI, now calling itself "a comprehensive global music rights company", reported revenue and EBITA growth for both of its divisions in the year to March 31. EMI Music had increased sales by 6.5% to £1.2bn ($1.8bn) and profits by 15% to £184m ($288m) and EMI MP revenues increased by 2.1% to £478m ($747m). Leoni-Sceti and (very briefly) Charles Allen on their appointment had announced new executive hirings and corporate restructurings in order to point EMI to the future, through a closer relationship with consumers, renewed emphasis on back catalogue and so forth. No such moves were made by Faxon, who did not seek to re-build EMI in his image, even though he had (theoretically) far greater control over the group than any of his predecessors. EMI's owners were not taking the long view, seeking to transform the debt-laden company into a profit machine; they were merely preparing it for a sale. Such a sale was widely consigned to the category of disaster merchandise.

But despite all indicators to the contrary, EMI was still getting hits. Its market share was static but its margins were rising. Take away the debts and EMI was in profit. Cost and job-cutting, restructuring, trying to making the consumer king and talking the talk of a "new" music company had done nothing, hadn't turned EMI round, but the hits — and from new acts — were there. EMI Music was in the curious position of generating more hit records while still unable to meet its debts. There was a growing sense that, whatever the current market conditions were, intellectual property was still very valuable.

A new killer business plan might be just around the corner. But who was to benefit from this possible renaissance?

And so we come to the lawsuit, a last-ditch attempt by Hands to conjure profitability out of imminent disaster. For Guy Hands (and Terra Firma, whose public face he was) the lawsuit he brought against Citigroup shattered old friendships and exposed best-kept-hidden financial practices. From the start the risks were incredibly high, with investors and commentators alike saying that the "adverse publicity" of a court hearing, as Hands despairingly put it, would wreck any attempt to rescue and or/retain control of EMI.

Hands accused Citigroup of tricking Terra Firma into buying EMI at an inflated price. The wealth of data and views in the filings of both sides added a little to the picture of Terra Firma and Citigroup's fading relationship. One intriguing detail was that in November 2009 Citigroup rejected a proposal by Terra Firma that it would invest a further £1bn ($1.69bn) in EMI in exchange for Citigroup foregoing a similar proportion of its £2.4bn loan to Terra Firma. It turned out that the proposal was far more complex than previously known, including on Terra Firma's behalf, "a complete restructuring of EMI" in which EMI Music and EMI Music Publishing (EMI MP) would be separated, thus saving EMI MP from slipping into Citigroup's hands if EMI Music defaulted on its covenants". More enlightening was that Hands valued EMI Music at less than £800m ($1.25bn) and EMI MP at £1.46bn ($2.28bn). This combined value was widely accepted as the starting price for the sale of EMI when Citigroup finally brought it to market in 2011.

But maybe Terra Firma, flush with punitive damages, if it won the case, wouldn't need Citigroup and could bring a revived EMI to the marketplace, transforming a disastrous deal into a profitable one. The lawsuit was in effect the traditional one of "you're a liar; no you are" with a few technical issues. To Hands' chagrin, the court hearing, which inspired many headlines and was covered in some depth, was decided on minor details – who remembered what – rather than on the grand issues he attempted to raise.

Hands launched the court case in December 2009. The lawsuit was a highly personal affair, setting Hands and Citigroup's David Wormsley, a long-time family friend and financial advisor, in direct conflict. The financial stakes were high for both parties. According to Hands some 70% of his personal wealth was tied up in the Terra Firma-EMI deal. Separately, Terra Firma reported that EMI's problems were largely responsible for the 43% fall in the venture capital firm's profits for the year ending March 1, 2009 to $1.9m ($3.4m) and that in protest at increases in UK capital gains tax and income tax in the UK, Terra Firma and Guy Hands were to move from London to Guernsey in the Channel Islands. The portents were hardly any better for Hands' reputation. To be "persuaded" to bid by an advisor to the seller, as Hands claimed, hardly suggests good business sense. Writing in the *Daily Telegraph* about the case, Tracy Corrigan made that point abundantly clear: "It is the job of a smart buyer not to overpay, whether or not bigger idiots are said to be lurking in the wings."

Citigroup was hardly in a better position. One of the four largest banks in the US, it suffered huge losses during the global financial crisis of 2008 and had to be rescued in November with a massive bailout from the US government, which took a 27% stake in the bank. Although the bank subsequently returned to profit the lawsuit meant that those practices which many alleged had helped bring about the crisis of 2008 would be aired. The legalities of the situation aside, offering advice to both seller and buyer and loaning money to the buyer – in court it was revealed that a jubilant Citigroup executive said of the deal "And we got paid on the buyside as well as the sellside!" – looked bad to outside observers. In addition, a loss in court, even if overturned on appeal, would likely open the floodgates to other former clients seeking redress from deals made in the run-up to the financial crisis that subsequently turned sour.

The first battle was about location. Terra Firma wanted the case to be held in New York, where damages, if awarded, were likely to be higher. Citigroup argued unsuccessfully for the hearing to be in the UK. After settlement talks failed, despite a late attempt by Citigroup to have the suit thrown out, a trial date was set for October 18.

Just before the commencement of the lawsuit EMI secured a last-minute settlement in its negotiations with its pension fund trustees that avoided an expected hearing before the UK's Pensions Regulator's determinations panel. EMI agreed to put £197m ($274.8m) into the EMI Group Pension Fund between then and April 2016, including an immediate £16m ($22.3m). While the settlement further increased EMI's debts, it saved EMI the embarrassment of a determinations panel hearing. However, when Citigroup came to sell EMI, its pension responsibilities, which would be borne either by the EMI Group if EMI was sold as a whole or by EMI Music if the company was sold in pieces were, along with the difficulty of raising credit, one reason that the prices offered by the various interested parties fell dramatically in the bidding process.

And so the lawsuit commenced. Terra Firma alleged that Citigroup tricked it into buying EMI at an inflated price in 2007 and that as part of this trickery David Wormsley, the head of Citigroup's UK investment banking business, lied. Terra Firma also argued that while previously it was relatively common for a bank to act as advisor to both seller and potential buyer of a property and provide the finance to the buyer, such a procedure was outmoded in the post-2008 economic climate. Citigroup responded by arguing that such a change in view had no legal implications, a view the court accepted. The presiding judge, Jed Rakoff, had significant experience in white collar business fallouts. He rejected the idea that this case was of great legal interest. When the jury was out of the courtroom, he noted that some press accounts suggested the case, which involved arcane Wall Street banking procedures, might be too technical for the jury to follow. He rejected this, saying that such cases as this one often came down to "credibility contests" between the plaintiff and defendant, which jurors could usually judge well enough for themselves.

Thus, the case came down to whether one believed Hands or Wormsley, or whether both might prefer the refuge of a darkened room to settle their differences in private. Having found an out-of-court settlement impossible, Hands' erratic memory proved to be his downfall. Citigroup's evidence was that Hands made no complaint to David Wormsley, even after he received an email in September 2007 from a senior director at Terra Firma indicating that Cerberus Capital, at the time perceived as Terra Firma's competitor for EMI, had not placed a bid for the company. Indeed, according to Citigroup, Hands and Wormsley socialised – going to the opera with their wives, for example – during a period when Hands apparently knew about the alleged fraud – while Hands mandated Wormsley to work on several deals for Terra Firma in the 18 months following the EMI purchase. The Citigroup defence was that Hands' decision to sue Citigroup for fraud was a retaliatory move following the bank's refusal in November 2009 to write off some of EMI's debts in return for Terra Firma injecting further capital.

In response Hands alleged that he only agreed to pay 265p (420¢) a share for EMI because Wormsley claimed another bidder, Cerberus Capital, was in the running and that he only realised this wasn't the case after a lengthy internal Terra Firma investigation that didn't start until 2008 or 2009. Hands, who testified over the course of four days, claimed that Wormsley lied to him during phone calls made the weekend before the auction, leading the private equity firm to overbid in a deal that lost money for all involved. Hands further argued that if he had known that Terra Firma was alone in the bidding, he wouldn't have submitted a bid. Instead, he told jurors, he would have tried to negotiate with EMI for a lower price and for more time to evaluate the company.

In his evidence, Wormsley said that his role was limited to helping arrange the financing of the EMI acquisition and that he wasn't part of another Citigroup team that acted as advisers to EMI in the bidding. This was rejected by Terra Firma, which cited a series of telephone calls at the time of the purchase in May 2007 in the course of which, it alleged, Wormsley made false statements that led Terra Firma to conclude the purchase.

The to-ing and fro-ing lasted a little over two weeks before on November 4, the jury reached its 8–0 verdict after less than a day of deliberations. In his summing up, District Judge Rakoff, who had earlier narrowed the range of possible real damages to $2.2bn from the $8.3bn requested by Terra Firma and ruled out punitive damages, called the suit "a catfight between two rich companies".

On news of the verdict Claire Enders, of Enders Analysis Ltd., predicted that "It's just a question of time before there's a covenant breach… I find it hard to believe that the Terra Firma partners are really going to face with equanimity the prospect of injecting capital into EMI, basically forever." In contrast Roger Faxon, EMI's newest CEO, said that the verdict case would have no impact on EMI. In a leaked memo to EMI staff he was Mr Optimism:

After more than sixteen years of working for EMI, I've become well used to the speculation that follows every single move that this company makes. Whether we're buying, selling, signing or dropping, EMI is never far from the headlines, as you will all have seen this weekend.

But like the sports star whose imminent transfer or trade occupies the back pages of the newspapers for weeks on end, most speculation contains only the smallest grain of truth. So while most people managed to correctly assert that Citigroup won the court case with Terra Firma, the tales of doom and destruction for EMI that followed had as much credibility as the idea that I might be the answer to the Yankees' pitching problems or Manchester United's defensive woes.

I know it's difficult not to be affected by these stories. So, I thought it would be worth me taking a look at some of the myths that have been bandied about over the last few days, and tell you why you should believe them as little as I do:

EMI WILL GO INTO CHAPTER 11 IF IT FAILS ITS COVENANTS!!

I'm sure that makes good copy, but it's more fairy tale than actual journalism. For a start, EMI is a British company and there's no such thing as Chapter 11 in the UK. And as our most recent results make very clear, EMI is easily meeting all its debt obligations, and paying all its bills, with room to spare. That's more than can be said about most of our competitors, and not the mark of a company that's in danger of going into any form of bankruptcy.

EMI TO SELL OUT TO ONE OF ITS RIVALS!!!

I don't know if you've looked at any of our competitors recently, but none of them are having a particularly easy time of it. As a result, their corporate structures absolutely are not geared up right now to stomach the financial demands of attempting to take over another big company. And that's before you even think about the regulatory issues that would almost certainly kick in if any one of the majors bid for one of their rivals. And having been involved [in] the doomed merger of EMI and Warner Music in 2000, I can tell you there is no easy route through those issues.

EMI TO SELL OFF CATALOG ASSETS TO STAVE OFF FINANCIAL RUIN!!!!

I think this is one of my favorite rumors, because not only is it completely untrue, but it's utterly idiotic into the bargain. Anyone can make a bit of money by selling off a piece of catalog here and there. But all that does is lower the value of the rest of the business. You might make a quick buck, but you're left with a company that is suddenly weaker than it was before. And nobody at EMI is interested in that. We're here to create long-term value 'for the artists and writers we represent, for our financial stakeholders, and for each other. And that's what we're going to do.

EMI TO BE BROKEN IN TWO IN SELL OFF SHOCK!!!!!

Let me just put this one to bed once and for all. Both Citi and Terra Firma understand that the best way to build value is for EMI to remain as one company. As was clear from the trial documents splitting the company up was looked along the way. But it went away because it simply would not work. Our Global Rights Management strategy, is not only the best way for EMI to create the maximum possible value for our artists and writers, but the best way to achieve the best possible value for the company overall. To be clear, the global rights management strategy for growth can only be pursued if the company is kept together. And so it will be.

So, there's a few myths firmly laid to rest. If you spot any more crazy headlines, don't hesitate to send them my way.

As I said to you all on Friday, let's focus on doing what it takes to be the best we can be. We have a great opportunity ahead of us here to build a thoroughly modern and vibrant company. Let's not let uninformed headlines or press chatter get in the way of us pursuing that goal.

"Roger."

A day later WMG was reported to be preparing a bid for EMI's record division, its shares rising by a little over 7% on the news. Then on February 1, 2011, Enders' prediction came to pass: Citigroup announced that it had taken ownership of EMI because EMI was insolvent and would be unable to make its covenant payments to Citigroup in March. In a remarkably speedy move, PricewaterhouseCoopers was appointed as the administrator to Maltby Investments Limited and instantly sold EMI and its holding company Maltby Acquisitions Limited to Citigroup, which in turn immediately effected a debt-for-equity swap to recapitalise EMI. The company's debt was reduced by 65% from £3.4bn to £1.2bn and it had in excess of £300m of cash available. Citigroup further announced that EMI's management team would remain unchanged, with Roger Faxon as the group's CEO.

Ever optimistic, Faxon asserted that "The recapitalization of EMI by Citi is an extremely positive step for the company. It has given us one of the most robust balance sheets in the industry with a modest level of debt and substantial liquidity. With that solid footing, we are confident in our ability to drive our business forward. We have already made great progress in meeting the challenges facing our industry. The closer alliance between our two operating divisions is already delivering impressive results on behalf of the creative talent we are privileged to represent. We have a clear vision for the future, a strong and committed management team, and now the right capital and financial structure in place to deliver successful outcomes for artists and songwriters."

At the same time, while repeating the one company mantra, Faxon accepted that Citigroup's sale of EMI was inevitable. And so began the rush to market of WMG and EMI, while UMG and SME concluded their complex game of musical chairs, all the time pondering which bits of WMG or EMI to pounce on.

Chapter 16

Hopes For The Future, Legislation And New Business Plans

The most dramatic events of recent years for the record industry had been the selling of EMI and WMG. The sale of EMI garnered more headlines – The Beatles for sale! – but the sale of WMG also made the mainstream news with its tale of yet another Russian oligarch buying into the American Dream. These were the big news stories, regularly appearing in the front pages of the world's newspapers as well as in the financial sections. They told of the struggle by majors to cut their costs through consolidation and of venture capitalists seeking access to new and as yet fully monetised assets. But these public tussles, for market share, for unrealised assets, and new opportunities, were only part of the restructurings of the record industry in the first decade of the new century. With far less public attention, the majors, by now aware that the digital revolution was a fact, that a paradigm shift had taken place, that past certainties no longer held true and that the growth of digital at the expense of physical sales had spectacularly reduced their revenues, started to seek new revenues sources with renewed enthusiasm and/or desperation. These searches involved a wide range of activities, 360-degree deals, (failed) negotiations with the former illegal P2P networks, such as Kazaa and Grokster, to set up legitimate licence paying versions of their pasts and licensing new ventures, such as Vevo and Spotify, which promised new revenue streams.

Piracy, as ever, remained a pressing problem for the record industry at the turn of the century, but it was also a useful calling card in a world where intellectual property had become a central element of international trade. The majors (and other content creators, such as film companies) found it easier to get a positive response from governments and the world's trade organisations when they suggested the protection of their rights should be part of treaty negotiations.

Previously, from the record industry perspective, a country's transition from being underdeveloped, to developing and then finally to being developed was accompanied by the shift from a cassette and piracy-dominated industry to a primarily legitimate industry with some CDs and then finally to a CD-dominated market with some piracy. The digital revolution transformed that process, making it possible for a country to move from a vinyl/cassette market to an online one in one move. This introduced a new level of piracy, with product aimed at both an international and national market. Moreover, the BRIC nations (Brazil, Russia, India and China) were economically vibrant – India had a space programme; Russia, oil and gas and Brazil and China were growing, while the Western economies were in recession. They were real markets and piracy (as much as bureaucracy) was seen as preventing their full exploitation. That piracy mostly concerned intellectual property aroused the interests of those bodies administering world trade, notably the World Trade Organization (WTO) and those interested in creating new trade agreements, such as the Ant-Counterfeiting Trade Agreement (ACTA), in a far more energetic manner than previously.

For the record industry this meant that it had serious levels of support in the battles it fought in Russia (with AllofMP3) and in China (with Baidu). In the 2000s Russian online music retailer AllofMP3.com had exploited contentious aspects of Russian copyright law (since changed) to sell low-priced digital music downloads. It offered a huge catalogue of recordings, including albums and individual tracks by The Beatles, which at that time hadn't licensed their recordings for online sale, for a fraction of the cost of tracks at Apple's iTunes store or other online music stores. AllofMP3 set its prices according to the size of the file to be downloaded. Full albums were available at around a $1, the cost of a single track on iTunes. Tracks from the Red Hot Chili Peppers' double album, *Stadium Arcadium*, cost between 10¢ and 16¢, while the latest hit album could be bought for just $1.40. Until 2006, AllofMP3.com appeared to be immune from prosecution under local copyright laws. In March 2005, the Moscow Southwest regional prosecutor's office ruled AllofMP3.com could not be indicted under Russian criminal law because it did not distribute physical goods. Separately the Russian courts accepted the claim of Media Services, the owner of AllofMP3.com, that it had licences from the Russian Multimedia and Internet rights society ROMS. When ROMS persisted in offering Media Services this defence, international association of authors' societies CISAC expelled ROMS in October 2004 for "issuing licenses to copyright users without the authority to do so from all relevant copyright owners" further noting that these actions "contravened internationally accepted collective administration principles, to the detriment of the creative community represented by CISAC".

What brought about the demise of AllofMP3.com was that it became an impediment to Russia's long-stated desire to join the WTO. In the course of the negotiations in 2006, the United States Trade Representative (USTR) Susan Schwab told the Russians, "The US is seriously concerned about the growth of Internet piracy on Russian websites … Russia's legal framework for intellectual property rights protection must meet WTO requirements … In that context, we continue to call on Russia to shut down websites that offer pirate music, software and films for downloading." Schwab specifically singled out AllofMP3.com as a prime example of rampant piracy and demanded that it be shut down, calling the website "a poster child for illegal music sales over the Internet". In response Russian Trade Minister Gref said that Russia could conclude its bilateral talks with the US on Russia's WTO accession, which it has been seeking for 13 years, within two weeks, noting that, "In principle we have agreed with the US on all questions connected with intellectual property rights and that other key disagreements were also close to being settled. Finally in 2012, Russia, which previously only had observer status, was granted full membership of the WTO.

A further blow for AllofMP3.com was the withdrawal of support by both the Visa and MasterCard credit card companies. That dramatically reduced the revenues of the company, which in 2005 were around $30m, from international users. The problems represented by AllofMP3.com, which faded away rather than went away completely, were in part a reflection of the difficulties of bringing online rights into the sphere of copyright without limiting the rights of users. These ongoing problems were particularly powerful in Russia where there was hostility towards foreign companies seeking reforms that were in their favour but that hindered the development of local businesses.

To some extent the Russian online market has opened up. At the time of writing there are at least 11 legitimately licensed online music services in operation in Russia, albeit no iTunes or Amazon MP3. Separately, led by SME the majors have expanded their presence there. Now a wide range of international repertoire can be downloaded legitimately in Russia. The result has been a period of online growth. Between 2006 and 2010 the value of digital sales rocketed by 3,400%, from $1m to $35m. This despite the fact that in the same period the trade value of physical sales fell by 63%, from $187m to $69m.

The situation facing foreign record companies in China was even more problematic. Over the period 2006–2010, the value of physical sales in China fell 71% from $55.5m to $16.2m, while digital sales grew, by 62%, from $31.5m to £58.1m. But it was not the majors who benefitted from this digital growth. It was another Apple. The online company Baidu was established in 2000 and offered a wealth of services, including the most frequented Chinese language search engine for websites, audio files and images. In 2010, it was estimated that there were 4.02bn search queries in China of which Baidu had a market share of 57%. On the back of this, Baidu's revenues grew from $122m in 2000 to $1.2bn in 2010.

One-click links to unauthorised free music download links via its search engine meant that international music and film companies were unable to benefit from their rights, while Baidu received revenues from the 53,000 companies – many of which were international businesses – whose advertisements ran alongside those searches. These links accounted for over a third of traffic on the search engine and led to two sets of lawsuits brought by IFPI on behalf of foreign record companies in China, both of which failed.

In 2008, Baidu was back in the news, facing new legal challenges, this time from Chinese companies using the country's new anti-monopoly law. These followed an exposé of Baidu's business model commissioned by state broadcaster CCTV, which showed that unlike most search engines, Baidu mixed disguised and very lucrative sponsored links with "genuine" search results, without making the sponsored links clearly evident. The CCTV programme showed that Baidu's customers could bid for search keywords with the link to the highest bidder's website appearing at the top of the search results and that the fees generated from these auctions accounted for almost all of Baidu's revenues as opposed to the conventional advertising revenue its competitors rely upon. The CCTV programme followed detailed research by online publication *The Register*, which revealed that Baidu was closely implicated in the "deep links" it provided to websites that hosted unauthorised copies of recorded music tracks. *The Register* also noted that when Baidu complied with a take-down notice directing users to a specific website, the material in question was moved to another website to which Baidu provided a new deep link.

After the failure of its lawsuits, IFPI, accepting that Baidu's dominance of the search market in China made it a valuable would-be partner, attempted negotiation. When those talks failed, in January 2009, three majors, Sony BMG, UMG and WMG, sued Baidu in the Beijing No.1 Intermediate People's Court for copyright infringement, seeking damages of Rmb0.5m ($71,000) per infringing track which represents a total claim of Rmb63.5m ($9m). The court was also asked to order Baidu to remove all links to files containing tracks owned by the companies. In April the court agreed to hear the claim for damages brought by the majors. The claim, which IFPI describes as a test case, was expected to expose Baidu to a multi-billion dollar liability.

However, when the case finally came to court, in 2010, Baidu was found not guilty of piracy. In a parallel case, another website, Sohu, was also found not guilty of copyright infringement. The court ruled that providing search results does not break copyright law. The decision was a setback in the attempts by the Music Copyright Society of China and the China Audio-Video Copyright Association, to raise the profile of the legitimate online music market in the country.

Despite these defeats in the courts, the government later took action to end online music piracy in China. In July 2010, over 20 music websites were shut down. This followed a ruling on July 9 by China's Ministry of Culture to the effect that, after preliminary investigations, 68 listed online music sites were operating without authorisation and as such were in violation of the *Provisional Regulations on Administration of Internet Culture* and other relevant laws and regulations. The Ministry of Culture subsequently tightened the regulations concerning online music providers, only granting operating licences to websites that agree not to distribute pirated music files. This was followed by a nationwide campaign against Internet piracy focusing on piracy of popular movies and TV series, newly published books, online games, music comics and animation, music, computer programs and other products under copyright protection. US government officials were especially active in pressurising the Chinese authorities for better enforcement, with Victoria Espinel, an intellectual property official in the Obama administration, stating that "China is the biggest problem that we face" in the theft of US music, films, pharmaceuticals and other goods, and "due to the scale and scope of manufacturing, its industrial policies and its potential as an export market, it's fair to say that China raises a particularly troubling set of issues".

The piracy problems facing record (and other) companies in China and Russia look to be on the way to being solved. However, it's difficult to see the majors significantly expanding their activities in China and Russia (or Brazil and India), places where local repertoire dominates and a new breed of nimble local entrepreneurs have forged media businesses in which music is but a part. When piracy was seen as an international issue that impacted on a wide range of rights holders, including computer software and film companies as well as record companies, the music industry could rely on governmental support. Piracy as a domestic matter is a more difficult nut to crack. Even with governmental support the struggle is mostly against ISPs, the gateways to unauthorised material and the delivery system to the computers of copyright infringers, companies that have the ear of government and deep pockets when it comes to publicity campaigns.

In a number of countries, including France, New Zealand, Sweden and the UK, there have been attempts to establish agreements between ISPs and rights holders, voluntarily or by law, under which, after an educative process followed by warnings, users would have their Internet connection terminated or severely limited if they continued to download unauthorised material. In every case the arguments of rights holders have been strongly resisted, largely on the grounds that the right of access to the Internet outweighs the infringements of the rights of a minor set of copyright owners and that it is not the job of ISPs to police the activities of their users. The debates concerning the establishing of HADOPI legislation in France show this rather well.

HADOPI (*Haute Autorité pour la diffusion des œuvres et la protection des droits sur internet*) had its origins in a landmark Memorandum of Understanding (MOU) concluded in November 2007 between French music and film copyright owners and the government. As part of the accord, which was hailed by IFPI as "the single most important initiative to help win the war on online piracy that we have seen so far", the French government agreed to establish an independent enforcement body, HADOPI, to operate a system of warnings leading to the suspension or termination of Internet subscriptions used for illegal file-sharing. The *Création et Internet* law established the HADOPI authority, enshrined the "three strike" concept and brought the termination of a user's Internet connection for copyright infringement, long lobbied for by rights holders, closer to reality, in France at least. In return the owners of French music copyrights agreed to make their entire repertoire available for sale online without DRM. French ISPs thus became the first to agree to a legally binding partnership with the music and film industries to filter and isolate potential copyright violations that might be made by their users.

The *Création et Internet* law benefitted from the receptivity of successive French governments to arguments about the preservation of national culture. Previously, the government had acceded to the music industry's call for a broadcast quota for French repertoire on condition that record companies (both local independents and the local branches of international firms) increased their rosters of new French acts. Now, at its signing, French president Nicolas Sarkozy described the new law as both "underlining my attachment to culture and my wish to see artists live from their work and have their rights respected on new platforms".

Nonetheless, passing the *Création et Internet* law and then its implementation proved far harder than expected. *UFC-Que Choisir*, the French consumer association, attacked the plans as "very harsh, potentially repressive, anti-economic and against the grain of the digital age", adding that illegal downloading was already punishable by a prison term of up to three years. Even members of President Sarkozy's UMP party deplored the proposal to confer judicial powers on an enforcement agency, saying the move "creates a truly exceptional jurisdiction for downloaders, contravening the principle of equality before the law".

After a series of mishaps – the parliamentary debates lasted for two years – *Création et Internet* was finally passed in 2009. The cost of its passing was the government's acceptance of several amendments, the most significant of which required that a judge would have to agree any termination of Internet access by the HADOPI authority.

Once the law enacted, technical problems quickly came to the fore. A search engine was established by the HADOPI authority for rights holders to track file-sharing. However, the search engine only carried a limited number of titles – as few as 10,000 film, game and music titles. Accordingly, from the start it was highly unlikely that copyright infringers who avoided sharing classic tracks and big hits in favour of jazz, folk, blues and classical music would be detected by the HADOPI search engine. Another problem was that once a rights holder identified a transaction involving the sharing of a track without authorisation, to initiate the HADOPI process that rights holder was required to send the information to HADOPI. However, he/she was not allowed to keep the information on file and as such was unable to point HADOPI towards serial copyright infringers. This was a serious limitation of the ability of a rights holder to administer (and in this case police) their rights.

There were other problems, some simply embarrassing but others that suggested the central thrust behind HADOPI was flawed. When HADOPI's agency logo was presented to the public by the Minister of Culture and Communication, observers noted that the logo used an unlicensed font, one created for and owned by France Télécom. The design agency that created the logo, Plan Créatif, admitted getting the font from a pirate site and using it without authorisation. The logo was redone with another font. Then Jean-François Copé, the leader in the National Assembly of the Union for a Popular Movement (UMP), had a change of heart and announced that "Illegal downloading will be marginalised not by restrictive legislation but by technological progress and changing patterns of usage." His view seemed to be in tune with a study by the University of Rennes, which found that the unauthorised sharing of copyrighted content on the Internet had increased in France since the passing of *Création et Internet*.

Following the passage of *Création et Internet* and prior to its implementation in 2010, HADOPI launched a campaign to highlight the evils of unauthorised file-sharing and its possible consequences. Over two weekends in August some 260,000 leaflets were distributed explaining how the three-strike scheme would work, about how warning letters would first be sent to those suspected of illegal downloading and that, in the event of repeat infringements, HADOPI would submit the file to a judge to approve or reject an order to cut the offender's Internet access for a specified time. The leaflet went on to explain that under the scheme, an Internet subscriber could be fined up to €1,500 ($1,905) as well as having their Internet access suspended for a month or longer.

More problematic, and not publicised by HADOPI – but leaked by its critics – was HADOPI's (failed) attempt to secure the right to require French Internet users to install spyware on their PCs with the aim of tracking their searches and analysing the applications installed on their PCs. As well as the opposition of consumer and Internet freedom groups, some of the law's supporters seemed to lose their belief in HADOPI. Jean-Claude Larue, the head of the trade group representing video game publishers, questioned the cost of tracking pirated works, after officials from HADOPI said they planned to pursue only the most prolific offenders, rather than all copyright infringers. He noted that the cost of monitoring 100 games would be more than €400,000 ($513,000). Another matter was who should pay for the running of HADOPI. Based on the costs of "the production and provision of communications data by communications operators" by the French Department of Justice in 2006, the implementation of HADOPI could cost France's four ISPs – Orange, SFR, Free and Numerique – at least $50m annually to operate a graduated response system of notifying infringing file-sharers and perhaps disconnecting them. These costs, which would not be reimbursed by copyright holders, would almost certainly result in the form of higher subscription fees for Internet users.

So, it would be costly, but would it work? No, said a number of observers, questioning the reliability of determining the activities of users at a given IP address or what was actually shared through such IP lookups. They point to tech-savvy users who know how to use virtual private networks (VPNs), proxies and other online tools to mask, conceal or make anonymous their online activities, which makes it less likely for HADOPI to find let alone catch them.

A year on, such debates seemed irrelevant when compared to the actual performance of HADOPI. In October 2010, the agency sent out the first warning emails to 650,000 French Internet users. Subsequently 44,000 people received a second strike letter. However, only 60 people were sent the final third strike notice and (by mid-2012) none had had their Internet connection cut off ... yet. Nevertheless, French president Sarkozy hailed the new law for reducing peer-to-peer piracy by 35%. Its critics argued that it neither educated the public about online piracy nor significantly helped the growth of the legitimate online market. This last point is debatable: according to IFPI, although the total value of recorded music sales in France in 2011 fell by 3.7%, the value of digital sales rose by 25.5%.

The future of HADOPI was set to be an important issue in the presidential elections of 2012. President Sarkozy announced the creation of a National Music Council (CNM) on the model of the current Centre National du Cinéma (CNC), to support the French music industry, using funding from a tax on Internet subscriptions. This was received with hostility by the country's ISPs. In response, the Socialist presidential candidate François Hollande said he would repeal the *Création et Internet* and concentrate on "commercial" piracy rather than targeting consumers. After his election in July, Hollande appointed former Canal Plus head Pierre Lescure to head a months-long revision of France's anti-piracy regime, with special reference to the punitive element HADOPI. In French some observers suggested that any modification of HADOPI would be seen as a retreat in the battle against piracy.

New Zealand is another country that has found enacting three-strike legislation difficult. The original draft of the *Copyright (New Technologies) Amendment Act* required ISPs to terminate the Internet access of persistent offenders. The Recording Industry Association of New Zealand and the Australian Performing Right Association campaigned on its behalf, but various ISPs, notably TelstraClear, argued against it. Separately, Google argued that the termination of a user's ISP account for copyright infringement was disproportionate, while the Creative Freedom Foundation highlighted various failings in the legislation, such as its lack of a precise definition of "infringer" and its suggestion of "guilt by accusation", which referred to there being no legal requirement for illegal downloading to be proved in court. There was also a number of "crowd sourced" oppositions, including a brief Internet blackout, the creation of several Facebook protest groups, and a petition, which received about 19,000 signatures.

In response the New Zealand government reworked the *Copyright (New Technologies) Amendment Act 2008* and when it came into law in September 2011, the termination clause, under which a District Court could order the closing of a persistent copyright offender's Internet account for six months, was left inactive. In Germany, the government was even more brutal, rejecting the three-strike policy saying that it was not a "fitting model for Germany or even Europe".

A similar scenario unfolded in Ireland, like New Zealand a small country in terms of recorded music sales. In January 2009, the largest Irish ISP, eircom, agreed, in an out-of-court settlement with the four majors, to introduce a graduated series of measures ending in termination in order to reduce its subscribers' P2P use. However, no other Irish ISP followed eircom's lead and in October the Dublin High Court ruled that the three-strike principle was not compatible with Ireland's copyright law and that, accordingly, Irish courts could not enforce it.

If it was widely accepted that copyright infringement was a serious problem, these three national cases indicated that the highly vocal opposition of ISPs and grass-roots groups to three-strike legislation made national governments reluctant to stand firmly behind termination of a users Internet connection as *the* solution and made them look for alternative solutions. The UK took a similar approach to New Zealand, passing *The Digital Economy Act 2010* (DEA) , which came into force in June 2010, but left various provisions, notably the notice and eventually termination clauses, to be decided by the existing regulatory body Ofcom. Although UK ISPs had opposed the DEA, they responded immediately when the High Court in April 2012 ordered five of the largest UK ISPs to block users from accessing illegal file-sharing website the Pirate Bay. The ruling, which followed the UK trade association BPI issuing legal proceedings against the ISPS, was accepted by the ISPs. However a spokesperson for Virgin Media noted: "As a responsible ISP, Virgin Media complies with court orders addressed to the company but strongly believes that changing consumer behaviour to tackle copyright infringement also needs compelling legal alternatives."

In the US in the course of the November 2011 hearings over the *Stop Online Piracy Act* (SOPA) it quickly became apparent that, despite a general acceptance that the online piracy of intellectual property was a real problem that needed to be addressed, there was a sense that the solution proposed was too severe. California representative Darrell

Issa noted simply, "I think it's way too extreme, it infringes on too many areas that our leadership will know is simply too dangerous to do in its current form" on the grounds that the bill would give the Attorney General the power to completely block IP addresses to shutter suspected rogues, without judicial court processes. Within the US the bill was attacked by the tech community: Google, Yahoo, Twitter and Facebook were among the most visible opponents.

John Naughton writing in UK newspaper *The Observer* summed up the problems posed by the attempt at covering all bases that the SOPA bill represents:

> *What's wrong with SOPA? Well, for starters it probably violates the US constitution and would certainly curtail free speech, threaten whistleblowers and undermine human rights. If implemented, it could put the US government on the same side of the line as China, Burma, Iran, Saudi Arabia and other authoritarian regimes which seek to control and censor the internet.*
>
> *But the most worrying aspect [is that it] would distort the architecture of the internet in ways that would cripple its capacity for enabling innovate... The proposed legislation would tamper with the Domain Name System (DNS) which is one of the core components of the net. This is the system which translates domain names (such as www.observer.co.uk) into a machine-readable code that enables any computer in the world to find the site.*
>
> *Sopa ... would give US authorities the power to block sites accused of copyright infringement at the domain level – in other words to make them disappear from the internet by rendering them unfindable ... and it's exactly what authoritarian regimes everywhere would like to do to sites that go on about democracy, human rights and other annoyances.*
>
> *Now you might say: what's wrong with that? Shouldn't a site devoted to wholesale piracy be 'disappeared'? ... But the problem with DNS-blocking is that it's indiscriminate. The vast majority of the world's (legitimate) websites and services are hosted on servers which exist under the umbrella of single domain names. A major hosting service (Blogger.com, for example) will contain many thousands of individual blog sites, a few of which may*

be fostering or practising piracy. But a DNS block would make the entire Blogger.com universe vanish.

There was also opposition from the European Parliament, which issued a joint resolution opposing cross-border, US-led shutdowns of suspected websites offering unauthorised material. The resolution "stressed the need to protect the integrity of the global internet and freedom of communication by refraining from unilateral measures to revoke IP addresses or domain names". A mark of the high level of concern that SOPA represented was that on January 18, 2012, when Wikipedia closed down its English-language website for the day, something it had never done before.

The problem that SOPA (and its sister bill PIPA which was presented in the US Senate) represented was that the protective measures granted on behalf of copyright holders were excessive. As originally proposed, the bill allowed the US Department of Justice, as well as copyright holders, to seek court orders against websites accused of enabling or facilitating copyright infringement. Depending on who makes the request, the court order could include barring online advertising networks and payment facilitators from conducting business with the allegedly infringing website, barring search engines such as http://en.wikipedia.org/wiki/Search_engine from linking to such sites, and requiring ISPs to block access to such sites.

Wikipedia's (and others) closure of its English-language website as a protest against the SOPA/PIPA was immediately effective. SOPA was withdrawn from Congress "indefinitely" by its main proposer as commentators, both right and left wing, mounted wounding attacks on the principles behind the bill. The report in *Forbes* magazine stands as a summary of this reversal:

The problem of stealing intellectual property and protecting property on the internet is important in our free markets. Censorship, increased government intervention and interference in our most important growth industry today, technology, would be a disaster. SOPA would make it impossible to advertise or conduct business with any website that infringes on the bill's guidelines. Additionally, SOPA could make it possible to ban internet service providers from hosting websites that do not comply. The goal of protecting property rights from theft needs to be accomplished with different moves from Washington. Enforcing the current existing laws nationally and globally would be the right path. Keeping the SOPA bill how it currently exists would increase government bureaucracy without having the desired effect. Legislation without enforcement is not the answer...

While the issue of stealing intellectual property is a serious one, there need to be better alternatives to solving the problem. Alternatives that would not infringe on freedom of information, start-up growth or creativity and alternatives that would not put small businesses at a disadvantage.

The debate generated by the attempted passing of SOPA/PIPA suggests that the battle between the interests of content owners and content suppliers will continue within the US, as already demonstrated in France and the UK.

Similar arguments were raised against ACTA, another US initiative seeking to impose an obligation on States to support "cooperative efforts with the business community" to enforce criminal and civil law in the online environment. Opponents of ACTA noted that such an obligation legitimised and promoted the policing and even punishment of alleged infringements outside normal judicial frameworks. Separately, a leaked document published by the European Parliament gave disconnection of users as an example of the private sanctions that could be imposed in such "co-operation". In effect, ACTA's objectors argued that ACTA represented a new set of trade agreements that undermined existing treaties, such as those in place through the WTO, by over-extending the rights of commercial bodies, particularly those based in the US.

However although ACTA was signed by the European Commission and 22 EU member states in January, it was never ratified. Australia, Canada, Japan, New Zealand and the US also signed ACTA, but none has yet ratified it in national legislation. The Commission's signing up to ACTA led to a series of protests in Belgium, the Czech Republic, Finland, Hungary – this one being organised by the Pirate Party – the Netherlands, Romania and the UK, against ACTA, all arguing that ACTA overly restricts civil liberties and freedom of expression.

The climax of this protest movement was the refusal of the European Parliament to ratify ACTA. The vote in Parliament was 478 opposed, 39 in favour, with 165 abstentions. Noting that "Never in history did a [European] Commission proposal only get 39 votes," David Martin, of the Parliament's International Trade Committee said "ACTA is dead, not only in the European Union."

As well as seeking the acceptance of ACTA as a basis of global trade in intellectual property, the US has also been accused of seeking to influence national laws, to adopt measures against users allegedly illegally downloading copyrighted music and movies from file-sharing networks. At the end of 2011, the Spanish Congress approved the so-called Sinde law which allows the closing down of websites deemed to illegally download copyrighted material. According to Wikileaks, the law was passed following US pressure threatening to put Spain on their Special 301 Report (a watch list of countries with "bad" intellectual property policies), a threat which they actually delivered. Such international pressures will never go away, but nor will the debate within nations about the rights of content owners as opposed to the rights of Internet users.

In November 2011, the EU Court of Justice struck another blow against the music industry's preferred solution, ruling that an ISP cannot be forced to prevent customers from downloading illegal music and video files. The case in question was brought by Belgian authors' society SABAM in 2004 against ISP Scarlet. The court ordered Scarlet to block illegal P2P downloads on the basis that despite Scarlet's protests it was possible for the ISP to insert a filtering system that blocked such downloads. Scarlet appealed, and the Court of Justice of the European Union ruled:

> *In adopting the injunction requiring Scarlet to install such a filtering system, the national court would not be respecting the requirement that a fair balance be struck between the right to intellectual property, on the one hand, and the freedom to conduct business, the right to protection of personal data and the right to receive or impart information, on the other.*
>
> *Accordingly, the Court's reply is that EU law precludes an injunction made against an internet service provider requiring it to install a system for*

filtering all electronic communications passing via its services which applies indiscriminately to all its customers, as a preventive measure, exclusively at its expense, and for an unlimited period.

On a more positive note in June Japan's parliament passed an amendment to its 2009 Copyright act imposing penalties of up to two years in prison or a fine of up to ¥2m ($25,320) on those who knowingly download music and video files without rights-holders' permission. The unauthorised uploading of content is currently punishable by imprisonment of up to 10 years or a fine of up to ¥10m ($126,600). According to the Record Industry Association of Japan (RIAJ) while in 2010 there were nearly 440m legal music downloads in Japan, there were nearly 10 times that number of illegal downloads.

As the survey above shows, national governments took seriously the problems posed to rights holders by the Internet but were as perplexed as rights holders themselves as to what the digital revolution meant. Outside of the safety zone of international trade agreements, they found it difficult to balance the conflicting demands of rights holders, users and ISPs.

If legislation was not the way forward, could the record industry come to some sort of contractual relationship with copyright infringers? All the attempts to remodel P2P networks as legitimate business had failed. But there remained a huge need by record companies to somehow grow a market that they could see on a daily basis was contracting. In the pre-paradigm shift new business plans were threatening – now any business plan that might produce growth was worth looking into.

WMG, the do-anything company, took up the challenge, seeking to legitimise not the P2P networks, but P2P's users, particularly those in US colleges and universities that offered their students high-speed Internet access, a lot of which was devoted to accessing P2P networks. In 2009, WMG funded Jim Griffin to establish a company, Choruss, which gained the support of SME and EMI, as a digital rights clearing house for the scheme.

In exchange for a compulsory payment included in their tuition fees, students would be allowed to download DRM-free content from

LimeWire, BitTorrent, and other P2P networks. College authorities would monitor the tracks downloaded to enable Choruss to distribute licence fees accurately. A condition of the licence would be that the universities and their students would not face legal action from the RIAA. In effect Choruss offered P2P users and broadband providers a covenant not to sue them if they paid rights holders a fee.

In mid-2009, Griffin said that he hoped to launch Choruss at six colleges by the autumn of 2009 and that he would seek to extend it to ISPs and, through them, to all US-based Internet users. Lawyers raised a number of issues over the "covenant not to sue", notably that, if only by implication, it was as something akin to a "blanket licence" and as such could be read as legitimatising P2P networks which would thus make it difficult for rights owners to sue them for copyright infringement outside the college/university environment. However, it was informational problems rather than legal ones that sank Choruss.

Choruss discovered that it could confidently identify only 30% of the material being downloaded and that on this basis it couldn't set up shop. Choruss wasn't the only organisation faced with this problem. SoundExchange, which collects performers' and record companies' royalties from digital music streams on Internet, satellite radio and cable television in the US, found itself with a sum of money that it called "unpayable royalties". It collected $204.2m (up 20% on 2008) and distributed $155.5m (up 55%) to recording artists. But SoundExchange also had a year-end balance in 2009 of $294m of which $111m it described "unpayable royalties". This included $43m in monies unclaimed by artists or record companies that hadn't registered with SoundExchange; $23m from tracks that couldn't be identified due to bad metadata; $23m in unclaimed money by foreign collecting societies; and $22m due to account issues and paperwork.

And then there's Google, which has hundreds of millions of dollars to whom it doesn't know to pay for music usage on YouTube. This issue, which can only be solved by the correct identification of the multitude of rights embedded in a music tract – composer(s), artist, record company, etc – is the current hot potato. All rights owners would benefit from a solution, but who will fund the expensive steps to that solution?

Whatever business plans and strategies emerge in the growing digital market – ISPs or telcos funding free access to music tracks; streaming: licensing music to a wide range of users from broadcasters to as yet underdeveloped uses (T-shirts, fridge doors, bus stops, etc); online sales: knowing what is played, who owns it (and where they own it) – is essential. Hence in 2010/2011, came the belated realisation of the need for some kind of a Global Repertoire Database to make the licensing process easier, by ensuring that rights holders were fairly and promptly compensated and music users were free of fear of litigation or cumbersome and lengthy negotiations. Plans were made, the EC made an intervention and the World Intellectual Property Organization said the issue was crucial.

Much detailed work needs to be done and the matter of who sets up and administers a GRD registry is hugely important, but the benefits are clear and recognised by a wide group of interested parties, who are in complete non-agreement as to how such a GRD should be implemented and administered. The creation of a GRD depends on the co-operation of a wide number of interested parties, rights holders, users and regulators and as such was bogged down in bureaucracy.

Initiatives depending on contracts rather than legislation or treaties have fared better. One such was Vevo. Established in late 2009, by UMG and SME, with the Abu Dhabi Media Company, Vevo, unusually for a record company initiative, has been an unqualified success. Within a year it established itself as the premiere destination for those seeking popular music videos online. In October 2010, Vevo attracted 47.6m unique viewers, the fourth highest among US online video channels that month, providing serious competition to MTVN, the reconfigured son of MTV.

Vevo hosts all of its owners' content plus videos from EMI and numerous independent labels and syndicates that to various websites, including YouTube, and AOL. It had over 200 advertising partners in 2001, including American Express, AT&T and Toyota. About half of Vevo's advertising revenue is returned to the participating record companies and artists. Vevo also produces some original content, mainly live performances and artist specials, virtually all of which is sponsored by major brands.

Hopes For The Future, Legislation And New Business Plans

Vevo is the most successful major-record company initiated content distribution platform to date, principally because of its relationship with Google and its YouTube subsidiary. Previously record companies struggled to deal with the free-for-all of user-uploaded content on YouTube. But following extensive legal wrangling and public arguments about YouTube's administration of copyrighted music YouTube became largely free of major record company-owned content. With quality control and imposed scarcity in place, Vevo, in the manner of Apple, was then able to charge premium rates to advertisers and significantly improve the ad revenues generated through users' access to the videos, which it then made available to YouTube.

Vevo achieved this near-instant prominence almost entirely through its deal with Google. Having withdrawn access to its videos to YouTube and established its rights Vevo then licensed YouTube. Since 2010, Internet users seeking any UMG, Sony or EMI artist videos have been directed straight to Vevo channels, or within YouTube to Vevo's own portal on that site. It's estimated that around 90% of Vevo streams are generated through YouTube searches, a fact the company has said it is not concerned about. As a result, every YouTube play of one of Vevo's 20,000 videos, from 7,000 artists, is reported as a Vevo stream. The advertising revenue generated is split between the two companies. EMI licensed its content to the portal just as it launched, however WMG chose to not provide material to MTV Networks, which also has a deal in place with Google/YouTube.

Vevo's success is due in great part to its exclusive premières of new videos from major artists. In early 2010, reportedly, 25% of Vevo's advertising profits at the time were being generated by Lady Gaga clips alone, notably the highly promoted extended video for 'Telephone', and 'Bad Romance', the latter being reported to be the most viewed music clip on the Internet to date.

UMG and SME's investment partnership with Abu Dhabi Media Company (ADMC), a non-music firm owned by the Abu Dhabi government, was an unusual move for a new major-initiated venture. That said, it presaged the new perception that entertainment bodies were the way into the market for new venture capital groups, especially those outside the US and Europe. Subsequently ADMC joined with Hollywood studio Warner Bros. to finance films and a theme park and joined the consortium that bought EMI MP.

The success of Vevo is simply stated: As of January 2012, five of YouTube's Top 10 videos of all time were controlled by Vevo with seven of the Top 10 being music videos. This gave Vevo access to significant advertising revenues. More significantly, Vevo enabled three of the majors to re-assert a degree of control of its ability to influence youth culture at a time when the legacy model, selling music recordings, was in decline even though music's connection with people – especially young people – has grown stronger in the digital age. Vevo also seems to have managed to monetise the transition in cultural consumption from ownership to access.

Vevo reported that for 2011 it had revenues of $150m and predicted that such was its rate of growth that revenues would "soon" grow to $1bn. As with Spotify, the average Vevo stream earns very little. *Billboard* calculated that the average Vevo stream in 2011 generated 0.43¢. However, whereas the majors are only minority shareholders in Spotify, the stake being granted as part of the licensing process, three of the majors co-own Vevo and as such receive more than just streaming revenues. That said, aggregated across the number of videos streamed, most of which are from the three majors, their revenues are becoming significant. As such Vevo has the possibility of becoming an important new recorded music revenue stream, but not for all record companies. WMG opted out and independents, most of which have tiny market shares, have noted that they receive very little from Vevo.

Another new revenue stream with a similar set of problems is audio streaming service Spotify, which had two basic tiers, free (with ads) and a paid-for service (no ads, bells and whistles). In a ghost-like repetition of the arrival of iTunes, it was first welcomed by the majors as opening the door to revenues from streaming and then when Spotify sought to enter the US market the "freemium" element was challenged as cannibalising sales. It took Spotify over a year to get the necessary licences to operate in the US.

In 2009, the value of recorded music sales in Sweden rose against the global trend by 10.2% to SKr 861.4m ($113.2m), making Sweden one of the few markets to report growth that year. One reason for the growth was the popularity of Spotify, launched there in October 2008 and since quickly established itself throughout Europe. Spotify carried 15m tracks, including repertoire from all the majors and most independent record companies. Users could register either for free accounts supported by visual and radio styled advertisements, dubbed the "freemium" mode, or for paid subscriptions without ads and with a range of extra features such as higher bitrates streams and offline access to music. Along with the introduction of the IPRED Directive anti-piracy laws, which threatened Internet copyright infringers with financial penalties if they continued to infringe, Sweden's Spotify, with its clean and easy to use interface, provided a more attractive alternative to P2P file-sharing. The "Spotify effect" was immediate. Legitimate digital recorded music sales in Sweden rose 119% in 2009 and UMG, the largest record company in Sweden, reported that its revenues from Spotify were greater than from iTunes. As Spotify expanded across Europe – by 2010 it was available in Austria, Belgium, Denmark, Finland, France, the Netherlands, Norway, Spain, Sweden, Switzerland and the UK – the "Spotify effect" continued. In 2010, Spotify paid some $60m in royalties to European record companies, making it their second largest source of digital revenues after iTunes. The "Spotify effect" also impacted on the larger European independent record companies. In 2010, the Beggars Group calculated that Spotify was one of its leading digital partners and predicted that following its huge success with Adele and Vampire Weekend, it would be their second or third source of digital revenue in 2011.

But there was also evidence that the "Spotify effect" was limited. In 2009, two European countries reported recorded music sales growth; none did in 2010. And there was the issue of the level of payments made to successful acts. Whereas the majors, because they controlled over 75% of the recorded music market, benefitted from the per stream revenues that Spotify generated – 75% of $60m was useful – for an artist who represented only a small percentage of those sales the per stream revenue was far lower, indeed minuscule. Lady Gaga reportedly earned just $167 (£108) from 1m plays of her hit 'Poker Face' in 2009. On this basis, Lady Gaga, a writer as well as performer, received 0.000167¢ per stream. Others have calculated that for a solo artist to reach the minimum US monthly wage of $1,160 they must have one of their tracks streamed up to 4.5m times a month, which would mean it being played continuously for 225 hours.

As Spotify's reputation as an Apple-like cool experience grew and Spotify sought to launch in the US, the majors became concerned that streaming might cannibalise iTune sales. Newly convinced Khunians, the majors had come to accept that digital was the game. Money and strategies would be available to support physical sales – dramatic cost reductions on catalogue, a new emphasis on high-priced vinyl versions of current and past releases – but digital was the only game in town. But what if digital 2, streaming, meant the death of digital 1, online sales, which were fast approaching 50% of all recorded music sales in the US?

There wasn't about to be another paradigm revolution, was there?

When Spotify sought licences to stream the majors' repertoire in the US, "freemium" became the key issue of what turned out to be highly protracted negotiations. The opening salvo came from Edgar Bronfman: "Free streaming services are clearly not net positive for the industry and as far as Warner Music is concerned will not be licensed. The 'get all your music you want for free, and then maybe with a few bells and whistles we can move you to a premium price' strategy is not the kind of approach to business that we will be supporting in the future."

Accordingly, Bronfman sought a streaming service that required payment and could appeal beyond those who currently pay for downloads in stores such as Apple's iTunes. In such a situation Bronfman was in favour of streaming, noting that, "The number of potential subscribers dwarfs the number of people who are actually purchasing music on iTunes."

And so Spotify began cutting back on its "freemium" and started placing restrictions on the amount of time its free European users could spend on the service. For the first six months, the freemium offer would be limited to 20 hours of listening a month; after six months, the limit would become 10 hours, and no track could be listened to more than five times in a month. US users will be subject to the same limitations. Spotify also offered the majors collectively the traditional sweetener in the form of an 18% share in the company, the individual proportions of that being set by a company's US market share. Spotify argued that by offering virtually all available music free, and sharing advertising revenue with record companies, it was removing the appeal of piracy, and consumers who had been lost to the industry could be lured back.

The move proved to be a deal clincher and in the summer of 2011 Spotify was licensed by the US majors with one-time critic Bronfman forecasting that licensing revenue from Spotify and other streaming services would be an "immediate source of growth" for 2011. Launched in July, Spotify secured 1m free and 175,000 paying subscribers within a month in the US, a conversion rate of 12.5%, close to that it had in Europe in 2010. In the US Spotify was faced with competition from established subscriptions services, notably Rhapsody, which claimed 800,000 US subscribers at the time of Spotify's launch. Spotify soon established itself as *the* service in great part of its ease of use interface, which, ironically, was developed from P2P networking practices, proof, as it were, that P2P represented a structural change in Internet transmissions.

And then the shit hit the fan. In November NARM released a report which showed that Spotify and similar access models were discouraging other forms of music purchasing, not encouraging them. In effect, the argument went, Spotify was iTunes mk2, a service that increased access to music, but also decreased the amount spent on recorded music. And then the representatives of small independents and artists started to speak out. The first was STHoldings which represented 234 independent record companies in the US. It removed their tracks from Spotify, simfy, Rdio and Napster, explaining: "As a distributor we have to do what is best for our labels. The majority of which do not want their music on such services because of the poor revenues and the detrimental effect on sales. Add to that, the feeling that their music loses its specialness by its exploitation as a low value/free commodity. Quoting one of our labels, 'Let's keep the music special, f--k Spotify.'"

STHoldings supported its decision with brutal figures. In the third quarter of 2011, its labels' revenues fell by 24% and, while Spotify,

Rdio, simfy and Napster accounted for 82% of all content "consumed", they provided just 2.6 % of overall revenues.

Other independents rushed to the Internet with similar revelations, culminating in the decision by Coldplay to withhold *Mylo Xyloto* from Spotify and other streaming services, notwithstanding EMI's comprehensive agreement with Spotify. Although it produced tiny royalties for artists, streaming had produced modest revenues for the majors. Spotify claimed it would change the game. For new acts that game change made sense, but established acts in complete control of the distribution of their product took a different view. Coldplay made a business decision, along the way demonstrating the power they had over their label. EMI wanted Coldplay to make *Mylo Xyloto* available to Spotify and so gain wide exposure. Coldplay took a contradictory position, preferring to have a smaller number of people listening to *Mylo Xyloto* to ensure that a larger number of them bought it. Coldplay won the battle. The album sold in greater numbers than was expected, shifting some 210,000 copies in the UK and 83,000 downloads in week one and almost 500,000 units (digital and physical) in the US, while charting at number one in 17 countries.

Spotify had presented itself as being the "new revenue stream", the magic business sought by the record companies. But as their major acts chose not to click the Spotify button, it became apparent that whatever increased revenues Spotify might represent, it was never going to be enough. Seen from this perspective Spotify was a divisive entrant to the market, rather than a generator of new revenues. For medium to large-sized record companies, it represented a new and workable business model, but for small companies or acts, who stood to lose significant online and offline revenues, Spotify was more problematic. This disconnectedness grew further when Spotify, following the path established by Apple, began to build a larger presence for itself, initially integrating with Facebook in search of greater revenues.

And it needed greater revenues. Spotify's turnover in 2010 grew fivefold to £63.2m (97.2m) but its net loss rose 60% to £26.5m ($40.8m). Advertising accounted for only 29% of revenue and 90% of total Spotify registered users were non-paying. In other words, 10% of

Spotify users, its paying subscribers, in 2010 generated some 71% of the company's revenues.

The majors wanted Spotify to migrate its "freemium" subscribers to its paid services. So did Spotify, but it took the view that in the crowded online subscription market it needed to offer more than just a music streaming service. It needed to become a platform. This chimed well with Facebook, which was facing the problem of monetising the most successful social networking service developed to date. Having started an integration process with Facebook, in November 2011, Spotify redefined itself as a go-to place that would allow other companies to build services and apps around Spotify's 15m music track database for its subscribers. Spotify became a platform in which, in the manner of MTV and Apple before it, its music licensing activities became the precursor of a range of business opportunities from which it, rather than record companies, would benefit.

A platform had been created and one in which social interactivity, not isolated usage, was central. Suddenly Spotify was radically different from its competing streaming services in the US, offering a growing number of extras and making itself a source for app developers. In the manner of Apple, having (finally) secured licences for the use of music in the world's largest recorded music market, Spotify set out to diversify as quickly as possible. Founder Daniel Ek's explained: "We have a ton of users that want to find more information around music, like buying concert tickets and so on."

Spotify's key partner in this transformation of self was Facebook. In the *Wired* roundup of 2011 (January 2012) Dave Rose, VP of partnership and platform marketing at Facebook, identified Spotify as a key add-on because it extended the value of Facebook to its users, "letting friends influence each other based on their browsing or purchasing history or likes". However, by mid-2012, following the collapse of the share price and status of Facebook, Spotify began to backpedal on its relationship with Facebook. Spotify was a service built around music by people who believed in music, but, in the manner of Apple and Facebook, it based its business model on technology. As such, to the extent that it needed to retain its music licences, Spotify would be a "friend" of the record industry, but it would always be seeking wider relationships. Music was Spotify's first strand of content, but it was the service, the medium not the message, that was of prime importance to Spotify.

A "better", and more reliable, friend to the record industry would be a company that was committed to music, in the manner of traditional music retailers, but facing similar problems in troubled economic times. And so in 2011, Live Nation, which a couple of years earlier had threatened to compete with the majors, signing Madonna and Jay-Z to recording and touring contracts, forged a broad-based strategic deal with UMG, covering ticketing, management and merchandising, which led to UMG becoming the distributor of Live Nation signed recording act Madonna. Central to the deal was the bundling of a wide range of music related assets, recordings, tickets, merchandise, etc. iTunes had led to the unbundling of recordings, largely reducing albums to collections of single track downloads; the Live Nation/UMG deal was an attempt to create and offer consumers even larger bundles than the album. There was similar reasoning behind the mega box sets featuring memorabilia, unreleased material and re-mastered albums and suchlike, that flooded the market in 2011. Bundling was the word de jour.

On September 19, Live Nation Entertainment's Front Line Management Group division and UMG announced that they would launch a joint-venture management company "aimed at managing and strengthening artists and their brands through a variety of worldwide sponsorships, strategic marketing campaigns and brand extension opportunities". The partnership, which was to be managed by Front Line, "will focus on developing direct-to-consumer bundling initiatives for select UMG artists in key markets around the world that bring together concert tickets and a variety of music products with artist websites," the release continues. In addition, ticketing and bundling products will be handled by Live Nation Entertainment's Ticketmaster division. Beyond the details announced loomed the possibility of UMG finding a new set of mega artists to flow through its distribution pipes, physical and digital, and extending the merchandising opportunities of its Bravado division, the second largest merchandising firm after Live Nation Merchandise. Such a deal offered simple opportunities to two partners locked into the sale of music and related items as their key products.

This was underlined in a statement from Irving Azoff, Executive Chairman of Live Nation Entertainment and Chairman and CEO of Front Line Management Group: "This is an unprecedented partnership that unites the world's top music artists with the world's leading artist management, live entertainment, event ticketing and sponsorship resources to drive innovation across our industry. We see tremendous opportunities to work together to create a broad range of products built on the power of music and the direct connection between artists and fans."

A decade earlier such a deal would have been anathema to a record company, but with merchandising a high-profit sector and physical sales, however troubled, still significant, a deal that promised higher sales in both revenue streams was a bonanza, giving Live Nation further visibility and opportunities outside the live arena and UMG the chance to find a few more cents' profit on a distribution machine that was ever in danger of being too costly for the revenues it produced. At the same time it seemed inevitable that Live Nation Merchandise and UMG's Bravado merchandising company would merge their manufacturing and distribution activities, at some point. If the deal flowers alongside such lines it will lead to more bundling of tickets, merchandising and UMG download content. And if, as seems likely, in an access world where music consumption shifts more toward the live side, the CD would be an add-on value to fans buying a ticket.

UMG could make the deal with Live Nation, because (as with the disappointing deal it made with Nokia for Comes With Music) it brought most to the table. Size mattered after all. And so began the final battle for WMG and EMI.

Chapter 17

Rush To Market: The Sale Of WMG And EMI

In 2011, WMG and EMI were sold, the former to an industry outsider, the latter to two insiders. Access Industries bought WMG for $3.3bn in cash, while Vivendi and a consortium headed by Sony's Sony/ATV divided the EMI Group between them. Vivendi bought the record division of EMI for £1.2bn ($1.93bn) and the Sony/ATV-led consortium bought EMI MP for $2.2bn. The sales shared a high level of melodrama, with sources "close to the key participants" regularly revealing the twists and turns of the negotiations and then, the deals made, of the regulatory process. In the WMG sale, the favourite romped home, while Citigroup's dismemberment of EMI saw the favourites, Access Industries and BMG RM, beaten in the home straight.

The sales of EMI and WMG represented the end of the independence of two high profile record companies in markedly different ways. WMG has gone through the seven ages of corporate existence. Born as an adjunct of a film company that eventually overcame its parent company as a revenue earner, it was then snapped up by corporate raider Kinney as part of the process of recognising the value of intellectual property. Kinney quickly disposed of its non-intellectual property interests and expanded its music interests before selling out to (merging with) Time, an old-fashioned media company that took the view that print might not be the future. So sure of this was Time Warner that it then merged with AOL – content meets the Internet – only to discover that there were more versions of the Internet than AOL represented. So WMG was sold to a venture capital consortium, which made a lot of money despite the company's falling revenues and then was neatly offloaded to a Russian oligarch, the latest cash-rich pocket to see intellectual property as worth a punt. The circle from Jack Warner, the son of Polish émigrés born in Canada to Blavatnik, Ukranian born but like Warner a naturalised US citizen, isn't quite complete aesthetically – it would be nice if the torch was passed from Russian to Russian – but the steps along the way detail a dramatic re-evaluation of what intellectual property represents and the changing view of how its administrators should be recompensed and valued.

The sale of EMI was equally revealing. Saved from disaster by the merger with Thorn and then unable to benefit from its success by being trapped in an old-fashioned company once sprung free of Thorn EMI always presented itself as available for sale. Financiers and venture capitalists had come to believe in the value of intellectual property, but EMI and its shareholders remained doubtful. So merger or purchase and then sale became the sad name of the game EMI played, a game that grew even sadder when movements in the financial markets meant EMI's second sudden run of success – it was a long time since The Beatles – was never enough to fund debts incurred by Terra Firma, which only too quickly discovered that while intellectual property might be intrinsically valuable, buying it at a top of the market price was not such a good idea when servicing debts suddenly became really difficult.

The sales also represented very different results for two long-time captains of industry. The failure of Access Industries to win EMI led to Edgar Bronfman, Jr., who had long made the winning of EMI a personal odyssey, quitting WMG, first as CEO and then as chairman of the board in January 2012. Things turned out far rosier for Marty Bandier, who had re-invigorated EMI MP before leaving the company for Sony/ATV when it refused to give him a minority share. The deal reunited Bandier with the EMI catalogue and made the expanded company once again the world's largest music publisher.

Executive shuffles also took place alongside the sales of businesses. SME's global head of digital Thomas Hesse quit to rejoin German media giant Bertelsmann, to oversee the company's stake in BMG MR, the joint venture with private equity firm KKR. Separately, Barry Weiss, the head of SME's RCA Music Group, defected to UMG when he was not offered the top job at SME. However, the most theatrical executive re-alignment was that of UMG's Doug Morris. At EMI MP the long expected scenario was that Bandier would exit to a well padded pension to be replaced by Roger Faxon and that control of the rudder would be seamless.

That didn't happen. Nor did the would-be seamless replacement of Doug Morris by Lucian Grainge at UMG. Grainge took the top job but, far from taking retirement and its muted glories, Morris jumped to SME to become its CEO. The move reflected both the desires of some to still get seats at the top table (rather than merely be remembered in celebrations of past success) and the high value that executives of a certain status represented. Such executives, as the story of their compensation from 1970 to 2010 demonstrates, had become more valuable than the artists signed by them, or their underlings. As Jon Landau, Bruce Springsteen's manager, noted of Morris: "He is a master at attracting and developing executive talent… No one is better at picking the people who pick the hit artists." In the battle between (the old) WMG and (the old) SME for US dominance in the 1970s as detailed earlier, the trump cards had been the artists – a Paul Simon trumps a Paul McCartney (*see* Chapter 4). No longer. In 2012 it was the executives that were the trump cards: you bet Grainge, I bet Morris; you up Weiss, I counter with Dr. Luke – one of Morris' first moves at SME was to offer top producer and songwriter Dr. Luke an exclusive deal, giving him a label and production entity. And so it went.

But the value and performance of a company was also important. In November 2010, WMG announced that its revenues for the year ending September 30, 2010 fell 6.7% to $2.98bn and that operating profit fell 12.3% to $348m. Both the recorded music and music publishing divisions of the company reported a fall in revenues, music by 7% to $2.46bn and publishing by 4.5% to $556m.

WMG explained the decline blandly as reflecting the "the continuing transition from physical sales to digital sales in the recorded music industry". Speaking at the press conference to announce the results WMG CEO Edgar Bronfman did not dwell on the disappointing overall results but boasted that in the last quarter of the year WMG's "digital and non-traditional revenue grew to a combined nearly 40% of total revenue compared to essentially zero in 2004 … [which] represents a fundamental expansion of our business model that we've implemented and executed since Warner became a standalone company". He added: "In the five years from 2004 to 2009, Warner Music has gained four points of global revenue share in the sale of both physical and digital recorded music."

The end of the rainbow spin was that WMG, re-energised under the Bronfman regime, was in the midst of a transformation process, the end of which promised greater revenues and increased profits. A more granular examination of WMG's results suggested otherwise. The significant contraction in the US market, which fell in value by 10% in 2010, meant that over the first nine months of 2010, WMG's physical recorded music sales fell from 53m to 45.1m units. This represented a considerable loss of revenues and profits: WMG's domestic revenues fell by 11.2% in 2009–2010. Understandably the company focused on matters digital, noting that its digital revenue at $759m grew 8.0% to represent 25.4% of WMG's total revenues.

However, after belatedly accepting the fact of the digital revolution ushered in by the CD, the majors were still finding its unforeseen consequences as perplexing as ever. The profits from online sales were growing, but clearly they would never compensate for the lost profits due to the continuing decline in physical sales. What was needed was a new significant profit centre.

But where to find it?

Subscription revenues remained modest at best; ancillary revenues, from performance rights, Vevo and 360-degree deals were growing, but not quickly enough. Moreover, there was strong competition for

360-degree deals from new entrants, such as Live Nation, or their own former acts now going it alone, such as the Eagles.

Nonetheless, one principle still had a substantial number of followers in 2010: copyright. The concept was under attack, from the likes of the Pirate Party and a growing number of academics who saw it as outmoded in the 21st century. However, copyright law and, running in parallel to it, patent legislation, were deeply embedded in the business structures of the world's mature economies, providing the economic basis for a wide variety of activities, ranging through cultural, scientific, engineering and similar structured industries. According to the 2011 report prepared for the IIPA by Stephen Siwek of Economists Incorporated, *Copyright Industries in the U.S. Economy*, the core copyright industries – those directly involved in the creation of copyrights, such as music, film, television, newspaper and computer software companies – generated 6.36%, $14.66 trillion, of the total US GDP in 2010. This share was virtually unchanged from 2007. The report further noted that these industries did better than the rest of the US economy over the period 2007–2010, growing at an annual rate of 1.1%, compared to 0.05% for the economy as a whole.

This belief in the actual and potential value of copyright was the underpinning mantra behind the sales of WMG and EMI. Currently, the argument went, the old means of monetising copyright – the selling of physical product – had been challenged and found wanting by the digital revolution and changes in the patterns of cultural consumption. However, recordings and the songs were still hugely valuable: witness their continued and expanding popularity across an ever growing number of social and cultural activities. Online music service *Digital Music News* reported that in the first half of 2011, seven of the 10 most followed people on Twitter were musicians. Among these were Lady Gaga with 15.1m followers, Justin Bieber with 13.9m, and Katy Perry with 11m, all ahead of fourth-placed US President Obama, who had 10.9m followers.

So, went the advice, buy copyrights now (while they are cheap, because of the distressed state of the record industry) and hope for a new business strategy that will bring about their full exploitation.

Such a strategy had its perils – witness the disastrous foray into the music business of Terra Firma – but also its successes – witness the Bronfman consortium which within a year of buying WMG was in profit. Accordingly, even as credit got tighter, as well as majors looking for economies of scale, outsiders, venture capitalists, would-be first movers were also potential buyers of record and music publishing companies.

There are two conflicting stories about how WMG was brought to market. One has Bronfman, who had long harboured the desire to buy EMI, proposing to the board that WMG sell Warner Chappell and so enable WMG to make a bid for the entire EMI group after it fell into Citigroup's hands. If WMG retained Warner Chappell, which most observers considered was less valuable than EMI MP (in great part because Warner Chappell's copyrights were older), so the logic went, the regulators would not allow WMG to buy the EMI group because the two publishing divisions would have around a third of the music publishing market. Combining WMG and EMI's recorded divisions might require some sell-offs, but the new company, with 25.1%, would have global market share relatively close to that of UMG (28.7%), and SME (23%).

Suddenly instead of there being two tiers of majors, there would be only one with three competing on a (relatively) equal basis. Moreover, in the new pragmatic perspective and with clear evidence that recorded music sales were in decline, the general consensus was that a merger of WMG and EMI's recorded music divisions made better sense than previously and that the regulators were likely to allow it with only minor divestitures.

The other view of the rationale behind the sale of WMG was much simpler. The consortium that had bought WMG had already made its money back and more. On this basis, the WMG board decided that the "long haul" view regarding WMG was over and that it was time to cash in further, before things got rockier.

In an interview with online news service *The Deal Pipeline* Bronfman expanded on this: "But when it became clear that EMI would be available in 2011, our board had to make a decision about what would maximise value for shareholders: to maintain the status quo, to become a bidder for EMI – which, might or might not be successful, and even if successful, would have taken several years to realise – or to put the company up for sale prior to EMI being available, and we chose to initiate the sale process." (The shareholders noted by Bronfman are not those who bought shares at the WMG IPO but the members of the consortium that bought WMG and sold it for more than they bought it for, despite the decline in the market.)

IFPI dubbed 2010 as "the year the industry broke the seal on subscription services, firmly establishing the concept in the market and among consumers" and quoted approvingly the finding by the NPD Group that: "Entertainment companies in the US are gradually moving towards a subscription and micropayment model, whether for digital books, game add-ons, or home video. The explosion in connected or smart devices in the home and in the mobile space has already begun to redefine the platforms for digital music."

The WMG board took a contrary stance and, in view of a fall in the company's revenues for eight consecutive quarters, decided to opt out and put WMG on the block in whatever form a buyer might choose. With EMI falling into Citigroup's hands sooner than expected, a beauty pageant seemed on the cards with EMI, suddenly free of debt and performing well in the market – the company had its first two successive US chart-toppers since 1998 when Amos Lee followed The Decemberists to number one in February 2011 – looking better placed than WMG. No such pageant took place and so in stages, rather than in competition, first WMG and then EMI were brought to the market.

In January, WMG opened its books and set in motion the auction. On offer was either the recorded music and publishing divisions as separate items or the whole company. The leading contenders were industry competitors: SME's publishing division Sony/ATV, UMG and BMG RM, the acquisitive joint venture established by Bertelsmann and equity firm Kohlberg Kravis Roberts, and a number of private equity groups, including those of Tom and Alec Gores, Ron Burkle and Ron Perelman and Len Blavatnik's Access Industries. It soon became clear that the regulatory concerns about the creation of dominant positions in the music industry that had scotched EMI's bid for WMG in 2006 remained in play. Accordingly, WMG rejected the bids of its competitors. (This led to minority shareholders, who had bought shares in the WMG IPO for $17 that were valued at $8.25 when the company was sold launching two class actions on the basis that WMG executives had failed to obtain "the highest value available for WMG in the marketplace", allegedly a higher bid from SME. The class actions were resolved in June 2011 in out-of-court settlements.)

In the end, after more than three months and three rounds of bidding, WMG opted for a deep-pocketed buyer with cash in hand – this last point would become a significant point in the EMI sale which took place in a much tightened credit market. The winner was Blavatnik, who paid $3.3bn in cash. He had a previous relationship with WMG, owning some 2% of the company and sitting on the board for four years. He also had a close association with Bronfman, buying a Manhattan property from him for $50m in 2007 and subsequently allowing Bronfman and WMG its use for various promotional events.

The timing of the purchase fell well for Access Industries. When Terra Firma had bought EMI, its financing partner Citigroup was unable to sell on the debt raised leaving with a huge debt burden. Access was far luckier: the resilient bond market of early 2011 allowed it to quickly transfer its unsecured borrowings into secured debt. Equally lucky were WMG's two top executives, Edgar Bronfman, Jr. and Lyor Cohen. Having already benefitted from dividends and bonus payments that followed WMG's IPO, both were granted another set of golden parachutes: payable in stock options at either the consummation of the merger or upon termination of their employment. Bronfman was due some $34m and Cohen $10m.

According to *Forbes* magazine in 2011, Blavatnik, a Ukrainian born naturalised US citizen with a fortune of some $10.1bn, was the 80th richest man in the world. His wealth came from investments in petrochemical firms and aluminium production. His media holdings, which included telecoms companies, wireless and mobile operators, Russian and Israeli TV production units and various UK interests, were small in comparison.

The history of Access shows a company shifting from physical to digital product. As a spokesperson said at the time of the WMG purchase: "Access is interested in content and content platforms that have the potential to take advantage of new media market opportunities." In effect Access Industries seems to have bought the mantra that the Internet, having changed things for the worse, could, if carefully tweaked, change things for the better.

This was further amplified by Jörg Mohaupt a senior Access executive in what seemed like a mission statement: "The music industry is at an inflection point where digital adoption is rapidly gaining momentum. Warner Music, as one of the most progressive forces in the music business, is well positioned to capture this opportunity for music creation and distribution."

The deal done, observers pondered whether it really was a sensible investment. The first to speak was Sean Parker, co-founder of Napster, an investor in Spotify and part of the investment group led by Ron Burkle and Doug Teitelbaum that failed to acquire WMG. He argued that the record industry was "on the verge of being fixed" with monetisation shifting from acquisition (downloading) to experience (streaming) and revenue shifting from newer to older music, the cost of which has already been assimilated by record companies. On this basis, Parker argued that the "back catalogues of record labels are going to become extremely valuable", noting that with reference to Spotify, "It's the back catalogue that is driving the consumption." Thus, according to Parker, WMG's significant back catalogue made it a valuable asset.

Another positive marker was the 2011 mid-year figures for recorded music sales in the US which showed that there was a flattening of sales rather than an increase in the rate of decline as had been the case in previous years. Through August 21, the 33rd week of 2011, sales of track equivalent albums (TEA) were up 4.8%. In contrast TEA had been down 0.7% the year earlier. Physical album sales were down only 4%, after being down 19% at the same point last year, with digital albums up 19.1% in 2011 after being up 13.5% in 2010. The trend towards catalogue sales, Parker noted with reference to Spotify, was also apparent in the physical market fuelled in part by price reductions.

The average retail price paid by consumers fell to $9.82 in 2010 from $11.07 in 2008, according to Nielsen, and anecdotal evidence suggests it fell further in 2011, primarily on the success of catalogue titles, which cost less than new releases and were heavily promoted by mass merchants, for whom they were more profitable than new releases. For the full year, according to IFPI, downloads in 2011 at $2.2bn grew by 9%.

There was a similar surge in the UK. Sales of digital albums in 2011 at 26.6m grew by 26.6% to account for a 23.5% share of total album sales, up from 17.5% for the same period in 2010.

Industry executives rushed to the microphone. Here's BPI Chief Executive Geoff Taylor talking about the fact that in the first nine months of 2011 there were more digital album downloads than in the whole of 2010: "It's encouraging to see such strong sales in the digital albums market before the Christmas gifting season gets properly underway. For the last five consecutive years, the final week of the year has been the biggest in terms of digital album sales, as consumers spend digital music gift vouchers received at Christmas and try out legal digital music services on their new iPods, tablets and laptops."

Online News service *Digital Music News* poked fun at the talk of the sales revival, noting in an October 2011 post "Haven't we seen this all before?" and quoting several comments from record company executives from 2003, a time when the industry saw a slight increase in album sales after years of declines. Among those whose 2003/2004 quotes were revived by *Digital Music News* were UMG President/COO Zach Horowitz: "There's a lot of good signs that a turnaround is beginning. We're all tremendously pleased by the impact of the Apple service." he told *The New York Times* (February 24, 2004); and David Munns, then chairman and chief executive of EMI Recorded Music North America who stated: "People are over this, 'I should get my music free...' I think there's a tide turn in the American psyche on that."

However, despite the recurrence of a general sense of optimism in mid-2011, the actual performances of the majors was less encouraging. UMG reported that in the first nine months of 2011 its revenues fell

2.9% to €2.84bn ($3.82bn). With a familiar refrain, Vivendi tersely noted that "the 11.3% increase in digital recorded music sales and higher license income only partly offset a lower demand for physical products". SME's performance was even worse with revenues for the six months ending September 30 down by 6.6% to $1.34bn. SME explained the fall in revenues as being due to the appreciation of the yen and lower album sales outside of the US. The reason for the disjuncture between unit sales, up – as reported by SoundScan in the US – and revenues, down – as detailed in the accounts of the major record companies – was simple. Lower prices had driven sales up. Thus, according to *Business Week*: "The lower pricing strategy is getting more music into the hands of consumers, though revenue from album sales remains lower than a year ago," citing details from an interview with Eric Garland, the CEO of BigChampagne, which measures entertainment sales.

One observer to address this decline in revenues and yet still find a way through to optimism was Hany Nada, a founding partner of GGV Capital, a venture capital firm with available assets of over $1bn. In October, he published the report *Music for Nothing and the Fans for Free*. Nada rejected the Internet mantra and accepted the consensus that "sales of recorded music are headed one way, down, but pointed to a new fan-centred music business: "When the dust finally settles between the artists, labels, and distribution companies, everyone will finally realise fans are more valuable than recorded music. As traditional monetisation models for recorded music sales slowly fade away, new monetisation methods centered on the fan will emerge."

Noting that there were a slew of new entrants to the music business – Pandora, Rdio, Spotify, YouTube, etc – Nada, in the manner of a Kuhnian scientist sure that a paradigm shift had taken place, argued that a transformation in the process of cultural consumption needed new methods of monetising those unique moments of creation and consumer enjoyment that music represents.

So how will labels offset the decline in recorded music revenue? How will artists capture more value for their creative work? The clear answer is from their fans. Musicians have never really engaged their fans, maybe every three years while they were on tour, but otherwise they just release albums and expected fans to buy them. Myspace was the first experiment with direct musician-fan engagement, and it started a trend that has continued. Now, over 300,000 musicians have BandPages on Facebook. Just about every musician has a Web site, e-commerce site, and a web strategy. Many are putting their music "out there" for discovery and promotion before it's ever part of an album. Soundcloud has seven million users who upload their music and recordings, for example, YouTube's most popular videos are music-related. Bands, managers, and labels understand this trend and are finding new and innovative means to monetise fans.

We anticipate a lot of "creative destruction" and changes to the value model based on fan-driven music marketing models. There are ways to make money from the music experience, and those channels — new and old, low- and high-tech — are creating opportunities for artists, labels, and music start-ups.

In Nada's vision the Internet has been the key disruptive force, challenging and destroying established business practices, but it has not yet provided a commercially viable new business model. Nada suggests that the Internet allowed for the expansion of social interactivity, which he sees as the only way forward in monetising the "music experience". Accordingly, for Nada the music industry will make money going forward by securing revenues from live music, patronage (ad placements and direct fundraising from fans in the manner of Marillion), whales (big spenders who will pay for exclusive access to stars) and little whales (who will buy merchandise).

Under the headline 'No one wants to pay for music. Yet investors are splurging on music firms', *The Economist* offered a decidedly contrary view: "Say what you like about the men who built business empires from the wreckage of Soviet communism. To money-losing Western outfits, they are angels. Roman Abramovich turned Chelsea football club into a winner. Alexander Lebedev rescued the *Evening Standard* and *Independent* newspapers. And on May 6 Len Blavatnik, an oil magnate, agreed to pay $3.3 billion for Warner Music Group.

The stunned reaction among music executives suggests that his is the greatest act of charity yet."

Rejecting the Nada thesis, *The Economist*'s analysis was simple: "Since 2003 global CD sales have roughly halved. Competition from pirates has crushed retailers and forced record labels to cut prices. Rising digital music sales, mostly through Apple's iTunes store, have not nearly made up for these losses. And it is still unclear whether music-streaming outfits such as Spotify will reverse the decline or accelerate it by drawing honest people away from buying music."

The Economist's caution was reflected in the financial community's post sale scrutiny that decided Blavatnik had overpaid for WMG. At the same time there was a widespread view that Access Industries had acquired a valuable asset. The question was, what would Access do next? On its own WMG was too small. How could it be grown?

The early moves of the "new" WMG answered that question, confirming that Access intended to hunt down EMI. If achieved, this would represent the culmination of the odyssey started by Bronfman in 2000. But then Access Industries promoted Lyor Cohen, the CEO of Warner's North American operations, to CEO of WMG's global recorded music interests, replacing Bronfman who was made chairman and given the task of handling the expected bid for EMI, and any regulatory challenges that would entail. And so Citigroup brought EMI to market.

During the 2007 auction of EMI, Blavatnik had unsuccessfully entered the bidding at a late stage, but his bid was rejected and EMI was bought by Terra Firma. Now, with WMG under his belt and a range of economies set in place Blavatnik, with Bronfman as point man, returned to the hunt. As an outsider he had won WMG, but it was the insiders who snatched both EMI's recorded music division and EMI MP at the last minute.

On June 20, just before it was announced that EMI was to be put up for sale, CEO Roger Faxon sent a memo to the EMI staff:

Well we are off to the races. In about a half an hour we will be announcing that we are beginning a strategic review process in earnest. We, along with Citi, intend to explore all possible alternatives, including a sale, recapitalization or IPO of EMI — all with the aim of setting the stage for the next chapter in EMI's ownership. That is not to say that Citi has not been a great owner — they have! They have been nothing but supportive of our strategy and our team. But from the moment of their acquisition of EMI in early February, we have made clear that their custodianship of this great company was always only going to be temporary.

Over the last few months, we have been preparing for the moment when we would formally begin this process. Many of you have worked very hard indeed during that time to gather all the information necessary, and while there is still some work to be done, we're now at a point where we can feel comfortable that we're ready to go forward in as ordered and well-prepared a fashion as possible.

So, how is this going to work? Normally there are three or four stages in processes like this. The first phase will involve engaging with and providing information about the company to potentially interested investors. After which, we will evaluate the investor interest and move into a more detailed diligence process. Simultaneously, we will be comparing and contrasting the various alternatives, including a sale, recapitalization or IPO. In the final phase, we will get into negotiating and executing on the desired alternative. If all goes according to plan that should mean that by Q4, we will have a good idea of who our new owners are likely to be. I will, of course, fill you in along the way on our progress...

I know that some of you will welcome this news with some trepidation, but really you should not. EMI is a great business. It has an incredible heritage and an even more exciting future. We are optimistic about the music market, and have a clear vision for the future which builds on the strengths of both parts of our business. Working together over these last months has demonstrated that the Global Rights Management approach will deliver the growth we seek because it delivers better outcomes for our artists and songwriters.

There will be a lot of people kicking the tires trying to figure out whether slicing and dicing the company will yield a higher value. But, we know that if you step back and see where we are going, where the alliance of these two businesses through Global Rights Management is taking us, the greatest value is in keeping the business together. That is why I believe that EMI will continue to be EMI for a very long time to come.

So I welcome this next chapter in EMI's history. We will come through stronger and even more prepared to meet the challenges of the future, empowered to continue to build a new kind of music company that is focused on delivering for our artists and songwriters.

Best wishes, Roger.

In the event "slicing and dicing" was Citigroup's chosen option. The sale of EMI was a more turbulent affair than that of WMG. There were "local" difficulties, notably EMI's pension problems and the possibility of regulatory issues if insiders won EMI. More importantly, there was a distinct change in the atmosphere between the sale of WMG and the marketing of EMI. Such changes can be short or long-lived. It's hard to determine exactly why Access or BMG RM didn't go the final mile, but it seems that caution set in. Access was beginning to see that while there might be potential there, WMG's performance, as shown in the first quarterly report after the acquisition, was problematic. On that basis buying another record company might not be the best move forward. WMG's revenues for the three months ending September 30 fell 6% to $707m, while annual revenues fell 4% to $2,87bn. An unexpected wrinkle was the willingness of the new WMG to sacrifice Bronfman and Bronfman, surprisingly, being equally willing to take the money and run, quitting as chairman in January after WMG's failed attempt to take over EMI Music. BMG RM took a similarly cautious view. And so the two companies widely expected to be the buyers dropped out of the auction leaving the way free for insiders, who could make immediate costs savings – Vivendi said on completion of the deal that it expected to make cost savings of some $135m by merging its own and EMI Music's back-office operations, but faced regulatory hurdles.

For Access Industries and BMG RM, it was the element of uncertainty that was paramount. And uncertainty was the name of the game in late 2011, as the general economic health of the world slipped. The earlier arrival of Spotify in the US and the sale of WMG for more than it had been bought for, hinted that success might be round the corner for recorded music. So in the first half of the year the number of start-ups seeking investment to finance a wide range of business models they thought might reboot the record industry grew. But the wind swiftly changed. "A fundamental mismatch is now starting to show," the *Wall Street Journal* reported in October, 2011. "While scores of web companies were founded in recent years, there isn't enough venture capital to keep all of them going indefinitely." In the third quarter of 2011, venture capital financing hit its lowest levels since 2003, according to the National Venture Capital Association. *Digital Music News* had predicted that music-related start-ups would garner over $500m in the full year, but it fell below that. And so it was insiders, companies that could make immediate cost cuts and find efficiencies of scale, UMG and the Sony/ATV led consortium, that dismembered EMI.

And then the wind changed again, bringing with it a new wave of optimism.

Just before the end of 2011, US trade paper *Billboard* predicted unit growth for calendar 2011 would be significant. UK trade association BPI similarly predicted that CD sales would soar in the Christmas period, which traditionally accounted for 22% of recorded music sales. The reasoning behind these two predictions was the fall in price of CD albums, particularly catalogue items, and the growing sales of Deluxe and Special Editions of albums, which cost more than standard releases. Special bundling clearly worked. In the 12 months ending September 2011, 10% of the Top 200 best-selling artist album titles in the UK was a Deluxe release, according to the BPI. The best-selling Deluxe album of the period was the *Hollywood* edition of Michael Bublé's *Crazy Love* which added a disc featuring new studio and live tracks to the original album. Also successful was the special edition of Lady Gaga's *The Fame Monster*, which added a further 16 tracks to the original album. Deluxe Edition reissues also proved popular for heritage acts. The Rolling Stones' re-release of *Exile On Main Street* in June 2010 added an extra disc of new material, and helped the group to their first number one since 1994. Classic albums by Nirvana, Pink Floyd, The Who, Queen and others were also given Deluxe edition reissues in 2011. In the wake of past dramatic oversells of the return to health of the industry, such predictions were treated with a higher degree of scepticism than in the past. Nonetheless, the forecast by PricewaterhouseCoopers that global music sales would return to growth in 2013 was greeted warmly.

And it might even be true.

SoundScan in January 2012 reported that in units terms albums sales in the US rose for the first time since 2004. Sales of CD albums fell by 5.7% to 223.5m units, but digital album sales rose by 19.5% to 103m downloads. The value question as ever was blurred, but later in the month global figures from IFPI confirmed that there had been a global recovery of sorts, or at least a slowdown in the decline of the value of recorded music sales (*see table below*).

The trade value of global recorded music sales in 2011 ($bn)

	Value	*% change*
Physical	10.0	−9 (−14)
Digital	5.2	+8 (+5)
Performance rights	0.94	+5 (+5)
TOTAL	**16.2**	**−3 (−8)**

Source: IFPI. The figures in brackets are the changes on the previous year

According to IFPI's figures, which are about value rather than volume, the digital revenues of the record companies were getting closer to compensating for lost physical revenues in some markets. In the US and South Korea digital accounted for more than half (51% and 54% respectively) of record companies' revenues, with digital channels accounting for around a third (32%) of their global revenues Thus, although physical sales continued to fall in value, but at a reduced rate, there was a sense of light at the end of the dark tunnel the record industry had for so long been in. In particular IFPI highlighted the fact that album downloads, with their greater margins, rose globally by 24% in volume terms – 19%, 27% and 71% in the US, UK and France, respectively – compared to an 11% rise in single track downloads.

This optimism was further extended when in January 2012 Global Industry Analysts (GIA) predicted that the global music recording industry would register steady growth over the next few years to reach $32.4bn in retail value by 2015. GIA, echoing Edgar Bronfman at WMG's 2010 annual results, argued that the industry was witnessing a transition phase in which the advent of digital technologies and the popularity of digital music had started to compensate for the decline in physical sales. Reading the report it is impossible not to be reminded of past extravagant examples of false optimism.

But the optimism was spreading.

At New York's New Music Seminar Tom Silverman trawled through the SoundScan's stats for 2011 and found only comfort, forecasting a "resurrection" for the record industry. It's an odd but apt choice of word. *Billboard's* Glenn Peoples was quick to see the implicit ironies: "Something has to die in order to be resurrected. Although the record industry didn't completely die in the 12 years from Napster to present day, many parts are completely gone (physical retailers), others have been transformed (distribution, marketing, ticketing) and still others have been born (digital distribution, social media)."

Piracy remains an issue for the record industry with one in four Internet users in 2011 regularly accessing unlicensed services, according to a survey by Nielsen and IFPI. However, there is some evidence that the spread of various versions of the graduated response laws have had an effect. Quoting a survey by Danaher *et al*, IFPI claimed that despite earlier evidence (*see* Chapter 16), France's HADOPI law helped to stimulate legitimate online sales in 2011. A further success was the closure of the Megaupload website in January 2012, following the indictment and arrest of its owners for allegedly operating as an organisation dedicated to copyright infringement. Piracy won't go away, but its impact seems to be growing less significant as legitimate online services find a commercial perch.

As oft repeated earlier, online sales have far lower margins for the majors. Those margins have been further threatened by a series of court cases raised by both current and heritage acts concerning the royalties due to them from the online sales of their recordings. In September 2010, Central District of California Judge Silverman of the US Ninth Circuit Court of Appeals in San Francisco reversed a 2009 federal jury decision in a lawsuit filed by F.B.T. Productions, the production company to which Eminem was signed, alleging that UMG had underpaid it royalties for digital downloads of Eminem's recordings on the basis that such recordings were licensed to iTunes and thus F.B.T. was due a higher royalty rate rather than the one paid by UMG to it for physical sales. The ruling meant that UMG owed original Eminem partner F.B.T. Productions 50% of digital royalties based on royalty rates for a licence rather than the royalty rate of 12% agreed on Eminem's physical sales. The case is likely to be significant for those acts whose contracts do not specify digital royalty rates and have a substantial back catalogue.

UMG presented the ruling as specific rather than generic: "The ruling sets no legal precedent as it only concerns the language of one specific recording agreement." Daniel Asimow, counsel for FBT took a decidedly different view. Speaking to *Digital Music News* after the appeal he said, "We are very pleased with the Court's decision as it vindicates our position that the agreements between record labels and iTunes and other digital music services are licenses, and record companies have to pay Eminem and F.B.T. under the royalty provisions governing licenses of their products."

All new recording contracts specifically eliminate the distinction between online and physical recorded music sales. However, if the F.B.T. case is accepted as a legal precedent, the ruling is likely to be called upon in support of previous lawsuits raised by heritage acts whose contracts did not specify online sales. A class action lawsuit was initiated by the Allman Brothers Band, Cheap Trick and others in 2006 against SME on the grounds that Sony (subsequently Sony BMG and now SME) had underpaid them for the download sales of their recordings via iTunes and other third parties. Just before the F.B.T. ruling, the case was settled out of court for $8m. In January 2012, the members of Sister

Sledge filed a class action lawsuit against WMG alleging they too had been deprived of royalties due them because of improper calculations of the royalties from digital music sales and subsequently a growing number of artists have launched lawsuits over the underpayment of revenues due them for digital downloads. The plaintiffs, some with careers stretching back to the 1960s and 1970s, include Motown vocal group The Temptations, country star Kenny Rogers, rocker Rob Zombie, R&B group Tower of Power, rock group Toto, rapper Chuck D and musical parodist "Weird Al" Yankovic.

Moreover, in the course of the investigations into the underpayments for digital downloads other issues have been raised. F.B.T. further alleges that not all money generated by foreign sales of Eminem recordings was returned to Aftermath, the Universal division that releases the rapper's music. Instead, the plaintiffs say that under an intercompany agreement at Universal, 71% of the revenue is paid to Universal's foreign affiliates while Aftermath only gets 29% . Then as part of the preparation for the final trial to assess the damages due them, F.B.T. made fresh charges about a range of issues. These included allegations about "Incorrect royalty Rates" referring to vinyl sales, sales at military bases, budget sales, record club sales and foreign licensing as well as digital downloads, as well as a variety of deductions made such as overstatement of the cost of television adverting. All in all F.B.T. itemised underpayments of $3.8m for the period 2005–2009.

Lawyers acting for Kenny Rogers, who had 11 US Top 10 hits, including two chart-toppers, 'Lady' (1980) and 'Islands In The Stream' (1983), produced an equally detailed set of allegations:

(1) In April of 2007, Kenny Rogers attempted to audit Capitol Records. However, because of a "purposefully complex and opaque royalty payment system," coupled with an inability to receive any documentation on digital sales, it took Rogers' auditing firm nearly two years to complete the process. "The accounting firm was unable to complete an initial audit report until March 9, 2009," the complaint read.

(2) That audit uncovered a number of payment issues, which Capitol Records promised to resolve in 2010. By 2011, Capitol told Rogers that

they were "still ironing out a few things," then the two employees assigned to the issue left the company (most likely laid off).

(3) The case was then passed to an attorney, who told Rogers in January of this year that he would "promptly try to resolve the Rogers audit." It was not resolved, leading to the lawsuit.

(4) Capitol Records systematically put a portion of Rogers' royalties into a "suspense file," for reasons that were not articulated. Rogers only found out about this file through the multi-year audit.

(5) Capitol refused to share any settlement amounts from lawsuits involving Napster, Kazaa, Audiogalaxy, Grokster, or BearShare. The label also refused to share what those amounts were.

(6) Capitol sold Kenny Rogers classics through record clubs, but did not pass those royalties on to the artist.

(7) Capitol Records provided inconsistent royalty statements to Kenny Rogers, based on the use of different royalty calculation and processing systems. One report would show royalties for certain albums in certain periods, while another report would not reflect those royalties.

(8) Capitol provided 'free goods' in foreign markets, but did not pay royalties on those freebies (as designated by the artist contract).

(9) Capitol charged Kenny Rogers for international taxes, even through they were receiving foreign tax credits.

(10) Capitol charged Rogers for 100 percent of video costs, even though the contract called for a 50 percent charge.

(11) Capitol charged more than $50,000 of inappropriate or mysterious expenses to the Kenny Rogers account, and never explained what these charges were.

(12) Capitol Records did not offer any accounting (or royalties) on foreign broadcasts.

(13) Capitol offered improper accounting on sales on a number of sales in foreign countries.

(14) After the findings of the audit, Capitol did not implement any changes to fix the issues discovered.

The contracts made by the majors (and the independents) with new signings over recent years have rectified many of the ambiguities.

However, the current court cases, coming at a time when the previously established economic patterns of the creation of musical works and their distribution are being challenged by the new contractual and distribution agreements, question the very structure of the modern record industry. Digital sales are now an essential part of a record company's revenues: in the US in 2011, they accounted for just over half of all recorded music sales. If the value to record companies of such sales were to be significantly reduced, bearing in mind the headlong decline of physical sales and the continuing huge importance of catalogue sales, the financial stability of the record industry would seem to be seriously threatened by the implications of the case won by F.B.T. and other cases currently challenging the status quo, particularly if accompanied by the lack of transparency that the subsequent investigations by F.B.T. and Rogers' people have uncovered.

MIDEM, the trade fair for the music industry, has offered real indications of the shifts in the music industry. Held annually since 1967 in Cannes, France, it began as a simple trade fair, offering attendees the opportunity to buy and sell territorial rights in recorded music and music publishing property. Over the years it grew to become a place where rights administrators, notably collection societies, would meet, while in the marketplace of the Palais des Festivals the latest would-be entrants to the music industry promoted their wares. Then in the first decade of the 21st century, as communications changes made it less necessary for the major players to travel to Cannes, MIDEM re-invented itself as a talk-fest. And so each year the business model/ *issue de jour* was debated. And in each year less business was done, the announcements notwithstanding. From this perspective MIDEM is a useful litmus test. Bringing together musicians, businesspeople, cultural policy makers, and journalists from many countries, it provides a forum for business talks, discussing political and legal issues, and showcasing new artists, musical trends and music-related products.

MIDEM 2012 was an odd mix, far less business but far more talk. Mega music publishing executive Marty Bandier, the requirement that he smoke his cigar outside the Carlton notwithstanding, was still a king, but legacy didn't cut the mustard anymore at MIDEM. Talk, not product, was what was being sold at MIDEM 2012. Tom Silverman's optimism didn't quite reach MIDEM. The Carlton bar was still jam packed with no table to be had, but it was the schmoozing and meetings around the trade fair rather than the fair itself that were the important diary dates.

Because, yes, the music business has changed dramatically in the course of the last 20 years.

The five majors have been reduced to three and their power to control the market has been shattered. As the digital revolution marched on, their power to set prices and determine the terms of distribution of their wares have fallen by the wayside. At the same time their control over artists has been eroded. Heritage acts, the Eagles, Radiohead, Rolling Stones and U2, have found being closely tied to a record company unnecessary and transformed themselves from signees to either partners or standalone operations. Such a move has been harder for new acts, but the huge success of Adele, the best-selling artist of 2011, and the emergence of acts like Arctic Monkeys, and the growing number of acts who want control rather than mega success, something that independent labels trade on, often through joint-venture agreements with majors, such as that of Mumford & Sons, has significantly reduced the earnings of the majors. The majors have certainly lost a degree of influence. Small and medium business enterprises mean cultural diversity and employment possibilities, two tunes that chime well with the regulatory authorities in Europe particularly as they produce more than 80% of all new music releases and around 80% of Europe's music industry-related jobs. The IMPALA argument is that their potential is enormous but is hampered by complex barriers to trade and severe market access problems. That said, the impact on diversity, consumer choice and pluralism is increasingly becoming clear. Over 95% of what most people hear and see, whether on radio, retail or the Internet, is concentrated in the hands of the majors.

Cultural and creative SMEs are now officially recognised by the EU as "the drivers of growth, job creation and innovation". In recognition of this, IMPALA has started to lobby the EC and its member countries to make key investment, digital and market access measures available to small and medium-sized businesses. Fostering Europe's economy of culture and diversity has been one of the EU's top priorities in becoming the world's leading knowledge economy. Culture is a bigger earner than any of chemicals, automobiles or ICT manufacturing and provides more than 3% of Europe's jobs. Despite small and medium-sized record companies being responsible for over three-quarters of new releases, according to a new study by the European Music Office, the majors accounted for 76.5% of tracks downloaded in Europe between September 2010 and August 2011 and 76% of tracks played on air over the same period. This was despite the success of Adele, whose recordings were issued by the British independent company Beggars Banquet.

The majors have lost a degree of influence. Small and medium-sized set-ups mean cultural diversity and employment possibilities. That said, the dramatic reduction in the cost of entry and the costs of digital distribution, especially after the creation of Merlin, which has successfully acted as an aggregator of independent music, making it far easier for online services to licence that music, has significantly reduced the problems of market access for the independents. Their greater flexibility and lower cost base mean that, despite the reduced margins on digital sales, they can survive on smaller revenues.

But survival also requires deep pockets, hence the lobbying of IMPALA for easier access to investment for the small outfits. UMG and SME, as divisions of huge conglomerates, both have access to deep pockets and parent companies committed to intellectual property. In 2011, Sony sold its 50% stake in its LCD television joint venture to partner Samsung for $939m. Television was once a core product for Sony, but the collapsing margins made it disposable. Two decades earlier Philips saw music as too dangerous a business and sold its music arm PolyGram. Then intellectual property was undervalued. However, neither Sony nor Vivendi, which ended up PolyGram's owners, while facing difficult times, has ever seriously considered quitting the intellectual property business.

Intellectual property works, but it requires a long view perspective. Elvis Presley's 'Heartbreak Hotel' will be featured in a film or two in 10 year's time; *Dark Side Of The Moon* will always be in the charts; 'Blowin' In The Wind' will always be on the radio. The trick is finding ways to monetise such assets, when you've lost control of their distribution.

EMI and WMG, for different reasons were unable to survive that loss. EMI always being available to be bought was rather like a Pooh stick – once dropped from a bridge it was never in control of its destiny, always the victim of the stream's current, going this way then that. EMI was an old-fashioned company that sank in modern, troubled times. Unlike EMI, WMG, in the course of its later history, played the trick of re-invention, the seven ages of corporate existence. Both stories were also the tale of the squeezed middle. Media heavy hitters need UMG and SME as partners because they have the repertoire, especially the back catalogue. They also need the independents because they have the edge. Economies of scale and high executive recompense are available to UMG and SME. Tight budgets and long working hours are possible for the indies.

But the middle?

The sale of the EMI group over, Faxon sent the staff another, more sombre, memo. It reads like a *billet-doux* to a long lost moment in time with a misty-eyed hope for the future:

> *"As all of you know, it was my ambition to keep EMI together as a stand-alone business in pursuit of our shared strategy. But that is not to be, not because there was no one interested, but because at the critical moment the credit markets seized up. With credit spreads widening and little access to debt capital it became difficult for financial bidders to formulate compelling proposals at the right price.*
>
> *"But the enthusiasm of trade bidders remained. They saw great businesses and were willing to step up. In the case of EMI Music, Universal won the day not only on price but also on other critical terms. As for Citi, it has always been clear that they were not long term owners no matter how much they admired our business and our team. In fact that is the reason they initiated the sale process to begin with. So, when faced with an attractive offer from Universal, they decided to sell.*
>
> *"So, the decision has been taken, the two parts of this great business are*

to move along separate paths. But, before ownership is transferred much needs to happen.

"Our biggest task will be to complete the legal separation of the two businesses, which many of you know is not a trivial matter. Equally, Universal will need to clear the necessary regulatory hurdles before they can take ownership. And that too will take time and effort. So, it is likely that EMI will remain much as it is today through and perhaps well past the end of our fiscal year.

"So, what is our obligation in the period to completion? It is very simple, to continue to drive each of our businesses to the very best of our ability. That is of course what Citi and Universal want but it is also the right thing for our artists. The promises we have made to each of them are not changed by the sale. While there is no doubt that for many of us the future will feel uncertain – how could it not – we must stay true to those promises. It is what has made EMI what it is and each of us who we are.

"We'll be having a number of calls and town hall meetings over the coming days, but I want to end for now by saying one last thing. You've heard me talk a lot about global rights management, and how I believe that this strategy has the ability to change the industry. For me, global rights management is not just a slogan. It is a philosophy built around a simple concept – to do the right thing – to act with passion, humanity and integrity. Over the next months together we will cement the legacy of EMI by our actions. I know I can count on you to play your part. I hope that every one of us will always remain true to that philosophy, both now and in the future.

"Best wishes, Roger."

But, of course, it wasn't over. UMG and the Sony/ATV consortium had won the bidding war. Now they had to win over the regulators.

Chapter 18

Battling The Regulators

The sale of EMI significantly changed the face of the world record and music publishing businesses. It reduced the number of majors to three and dramatically changed their positions. Where before there had been two companies with 20+% market shares and two with 10+% shares, *Music & Copyright*'s *pro forma* market shares for 2010 saw UMG with a 38.9% global market share, SME with 23%, WMG third with 14.9% and the independents with 23.2%. Henceforth UMG and SME would have the advantage of size, the independents the advantage of speed and greater flexibility, leaving WMG in the squeezed middle and with less room to manoeuvre. WMG's music publishing division, Warner Chappell, was in the same position with a 13.9% global market share, with Sony/ATV (32.2%) and the independents (31.4%) having 30% plus shares and UMPG some 10 percentage points less (22.6%).

Both sales required regulatory approval, a process that took up most of 2012. The consortium's purchase of EMI MP had the easier ride, in great part because Sony/ATV only represented 38% of the consortium and although it would supply back-office operations EMI MP would not be rolled into Sony/ATV. Sony/ATV had to make some divestitures, but far fewer than UMG, to placate the regulatory authorities, particularly in Europe. A mark of the confidence of Vivendi and the Sony/ATV-led consortium was that both agreed to pay Citigroup upfront and take upon themselves the regulatory burden. The regulatory process began in January 2012, with the various parties drawing their various lines in the sand. However, as the process unravelled the lines quickly blurred in the face of the extended public inspection of the UMG-EMI deal and an element of desperation appeared.

AIM, which said at the time of the sale of EMI Music that it represented "bad news for almost everyone" delivered its opening salvo in January, issuing its members with a letter to send off to their local MPs seeking to encourage the Secretary of State for Business, Innovation and Skills to intervene: "The increasing concentration of the music market in the hands of a decreasing number of gigantic multinationals has undoubtedly damaged competition. The proposed sale of EMI threatens further damage so great that it must be reviewed and resisted by the UK Coalition Government with the full support of the Opposition… The move will undoubtedly concentrate the global music market still further into the hands of two dominant major companies – UNIVERSAL and SONY. That itself is enough to demand that the UK Government looks closely at and opposes the proposed sale of the only UK major music company to the remaining gigantic multinational."

In a surprise addition – AIM represents independent record companies – the AIM letter concluded: "If the deals with Universal and Sony are allowed to go ahead Warner Music will effectively be relegated in size to a position where it can offer no real global competition, and the global music market will be in the control of just two huge companies – one French [Vivendi/Universal] and one Japanese [Sony]."

This concern was echoed by the pan-European trade body IMPALA, to which AIM is affiliated, which, playing the cultural diversity and small business cards, argued that further consolidation in the music industry was bad news for the wider creative sector, and especially small and middle-sized enterprises, which would find it even harder to compete with ever bigger major players.

Rich Bengloff, the president of AIM, said: "The increased concentration of copyright ownership, historically, has always hurt the independent label community in terms of achieving economic parity and market access. We join our European Impala Independent music label colleagues in their concern over this acquisition and await more detail."

In previous merger attempts the major battlefield had been Europe where the Commission had been highly excited and involved in the issues such mergers raised, but this time round the US Federal Trade Commission (FTC) seemed equally interested. Accordingly, WMG, now the smallest of the majors, hired Brownstein Hyatt Farber Schreck, lobbyists who specialise in competition policy and corporate mergers, to argue their case before the FTC. Just as UMG had argued against the first proposed merger of EMI and WMG in 2000, so WMG took the same position *vis a vis* UMG's takeover of EMI Music. UMG responded in kind, hiring Bingham McCutchen to lobby on its behalf on competition matters.

Past merger and takeover attempts that required regulatory approval were invariably accompanied by protests from competitors that they would be disadvantaged if such an acquisition/merger were allowed to take place. Thus, for example, UMG argued that the first attempted merger of EMI and WMG in 2000 would result in an unlevel playing field and when SME and BMG merged in 2004, EMI, UMG and WMG all filed statements of objection to the deal with both the FTC and EC. However, whereas IMPALA had always raised its concerns in public, the majors previously had raised their objections privately in statements filed with the regulatory authorities. Not so with regards to the dismembering of EMI.

On his last day as chairman of WMG, Edgar Bronfman, Jr. at the Los Angeles *D: Drive Into Media Conference* said UMG's acquisition of EMI "would create what I call a super-major that would basically determine the future of not only recorded music but really any kind of digital initiative as well". He further argued that given that the expanded UMG would have a global market share of some 40% the deal would not only effect the digital marketplace, but it would drive down the economics of artists deals and, echoing one of IMPALA's key themes, the impact of cultural diversity.

The contrast between the Sony/ATV consortium's approach to seeking regulatory approval for its purchase of EMI MP and that of Vivendi in search of the same for its purchase of EMI Music couldn't have been greater. Vivendi's, as we shall see later, was conducted in the full glare of publicity and ill fortune. At the start Vivendi took the position that the regulators would naturally authorise its buying of EMI Music. Despite the huge market share the combination of UMG and EMI would generate (over 40% in some European territories and close to that in the US), Vivendi opened the bidding with no offers of divestitures, beyond the sale of various properties to help fund the purchase. The divestitures included its classical, Christian and other music publishing catalogues, which were expected to raise some $200m, and various bits of real estate valued at around $500m. These sales had the function of narrowing the focus of UMG to a company based on popular music.

The Vivendi view seemed to be a quiet word here, a nod and a wink there and the European regulators – it was assumed the US regulators would just rubber stamp the deal – would see sense. Deal done! And then the wheels fell off. Vivendi's share price took a battering, its CEO was replaced and very significant disagreements erupted, culminating in a couple of weeks of public horse trading.

Not so the consortium's stately march to approval. The consortium planned for Sony/ATV to administer EMI MP, but it would be doing so on behalf of the consortium, to which it would be financially responsible. At the same time EMI MP would be kept separate from Sony/ATV for all but administrative purposes. The benefits to Sony/ATV were immediate. Under its arrangement with the consortium, it would administer EMI MP's business, which involved processing royalties and making licensing deals. In exchange for eliminating about $120m in overhead expenses, Sony/ATV would get 15% of the net publisher's share – its revenue minus royalty payments to songwriters – as an administration fee. This was likely to net Sony/ATV around $50m a year, while reducing EMI MP's operating cost by $70m.

The consortium's first slice of luck was that raising the funds to make the purchase turned out to be far easier and cheaper than expected. The anticipated interest rate on the bonds when the bid was put together in November 2011 was 12%. In actual fact, when the deal was concluded in February it was only slightly over 5.5%, a reflection of the perceived high value of music publishing and of EMI MP in particular. EMI MP controlled 1.3m copyrights, which represented a broad range, from new artists, such as The Black Eyed Peas, Rihanna, Kanye West and historical classics from Motown as well as a large number of standards, such as 'New York, New York' and 'Over the Rainbow'.

In March the consortium was apprised by the European Commission that although it had presented Sony/ATV and EMI MP as separate companies, the Commission saw the two as a single entity when it came to negotiations with users and that with a 31% plus market share in the European Economic Area it would be able to exercise a greater degree of control than was thought to be appropriate with regard to the online licensing of Anglo-American chart repertoire, which the Commission noted was "an indispensable part of any online platform offering to consumers". In particular the Commission noted that in the UK and Northern Ireland Sony/ATV and EMI MP would either own or have a share in the publishing rights to over 50% of chart hits. In response the consortium offered a clutch of divestitures. When these were deemed not to be enough, the consortium swiftly upped the divestitures to include the worldwide publishing rights of Virgin UK, Virgin Europe, Virgin US and Famous Music UK catalogues. In addition, the rights to recent and future musical works of a number of Anglo-American authors, such as Gary Barlow, Ozzy Osbourne, Robbie Williams, Ben Harper, Lenny Kravitz, Placebo and The Kooks, would also be sold. The value of these divestitures, all of which were made in private and were only made public after the deal was approved, was in the region of $25m, which represented slightly more than 2% of the combined group's revenues. In the light of these the Commission authorised the deal in April 2012, on the basis that the transaction "would not significantly impede effective competition in the EEA or any substantial part of it".

Approval granted, the consortium immediately set about implementing the restructuring of EMI MP that was leaked to *The New York Times*. In February, a confidential report, prepared as part of raising the necessary funding, revealed that Sony/ATV planned to eliminate some 60% of EMI MP's staff within two years as part of the $70m in annual savings sought. According to the document, 152 people would be laid off in the first year, and 174 would be "used on a temporary, transitional basis". The elimination of those 326 positions represented about 63% of EMI Publishing's then workforce of 515. The price of the efficiencies that the deal represented to the consortium was lost jobs. Nonetheless deal done, book closed, cuts started.

Vivendi's first piece of bad news was the decision of Senator Herb Kohl, chairman of the US Senate Judiciary Committee's antitrust panel, to hold hearings on the merger. Even though the committee had no official influence over the federal government's antitrust regulators who would decide on the matter, it guaranteed extra publicity for the issue, gave opponents of the deal fresh opportunities to make their case, and made it more difficult for the FTC to simply nod through the deal.

Prior to the June hearings, the deal won approval from the Brazilian and New Zealand regulatory authorities (and later from the Australian, Japanese and Canadian authorities) and the support of the artists' and musicians' unions (SAG-AFTRA and AFM), but the June Senate hearings soured any pleasure Vivendi might have had from that. The hearing saw leading executives offering wildly different portraits of the future of the music business.

Appearing as a witness, Lucian Grainge, Vivendi's CEO, made the case that market share did not mean market power that resided with the consumer. He further argued that an expanded UMG and revitalised EMI would help stop piracy, in short: "Through our acquisition of EMI, Universal will enhance the creative investment in the company and further broaden the support for digital services. This will provide more opportunities for artists and more music and choice for consumers than ever before."

Grainge was supported by an equally voluble Roger Faxon, EMI's CEO, however Edgar Bronfman returned to the issue of market share, which he suggested did lead to market power:

> The potential level of concentration that would result from the proposed Universal/EMI merger has never been seen before in this industry. No record company in the SoundScan era has had a U.S. market share greater than the more than 30% that Universal commands today.
>
> Again, a combined Universal/EMI would have about a 42% U.S. market share. This is high by almost any standard. Consider other industries: General Motors has about a 20% market share. The largest airline – Southwest – has an 18% market share.
>
> The story is the same for the media industries.
>
> To put it in context, last year, the largest movie studio, Paramount, had a market share of around 20%. Random House, the largest trade book publisher, was less than 20%. And Comcast, the largest cable operator, had just over 20% of pay television.
>
> So who would be hurt by this merger, and how?
>
> Universal, currently the world's largest recorded music company and the world's largest music publisher, would become the dominant firm in recorded music. It would effectively become a bottleneck. It would impede technological innovation. It would significantly reduce competition among record labels to sign artists. And it would interfere with its competitors' access to effective distribution with both physical and digital retailers.

Bronfman also offered two examples of UMG using the leverage that comes from market power, firstly quoting a story from *The Wall Street Journal*:

> In some cases, Universal has already used its market power to extract favorable terms from online music services. In early 2008, David Pakman, then the CEO of eMusic.com Inc, was negotiating to add major-label releases to his company's catalog of independent music. David Ring, a senior digital executive at Universal Music, told him Universal's massive catalog entitled it to more favorable terms. He said, 'We get more, because

we're Universal. That's just the way we roll,' Mr. Pakman recalls. That stance, Mr. Pakman adds, applied to 'every dimension of our contract: the rate you pay per unit sold; the promotion you agree to do.' The companies reached an agreement ... later, after Mr. Pakman had left and eMusic raised its prices sharply.

And then Bronfman brought up the case of Deezer:

Another example of Universal trying to dictate a new service's business model was evidenced by the 2011 Deezer judgment in a French court. The court rejected Universal's attempt to prohibit Deezer from using its catalogue of songs finding that Universal was abusing its dominant position by the new terms and conditions it was trying to foist on Deezer.

Independent record company owner Martin Mills played the indie card:

The transaction will lead to a loss of consumer choice, injury to competition, increased barriers to entry, impairment of innovation, further entrenchment of the Majors to the disadvantage of independent recorded music, increased moulding of the online market and ultimately increased prices/reduced terms for consumers. This transaction should not be permitted to go forward.

The most combative witness was Irving Azoff, the Live Nation Entertainment/Front Line Management chairman. Philosophically he agreed with Lucian Grainge: "Bottom line: The people concerned that a combined EMI-UMG would have too much 'power' really just don't get what has happened to this business over the last decade. Labels don't control artists. Those days are gone. And no label in the world can control the supremacy of the modern music fan. The power shift has already taken place – and no one should worry for a minute that it rests with the labels any longer."

And then came realpolitik. According to Azoff, WMG had had a chance to buy EMI Music but fluffed it. It was now opposing the deal because if it failed EMI would come back to the market at a reduced price, thus giving WMG a second chance again against less competition, thus possibly winning an increased market share, rather than facing a position in which it would be the smallest of the majors if the deal went ahead.

Online music essayist Bob Lefsetz summed up the hearing in a typically acerbic fashion:

Be afraid, be very afraid. Especially when Lucian Grainge makes Edgar Bronfman, Jr. look like a paragon of openness and reasonableness.
If you were watching this hearing, and you knew nothing about the law, were just deciding whether the Universal/EMI merger should go through on fairness, you'd say NO WAY!

Lucian Grainge was so evasive and duplicitous you'd be afraid to go to dinner with him for fear he'd steal your watch. It was so obvious that both the panel and the chairman/senator had to remark upon it, that he didn't answer a single damn question.

Roger Faxon was eloquent. But it was hard to figure out exactly whose side he was on. What I mean by that is isn't he up for a job at Warner? And isn't this sale from Citi to Universal guaranteed? And he said if the merger goes through he's gonna lose his job, but admitted with a send-off paycheck, ain't that the American way.

At least Irving Azoff was honest. He said that Warner was blocking this merger because they didn't want to overpay for EMI, but they still wanted to own it. Truth is always refreshing. Irving was the only one who really talked about the new music business. Still, the concept that recorded music income is going to drop off a cliff and be nonexistent in the future is just plain wrong. The majors may not control the music of all of his acts, but they can determine on which terms they engage with the public in the marketplace.

Martin Mills made you want to sign to his company. He wasn't sleazy, he was direct, and forceful …

And the inquisitors were quite informed. Star of the panel was Al Franken, who even corrected Azoff, putting in the record that Universal was not first on Spotify, but third, after EMI and SME. Franken had done his homework. He cornered Grainge. But like the weasel Lucian is, he refused to respond to the inquiry, again and again and again. Hell,

Grainge wouldn't even answer Kohl's question as to why he bought EMI. Can you imagine that, someone spending $1.9 billion and not being able to articulate why?

This hearing is meaningless. But the proposed merger is not.

As it turned out the hearing wasn't meaningless. It had an immediate effect on the press coverage and even more dramatic delayed one (*see below*). The issue of market share/size/power had legs. At the hearing Bronfman, in response to questions, reiterated his earlier point about market share:

Universal has tried to portray its market share as lower than it actually is by excluding labels that it distributes. But that's disingenuous. Owned and distributed market share is the metric Universal uses when talking to potential purchasers of its parent Vivendi shares, that's the metric it uses when seeking better economics from the Copyright Royalty Board, and most importantly, that's the metric it uses when negotiating the terms of its digital deals. When it comes to market power, especially in digital where market share includes all music under distribution, there is no distinction between music that is distributed and music that is owned.

A few days after the hearings the *New York Post* reported that IFPI had postponed the publication of its *Investing in Music* report. The reason UMG, which like all the majors had to OK the publication, declined to do so was because it would include market shares which it clearly preferred not to be made public.

In July the circus moved to Europe. Vivendi's bravado notwithstanding, after its initial examination into the Vivendi/EMI Music deal, the Commission issued a 194 page Statement of Objections (SoO) and initiated a phase 2 review, which required more than pleasant words in response from Vivendi. The Commission disagreed with Universal's statement of its market share, which excluded the recordings it distributed on behalf of independent record labels, and was not impressed by either the company's description of the power of Apple or the pressures on the majors from piracy. Vivendi sought to pour oil on troubled waters: "We are preparing a detailed response to the Commission's statement which will address the concerns outlined in this procedural document. We will continue to work closely with the Commission and look forward to securing regulatory clearance."

More significantly, Vivendi changed the team negotiating with the Commission. In the same week of the SoO, Jean-René Fourtou, Vivendi's chairman, took direct charge of negotiations with the Commission. The move, which swiftly followed the exit of Vivendi's former CEO, Jean-Bernard Levy who was widely thought to be less supportive of the bid and of Vivendi's high level of involvement in music, was accompanied by a change of tone. Vivendi, it was stressed, was a *European* company. Hence, there was much mention of The Beatles and Charles Aznavour. And concessions and divestitures were now on the table, so much so that Vivendi asked for an extension to respond to the SoO and – remembering Grainge's difficulties at the Senate hearings? – turned down the offer of an oral hearing before the Commission.

The first sign of Vivendi's change in stance was the *Manifesto for a New Music Industry*, in which Grainge described the philosophy behind the EMI deal. Only privately circulated, it presented UMG as concerned with heritage, determined to keep EMI "as intact as possible", re-dedicating to A&R and aiming to be collaborative rather than antagonistic towards the independent music community. Little more than a week later in an open letter to IMPALA Grainge detailed the concessions behind the *Manifesto*: There would be a significant offer of more than €150m in divestments of owned repertoire and more than €100m of licence, compilation and distribution rights, which together represented $304m of EMI Music's European revenue, but only if IMPALA supported the takeover. The package promised:

- *A commitment to continue the support of the CD format for five years*
- *Label divestments including Virgin Records, Chysalis UK (without Robbie Williams), Mute, Ensign, EMI Classics, Virgin Classics, Sanctuary (plus sub-labels Trojan and Noise), Co-Op, Roxy Recordings, MRS, Jazzland, EMI Music Belgium, EMI Czech Republic and Universal Music Greece*

- Guarantees that Universal wouldn't insert 'Most Favoured Nations' clauses in its future digital agreements and wouldn't oblige digital services to offer terms disproportionate to market share
- A €25m 'innovation and cultural' loan to help fund the purchase of assets and strengthen the combined might of the indies, which Universal recommended was split between IMPALA and Merlin
- A recommendation to either create a new global trade body between indie and major labels or a guarantee that Universal would vote for IMPALA to have a seat on the IFPI Main Board.

The letter, intended for the sight of the Commission, but addressed to IMPALA, revived memories of WMG's attempt to get the support of the independents in the course of its last failed attempt to merge with EMI Music and represented a momentous repositioning of UMG's presentation of self. The accepted view until then had been that divestitures would be made and that WMG would be the beneficiary of any sell-offs. Suddenly UMG seemed to be saying that it should be the independents, not its larger competitors that should benefit from any divestitures required. Just as WMG's offer to IMPALA caused ructions within the independents' trade group so did UMG's. IMPALA's board rejected the offer only to have to report that more than 50% of its board, including the likes of Domino, Ministry of Sound, Mute, PIAS and Union Square, had voted in favour of the offer. Then Patrick Zelnik, IMPALA's co-president and owner of the French independent Naive label, announced his support for the deal in an opinion piece, "A Universal/EMI merger could rescue the music business" for the *Financial Times*.

For 12 years at IMPALA ... I have fought concentration in the music industry. However, as Universal Music awaits regulators' verdict on its £1.2bn bid for EMI's recorded music division, I think it could be just what the sector needs... as I contemplate EMI's fall from grace and the way it was ravished by private equity, I can see that in the right circumstances this merger could create a more competitive industry, while offering stability to EMI's artists ...

> *The industry has lost more than half of its revenue, EMI was seized by bankers, other big companies cut staff and artists and the independents are, with few exceptions, fighting for their lives.*
>
> *Moreover, we can use Universal's acquisition as a model to create online competition that reflects music retailing when it was healthy – when specialists, independents and mass merchants had easy, non-discriminatory access to all repertoire. Emulating this online could give a huge boost to digital sales, streaming options and choice.*
>
> *Today, we can change this. I call on all sides to create a new pro-growth industry forum – without the vested interests of the current bodies – to balance the market between majors and independents and ensure that content owners, creative entrepreneurs, artists and consumers all benefit from the opportunities created by the internet. I call on regulators to bring Universal and the independents to the table to redress competition concerns and show the world they are capable of vision in transforming troubled industries.*

Just as Grainge's offer was self-seeking, so was Zelnik's. Shortly after the opinion piece, it transpired that Zelnik and Richard Branson had been talking about a possible re-entry for Branson into the music business with a possible offer for Virgin. For a few days, Branson basked in such publicity, before it became apparent that the caravan had moved on.

The differences within the IMPALA board notwithstanding, IMPALA reiterated its opposition to the deal, announcing on July 16 that:

> *Our board took a clear decision yesterday to continue its opposition to the Universal/EMI merger, rejecting remedies which do not deal with the specific problems set out in the EC's statement of objections. The issue isn't just digital, it's physical and access to media-exposure for new artists, as well as the foreclosure of independents when it comes to signing artists. We all respect Patrick Zelnik's view, but the FT article is the Naive position, not the Impala position.*

And then the artists, whose recordings UMG was offering to sell to whoever, stepped in with yet another letter to the *Financial Times*:

Sir,

The views of Patrick Zelnik ("A Universal EMI merger could rescue the music business", Comment, July 17) were as welcome as they were needed. His analysis was incisive, but his solution stopped one step short of perfect.

Divestments in the wake of mergers should first offer copyrights, at market rates, to the artists who created them. To sell them to other corporations, whether large or small, is just a perpetuation of an old business model, which has seen the recorded music business halve in value over 10 years. During that time, the technological revolution has displaced the old music business players. We do not need to repeat the mistakes of the past.

It would be good to have music business people rather than financiers owning and running music companies again. It would be even better to have artists owning their work and entering into partner relationships with service-providing major and independent record companies with all the finance and expertise an artist needs to develop their own business.

Top management at Universal has already concurred with this view. The concept of "turning the taps on" so that music catalogues are much more readily available to users, and copyright ownership is not an impediment to new services, would help build the artist-centric new music business that will benefit creators, investors and consumers.

Ed O'Brien, Radiohead, Nick Mason, Pink Floyd, Sandie Shaw, Co-Chairs, The Featured Artists' Coalition.

However, the Commission remained unhappy with the concessions offered, so UMG went back to the drawing board and came up with a neat idea that developed from its July 13 offer to IMPALA. Over the weekend of July 22, UMG offered a new package of concessions with the twist that it expected BMG RM, not its leading competitors, SME and WMG, to benefit from any divestitures required by the Commission. SME, the world's second-largest recorded music group by revenues, had been seen as a likely bidder for classical music labels, while WMG had been expected to snap up any pop repertoire that might be sold.

The news won UMG plaudits but also queries, with a number of independent label executives being interviewed by the *Financial Times* saying they wanted to buy assets but were unsure how to fund such deals. "They're saying their preference is to sell to the independent community," said Kenny Gates of PIAS, the independent distributor and owner of the Play It Again Sam label. "The funds are the problem for the independent community." Daniel Miller, who sold his Mute label to EMI, said he wanted to buy it back, but "it depends how much they want. I can only hope I can do it", while "We'd sure as hell like to try" to buy some of the labels Universal is offering, was the opinion of Laurence Bell of Domino Records.

And then another problem emerged. Under the original deal with Citigroup, Vivendi had agreed to pay it some 90% of the agreed purchase price by September 9 whether or not it had secured regulatory approval. However, as Vivendi had asked – and would continue to do so – for various extensions to allow it to better plead its case, it became clear that approval, if granted, would not be before mid-September at the earliest. One reason for this was the difficulty that UMG was having in reducing its European market share below 40%, which for the Commission, observers suggested, had become the essential requirement of the deal.

UMG returned to the table. On July 27, it proposed further concessions. Roger Faxon detailed these in a memo to EMI staff:

Subject: EMI Music – UPDATE

Dear All,

There has been a huge amount of speculation surrounding EMI in the press over the last couple of weeks, as the regulatory process surrounding EMI Music's proposed acquisition by Universal continues. I wanted to be sure that you heard the truth direct from me rather than on the industry grapevine, which is why I am writing to you all today.

The intricacies of the anti-trust world are an impenetrable mystery to most of us, but obviously it's important in any transaction of this nature that the regulators make a full review to ensure that consumers are protected from anti-competitive behaviour. UMG and each of the regulators around the world have been working closely together for many months now to achieve that. Since the market is different in each region of the world, the issues and the difficulty of resolving them also tend to be different. In a number of jurisdictions, such as Japan and New Zealand, Universal has been able to resolve the issues and has already received clearance. Now the focus is clearly on resolving the issues in the largest and most complex markets – and none is more important than Europe.

As I am sure you will have read, the European Commission has raised formal objections about the effect of bringing EMI and Universal together, and the two parties have since been working to find a potential remedy. As you can imagine, there are often significant differences in view between the regulators and the company applying for approval, but in the end, the two need to find a way of bridging those differences so that the merger can go forward.

In the last few days, Universal has identified a possible set of solutions that it believes should resolve the Commission's concerns. I emphasize the word 'possible' because before a resolution can be finalized the regulator will seek the input of a variety of third parties. The market testing of a proposed set of remedies is designed to help the regulator understand the implications of the proposed package, before they make a final determination. So, following the feedback from the market, there is obviously the chance that the proposed set of remedies will change before they become final.

The EU regulators will soon be putting the remedy package proposed by Universal into that market testing. Inevitably much of what is in that package will leak to the press, and that has already started to happen. As such, I wanted to make sure that you heard what is really going on directly from me.

Here is what is included in the package of proposed divestments:
– In the UK, an entity composed of the rosters and catalogues of Parlophone (excluding the Beatles, both as a group and individually), Mute, Chrysalis (excluding the Robbie Williams catalogue) and Ensign would be sold. Included in that disposal would also be the Pink Floyd catalogue and the recently concluded new deal with David Guetta, along with his catalogue. Note that these disposals only relate to exploitation of this repertoire within the EEA.
– EMI Classics and Virgin Classics would also be divested in the EEA.

- EMI's share of the NOW brand and compilation business in the EEA would also be sold. However, Universal would keep its share and participation in the Now compilation venture.
- The proposal also includes the divestment of a number of EMI's operating businesses in Continental Europe. Those local operating companies are EMI France, EMI Belgium, EMI Czech Republic, EMI Poland, EMI Portugal, EMI Sweden and EMI Norway.
- Universal is also proposing to divest some of its own businesses, principal among which are Sanctuary, Co-Op, and UMG Greece plus several European jazz labels.
- They would also commit to terminate or not to bid for a number of high-profile European licenses for major Anglo-American and domestic repertoire, namely Disney Records, Hollywood Records, Ministry of Sound, and Restos du Coeur in France.

Clearly it's an understatement to say that there are huge implications here for EMI, our staff and most especially, our artists. You will have hundreds of questions, as do we. As this is still a proposal right now, it is difficult for us to answer any of them right now, but over the coming days and weeks, we will be working very hard to address as many of them as possible. We have a lot of time to work through how all of this is going to unfold and how it will affect each of you. So as soon as we are able, we will be working with you to achieve just that.

So what happens next? Obviously the remedy proposal needs to proceed through market testing. That testing should not take long, but a final decision by the EU College of Commissioners will not take place until the second half of September. Of course, regulatory reviews elsewhere – particularly in places such as the United States and Australia – will also need to be completed, as well as a number of practical logistics.

With all that in mind, it's possible that with a wind behind our backs we could close the sale and EMI could pass to UMG as early as the end of September. However I think it is more realistic to plan for a close at the end of October. It is only at that point that any of the disposals could be put up for sale – and even then it will take some additional time for the sale to be completed of any businesses that are being divested. So as I say, we have some considerable time to make plans that take *into account the needs of our artists, and in the meantime we will be working as hard as ever to deliver the successful outcomes that our artists so richly deserve.*

All of this is a lot to digest, I know. While there is not much more that any of us can say right now, I am sure that you will want to talk to senior management here at EMI, and we will be reaching out directly to as many of you as possible over the coming days and weeks. As soon as I have any more concrete news for you, rest assured that I will contact you all right away.

Best wishes,
Roger

This meant that in total, UMG was willing to commit itself to selling some €360m ($440m) of recording, merchandising and other revenue, around 28% percent of EMI's €1bn ($1.6 billion) European sales in the year to March 31, 2011. UMG had anticipated $160m of annual cost savings, however, assuming profit and synergies were proportional to revenue, the EMI businesses UMG would retain were worth some $530m less than the deal price. On the basis of the July 27 proposal Vivendi would be paying about seven times EBITDA for EMI, or around 4.5 times, adjusted for synergies. If it could dispose of the requisite EMI pieces for same level of EBITDA, it would recoup about $330m, which would mean that it would be about $200m out of pocket plus the costs of the transaction.

But what would happen if the American regulators sought concessions too? Then on August 3, US senators Herb Kohl and a fellow member of the Senate Judiciary Subcommittee on Antitrust, Competition Policy and Consumer Rights, Mike Lee, co-signed an open public letter to the Federal Trade Commission (FTC) chairman Jonathan Leibowitz in which they stated that Universal's proposed acquisition of EMI Music "presents significant competition issues that merit careful FTC review". The letter recounts the arguments made before the committee and stresses the factual disputes in the evidence presented to it:

Without reaching any final judgment as to the legality of the deal under the antitrust laws, we believe this proposed acquisition presents significant competition issues that merit careful FTC review to ensure that the transaction is not likely to cause substantial harm to competition in the affected markets. In the course of this review, we also urge the Commission to be mindful of the changes in the music industry in the last decade, particularly the shift to online distribution as the preferred way consumers purchase music.

We urge the Commission to pay close attention to the impact of this deal of digital music distribution services in assessing competitive consequences. There are considerable factual disputes in our hearing record as to (1) whether this acquisition would make universal a greater gatekeeper of digital distribution platform success, (2) whether EMI is presently more open to licensing new services other than other major record companies, and (3) whether Universal has been hostile to licensing such services in the past. Our Subcommittee has not reached any conclusions as to the merits of these factual disputes. Resolution of these issues will be vital in determining whether or not this acquisition will substantially harm completion in the digital music distribution market.

We also urge the Commission to consider the impact of this acquisition on the sale of physical recordings, which still account for half of music industry revenues. The deals critics argue that given the substantial increase in market concentration as a result of this acquisition, the deal may result in a price increase for CDs sold to consumers. These concerns are heightened because of the limited space available to sell CDs in retail stores.

The advent of digital music distribution has eliminated nearly all of the chain record stores selling CDs. With the exception of a few 'mom and pop' local record stores, most CDs purchased today in brick-and-mortar stores are sold in the so-called "big box" national chains such as Wal-Mart, Target and Best Buy. These retailers have very limited shelf space available for CDs and generally seek to offer current hits and top sellers, leaving little room for inventory of non-top sellers. Obtaining promotional placement in these stores can be crucial to a record label, in what is known as "end cap" and other high traffic space.

The deal's critics argue that experience supports the proposition that piracy is not a significant constraint on music industry price increases. For *example, in 2009, Apple iTunes imposed a 30 percent price increase (from $0.99 to $1.29) on most digital singles without any appreciable loss in sales. Although piracy has clearly caused significant declines in music sales in the last decade, the rise of popular legitimate sites such as Apple iTunes has led to more recent growth in legal music purchases. In light of these trends, we encourage the Commission to examine the extent to which piracy would serve to constrain the ability of a combined Universal/EMI to raise prices.*

Finally, we urge the Commission to consider the impact of this proposed acquisition on independent labels and new artists. Our subcommittee has long recognized the importance of maintaining the fullest possible diversity in media, and this includes a diverse music industry. Independent record labels are an important avenue for new and varied artists to reach consumers. Our Subcommittee heard evidence of the potential dangers to the survival of independent record labels, including the testimony of Martin Mills of the Beggars Group. Whether this acquisition will likely lead to these effects is an important issue for the FTC to examine.

In sum, we argue the Commission to consider the issues discussed above in determining whether Universal's proposed acquisition of EMI will substantially injure completion in violation of antitrust laws. The Commission should consider whether this deal may help revive the declining EMI record labels to benefit the music industry and consumers. It should also carefully analyze the acquisitions likely effects on the ability of new and innovative digital music services to enter the market, on competition for music sales and prices for consumers, and on the welfare of independent labels and artists.

The music industry has undergone a transformation in the last two decades as consumers' access music through new online forms of distribution and as the market faces the challenge of piracy. Yet, in this as in other industries, robust completion remains the key to restraining prices, ensuring new and innovating from of distribution, and maintaining diversity of choice available to consumers.

The letter had an immediate impact in the US, leading to the US trade association of independent record companies, A2IM, to call for the FTC to insist on divestitures of US assets of UMG/EMI if the deal was to go through. Historically, the FTC considers the impact of a deal on consumer pricing, whereas the EU also takes a broader examination on whether a deal will impact competition in an industry. The significance of the senators' letter to the FTC is that it went beyond pricing and asked FTC to consider how the deal would impact competition in the music industry overall, bringing the issue of US divestitures to the fore.

Then it transpired that the Commission was also concerned that the proposed divestitures, while looking dramatic – the back catalogue of Coldplay, Pink Floyd and Radiohead, for example – were limited to Europe. At the same time – by now the approval process of the deal was being conducted in a glare of publicity – further details of the Commission's actions were leaked to the press. The Commission had test marketed the divestitures offered by Vivendi, sending out a detailed 30-page questionnaire asking UMG's rivals if they were satisfied with the promised divestitures. Surprisingly, many were, but the Commission remained unconvinced. Maybe global divestitures, which the Sony/ATV-led consortium quickly agreed to earlier, were required.

In the midst of all this, Citigroup published EMI's accounts for the year ending March 31, 2011. These showed that group revenues had grown by 1.3% to £1.47bn ($2.35bn) with losses, which included the writing down of its two sold divisions, falling to £349m ($558m). Revenues at EMI Music rose by just under 2% to £1.04bn ($1.66bn) during the year, while revenues at EMI Music Publishing remained flat at £434m ($694m). Both EMI Music and EMI MP, it would seem, were solid, healthy operations with losses that would disappear with restructuring. According to Vivendi's accounts UMG's revenues in calendar 2011 fell by 6% to €4,197m ($5,804m). EMI Music was a good buy.

However, when the deal was finally approved it transpired that UMG would benefit from significantly less of EMI Music's revenues. By the time of the Roger Faxon letter of concessions (July 27), UMG had increased its offer to sell of around 28% of EMI's European assets. Two weeks later that offer had risen to 60% with the possibility that some divestitures, to satisfy the FTC, would be global, pushing the deal into a position where the efficiencies it offered might not be sufficient for

Vivendi, a company saddled with major debts and investor pressure to increase earnings. In response to that offer, Vivendi's share price, which had fallen 3.8% since the start of 2012, fell a further 1%, valuing the company at €20.5bn ($28.5bn), its lowest for several years. But, if parent company Vivendi was having a difficult time in 2012 – revenues fell 1.2% to €14.1bn ($17.7bn) and EBITA by 12.7% to €2.9bn ($3.6bn) for the first half of 2012 and the company announced lay-offs – UMG saw a rise in both revenues (up 3.2% to €1,922m; $2,504m) and EBITA revenues and EBIDTA (up 18.2% to €156m; $196m). The music business could still be profitable.

In the same week two members of the House Judiciary Subcommittee on Intellectual Property, Competition and the Internet sent a letter to executives at Universal and two other major labels, asking pointed questions about how the merger would affect competition in the music industry. The letter put further pressure on the FTC as did the paper by the American Antitrust Institute, a Washington-based education, research, and advocacy organisation, *Music Industry Consolidation: The Likely Anticompetitive Effects Of The Universal/EMI Merger* that urged the FTC to block the deal because "Based on an analysis of publicly available information, we believe Universal's acquisition of EMI's recorded music division may substantially harm competition in the U.S. markets for physical and digital recorded music services."

However, the time for principled opposition to the deal was over. As the daily leaks confirmed, in Brussels UMG and the Commission were horse-trading with a vengeance, UMG desperately seeking a deal before it was due to pay Citigroup the $1bn due on September 9 and the Commission, confident UMG would accept severe conditions, simply seeking an end. The dealmaker was UMG's offer in addition to those proffered in the Faxon memo, to divest itself of Parlophone, not merely in Europe but globally, thus giving up the rights to Coldplay, Radiohead, Blur, Pink Floyd, Kylie Minogue and others, and only keeping the Beatles catalogue.

And so it came to pass. On September 21, both the European Commission and the FTC approved the sale of EMI Music and on September 28, UMG took operational control of its acquisition. On that day, Roger Faxon, who had earlier signed off with a "keep your chin up" style memo, quit as CEO, leaving UMG's Lucian Grainge in charge.

The FTC approved the deal with no conditions, but the Commission, as expected, required the global divestiture of Parlophone in addition to the European sell-offs announced by Faxon earlier (*see* pages 331–2). The total value of these, set at a little less than 30% of EMI's revenues, was around $450m. Following these sales, which the Commission demanded UMG make within six months, the expanded UMG would have a market share of less than 40% in Europe and of around 35% in the US. In addition, Universal committed itself to selling EMI's 50% stake in the popular *Now! That's What I Call Music* compilation joint venture and to continue licensing its repertoire to the series for the next 10 years.

At one moment in the horse-trading process UMG suggested it would favour the independents when it began its divestiture programme. It's unclear whether that will actually happen. A late addition to the conditions imposed on UMG was that it must sell the assets to purchasers that are either already active as record companies, or have a proven track record in the music industry. This is likely to eliminate private equity groups, unless they act in support of music companies. It makes it all the more likely that BMG RM and WMG will be the main bidders. The hostility between UMG and WMG, which intensified at the US Senate Judiciary Committee antitrust panel hearings, led many observers to suggest that UMG would seek reasons for not selling to WMG. But with parent company Vivendi carrying a high level of debt and the economies of scale offered by the deal diminished by the divestitures required, it could be that price alone will determine who benefits from the coming sales of UMG/EMI companies. That said, just as WMG faced a deadly serious contender when EMI Music came to market, when the EMI scraps come to market WMG will face in BMG RM a deep pocketed company in need of recorded music rights to add to the catalogue of over 1m compositions it has built up remarkably quickly.

In the digital arena, the Commission secured UMG's agreement not to include Most Favoured Nation (MFN) clauses in its favour in any new or renegotiated contract with digital customers in the European Economic Area for 10 years. A Commission spokesman explained:

> *Most-Favoured Nation clauses provide that if a digital customer negotiates an attractive licensing deal with Universal's competitors, this customer needs to offer the same terms to Universal.*
>
> *The effect of these clauses is two-fold. First, the licensing cost of this customer increases as it needs to offer the favourable conditions to both Universal and its competitor[s]. Second, Universal's competitors may be constrained in their negotiations with digital customers, as these negotiations take place under the threat that customers need to extend any favourable treatment, agreed between the customer and Universal's competitor, also to Universal ...*
>
> *This commitment should assist digital customers in preventing increases in their licensing cost. It also assists competitors in competing effectively with Universal, as they will no longer negotiate with digital customers under the constraints of Universal's MFN clause.*

The ending of the MFN clause should make competition for digital deals marginally fairer. However, surprisingly, the Commission did not question UMG's tactic of seeking to only grant a licence to a digital music service provider if it, as the market leader, was able to get a greater share of licensing revenues than was due to its actual market share. One can only assume that that practice will continue.

The usual suspects complained that the divestitures were not sufficient and others that the level of divestiture meant the deal made less economic sense. However, all were agreed that neither UMG nor SME, the two largest record companies with annual revenues of around $6.5bn and $6bn respectively (assuming the divestitures required of them), could seek to grow further through acquisition.

The different tracks that the approval of the dismemberment of EMI took are fraught with significance. In music publishing it looks as though the consortium and Sony/ATV, being very large, might generate the "disproportionately high profits" that Thomas Middelhoff famously noted followed market leadership "in clearly defined market segments". Sony/ATV successfully argued that although more people would want to make deals with them because of their increased size, they wouldn't be able to deform the market or set their own deals, because most of their activities went through the collection society environment. That argument is challengeable, particularly as the major publishers are increasingly seeking to make deals outside the society environment, but it certainly won the day for Sony/ATV. The Sony/ATV's consortium's takeover of EMI MP was a stage in an inevitable process. In the world of music publishing big makes sense. That view might be questioned by the efficiencies represented by Kobalt, which administers but does not own rights, and BMG RM; but even Kobalt and BMG RM wanted to grow.

The meaning behind Vivendi's takeover of EMI Music was far more problematic. Previously, the argument that increased size was essential to fight piracy and prepare for the digital age had been widely accepted. In far happier times, UMG had been invited to swallow PolyGram. In more difficult times Sony, albeit with a hiccup or two, was allowed to merge with and then gobble up BMG. By the time of the Vivendi takeover of EMI Music, the logic behind such takeovers had been tarnished. Moreover, the European Commission was increasingly fretful about their impact on jobs and culture and, suddenly, the American regulators seemed to be moving from simple consumer concerns to taking on board competition issues. Increasingly small was seen as positive – the independents represented job creation; takeovers represented job losses – and very large was questionable.

And yet both the consortium and Vivendi were able to argue that size didn't matter while both got bigger. The clever construction of the consortium, in which Sony/ATV was only a minor partner, and the professional manner in which it approached the Commission won it EMI MP. Vivendi's route to continued market dominance was far more difficult, depending upon on concession after concession, each of which marginally lessened the economies of scale the deal promised. A further irony was that the central plank in Vivendi's argument was that yes, it wanted to get bigger but that being big didn't matter because it was powerless in the digital world where the digital services oversaw consumers' access to music.

UMG, having the greatest global market share and knowing that physical was more profitable than digital because physical was bundles and digital was (primarily) tracks, was the company that did the most to support the CD album. It created innovative pricing campaigns in the US and Europe and experimented with making the bundle bigger, adding DVDs or books to CD reissue packages. Similarly UMG was the company that always bid for back catalogues looking for a new home, such as the Rolling Stones and Queen, and did distribution deals for people able to self-finance their own recordings, such as the Eagles. Part of the logic of getting even bigger through the acquisition of EMI was that it would have even more product to flush down its marketing/promotional/distribution pipes. Not all would be equally profitable, but all would help fund the company's fixed costs, producing economies of scale not available to smaller companies, such as WMG.

In the public and leaked debates that were part of the EC's approval process, UMG was repeatedly described as a company possessing greater leverage than it derived from its market share of owned repertoire and as a company that regularly used that leverage in making digital deals to its own special advantage. The Commission took the view that, whether that was the case or not, the likes of Apple and Amazon could look after themselves. In the digital world UMG may be powerful but that power was to a degree intangible: Amazon, as in the Lady Gaga promotion, could easily upset UMG's apple cart. But in the purely physical world, where market dominance was tangible, the Commission decided the 40% maximum market share that it had relied on in the consortium's bid for EMI MP was a hard and fast rule.

In effect the Commission's decision and UMG's deal-making in seeking approval marked the final, if belated, acceptance that while the physical world still was more profitable than the digital, competition within was no longer the central issue. The Commission, seeking to invigorate a Euro-wide digital music market for several years, has failed to find the plan, but remains committed to the task. UMG, in the manner of a Kuhnian scientist with a new mindset, has accepted a lesser degree of dominance of the physical recorded music market to pursue the possibility of increased power within the digital market. Further confirmation of this is that within UMG the rising executives are those with digital rather than physical responsibilities and that within UMG's labels digital and physical responsibilities have largely been melded.

In the past Nokia wanted to be a friend of UMG (and the other majors) in the fashion of record retailers of old. Maybe Amazon or Apple could take such a view; it's unlikely but well worth positioning oneself for it in case it became possible.

The independents, as ever, squabbled among themselves, some seeking to make personal advantages of the situation, some accepting the inevitability of it and some resisting. Nonetheless, of all the parties the independents emerged with the greatest credit from the Vivendi-EMI Music circus. In the failed WMG-EMI takeover, the independents won the funding of Merlin as the cost of their support, as part of the Vivendi-EMI Music they won even greater visibility. However, when the deal went through they collected few of the crumbs the EC forced Vivendi to divest. It was the larger 'indies', for example BMG RM, which even before the Commission granted its approval, was in discussion with UMG about the sale of Parlophone, that had the deeper pockets and was expected to snap up Vivendi's leavings. In the new record market there was one company (UMG) with a global market share in the high thirties, another (SME) a share in the high twenties and WMG a market share in the mid tens.

The story of *Download* is of the record industry's move from rejection of the digital revolution to a belated embrace of it. A key feature of this rejection was the loss of control of the sale of its product. This meant that new entrants, such as Wal-Mart in the physical world and Apple in the digital world, could make use of recorded music for their own ends. As the story has evolved, the industry has been reshaped. The first attempt was to reject the digital world on the basis that it made little sense because the profits were elsewhere. Then, ill-advised and caught between the known (the physical world) and the unknown (the digital world), the industry attempted a last-ditch attempt to control the emerging digital world before finally accepting that it was the future, even if it represented a smaller business. Just as the paradigm shift that was the Copernican Revolution represented an acceptance that the earth was no longer the centre of the universe, so the story of the record industry over the last decade culminating in the takeover of EMI by UMG represents the, belated, acceptance that digital is the future.

The deal and the story that led up to it confirm one thing. The view of Thomas Middelhoff Bertelsmann's CEO in 1988 was that: "The position of the biggest media company is of no value in and of itself. But in clearly defined market segments, market leadership is associated with disproportionately high profits." Over the last 20 or so years EMI, SME, UMG and WMG have undergone various struggles to attain that position. UMG has now achieved it, but at a time when the modern record industry is no longer a "market segment" from which "disproportionately high profits" will flow.

One company has achieved such profits – Apple, the first entity to see the commercial implications of the dissemination of digital music. Most of the new digital upstarts met with little success, as the majors delayed and delayed and/or sought high upfront licences for the use of their repertoire. Not so Apple. In August 2012, Apple's market capitalisation reached $619bn, overtaking Exxon Mobil ($405.6bn), which had held the top spot since 2005, making Apple the most valuable company in America.

In contrast, the value of recorded music sales fell, by over a third from a trade value of $23.35bn in 2000 to $15.4bn in 2011. If there was ever a company to mine the "disproportionately high profits" that came from being "the biggest media company" it was Apple.

Endings

This book is about the impact of digital and changes in patterns of cultural consumption on the record industry. But, those changes also had a deep impact on the production of music. It seems sensible to address them briefly.

Just as the tape recorder reduced the cost of entry into the record industry so the digital audio workstation (DAW), Pro Tools, developed and manufactured by Avid Technology, changed the production process. Tape recording had introduced editing to the recording process, but with difficulty: tapes had to be spliced. Pro Tools, launched in 1991, was digital and tapeless. And you didn't need a studio with the all-important console to mix what was recorded. You could do that in Pro Tools itself, in the box, as Pro Tools dubbed it. Thus began the demise of specialist recording studios known for their distinct ambiances and special sounds. Greg Milner calculated that by 2007 between 70% and 80% of all pop music recording and virtually 100% of hip hop, R&B and dance recording were "mixed in the box". The first calling card of Pro Tools was price. That was emphasised when Apple included a similar tool, GarageBand, with its Mac computer lines from version OS X onwards, making it realistic for would-be performers to make a recording without going into a studio. The bedroom studio was born.

And then came the plug-ins, the most influential of which was Auto-Tune, a programme that corrects the pitch of vocals. Greg Milner again:

"Although Auto-Tune was designed as a corrective device, it broke into the mainstream as a creative sound processor." While working with Cher on the song 'Believe' in 1998, producers Mark Taylor and Brian Rawling discovered that if they set Auto-Tune on its most aggressive setting, so that it corrected the pitch at the exact moment it received the signal, the result was an unsettlingly robotic tone. When 'Believe' became a huge worldwide hit, Taylor and Rawling initially tried to keep their Auto-Tune trick a secret, although word soon got out and the "Cher effect" became a ubiquitous production tool over the next few years.

At the same time, Auto-Tune was steadily infiltrating the recording world in more insidious ways. For obvious reasons, producers and musicians often don't admit that they use Auto-Tune to fix voices that are out of tune, but it's obviously used to make singers out of people who cannot actually sing. The Spice Girls, who broke out around the same time, were clearly Auto-Tuned to the gills. Since then, Auto-Tune has done as much as Pro Tools itself to change the sound of pop music.

What Pro Tools and Auto-Tune represented was a dramatic shift in what being a performer meant. Talent became less important than the "journey" as we entered a new world in which not only was it reasonable to simply want to be famous, but there were academies and television shows to facilitate that "journey". Singing out of tune was a problem that could be fixed – so could bad teeth, but that was more expensive.

In the UK there was the London School for Performing Arts & Technology (most commonly known as The Brit School), established in 1991, with a mandate to provide education and vocational training for the performing arts, media, art and design and the technologies that make performance possible. The school is funded by the UK government with additional support from the UK record industry, via the British Record Industry Trust. A number of successful acts have come from it, including Adele, Amy Winehouse and The Kooks. The Brit School has operated in a similar fashion to long-established theatrical schools and the creative writing courses established by a number of universities in the UK and US.

However, elsewhere such academies have taken on a rather different slant. The most notable example of this is in South Korea. Idol pop has long been common throughout Asia. From China to Indonesia and Thailand, cuteness abounds, but South Korea has embraced this in an extreme fashion. A recent survey there showed that 51% of children chose singing and acting as their preferred profession as adults, compared to a similar survey in the early 1980s that showed that hoping to be a scientist, teacher or judge accounted for the same proportion of the population. This trend is not restricted to elementary schoolchildren. Young South Koreans have become fixated on becoming stars, with talent searches drawing 20,000 or more applicants. Even entry into university courses that teach entertainment-related fields is so competitive that students must beat hundreds of others for a place.

This led to a boom in the number of performing arts academies, which have more than doubled from 300 to 700 during the past five years. Students from these institutes need such basic skills before trying to get into the even more severe academies operated by the music companies themselves. Typically grooming artists for three to four years with choreography, vocal training, acting and language classes, the leading domestic music companies have put considerable efforts into reducing the risk of such a long-term investment. Essential to grooming is being able to speak and sing fluent Japanese and Chinese, and being of such a compliant personality that disputes with managers/record companies are unlikely to occur as artists grow up and begin to think for themselves. Such acts, which in the course of 2011 were responsible for a "South Korean Invasion" of Japan as K-Pop represent the virtue of control for a record company, at least over its (would-be) stars. In South Korea 360-degree deals are the norm.

In Europe the growing number of television talent shows initially followed long-established traditions of just being that, a talent show, but they quickly changed following the success of *Pop Idol*. Consider for example, *Operación Triunfo* (*OT*), the television talent show developed by Spanish public broadcaster TVE, once one of the most successful *Pop*

Idol style shows anywhere in the world. Viewing figures for the final programme of the first series in November 2002 peaked at 12.9m, or 68% of the television audience. This was the highest rated programme in Spain since the current audience measurement system was introduced in 1992.

If *OT* was a hit for TVE, it transformed the fortunes of Vale Music, a (then) small independent record company that was established in 1997 as a compilation and dance company. As noted earlier (*see* Chapter 12), Vale secured the rights to almost all the recordings associated with the show. Such was its success with *OT* related recordings that in 2002 the Barcelona-based company's Spanish market share rose to 21%, putting it ahead of all the majors with, I calculated at the time, some 65% of Vale's 2002 revenues coming from *OT*. This meant that records linked to the programme accounted for 17% of the trade value of the Spanish market that year.

However Vale's success was dwarfed by that of Syco, the joint venture between British impresario Simon Cowell and SME created to exploit the music, television, film and digital content from the various talent shows mounted by Cowell, notably *The X Factor*. In 2009, Syco artist Susan Boyle released the world's best-selling album of the year, *I Dreamed A Dream*, and in 2010, she was responsible for SME's best-selling album of the year, *The Gift* and for the best-selling album of the last quarter of 2011, *Someone To Watch Over Me*. Television and the "journey" had taken stage centre.

In 1995, Marcus Breen in his article, *The end of the world as we know it: Popular music's cultural mobility*, noted that: "Popular music has moved to the centre of economic life, suggesting a shift in the political economy of advanced societies. The transition has been marked by a concomitant shift in the centrality of popular music in social life, assisted by new technologies. More importantly, the changes have been brought about by the reorganisation of record company ownership and activity since the 1980s … The use of popular music as a feature of the corporate economy has involved the expansion of all forms of entertainment into the information economy."

This transformation of the role of music has been greeted with pleasure in some circles. Consider *The Tanning of America*, written by Steve Stoute, a former music executive turned brand marketing guru. His book tells the story of how bling and rap culture became mainstream, along the way discovering that the musical element of music was less important than the commercial factor that could be liberated through a deal with a headphone manufacturer or Courvoisier. Such uses of music are liberating but they are also transformative.

Popular music has always been a commercial activity, but in the past there was a sense that the troubadour – say Randy Newman – or his employer – say Mo Ostin – were also committed to their joint economic venture also being a cultural activity.

Music from this perspective has a social dimension. This view was famously articulated by Langdon Winner in 1968 when he offered the view that: "The closest Western Civilization has come to unity since the Congress of Vienna in 1815 was the week the *Sgt. Pepper* album was released."

The view has been challenged by historians on grounds of accuracy, but the point, especially if you transfer the moment to the Band Aid television transmission, which was available more or less around the world, remains compelling.

Music mattered. It had hidden social dimensions. As noted by Steve Stoute, music can bring sudden riches to individuals. But it also moves in smaller and more complex ways. This was captured most eloquently by Bill Millar in his entry on George Goldner in *The Encyclopedia Of Rock*: "Goldner never worried about creed or colour. Provided you could sing falsetto ballads, or hot impromptu scats, he would give you a chance on one of his numerous labels. Consider this list, most of whom had major hit records: on Gee – the Cleftones, the Heartbeats, the Regents; on Gone – the Channels, Jo Ann Campbell, Ral Donner; on End – the Chantels, Lewis Lymon and the Teenchords, the Flamingos, Little Anthony and the Imperials; on Mark-X – the Isley Brothers; and on Golddisc – the Temptation, the Royaltones…

"He was the original fifties bubblegum king without a mind for stone blues. Nor was he entirely punctilious over royalty payments, but he cut a lot of wonderful records and did more for integration than the Supreme Court."

One hopes that, half a century later, music would still have that power.

Appendix
The Guy Hands Memos

Guy Hands, particularly in the early days of Terra Firma's ownership of the EMI Group, spoke about the challenges that EMI represented for Terra Firma. He spoke more frequently and in more detail than most CEOs do about their latest acquisition, especially when it was a controversial purchase. He also sent memos to the staff on a regular basis, seeking to co-opt them into the vision of an outsider's view of what a modern record company might be. The memos were widely leaked on the Internet. I publish the key ones below in the interests of history. There are no comparable memos between the Bronfman consortium group and WMG staff, in great part because the Bronfman consortium, as I have shown earlier, understood the ways of the record industry as it was. Guy Hands and Terra Firma had no such insider knowledge of record industry practices. His memos are of interest because they both show the gap twixt cup and lip and the difficulties of interrogating that gap, particularly when the surrounding economic climate is decidedly unhelpful.

August 29, 2007
Guy Hands offers a glimpse of his strategy in a statement accompanying the announcement that EMI CEO Nicoli is to step down

"Terra Firma's success is founded upon the real commitment it makes to the businesses in which it invests," he said. "The new management structure will allow EMI to benefit from Terra Firma's experience in strategically transforming businesses and driving operational change. The initial focus will be to maximize the value of the significant assets in EMI's publishing business and to realize the digital opportunity in recorded music. We will invest in the business to ensure that it grows both organically and by acquisition. The goal is for EMI to be the world's most innovative and consumer-focused music company and the best home for musical talent."

September 17, 2007
Hands outlines the Terra Firma philosophy: buy the worst-run company and fix it. The results: profits
Dear colleague,

Last Friday, I was on a panel on embracing change at the UK's annual major convention on broadcasting at which all the industry's major players were represented and which received some press coverage.

I made the point that Terra Firma's biggest successes over the years had been when we had bought those businesses in need of the most change and in sectors facing the biggest challenges and that EMI fits that model perfectly. I went on to say that Terra Firma's model transforms companies that have been in the past poorly managed and have lost their direction and EMI had to date not disappointed in its potential for transformation. However, this is not just an EMI issue as the recorded music industry as a whole has not positioned itself well for the changing environment over the last ten years and has failed to anticipate or adapt to the new market place.

With regard to EMI specifically, I believe that there has been too much management focus over the last seven years on a potential merger with Warner and on a continuous cost-cutting program which has failed to deliver a new business model and sadly has led to the loss of many talented people from the business. Terra Firma has inherited EMI past management's business plan which is currently being executed. However our future focus is to develop a plan that ensures that EMI's

Recorded Music business, as an independent company (i.e. without a merger with Warner), can best serve its artists, the music industry, its customers and employees. Put simply, focusing alone on the production of multi-million selling albums cannot produce a sustainable business model. In developing the business plan for EMI Recorded Music, we intend initially to look at these areas:

- The relationship between EMI and its artists and what contractual relationship best serves those artists
- Digitalization and how EMI's recorded music business can embrace and benefit from it
- How EMI can be the most efficient partner in recorded music for artists who are likely to sell less than 200,000 copies of their albums
- How EMI can develop a closer and more valuable relationship with its customers
- What services and products EMI should be developing and delivering to its artists and customers
- How EMI can provide multi-million selling artists with a top quality service internationally.

In short, how EMI can be big enough to serve anyone but small enough to truly care.

So far, we have not spent a huge amount of time on analyzing what might be done with EMI's publishing business. As I said at the broadcaster's convention "if it ain't broke, don't fix it." However, Roger Faxon has a number of new initiatives which he is intending to roll out to ensure that EMI Publishing will continue to grow and prosper which Terra Firma supports.

In the near term, I am embarking on a roadshow over the next month in which I intend to meet as many of EMI's employees as possible. At those meetings, I will be happy to answer your questions. Additionally, feel free to email me in confidence on the following email (guy.hands@terrafirma.com) any ideas as to how we can make the business work better to the benefit of EMI, its staff and its artists.

In spite of a lack of clear direction and an extremely challenging market, EMI's artists and employees have delivered a huge number of successes in recent years and have much to be proud of. I continue to be impressed by your commitment and creativity and would simply ask that you continue to be focused on the work you are doing for EMI and its artists. Terra Firma's commitment to EMI is total and we have invested more financially, both personally as individuals and as an organization, in EMI than any other company in our history. We are absolutely committed to making EMI the world's most innovative and consumer-focused music company and the best home for musical talent. I look forward to working with you in order to achieve just that.

Guy Hands
Chairman

October 5, 2007
The Radiohead debacle
Dear all
RADIOHEAD
As you know, Radiohead, a band with whom we have enjoyed a long and productive history, have decided to release their new album, *In Rainbows*, directly to consumers via their own web-site. They have also allowed fans to download the digital album at a price to be set by the consumer. While some recorded music executives and other firms have expressed shock and dismay at this development, it should have come as no surprise. In a digital world, it was inevitable that a band with the necessary financial resources and consumer recognition to be able to distribute their music directly to their fans would do so. Radiohead is one of the most iconic, original and successful bands in the world, and one of the few with a fan base large and devoted enough to support the costs of such an initiative.

However, whilst most bands, including many successful names, will not be able to – or want to – follow in their footsteps, there are some important lessons to be learnt which support our analysis of what needs to change in the recorded music business model and which many of you have touched on in your letters and emails to us since Terra Firma bought EMI.

In this note, I want to address what Radiohead's decision means for EMI and what it means for artists generally.

For EMI, this is a welcome reminder of the new digital world in which we operate and the need to focus on the services we provide to our artists. Those artists break down into three categories:
- Those who are already established and in whom we have invested heavily;
- Those with whom we are working to make really successful; and
- New, start-up bands.

EMI needs business models which work for all three categories, the reality being that the vast majority of the third category will fail to achieve commercial success and have historically been cross-subsidised by the first category.

EMI Recorded Music still has value to the vast majority of artists – in funding their development and in distributing and marketing their music – but highly successful bands have other alternatives for making money (such as touring) and a few, especially the more established ones, may be able to abandon their label and try to go it alone. You can see why they might choose to do so. Why should they subsidise their label's new talent roster – or for that matter their record company's excessive expenditures and advances – particularly when they are providing income to their record company through their catalogue sales?

We will need to give artists at all levels a deal that is fair to both sides, perhaps one that moves away from the large advances model of old and provides a true alignment of interests and transparency.

However, for every artist being signed to us, regardless of level, we need to deliver them maximum value and a world-class service; we need to develop products that the consumer wants. We need to develop revenue streams both for our artists and for EMI that come from many channels and not just from CDs. We need to be best in class at identifying and developing these revenue streams where best in class is not being judged against the recorded music business, but against international businesses of all types. We are determined to do so and to ensure that EMI Recorded Music has the people with the skills to provide such a worldwide service. It is only by doing this that we will be the best home to musical talent and the most innovative and creative music company.

In effect, the recorded music business needs to become more like the music publishing business which provides its writers multiple opportunities for distribution of their product in order to maximise copyright fees and royalties. In this effort, EMI publishing continues to be at the forefront of innovation and provides a broad range of services.

The recorded music industry, while seeking to develop some of these services, has for too long been dependent on how many CDs can be sold. The industry, rather than embracing digitalisation and the opportunities it brings for promotion of product and distribution through multiple channels, has stuck its head in the sand. Radiohead's actions are a wake-up call which we should all welcome and respond to with creativity and energy.

If you have any comments, please do feel free to email me as usual.

With best wishes
Guy

October 31, 2007
EMI needs a new breed and type of executives
Dear all:
I want to thank all of those whom I met on my recent trip to the United States for making me so welcome. I found it incredibly stimulating and encouraging. EMI has a huge number of highly skilled and dedicated people and it is my job to ensure that this enormous potential is unlocked. There were a few particular questions I was asked on the trip which may be of interest to many. Let me take each of them in turn:

My initial views on what we need to do to make EMI recorded music successful:

Clearly after only a few weeks' involvement with EMI, this is not something on which we can as yet give great detail. However, I do see a need for fundamental change in how we approach the music business and how we deliver the interconnected triangle of the consumer, EMI and the artist.

The first leg of the triangle, in my view, should be EMI's position and relationship with its consumers, be they B2B or B2C. We need to communicate with them, understand fully what we can provide them with, and ensure that we are not purely reliant on others to do so. Technology should be seen as an enabler, rather than a threat to our long-term economic success and, as I have said before, we need to embrace it.

We also need to focus on how we can develop a direct relationship with consumers and not rely on or blame others. If we do this throughout EMI (and in parts of the business, we are already doing so very successfully), we will find ourselves being in demand from artists as we will be able to give them solutions that will help them both increase their revenues and additionally protect and develop their artistic integrity. Please feel free to send me any ideas you have on products or services involving music that could be appropriate for either B2B or B2C channels that EMI could provide.

The second leg of the triangle is EMI as an organisation. While individually there is incredible strength within the organisation, there is not currently a universal culture of working together. This is not the fault of the individuals within EMI, but is due to a compensation and management system put in place over the last 20 years which does not encourage the right behaviours or reward the right actions. However, I am hugely encouraged that most of the people I have met want to work together with great enthusiasm for the good of EMI and of music generally. What worries me is that the existing structures have been put in over a couple of decades and unpicking them in a way that releases the good in the company is not going to happen overnight.

The third leg of the triangle is the artist and the artist's representatives. Here, I believe that if we offer better products and have the right culture which has at its core honesty, transparency and performance, then we will be able to attract, retain and develop the very best artists. Additionally, at the point where we are really world-class in the service we are offering to artists, there is no reason why we should not be more selective in whom we choose to work with. There has been a lot of talk about what labels offer to artists and to the consumer. However, there is not much talk about how artists should work with their label. While many spend huge amounts of time working with their label to promote, perfect and endorse their music, some unfortunately simply focus on negotiating for the maximum advance...advances which are often never repaid. However, once EMI has the best products and services in music and the best culture for working together then, as already exists within some of our labels, it will be open to us to choose which artists we wish to work with and promote.

Hiring of new people for EMI?

Whenever Terra Firma invests in an industry or business in need of transformation, we seek new people – both inside and outside of the industry – in order to inject into the business fresh perspectives on different business models that might drive further revenues and services or reduce costs. When we acquired EMI, we broke this search down into five groups:

- Current executives in the major labels
- Former executives in the major labels
- Executives and entrepreneurs in the music industry not attached to major labels
- Senior professionals in the entertainment and media industries and
- Executives in other industries.

In the first two categories, while we have interviewed and seen many people, we have not seen many who, in our view, add anything over and above those we already have in EMI. The other three categories, however, do have people who could add additional skills and experience to that which already exists within EMI and we expect to hire people from these categories to work with current EMI people and to advise Terra Firma on how to put new products and services into EMI's offering. However, I should add that the press speculation with regard to them taking very senior management roles at this time is completely false.

I might also take the opportunity to add that, as you know better than me, the music industry lends itself to media commentary which is at best speculative and to advise you to take much of what is written with a pinch of salt. Only this week as an example, we have seen one US-based newspaper suggest that Terra Firma selling a small part of its equity in EMI was somehow significant. If they had bothered to do a little research, they would have found that in all major private equity deals, equity is sold by private equity managers, to their investors and other private equity firms. Indeed, Terra Firma has done this on all previous deals it has done and it is something we proactively market to our investors. Importantly, however, EMI is Terra Firma's largest investment and Terra Firma will continue after the sell down is completed (which in the past on previous deals has on occasion taken up to 18 months) to hold a substantially higher proportion of its fund in EMI than we are aware any other private equity firm has with any other investment. Similarly any suggestion as to what may or may not come out of the strategic review we are conducting should be seen as just that, speculative suggestion and nothing more.

Further communication on Terra Firma's vision:

We are continuing to refine and develop our vision for EMI. There has been, and continues to be, a fantastic response from both the employee and artist communities to our consultation on the future vision for EMI. The Investor Board are working hard on bringing together all the ideas and suggestions and evaluating them. Once we have pulled together a coherent, high-level vision, we will hold a series of meetings to brief the management teams around the world. We will then roll out the agreed vision to individual employees in a series of town hall sessions similar to those held in September/October. The timeframe for all of this will be early 2008.

Please feel free to come back to me with any questions or comments.

With best wishes
Guy

November 19, 2007
Hands details his plans for "repositioning" EMI
Our latest acquisition, that of EMI, is a great example of a quintessentially Terra Firma deal. EMI draws on Terra Firma's full experience in strategically transforming businesses, repositioning assets, driving operational change, and growing and stabilizing cash flows in an industry that is out of favor. It has all the attributes of a Terra Firma transaction:
- Asset-rich business Publishing and Recorded Music catalogues;
- Industry in transformation Impact of market change on consumer and artist behavior;

- Potential for consolidation Acquisition of assets from other market participants;
- Potential for greater efficiency Ability to use technology to reduce the cost base; and
- Opportunity for strong financing An attractive initial financing package that took advantage of the pricing and terms that were available at the time and which provides the flexibility needed for Terra Firma's planned changes.

Terra Firma plans to add value in many ways, including:
- Bringing focus Making the people in the business understand what it is they are supposed to be doing, that is, that they are there to serve the customer and the artist and not to try and be or act like artists themselves;
- Driving operational change Forcing the business to simplify its operations, reduce costs and start making decisions based on sound financial judgements;
- Repositioning Recorded Music Helping Recorded Music tackle the B2B and consumer digital opportunity/challenge;
- Exploiting assets Moving the prioritization of the exploitation of the catalog from the bottom of the pile to the top; and
- Intervening Changing the culture and displaying leadership where previously there was little and, what little there was, was confused.

These changes will not be easy and will require both extensive effort and resources. We are driving these value-added changes by putting approximately 45 people, both from Terra Firma and outside our firm, into the business. This total includes three seconded MDs, and I have taken on the role of non-executive Chairman.

There is no doubt that EMI is a tremendous challenge, but it is also a huge opportunity and our success or failure will not be correlated to the markets, but to our ability to effect change, quickly and decisively. It is this type of deal that Terra Firma focuses on and from which it makes money.

But, EMI is a done deal, so going forward, what type of deal should Terra Firma do? You won't be surprised to hear me say, more of the same. Our contrarian interventionist strategy focuses on assets that need transformation in how they are managed and is well suited to making money in more challenging environments such as that which we now face.

Terra Firma intends to focus on the same type of deals that we have always done. Having been formed in recession, we are not frightened or dismayed about the times ahead and feel that we are well-positioned to take advantage of the opportunities that will be presented in this changed environment. It will not be easy, but I believe it will be profitable for all of us.

Best wishes, Guy Hands, CEO, Terra Firma

January 17, 2008
Hands' general plan to "move forward" EMI's recorded music business
Dear All,
I am writing to you today, as we are announcing the first steps towards achieving our goal of becoming the world's most innovative, artist friendly and consumer focused music company, by reshaping and streamlining the structure of EMI's recorded music division.

After in-depth research and hundreds of discussions with artists, managers, industry insiders and business partners, we have concluded that dramatic and immediate change is warranted. You yourselves have been strong advocates for change, in the many letters and emails I have received from around the globe.

Constructive change must be built on principles and we have been guided by three of them:
- We believe in our artists for the long term.
- We will respect and collaborate with them
- We must establish a true partnership with our artists and their advisors, based on openness, trust and honesty

As you are aware, the current economic model at EMI is unsustainable. We have analysed recorded music in detail and while some areas are profitable, the business as a whole is not. This type of analysis is something we have done across hundreds of businesses, and in the case of EMI the conclusions show that change is necessary.

Therefore, we have to change our organisational structure and the ways in which we do business. Some of the organisational changes will come immediately and other parts will be implemented in stages in order to protect existing projects. However, by summer the revised organisation will be in place.

To explain these structural changes to you more clearly, please find attached, a document showing the new global functional organization. As you will see, the changes to the global company can be explained as follows:

- Repositioning EMI's labels to ensure they will be completely focused on our artists and A&R, maximising the potential of all our artists.
- Developing a new partnership with artists, based on transparency and trust, and helping all artists monetise the value of their music by opening new income streams.
- Bringing together all the group's key support activities including sales, marketing manufacturing and distribution into a single division with a unified global leadership.
- The elimination of significant duplications within the group to simplify processes and reduce waste.

This structure is designed to serve your artists needs, to allow EMI to tailor services to you and your artist's specific requirements, and to enable EMI to be a sustainable and growing enterprise. In simplified terms, the new divisions will be as follows:

- Labels / A&R putting the artist first
- Music Services delivering music products and services for today's consumer
- Support Services achieving operational excellence

The change in the organisation cannot be accomplished without considerable pain. Eliminating duplication and bureaucracy, and reducing cost will necessitate substantial staff reductions. Sadly, between 1500 and 2000 jobs will have to go. While these reductions will be undertaken with great care and fairness, we may have to remove an individual or two who has been helpful to your artist, or, you.

EMI currently has 14,425 artists on its roster, and in the last year, we tried to break 1,300 globally. This is clearly unsustainable; we need to focus on those artists for whom we have both the time and expertise to support properly and with whom we can be successful. The roster is too large and the number of album releases are too many, to apply proper focus or expertise.

As of today, I cannot tell you the future size of the reduction in EMI's roster. We are going through a systematic process of categorising artists signed to EMI:
1) Those currently profitable, which is currently only about 3%.
2) Those we believe can be profitable, which we clearly hope is as large as possible.
3) Those whom will never be profitable, no matter how we change the model.

Sorting out the roster and finding solutions for artists who cannot be profitable under any model, is of great importance. We believe there are alternative models outside of the profit model required by EMI to support these artists, such as local and corporate sponsors and angels.

I want to assure you that our artists and our staff are at the centre of our planning and we are using all our energy, determination and focus to create a stronger, healthier EMI. I have enormous respect for EMI and our artists. EMI is an iconic brand with a rich history and we want to ensure that the creation of music by the incredible talent signed to this label, continues for generations to come. This will only be possible, if the recorded music division becomes a sustainable business.

Once you have reflected on our plans, please, reach out to Caryn Tomlinson, so she can quickly direct your questions or issues to the appropriate member of the Music Management Board....

I believe that, with your help, we can turn EMI into the most creative, most expert and most profitable company in the world. We will give this Company the success that its famous name, our artists and our staff deserve. That is my commitment.

With best wishes,
GUY HANDS

March 3, 2008
The reorganisation of EMI Music, Mk2
I would like you to know that the big operational and strategic decisions with regard to the future of EMI are now behind us and,

from hereon in, our focus will be on execution. I would like to thank everyone who wrote to me and my team for sharing their thoughts and vision for the business. While clearly we could not incorporate all the ideas proposed to us, we have taken on board many of the suggestions given to us by artists and their representatives and we all thank you for these.

EMI has now started the process required to move to a collaborative matrix structure, focusing on the three streams of business activity I announced in January: Labels/A&R, Music Services and Support Services. Today our staff will shift their reporting lines to a matrix system, moving from the current locally centralized model to a global functional matrix model. Staff will report first to their functional head, with a secondary reporting line linking them to their Country or Label Head.

As a result, we will start to feel the benefits of a global matrix organisation almost immediately. Our aim is to think globally but act locally. This means we can act in markets using our global reach, leverage, speed and efficiency, without losing the many benefits of local presence which, we all know, is essential to this business.

As you can imagine, the real and difficult work starts now as we have to make individual decisions on people. We regard ourselves as a client business, where we have two major clients, our artists and the consumer. While we have a vast fund of information on what the consumer thinks about our performance, we have less on what our artists actually think. I would, therefore, like to invite you and our artists to give us any feedback which could help inform these decisions. Your comments will be assimilated with feedback from many others and will contribute to good decisions being made. We will treat any contribution you make in the utmost confidence. Clearly we will not be able to please everyone with all the decisions made but your feedback is crucial and will be taken into account.

We are now rolling out the strategy that will ensure a positive and successful future for EMI and our artists, please rest assured that we have systems in place to ensure that those of you who have releases currently active or soon to be released, will get the service and commitment you deserve. Please if you have any concerns with regards to this, let Caryn Tomlinson know and she will ensure that the appropriate functional head follows up with you.

We know this is a tough time for the music industry, for our staff, our artists and our partners, but we are working towards a more efficient, dynamic, innovative and financially successful EMI, which will benefit us all and address the challenges we all face. We are all impressed by the level of commitment our staff have been maintaining under pressure, the evidence of which is the encouraging results, chart positions and awards our artists are receiving around the globe. Last but most importantly I wish to thank many of you for the dignified and solid support you have shown over the last few months. Change is never easy and always disturbing but with your help we will come through stronger than ever.

With best wishes,
Guy

April 16, 2008
Hands splits board into two, announces promotions, restructuring:
The Chairman's Board, led by Hands, will focus on developing long-term strategy and dealing with major strategic topics such as acquisitions, meeting on a monthly basis.

The Operating Board will drive the operational management of the business and will deal with all day-to-day business decisions, meeting every two weeks. Chris Roling, named President and Chief Operating Officer of EMI Music, will chair.

Roling has been working as CFO of EMI Music and COO of International Labels since January. In his new role of President and COO, Chris Roling will be focusing full-time on managing the business on a global basis and on leading the Operating Board.

Kennedy has been promoted to the global role of Chief Financial Officer of EMI Music. Chris has worked for EMI since 1993 and will now transition his current financial, investor relations and restructuring responsibilities to Pat O'Driscoll, with whom he'll spearhead the company's reorganization.

Clasper's executive responsibilities in operations are being passed to Douglas Merrill and Gareth Thomas, Head of Global Procurement and Logistics. Clasper will now serve as Deputy Chairman of the Operating Board, assisting Roling in his new role.

With Roger Ames having completed his work on the reorganisation of EMI Music in North America and the UK, he will now leave the operational side of the EMI business and work with Hands and Terra Firma on strategic acquisitions.

Said Hands: "Roger's advice to EMI over the past months has been invaluable and I would like to thank him for his contribution." Until Gatfield joins the company, Ashley Unwin will become head of North American and UK A&R, with all label heads in those countries reporting to him in the interim.

With the appointment of Douglas Merrill, Hodgkinson, who has been largely responsible for the digital area, along with marketing, will move to become President of Business Development and will report directly to Hands, assigning Merrill in the transition.

Van der Feltz will assume responsibility for Global Marketing, bringing over 20 years' marketing experience at a senior level from multinational consumer goods company Unilever where he was a member of the Board. He has successfully lent his marketing skills to several companies in the Terra Firma portfolio including, most recently, Odeon Cinemas.

Best wishes, GUY.......

July 7, 2008
The last memo: Hands steps back from direct involvement in EMI
Dear all

I am writing to you today, as I am pleased to announce that we have completed the difficult, but necessary organisational restructuring of EMI and, having finalised our strategic planning, are entering a new phase of positive development and innovation across the business.

First, I am delighted to inform you that I have appointed Elio Leoni-Sceti as Chief Executive of EMI's recorded music division.

Elio joins EMI from Reckitt Benckiser, the global consumer brands company, with £3 billion in sales and 10,000 staff, where he has been Executive Vice President, Europe.

During Elio's stellar 16 year career with Reckitt Benckiser he led some outstanding brand successes and business turnarounds in the United States and across Europe. His career achievements and excellent leadership qualities are ideally suited to ensuring that EMI is a successful business and a strong creative partner for our artists.

Elio has the passion, drive and belief in the future of the music industry to realise the ambitions we all have for EMI. Elio joins at the right time to shape, drive and lead EMI to become the world's most artist focused and consumer friendly music company.

Second, with Elio's arrival as Chief Executive, I will step back to become Non Executive Chairman of EMI. I would like to thank you, and our artists, for your continued support and for your contribution to the positive results currently being achieved by our artists, in collaboration with EMI staff globally.

Elio, EMI's board and I believe the potential that can be realised in this industry, for our artists and EMI, is massive. Music consumption is growing more than ever across the world and EMI is now poised to take the lead in ensuring our artists reach more consumers, are rewarded financially for their creativity, work in true partnership with EMI and are able to collaborate closely with our newly empowered staff to make the best possible decisions for their careers.

Third, I wanted to inform you that JF Cecillon and I have amicably agreed that he will step down from his executive positions as President, A&R Labels, International, and President, EMEA, at the end of this week. I would like to thank JF for his many contributions to EMI. He has nurtured great talent, both artistic and executive.

Billy Mann, EMI Music's Chief Creative Officer based in New York, will assume the additional role of President, A&R Labels, International, assuming JF's responsibilities for artist development in countries outside North America and the UK. With Nick Gatfield leading our A&R efforts in North America and the UK from the 15th of July, complemented by Billy Mann in the rest of the world, we have two strong, artist-driven talented executives who can help us move into a new phase of creativity and who can ensure we work in a collaborative partnership with our artists.

David Kassler will take over JF's regional duties as President, Europe/Middle East/Africa, in addition to his other role of President, Global Artist Projects. Ashley Unwin will assume David Kassler's former duties as President, UK and Ireland. Ashley, who has been interim President, A&R Labels, North America and UK, will step down from that role when Nick Gatfield joins EMI on the 15th of July. At EMI France, where JF was President and CEO, Nathalie Collin now moves into the lead management position there as Chairman, EMI Music France, reporting to David Kassler.

We all look forward to working with you over the coming year and to ensuring the success of your music.

With best wishes,
Guy Hands

Bibliography

Books and selected reports and articles

John Alderman, *Sonic Boom: Napster P2P and the battle for the future of music*, Fourth Estate, 2001

Louis Barfe, *Where Have all the Good Times Gone?: The rise and fall of the record industry*, Atlantic Books, 1994

Robert Burnett, *The Global Jukebox: The international music industry*, Routledge, 1996

Stan Cornyn with Paul Scanlon, *Exploding: The Highs, Hits, Hype, Heroes, and Hustlers of the Warner Music Grup*, Harper Entertainment, 2002

Clive Davis, *Clive: Inside the Record Industry*, Morrow, 1975

Frederic Dannen, *Hit Men, Power Brokers and Fast Money Inside the Music Business*, Vintage, 1991

Anita Elberse, 'Bye-Bye Bundles', *Journal of Marketing*, May 2010

Enders Analysis, *Recorded Music and Music Publishing*, Enders, March 2007

Nicholas Faith, *The Bronfmans: The rise and fall of the house of Seagram*, St Martins Press, 2006

Bruce Feiler, *Dreaming Out Loud: Garth Brooks, Wynona Judd, Wade Hayes and the changing face of Nashville*, Avon Books, 1998

Roland Gelatt, *The Fabulous Phonograph, 1877–1977*, Cassell, 1977

Danny Goldberg, *Bumping Into Geniuses: My life inside the rock and roll business*, Gotham Books, 2009

Fred Goodman, *Fortune's Fool: Edgar Bronfman Jnr., Warner Music and an industry in crisis,* Simon and Schuster, 2010

—*The Mansion on the Hill: Dylan, Young, Geffen, Springsteen and the head-on collision of rock and commerce,* Times Books, 1977

Robert Greenfield, *The Last Sultan,* Simon & Schuster, 2011

Pekka Gronow and Ilpo Saunio, *An International History of the Recording Industry,* Cassell, 1999

Phil Hardy and Dave Laing, *The Encyclopedia of Rock: Volume 1, The Age of Rock'n'Roll,* Panther, 1975

Bruce Haring, *Off The Charts: Ruthless days and reckless nights inside the music industry,* Birch Lane Press, 1996

The International Federation of the Phonogram Industry, *The Recording Industry in Numbers,* published annually

Steve Knopper, *Appetite for Destruction: The spectacular crash of the record industry in the digital age,* Free Press, 2009

Thomas S. Kuhn, *The Copernican Revolution,* Vintage Books, 1959

Robert Levine, *Free Ride: How the Internet is destroying the culture business and how the culture business is fighting back,* The Bodley Head, 2011

Stephen Levy, *The Perfect Thing: How the iPad shuffles commerce, culture and coolness,* Ebury Press, 2006

Greil Marcus, ed., *Rock and Roll Will Stand,* Beacon Press, 1969

Peter Martland, *EMI, the First 100 Years,* Batsford, 1977

Rod McQueen, *The Icarus Factor: The rise and fall of Edgar Bronfman Jnr.,* Doubleday Canada, 2004

Greg Milner, *Perfecting Sound Forever: The story of recorded music,* Granta, 2009

Keith Negus, *Music Genres and Corporate Cultures,* Routledge, 1999

Russell Sanjek, updated by David Sanjek, *Pennies From Heaven: The American music business in the twentieth century,* Da Capo Press, 1996

Brian Southall, *The Rise and Fall of EMI Records,* Omnibus, 2009

Steve Stoute with Mim Eichler Rivas, *The Tanning of America: How hip-hop created a culture that rewrote the rules of the new economy,* Gotham Books, 2011

George W. S. Trow, *I-eclectic, Reminiscent, Amused, Fickle, Perverse, New Yorker* magazine, May & June, 1978

Bibliography

Michael J. Wolf, *Entertainment Economy: How mega media forces are transforming our lives*, Times Books, 1999

Walter Yetnikoff with David Ritz, *Howling at the Moon*, Random House, 2004

Albin J. Zak III, *The Poetics of Rock: Cutting tracks, making records*, University of California Press, 2001

Magazines and newsletters consulted

Billboard, billboard.biz, *Digital Music News, Hits Daily Double, Music & Copyright, Music Week, theviewfromtheboundary* (all issues of which are available for free at theviewfromtheboundary.com)

Notes And Sources

Beginnings
Noria Ohga demanded, Knopper, page 21
Akio Morita could listen to operas: Akio Morita Wikipedia entry

Chapter 1
Suddenly, the PolyGram prospectus, interview, Dec 2011
A classic example of this was the battle of the speeds. For a more detailed account of the speed wars and the introduction of stereo see Gelatt, pages 290–302

Chapter 2
At a meeting senior representatives, EMI archives

Chapter 3
Over the heads of his label leaders, Cornyn, page 128
In 1970, Nesuhi divided the world, Cornyn, page 191
Art Director Ed Thrasher, Cornyn, page 127
Bidding wars for hot acts, On a trip to New York
I [had] deep CBS money, Yetnikoff, page 93
With Warner movies and Warner music at his command, Ross, Yetnikoff, page 93
On a trip to New York, Cornyn, pages 446–447
Daly's and Semel's contracts, Cornyn, pages 449

Notes And Sources

Nothing will be the same again, Faith, page 265

Chapter 5
Ultimately the deal, like Guy Hands' takeover of EMI, represented a huge miscalculation. For a brief but comprehensive review of the merger, based on extensive interviews with the participants see *How the AOL-Time Warner Merger Went So Wrong*, by Tim Arango, *New York Times*, Jan 11, 2010
The merger, the largest in American business history, Arango
The business model sort of collapsed under us, Arango
We did 120 deals, Southall, page 96
Musicmaker, which offered, Southall, pages 90–91
Look Kearby, my job is to keep you down, Knopper, page 120
In a nod to the future, Alderman, page 178

Chapter 6
I worked for Virgin Records, *Daily Telegraph*, Jan 17, 2008
Ken and Nancy's rock'n'roll Circus, Patrick Reilly, reprinted in *The Independent*, Feb 27, 1998
I knew that our record company, Cornyn, pages 234
If you are getting no US repertoire, Southall, page 147

Chapter 7
According to Stan Cornyn, Cornyn, page 303
The motivation of those big companies, interview, Sept 2011
According to Larry Kenswil, interview, Feb 2007
To obtain Internet Music from all major record labels, court papers

Chapter 9
Industry observers say the rapid decline, Ed Christman, *Billboard*, Jan 15, 2000
I don't think we're going to make a lot of money, but [Jobs] is going to sell a lot of iPods, quoted in Knopper, page 172
Coldplay's 2002 smash A Rush Of Blood To the Head, Knopper, page 177
Sony Music chairman Rolf Schmidt-Holtz had a heated Christmas Eve phone call, *The New York Times*, Feb 2, 2009

eventually sold more than 14m records generating around $75m in profit for Warner Music, Goldberg, page 236
When I was at Mercury Records, Goldberg, page 244
According to Brooks in conversation, Feiler, page 277 ff
These devices are just repositories for stolen music, Houston Chronicle, Nov 21, 2006

Chapter 11
His reputation as a financial steward has been the butt of jokes, The New York Times, Nov 30, 2003
I thought it crazy to go to the EU, Goodman, *Fortune's Fool*, page 184

Chapter 12
The deal with Edgar is, he does a good job or someone else comes in who does a good job, The New York Times, Nov 20, 2003
While WMG continues to reduce staff and scale back compensation, quoted in Digital Music News, April 27, 2011
It's becoming more and more apparent that this is nothing more than a financial play, The New York Times, April 17, 2005
They're very smart money guys, The New York Times, April 17, 2005

Chapter 13
We believe that the global music industry, Global Equity Research, company focus, Deutsche Bank, April 4, 2005
He is a master at attracting and developing executive talent, The New York Times, Nov 7, 2011
Imagine a world, posted, Feb 2, 2007
Terra Firma's success is founded, memo, Aug 29, 2007

Chapter 14
The software, hardware and communication technologies of the Internet age, Recorded Music and Music Publishing, page 5
However, Abbey Road recording studios appear to be very dear to the nation's heart, National Trust website

Notes And Sources

We have no record contract as such, Radiohead website
dreaded going to see them. Everybody at EMI had become part of the furniture, The Times, Dec 14, 2007
I would like to say at the outset, Maltby Capital Ltd, Annual Review, Year ended, March 31, 2008, page 5
The numbers presented here, Maltby, page 8
EMI – and much of the industry and its commentators, Maltby, page 7
EMI Music has not made the most of its top 250 artists, Maltby, page 20
EMI Music… lost touch with a customer base, Maltby, page 18
Recent years have seen the emergence, Maltby, page 18
[Its] approach to travel and expense policies was more than generous, Maltby, page 24
We have dwelled on these historical issues too, Maltby, page 8

Chapter 15
It is the job of a smart buyer not to overpay, whether or not bigger idiots are said to be lurking in the wings, Daily Telegraph, Oct 20, 2010, quoted in Bloomberg News, Nov 5, 2010

Chapter 16
The US is seriously concerned about the growth of Internet piracy on Russian websites, quoted in Wired magazine, Feb 6, 2006
A poster child for illegal music sales over the Internet, Wired, Feb 6, 2006
What's wrong with SOPA, The Observer, Jan 8, 2012
The problem of stealing intellectual property, Forbes, Jan 23, 2012
The average Vevo stream in 2011 generated 0.43¢, Billboard.biz, Feb 1, 2012
Free streaming services are clearly not net positive, quoted in The New York Times, Jan 28, 2011

Chapter 17
Would create what I call a super-major, quoted in Billboard.biz, Feb 2, 2012
The majors were required to provide a detailed analysis of online and mobile sales, Billboard.biz, Feb 2, 2012
No one wants to pay for music. Yet investors are splurging on music firms, The Economist, May 12, 2011

While scores of web companies were founded in recent years, there isn't enough venture capital to keep all of them going indefinitely, The Wall Street Journal, Oct 2, 2011
Something has to die in order to be resurrected, Billboard.biz, Jan 30, 2012

Chapter 18
through our acquisition of EMI. This and all the subsequent quotes from the witness statements are from transcripts the US Senate Judiciary Committee's antitrust hearings of Thursday, June 21, 2012.
Be afraid, be very afraid, bob@lefstetz.com, archives

Endings
Mixed in the box, Milner, page 340
Although Auto-Tune was designed as a corrective device, Milner, page 343
The closest Western Civilization has come, in 'The Strange Death of Rock and Roll', in *Rock and Roll Will Stand*
Goldner never worried about creed or colour, Hardy/Laing, page 147

Index

A&M Records, 2, 4, 43
ABC Records, 20
Abu Dhabi Media Company, 280, 281–2
Access Industries, 189, 290, 297, 298, 302, 304
AC/DC, 128
Adele, 312, 313, 343
Aftermath, 309
Allen, Charles, 250–1, 253
Allen, Charlie, 28
Allen, Lily, 135
The Allman Brothers Band, 308
AllofMP3.com, 263–5
Amamou, Slim, 133
Amazon, 115, 119, 144–5, 188, 213
Ames, Roger, 48, 163, 183
The Animals, 18
Anthony, Dee, 31–2
Anti-Counterfeiting Trade Agreement (ACTA), 276–7
AOL, 41–2, 54, 60, 62, 65–667
AOL Time Warner, 107, 147, 149, 153–7
Apple, xvi–xvii, xviii, xix, 6, 98–9, 113, 115, 120, 131, 134, 135–8, 211–12, 213, 341
Arcade Fire, 145
Arctic Monkeys, 229, 312
Ariola Records, 64
Arista, 65, 97
Asimow, Daniel, 308
Associated British Picture Company, 19
Association of Independent Music (AIM), 214, 317–18

Asylum Records, 35, 202
Atlantic Records, 28, 30, 35, 139, 186
Australian Performing Right Association, 272
Auto-Tune, 343
Azoff, Irving, 162, 289, 323–4

Backstreet Boys, 72, 148
Baidu, 265–6
Bandier, Martin, 21, 77, 207–8, 291, 311–12
Barlow, Gary, 320
Bates, Tony, 85
The Beach Boys, 20, 34, 143
Beastie Boys, 97
The Beatles, 17, 18, 20, 80, 230, 243, 247, 264, 337
Beggars Banquet, 313
Bell, Laurence, 330
Bengloff, Rich, 318
Berry, Ken, 76, 77–8, 82, 83, 85
Berry, Nancy, 76, 77–8, 85
Bertelsmann, xiv, xvi, 32–3, 50, 54, 60, 64–5, 69–72, 103, 107, 109, 147–9, 153–8, 163–7, 170–1, 173–6
Best Buy, 112, 118, 120, 121
Bieber, Justin, 293
Bilk, Acker, 17
Birt, John, Lord, 192, 233, 235, 236–7, 241–2
The Black Eyed Peas, 320
Blackwell, Chris, 33
Blavatnik, Len, xii, 189, 297, 301–2
The Blues Band, 245–6
Blur, 337

375

BMG (Bertelsmann Music Group), xxii, xxiii, 20, 36, 49, 51, 65, 72–5, 81, 92, 148–9, 158–9
BMG Music Publishing, xiv, 72, 180–2
BMG Rights Management, 170–1, 240, 290, 296, 304, 340
Bowen, Jimmy, 140
Bowie, David, 140
Boyle, Susan, 345
BPI, 52, 117–18, 237, 273, 299, 305
Branson, Richard, 33, 328
Breen, Marcus, 345–6
Bronfman, Edgar, 41–2, 46–7, 149–50, 161–3, 183–6, 189, 201, 207, 212, 284, 291, 293, 295–6, 297, 302, 304, 318–19, 322–3, 325
Brooks, Garth, 49, 78, 128, 140–1
Browne, Jackson, 35
Bryan, Luke, 243
Bublé, Michael, 305
Bug Music, 240

Calder, Clive, 148
Capitol Records, 16, 17, 19–20, 86, 140–1, 309–10
Carey, Mariah, 79, 83–4
Caruso, Enrico, 11
Casablanca Records, 20
Case, Steve, 66
CBS Records, 34, 35, 82, 141
Charles, Ray, 197
Cheap Trick, 308
Chemical Brothers, 77
Cheng, Norman, 91
Cher, 343
Choruss, 278–9
Christman, Ed, 117
Chuck D, 309
Church, Eric, 243
Citigroup, 215, 220–1, 233–4, 248–51, 254–8, 260, 302, 304, 336
Cohen, Lyor, 34, 186–7, 188–9, 190, 191, 192, 210, 297, 302
Cohen, Ted, 136–7
Coldplay, 77, 91, 136, 144, 205, 208, 232, 238, 243–4, 286, 336, 337
Cole, Nat King, 16
Columbia, xxii, 13–15, 31
Columbia Graphophone Company, 10, 11–13
Concord, 197

Conklin, Jim, 26
Cooper, Ray, 86
Cornyn, Stanley, 28, 31, 38–40, 41, 99
Cowell, Simon, 345
Creative Freedom Foundation, 272

Daft Punk, 77
Daly, Robert, 37, 41
The Dave Clark Five, 17
Davis, Clive, 29, 31, 65
Davis, Sammy Jr, 27
Decca Records, 13, 18, 99
The Decemberists, 296
Def Jam, 82
Delfont, Bernard, 19
Department of Justice (US), 108, 181, 275
Department of Media, Culture and Sport, 22–3
Domino Records, 327, 330
Dornemann, Michael, 69
Dr. Dre, 197
Dr. Luke, 292
Dylan, Bob, 29

Eagles, 128, 144, 187, 312
Echo, 112–13
eircom, 273
Elberse, Anita, 141–2, 143
Elektra Records, 26, 30, 186
Ells, Stuart, 86
EMI, xiii, xxii, 7, 10, 13–25, 44–7, 48–51, 53–63, 67–8, 71–3, 79–94, 107, 110, 126, 134–5, 140–1, 150–1, 158, 163, 185–6, 204–11, 213–21, 223, 225–7, 228–42, 243–4, 246–60, 290, 291, 295–6, 302–4, 314–15, 316–19, 330–3, 336
EMI Music Publishing, 21, 44, 46, 55, 60, 77, 80, 87, 88, 92–3, 217, 290, 316, 319–21, 338
Eminem, 67, 110, 308
Enders Analysis, 222, 258
The Entertainment Network, 51
EquaTrax, 174
Ertegun, Ahmet, 28, 29, 31, 32, 33, 190
Ertegun, Nesuhi, 28, 30
European Commission, 8, 54, 55–63, 65, 71–5, 108, 135–6, 155, 159, 165–70, 171–3, 176–82, 207, 276–7, 320–1, 325–6, 339–40
European Court of Justice, 176–8, 207, 277–8

Index

Everly Brothers, 27
Exigen, 174

Facebook, 274, 287
Fanning, Shawn, 70, 98
Faxon, Roger, 86, 253, 258–60, 302–4, 314–15, 322, 330–3
F.B.T. Productions, 308, 309
Federal Trade Commission (US), 108–9, 123–4, 164, 318, 333–6
Festival Mushroom Records, 201
Fifield, Jim, 21, 140
Ford, Tennessee Ernie, 16
Fourtou, Jean-René, 326
Freddie & the Dreamers, 17
Front Line Management Group, 288–9
Fuchs, Michael, 37

Gainsbourg, Serge, 82
Garland, Eric, 300
Gates, Gareth, 166
Gates, Kenny, 330
Geffen, David, 31, 35
Gildersleeve, John, 93
Global Industry Analysts, 307
Goldberg, Danny, 139
Goldner, George, 346–7
Goodman, Fred, 37
Google, 272, 274, 279, 281
Gorillaz, 205, 208
Grade Organisation, 19
Grainge, Lucian, 292, 321, 323, 326–7
Gramophone Company, xxi, 10–13
Grateful Dead, 27, 65, 78
Green Day, 198
Griffin, Jim, 99, 278–9
Grokster, 98, 104, 132
Gulf & Western, 19

HADOPI, 268–72, 307
Hallyday, Johnny, 82
Hammond, John, 29
Hands, Guy, xii, 49, 78, 214–21, 223, 224–5, 226, 228, 231, 233, 240–1, 248, 254–7, 348–65
Harper, Ben, 320
Herman's Hermits, 18
Hesse, Thomas, 292
Hikaru, Utada, 49, 91
HMV, xxi, 16, 45, 52, 88, 115–16

Hollande, François, 272
The Hollies, 17
Holzman, Jac, 30, 202
Hootie & the Blowfish, 139
Horowitz, Zack, 48, 299
Houston, Whitney, 65
Hunter, Tab, 26
Hyman, Eliot, 28

Ice-T, 36–7
IFPI (International Federation of the Phonogram Industry), xviii, 40, 95, 96, 221, 231, 266–7, 296, 306–7, 325
Imperial Records, 17
Independent Music Companies Association (IMPALA), 53, 155, 156, 163–4, 165, 176, 179, 181, 213, 312–13, 317, 326–7, 328
Integrity, 197
International Intellectual Property Alliance, 22
Intertrust, 110
Iovine, Jimmy, 34
Island Records, 2, 4, 33, 43
iTunes, xvi, xix, 6, 113, 130–2, 133–4, 137–8, 143, 144, 202

Jackson, Janet, 78
Jay-Z, 197, 288
Jobs, Steve, xii, 99, 131, 134, 137, 211–12
Jones, Norah, 91, 94, 135
Journey, 128
Jump Start, 124–5

Katzmann, Robert, 111
Kazaa, 98, 132
Kearby, Gerry, 69
Kenny G, 72
Kenswil, Ken, 110
The Kinks, 18, 27, 65
Kinney Corporation, 28, 29, 30, 290
Klein, Joe, 109
Kohl, Herb, 321, 333–5
The Kooks, 320, 343
Kramer, Billy J., 17
Krasnow, Bob, 37
Kravitz, Lenny, 320
Kronemeyer, David, 20, 35
Kwatinetz, Jeff, 162

Lack, Andrew, 147, 164, 175

Lady Antebellum, 232, 243
Lady Gaga, 188, 281, 283–4, 293, 305
Lane, Brian, 31–2
Led Zeppelin, 19, 200
Lee, Amos, 296
Lee, Mike, 333
Lefsetz, Bob, 324–5
Leibowitz, Jonathan 333
Leoni-Sceti, Elio, 231, 246, 253
Levin, Gerald, 36, 41, 42, 66
Levy, Alain, 47, 82–3, 86–8, 93, 135, 147, 174, 205, 210
Levy, Jean-Bernard, 326
Lewis, Edward, 99
LimeWire, 98, 104, 133
Linkin Park, 196
Liquid Audio, 69, 110–11
Live Nation, 234, 288–9
Lockwood, Joseph, 15, 16–17
London School for Performing Arts & Technology, 343–4
Lott, Roy, 86
Ludacris, 197

Macrovision, 110
Madonna, 84, 143–4, 201, 202, 229, 288
Maitland, Mike, 27, 28
Maltby Capital, 192, 223, 232, 233, 241–2, 253
Manfred Mann, 18
Manilow, Barry, 65
Marillion, 244–5
Martin, Dean, 16, 27
MCA, 33, 36, 46, 147
McCartney, Paul, 34, 141, 229
Mellencamp, John Cougar, 128
Merlin, 179, 214, 313
Merrill, Douglas, 246
Messier, Jean-Marie, 41, 150, 161
Metallica, 37, 67
MGM, 14, 18
Microsoft, 96, 107
Middelhoff, Thomas, xiv, xvi, 50, 70, 338, 341
MIDEM, 165, 311–12
Millar, Bill, 348
Miller, Daniel, 330
Miller, Mitch, 32
Mills, Martin, 323
Ministry of Sound, 214, 327
Minogue, Kylie, 84, 201, 337
Mitchell, Joni, 27

Mohaupt, Jörg, 298
The Moody Blues, 18
Morgado, Robert, 37
Morita, Akio, xxii
Morris, Doug, 32, 34, 37, 48, 131, 144, 190, 208, 292
Morrissette, Alanis, 97
Mossberg, Walter, 97
Motown Records, 43, 82
Mottola, Tommy, 147
MP3.com, 98, 107, 111
MTV, xxii–xxiv, 68
Mumford & Sons, 229, 312
Munns, David, 83, 210, 299
Musicland, 108, 121
Musicmaker, 68
MusicNet, 94, 107–8, 110, 111–12
Mute Records, 88, 327, 330

'N Sync, 72, 148
Nada, Hany, 300–1
Najafi Companies, 154, 176
Napster, xix, 67, 69–71, 98–9, 102–4, 107, 113
National Association of Record Merchandisers, 121, 127
Naughton, John, 274–5
Nelson, Ricky, 27
Newton, Ashley, 86
Newton-John, Olivia, 201
Nicks, Stevie, 118
Nicoli, Eric, xi, 49, 77, 90, 151, 207, 210, 216
Nirvana, 128, 306
Nyro, Laura, 35

Oberstein, Maurice, 45
Ofarim, Esther & Abi, 18
Ohga, Norio, xviii
Ondrejka, Cory, 246
Osbourne, Ozzy, 320
Ostin, Mo, 27, 30, 31, 34, 37
Otto, Frank, xxii

Page, Jimmy, 200
Pakman, David, 322–3
Paradis, Vanessa, 82
Parker, Sean, 298
Parsons, Richard, 67
Paterno, Peter, 196–7
Pearl Jam, 197
Peoples, Glenn, 307

Index

Perry, Katy, 232, 239, 243, 293
Peter & Gordon, 17
Petty, Tom, 97
Philips, xxii, 2, 5, 6, 18, 43–4, 47, 82–3, 110, 147
PIAS, 327, 330
Pink Floyd, 18, 143, 230, 306, 329, 336, 337
Pirate Bay, 273
Piratpartiet, 133
Placebo, 320
PolyGram, xiv, xvii, xxii, 2–4, 6, 7, 20, 24, 43, 47–8, 82–3, 147, 313
Presley, Elvis, 72
Pressplay, 94, 107, 108, 110, 111–12, 113, 131
Prince, 78
Pro Tools, 342
Public Enemy, 97
Pye, 18

Quartararo, Phil, 91, 92
Queen, 18, 144, 229, 306

Radiohead, 144, 226–8, 312, 329, 336, 337
Rawling, Brian, 343
RCA, xxii, 13–15, 65
RealNetworks, 107
Recording Industry Association of New Zealand, 272
Red Hot Chili Peppers, 264
Reed, Lou, 65
Reprise Records, 27
RIAA (Recording Industry Association of America), 67, 95, 96, 97, 102, 104–6, 109, 111, 190, 212
Richard, Cliff, 17, 228–9
Rihanna, 320
Rogers, Kenny, 309–10
The Rolling Stones, 18, 91, 144, 229–30, 305–6, 312
Rose, Dave, 287
Rose, Philip, 30
Ross, Steve, 28–9, 30, 34, 35, 37
Roxio, 110, 113, 131
RTL, 165–6
Russo, Wayne, 191–2

Samit, Jay, 68, 236
Sandall, Robert, 76–7
Sarkozy, Nicolas, 269, 271–2
SBK Entertainment World, 21

Scarlet, 277–8
Schmidt, Andreas, 70
Schmidt-Holtz, Rolf, 137, 164, 175
Schulte-Hillen, Gerd, 163
Schwab, Susan, 264
Scorpio, 31–2
Scott-Heron, Gil, 65
Seagram, 33, 44, 46
Secure Digital Music Initiative, 95–7
The Seekers, 17
Semel, Terry, 37, 41
Semenko, Serge, 28
Serletic, Matt, 86
Seven Arts, 28
Shaw, Sandie, 18, 27, 329
Sherman, Cary, 190
Silver, Jeremy, 68
Silverman, Tom, 307
Simon, Paul, 34
Sinatra, Frank, 16, 27
Sister Sledge, 308–9
Smith, Al, 69
Smith, Chris, 22–3
Smith, Joe, 27, 30, 31, 78
Smith, Patti, 65
Sonopress, 72–5
Sony, xxii, 5, 96, 97, 106, 110, 147, 158, 171, 173–4, 313
Sony BMG, 174–5, 176, 178, 266–7
Sony Music Entertainment, xiii–xiv, 49–50, 51, 85, 107, 127, 147, 158–9, 163–7, 280–1, 292, 308, 314, 316, 345
Sony/ATV, 208, 290, 296, 316–17, 319–21, 338
Sorkin, Andrew Ross, 184–5
SoundExchange, 279
Southgate, Colin, Sir, 44, 45, 49
Spears, Britney, 72, 84, 148
Sperling, Scott, 162–3, 183–4
Spice Girls, 77, 84–5, 343
Spitzer, Eliot, 201
Spotify, xviii, 282–8, 298
Springfield, Dusty, 18
Springsteen, Bruce, 78, 175
Starbucks, 120
Stewart, Al, 65
Stewart, Rod, 19, 34
STHoldings, 285–6
Stigwood, Robert, 31
Stop Online Piracy Act (SOPA), 273–6
Stoute, Steve, 346

379

Streamwaves, 110
Swift, Taylor, 209
The Swinging Blue Jeans, 17
Syco, 345

Taylor, Geoff, 299
Taylor, James, 34
Taylor, Mark, 343
TelstraClear, 272
Temptations, 309
Terra Firma, xiv, 49, 192, 214–16, 220–1, 223–4, 230–6, 237, 248–58
Thielen, Gunter, 149
Thorn EMI, 20–1, 44
Thrasher, Ed, 31
Time Warner, 36–41, 46, 49, 54, 60, 62, 66–7, 107, 162
TOEMI, 16, 21
Toto, 309
Tower of Power, 309
Tower Records, 108, 121, 127–8
Trans World Entertainment, 108, 112
Transamerica Corporation, 29–30
The Troggs, 18
Turner, Tina, 140
Twain, Shania, 84, 139–40
Twitter, 274

U2, 141, 312
Union Square, 327
United Artists, 20, 29
Universal Music Group, xiii–xiv, xvii, 44, 46–8, 51, 81, 85, 89, 96, 100, 107, 110, 124–5, 126–7, 149–50, 151–2, 166, 174, 188, 197, 229, 239–40, 266–7, 280–1, 288–9, 296, 308, 314, 316, 318, 322–3, 325, 326–33, 336–7, 339–40
Universal Music Publishing, 180–1

Vale Music, 170, 345
Vanderbilt, Dick, 32
The Verve, 77
Vevo, 280–2
Victor Talking Company, xxi, 11

Virgin Media, 273
Virgin Records, 21, 62, 76–7, 86
Viva, xxiii, 90
Vivendi Universal, 34, 41, 81, 107, 149–50, 161, 176, 180, 182, 197, 290, 304, 317, 319, 321, 325, 330, 333, 337, 338–9

Wadsworth, Tony, 90–1, 231
Wainwright, Loudon III, 65
The Walker Brothers, 18
Wallichs, Glenn, 16
Wal-Mart, 119, 120, 125, 127–8, 130
Warner, Jack, 27, 291
Warner Chappell, 35, 55, 60, 194, 201, 227, 316
Warner Music Group, xiii, xxii, 26–42, 49–51, 53–63, 99, 148, 149, 174, 183–7, 189–90, 193–203, 207–8, 213, 249, 266–7, 278, 290–1, 292–3, 295–8, 302, 309, 314, 316, 318
WEA International, 30, 35, 36, 37, 186
Webnoize, 103
Weiner, Jeremy, 197
Weiss, Barry, 292
West, Kanye, 145, 320
Wexler, Jerry, 28, 29
Wherehouse Entertainment, 112, 121
White, Adam, 2–4
The Who, 306
Wikipedia, 275
Williams, Robbie, 84, 93–4, 320
Winehouse, Amy, 343
Wippit, 135

Yahoo, 274
Yankovic, Al, 309
Yetnikoff, Walter, 34–5
YouTube, 281

Zelnick, Strauss, 69
Zelnick, Patrick, 327–8
Zomba, 55, 71, 72, 111, 148
Zombie, Rob, 309
ZZ Top, 78